Proceedings of the First iKMS International Conference on Knowledge Management

People, Knowledge and Technology:

What Have We Learnt So Far?

Singapore   13 – 15 December 2004

Editors

Bruno TREZZINI

Nanyang Technological University, Singapore

Patrick LAMBE

Straits Knowledge, Singapore

Suliman HAWAMDEH

University of Oklahoma, USA

 **World Scientific**

NEW JERSEY · LONDON · SINGAPORE · BEIJING · SHANGHAI · HONG KONG · TAIPEI · CHENNAI

Published by

World Scientific Publishing Co. Pte. Ltd.

5 Toh Tuck Link, Singapore 596224

USA office: 27 Warren Street, Suite 401-402, Hackensack, NJ 07601

UK office: 57 Shelton Street, Covent Garden, London WC2H 9HE

British Library Cataloguing-in-Publication Data
A catalogue record for this book is available from the British Library.

PEOPLE, KNOWLEDGE AND TECHNOLOGY: WHAT HAVE WE LEARNT SO FAR?
Proceedings of the First iKMS International Conference on Knowledge Management

ISBN 981-256-149-8

Printed in Singapore by World Scientific Printers (S) Pte Ltd

PREFACE

This is a volume born out of passion and commitment. You are holding in your hands the proceedings of the *First International Conference on Knowledge Management* (iCKM 2004) organized by the *Information and Knowledge Management Society* (iKMS) and held in Singapore from December 13 to 15, 2004.

iKMS is a non-profit society which started as a knowledge management interest group in Singapore in 1999 with the objectives of promoting awareness of KM research and practice and discussing issues related to the development of knowledge management locally and internationally. The degree of interest and participation grew rapidly, so the founding members decided to register a society. As a result, iKMS was officially born in January 2001. Besides having become a major force in the local KM scene, iKMS created an international presence by publishing the first international refereed journal in knowledge management. The *Journal of Information and Knowledge Management* (JIKM) is the Society's flagship and is currently published by *World Scientific* (www.worldscinet.com/jikm/jikm.shtml). In many ways, iCKM 2004 marks another important step in the coming of age of iKMS.

By choosing the conference theme "People, knowledge and technology: what have we learned so far?" we wanted to elicit contributions that would shed some light on the current state of the art in KM as well as on the future challenges that lie ahead. How much has KM come of age as an academic discipline as well as a professional practice? In particular, we wanted to bridge the too frequent gap that exists between KM research and KM practice, by bringing academics, practitioners and providers into the same space, to discuss their common issues.

It is not especially easy to strike a balance between the particular needs and interests of academics, practitioners and solution providers in a conference program. However, we hope that in the end we managed to devise a flexible and productive program that allowed for maximal cross-fertilization between the different constituencies within the KM arena. The first and second conference days focused on insights and cases from KM research. On the second day country reports were also scheduled, offering insights into the state of KM adoption and practice in the Asian-Pacific region, the natural geographical focus of this year's conference. The focus of the last day shifted to the specifics of KM practice in Singapore, with case studies from Singaporean organisations. The final afternoon of the conference was devoted to knowledge sharing between speakers and delegates in a forum facilitated according to the principles of open space technology.

We are particularly pleased to have secured the support of four eminent personalities in the field of knowledge management as keynote speakers for iCKM 2004. In their addresses they shared their ideas on the power of social networks (Rob Cross), knowledge strategies for innovation (Josef Hofer-Alfeis), the future of KM (Dave Snowden), and metadata and taxonomies (David Weinberger).

This volume contains 32 oral presentations as well as the abstracts of the four keynote addresses and 37 poster presentations. The papers were grouped into six major themes, reflecting common concerns addressed by the authors: (1) communities and collaboration; (2) knowledge sharing; (3) culture as context; (4) knowledge management strategies; (5) knowledge creation; and (6) knowledge discovery. Many of these papers reflect the growing interest in non-technological aspects of KM. The insight that information technology is no panacea has become somewhat of a truism in the KM field. Technology continues to play an enabling role, but it is often subsidiary to social and cultural success factors.

Organizing an international conference is no mean feat for such a young organization, and it would certainly not have been possible without the dedication and active support of all iKMS executive committee members in a period of planning that spanned two years. We are also particularly grateful to our reviewers and the members of the international program committee for their advice and support in preparing the program. To these contributors, who freely gave of their time and insight, we offer our deepest thanks.

We would also like to thank Max Phua from *World Scientific* as well as Jane Lim and Khoo Cheng Hoon from *Meeting Matters International* for their logistic and administrative help in organizing this conference. Last but not least, our thanks go to all speakers and conference participants who made this event a worthwhile one.

Preparations for the second and third iCKM are well under way, and we hope that we will see many of you again in Tulsa (Oklahoma, USA) in 2005 and in London (University of Greenwich) in 2006.

Bruno Trezzini
Patrick Lambe
Suliman Hawamdeh

ACKNOWLEDGEMENTS

We would like to thank the following people who served as members of the international program committee and/or as anonymous reviewers (the latter are marked with a *):

ABRAHAM Ajith *
ALLAN Neill
ALQUDSI Taghreed

BARACHINI Franz
BARTH Steve
BARUCH Lev
BHANDAR Mamata *
BOCK Gee Woo *
BOISOT Max
BONTIS Nick
BURSTEIN Frada *

CALABRESE Carmen *
CALLAHAN Shawn *
CHAI Kah-Hin *
CHANG Meng Lai Calvin *
CHANG Yun-Ke *
CHATTERJEE Jayanta *
CHAUDHRY Abdus Sattar *
CHEN Hsueh-hua
COLEMAN David *
COLLIS Betty A.

DANESHGAR Farhad *
DAVIS Charles
DAWSON Ross

ELLIS Steve

GILBERT A. Lee *
GOH Su Nee *
GURTEEN David

HANDZIC Meliha
HARRISON Alan
HART Thomas
HASAN Helen
HOFER-ALFEIS Josef *
HSIAO Ruey-Lin

KAN Siew Ning *
KANKANHALLI Atreyi *
KONG Wei Chang *
KUMAR Prem *

LANG Josephine *
LAYCOCK Martyn *
LEE Chu Keong *
LEE W. B.
LEE Wai Peng *
LEE-PARTRIDGE Joo Eng *
LEMOULT Diane
LESTER June

LIM Ah Seng
LIM Thou Tin *

MANSOR Yushiana
MAYSAMI Ramin *
MENKHOFF Thomas
METAXIOTIS Kostas *
MORALES ARROYO Miguel A. *
MYBURGH Sue

NICHANI Maish

ORDOÑEZ DE PABLOS Patricia *

PAN Shan Ling *
PATTERSON Lotsee F. *
PERVAN Graham
PHANG Chee Wei *
POWERS Clair *
PROBST Gilbert
PULIC Ante

RAHMAN Naseem J. *
RAMCHAND Anand M. *
RAO Madanmohan *
RAVISHANKAR M. N. *
RITTER Waltraut *
RIVERA Melagros

SAJJAD Ur Rehman
SANKARA Shankar *
SBARCEA Kim *
SHAHEEN Majid
SNOWDEN Dave *
SPIRA Jonathan B. *
SRIKANTAIAH Kanti
SRIRAMESH Krishnamurthy *
STEINHEIDER Brigitte *
STEPHENSON Karen
SUTANTO Juliana *
SYEED Zakir

TIMBRELL Greg *
TRONDSEN Eilif
TSUI Eric *

VAN UNNIK Arjan *

WALLACE Danny
WEINBERGER David

YAMAZAKI Hideo
YEUNG Kwok Tung Christopher *
YOUNG Ron

ZOECKLER Mark *

CONTENTS

PART III Knowledge Sharing

PART IV Culture as Context

PART V Knowledge Management Strategies

PART VI Knowledge Creation

PART VII Knowledge Discovery

PART VIII Abstracts of Poster Presentations

PART I

Abstracts of
Keynote Addresses

THE HIDDEN POWER OF SOCIAL NETWORKS

ROB CROSS

McIntire School of Commerce, University of Virginia
robcross@virginia.edu

In today's flatter organizations work of significance demands effective collaboration within and across functional, physical and hierarchical boundaries. In all but the most rote manufacturing and service environments work has become a collaborative endeavor accomplished less through standardized processes and formal structure than informal networks of relationships. This presentation will demonstrate why and how to pay attention to the health of networks based on in-depth experience with over 60 organizations in the last five years. Specifically, the session will:

- Demonstrate the importance of networks in terms of performance (organizational and individual), learning, innovation and quality of work life.
- Provide case examples of strategic problems organizations uncover when conducting a social network analysis and means of correcting them.
- Characterize networks of high performing individuals and provide diagnostic questions that people can apply to assess their own networks.
- Describe new work assessing energy in networks, both how it is created and transferred as well as its impact on performance and innovation.

KNOWLEDGE STRATEGY AND INNOVATION

JOSEF HOFER-ALFEIS

Corporate Technology, Siemens AG, Munich
josef.hofer-alfeis@siemens.com

The state and value of KM in today's business can be exemplified by the wide variety of successful KM instruments and solutions implemented at Siemens. A sustained KM approach needs basic concepts driving the cross-discipline value of KM, e.g. the comprehensive knowledge quality model and the socio-technical KM system model with its architecture and major knowledge flows. Typical usage and implementation indicators demonstrate broad application and high maturity of such KM systems at Siemens.

The crucial success factor for KM is its strategic and organizational positioning. Defining and executing knowledge strategies enables business owners and management teams to focus and coordinate knowledge improvements in order to achieve their primary business ambitions. And it keeps KM and its partner management disciplines, i.e. HR, IT, Process/Organization and Innovation, aligned with the business strategy.

Using KM to drive innovation underscores that KM is not just about "recycling" knowledge already owned by the organization, but is equally decisive for creating new knowledge, e.g. ideas, next practices and new technology understanding. Knowledge strategies and KM solutions can support this, e.g. by customer interfaces for effective knowledge flows.

In the future organization, innovation, knowledge and intellectual property managers will collaborate in a harmonized intellectual capital management process; and the strategic alignment of the intellectual capital in business processes will be a major challenge.

THE FUTURE OF KNOWLEDGE MANAGEMENT

DAVE SNOWDEN

Cynefin Centre
dave.snowden@cynefin.net

Knowledge was managed before the advent of "KM" in the mid 90's and will be managed after the formal title has faded into the "business as usual" graveyard of most management "fads". However KM has certain important differences with other "fads": firstly, it did not arise from a single school of thought or author and has multiple origins from the measurement of intellectual capital (Stewart, Edvinsson), to the use of distributed computing (Buckman) and from advanced understanding of information management (Prusak, Davenport) to organic and narrative models of human organizations (Snowden, Ward). This rich diversity has produced a movement that has defied many a prediction of its immanent demise, attracting a cadre of "true believers" or evangelists for a new way of thinking about the organization. This presentation will look at the development of the various historical movements that produced KM and will also examine its future direction and focus. Where should the KM function be located? Information Technology, Human Resource Management, Strategy? It will argue that KM was the trigger mechanism of taking a whole new scientific paradigm in to management thinking, not just another business process reengineering, but a replacement of the Taylorist approach to "scientific management" which has dominated the last century. Having established that principle it will explore the future directions and implication for governance in both organizations and society.

METADATA SPEAKS:
THE THIRD ORDER OF ORDER AND THE VALUE OF THE UNSPOKEN

DAVID WEINBERGER

Berkman Center for Internet & Society, Harvard Law School
self@evident.com

For thousands of years, we have organized information into taxonomic trees - the tree of life, family trees, organizational charts, the Dewey Decimal System, etc. This made sense when we were organizing physical objects, whether they were shirts hanging on a rack or the card catalog for the 11 million images in the Bettmann Archive. The digitizing of information, however, is undoing our traditional assumptions. For example, digital information can be stored in dozens of "buckets," and having lots of messy lines among them enriches the value of the system.

The biggest change, however, is that the owners of the information no longer own the organization of that information. Users do. Information architects and knowledge managers are finding that their primary job is to create a pool of information objects so enriched with metadata that users can sort and classify them as they want.

But, users creating their own taxonomies fragments the "knowledge space." And it requires us to make explicit that which thrives best as implicit. How will these changes affect the shape and authority of knowledge?

PART II

Communities and Collaboration

EFFECTS OF COMPANY SIZE AND WORKER'S EXPERIENCE ON KNOWLEDGE DELIVERY FACTORS VIS-À-VIS SOFTWARE DEVELOPMENT EFFICIENCY

SAMUEL A. AJILA

Department of Systems and Computer Engineering, Carleton University, 1125 Colonel By Drive, Ottawa, ON K1S 5B6, Canada ajila@sce.carleton.ca

ZHENG SUN

Hummingbird Ltd, 80 Aberdeen Street Ottawa, ON K1S 5R5, Canada Bill.Sun@Hummingbird.com

In this empirical research study, we first investigate the effects of knowledge delivery factors on software development efficiency and later examine the effects of company size and knowledge worker experience on knowledge delivery factors. Data were collected from 41 software development companies in North America (Canada and the USA). The data were used to test hypotheses concerning the relationships between knowledge delivery factors and software development efficiency. Results obtained show that pull approach of knowledge delivery is more effective than push approach; that software development will be more efficient if knowledge is delivered close to the time it is needed; and that software development efficiency is not affected by how deeply knowledge delivery is embedded in the development process. In addition we found that software development teams with low-level experience have stronger needs for deeper embedded-ness of knowledge delivery in software development process and that high-experienced teams tend to use documents more than inter-personal communication.

1   Introduction

Software product development (SWD) like any New Product Development (NPD) practices is a human and knowledge intensive engineering process. There is constant technology change with new problems being solved and new knowledge created every day. There are occasions when organizations have problems keeping track of this knowledge – how to create it, how to disseminate it and how to manage its use. Studies show that employing (KMS) might introduce risks as well as benefits [5]. There is therefore the need to find an effective way of managing knowledge in software product development.

The main asset of a software development organization is its knowledge repository otherwise known as *intellectual capital* [6]. The ability to access and utilize in-house intellectual capital will provide the necessary expertise needed to make timely and better decisions and, to resolve problems through proactive actions. It can also take advantage of best practices, eliminate redundant efforts and speed products to market, thus saving company unnecessary development cost, improving development team's productivity and increasing the quality of the product [7], [8], [9]. Some of the benefits in applying KMS

9

include [18]: decreasing development cost, decreasing time to market, knowledge sharing, and collaboration.

Knowledge management is a cyclic process involving three related sub-processes [9]: *creation, integration,* and *dissemination.* A knowledge worker constantly creates knowledge and this is formalized and integrated into organization's memory. It is worth noting KMS can only deliver knowledge to potential users but it cannot dictate what they do with it [8]. Therefore, to provide better KMS to SWD organizations, it is necessary to investigate (i) what better means of knowledge delivery and (ii) what are the desirable characteristics of KMS that will impact positively on software development efficiency as well as reduce the risks brought by it. The aim of this research therefore is to answer the question: how do different characteristics (or variables) in KMS affect software development efficiency? In other words, we seek to investigate the effect of knowledge delivery factors on software development efficiency based on the assumption that after the knowledge is delivered to the receiver, it will be applied in their work environment.

2   Background and Motivation

Knowledge Management (KM) is an emerging discipline especially when one considers *how to manage and capitalize an organization's internal intellectual capital* [8], [16]. In software organizations, knowledge is "embedded not only in documents or repositories, but also in organizational routines, processes, practices, and norms" [8]. Knowledge can be categorized as explicit or tacit [15]. One of the most important characteristics of knowledge is that it has several levels of refinements [18]. Current research literature on knowledge management deals with the specific elements of knowledge enterprise in general, such as knowledge transfer [19], organization memory [6], knowledge strategy [20], and design of knowledge management models [1], [13]. In addition, there are various research models, mostly conducted by case studies, to address KM challenges in software development [10]. However, there is a lack of empirical research on how knowledge delivery factors affects performance in Software Product Development. So the major goal of this research is to fill such research gap. In particular, this research is largely motivated by Cooper's paper [5] "A research agenda to reduce risk in new product development (NPD) through knowledge management: a practitioner perspective." According to her, some NPD organizations were suffering frustrations introduced by KMS. She divided the frustrations into three categories: (i) disrupting the natural flow of activity; (ii) altering roles; and (iii) lack of context. This paper focuses on one of the research challenges in Cooper's paper [5]. Thus, the objectives of this study are to:

(1) Identify the key knowledge delivery factors in software development process;
(2) Explore the relationships between these key factors and software development efficiency;
(3) Quantitatively analyze the impact of knowledge delivery factors on software development efficiency;

(4) Examine the effects of company size and knowledge worker experience on knowledge delivery factors; and
(5) Present the desirable characteristics of knowledge delivery factors relevant to software development process.

The first part of the study is based on an extensive literature review within the fields of knowledge management in Software Engineering, New Product development, and organization learning. From this, we developed four testable hypotheses. A research model was designed and variables were identified. A questionnaire was developed, submitted to Carleton University research ethics committee for clearance and approval. The approved questionnaire was sent to 102 selected software development companies. A total of forty one usable questionnaires were returned (response rate of 40.2%). The respondents companies represent both small/medium and large sized organizations. Forty six percent of the usable questionnaires came from large organizations with more than 1000 employees and the remaining 54% from small to medium sized companies. The study period was between January 1999 and December 2003.

3   Research Hypotheses

From literature review, we highlighted four major factors relevant to knowledge delivery [7], [9], [10], [12], [16], [18]:

(1) Which approach is better to deliver knowledge – pull or push?
(2) When is the best time to deliver knowledge?
(3) How is knowledge embedded in software development process?
(4) Which form of knowledge delivery is better – inter-personal communication or reading documents?

In what follows, we review each of these factors and we formed four testable hypotheses (one for each factor) to guide our research.

3.1 How knowledge is delivered

There are two ways of delivering knowledge reported in the literature: 'pull' and 'push' approaches [12], [19]. The former refers to technologies that aim at drawing knowledge from existing knowledge repositories or organization memories to knowledge users. On the other hand, 'push' approach aims at providing knowledge to users without prior interaction [12]. When knowledge is pushed to users, it is assumed that the knowledge being delivered is useful to the knowledge worker and it is more likely to be reused in the future. Yet, in a real working environment, this assumption is problematic, because it is very difficult to forecast which knowledge is more useful in the future. In contrast, by using the pull approach, knowledge workers already know what kind of knowledge they will need for their work, and they take initiatives to search for such knowledge. Hence, from the above considerations, we form the first hypothesis:

H1:   *Software development is more efficient if majority of knowledge is delivered by pull approach rather than push approach.*

3.2 When is the best time to deliver knowledge

Successful knowledge delivery must provide users with the knowledge required by a task at the time of performing the task [4]. According to Cole [4], "Just in time" knowledge delivery is a situation whereby knowledge is delivered "soon enough that it is applied to the appropriate situation, and late enough that the user does not have to go through training or information overload." If knowledge is delivered to software engineers too early, the knowledge may turn obsolete and not useful by the time such knowledge is needed. On the other hand, software engineers expect knowledge to be delivered not too late after the time they need it.   These considerations lead to the second testable hypothesis:

H2:   *Software development efficiency is impacted positively if the knowledge required is delivered "just in time."*

3.3 How knowledge is embedded

Studies show that people are often not aware of the information that might be relevant to their work, even though such knowledge has been explicitly stored in the company's organizational memory [12]. This is especially true for business with a rapid changing environment, like software development [1]. To address this challenge, many researchers turn to active task-oriented or process-oriented knowledge delivery approach where the knowledge delivery system would be aware of specific tasks performed by users at specific time, and deliver necessary knowledge to accomplish that task [1], [2], [13]. There are two major research streams advocating process-oriented knowledge management: MILOS (Minimally Invasive Long-term Organizational Support) [13] and DÉCOR (Delivery of context-sensitive organizational knowledge) [1]. The literature review on the process-oriented knowledge management leads to the third testable hypothesis:

H3:   *The more deeply knowledge delivery is embedded in the software development process the more efficient the software development activities are.*

3.4 Form of Knowledge delivery

Software development involves many document-driven processes and activities [3]. However, learning from documents is not enough in software development organizations. Software engineers tend to talk directly with other people who have the knowledge they need either by discussing face to face, or via electronic means like telephone, and e-mail [10]. As these two forms of learning knowledge exist in current software development practice, it is desirable to investigate how they affect software development productivity. Moreover, it may be difficult to keep static documents updated in order to deliver the latest information or knowledge. Therefore, we hypothesize that:

H4:   *Learning directly from people by inter-personal communication is more positively associated with software development efficiency than reading documents.*

4   Research Methods

Information required to test hypotheses is collected by questionnaires as stated in section 2. Companies involved in software development are considered as the target population for this study. This population includes companies of different sizes. These companies should have their headquarters in North America and with over fifty employees. Key people in the software development projects teams are targeted as respondents to answer the questionnaire.

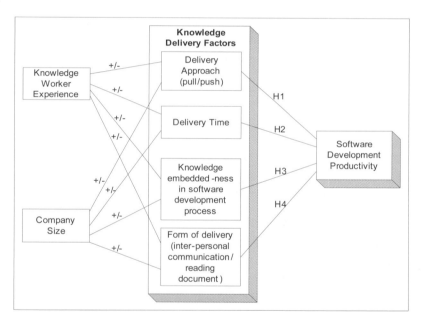

Figure 1. Research model

Out of 43 questionnaires returned, 41 were valid. The response rate is therefore 40.2% (41/102). In the sampled projects, 46% (or 19/41) are from large organizations that have more than 1000 employees, and 54% (or 22/41) are from small or medium-sized companies with less than 1000 employees.

4.1 Research Model, Variables and Measures

Figure 1 represents the research model used in the study.   It consists of three components – knowledge delivery factors which constitute the independent variables, software development productivity (the dependent variable), and organization size and knowledge worker experience (control variables).

4.1.1 Independent Variables

- How knowledge is delivered is categorized by two approaches: *pull* and *push* [12].
- Time to deliver knowledge is measured by the period between the time knowledge is delivered and the time when such knowledge is needed. Respondents were asked to use 7-point Likert scale. A "4" means the time of obtaining knowledge is same as the time such knowledge is needed. If the time of obtaining knowledge is earlier than the time such knowledge is needed, respondents are expected to answer 1 – 3. Otherwise, if it is late, the expected answers are 5 - 7.
- How knowledge delivery is embedded in software development process. There are two major attributes:
  - o Is the required knowledge for each task clearly defined during the enactment of development process?
  - o How easy is it for the knowledge worker to access the necessary knowledge for a specific task during process run-time?

  A 7-point Likert scale that ranges from "totally disagree" and "totally agree" is used to obtain score for each attribute.
- Form of knowledge delivery falls into two categories: *reading document* and *learning directly from other people via inter-personal communications*. Respondents were asked to identify which one is the most often used to obtain work-related knowledge in their project development.

4.1.2 Dependent Variable

Human effort is the most important resource consumed in software development and productivity takes both human efforts and time into account, thus *Development Productivity* is used as the major metric to measure software development efficiency. It is calculated by dividing software project size with development efforts. Function point (FP) is used to measure software project size and person month is used to measure development efforts [11], [14]. Participants in this research can indicate the size of their projects by either LOC or FP. In the data analysis, LOC is converted to FP.

4.1.3 Control Variables

There are two control variables – *organization size* and *knowledge worker's experience*. Organization size is measured by the total number of employees in the company. The effectiveness of knowledge delivery approach is dependent on the receiver's capabilities to identify what knowledge is needed for the work at hand [11].

5 Research Results

Six of the variables used in this study have numeric values. Table 1 presents the descriptive statistics of the sampled data for these variables. The skew-ness and kurtosis indicates that sampled data for these variables are normally distributed.

Table 1. Descriptive Statistics (sample size = 41)

	N	Mean	Std.	Skewness		Kurtosis	
	Stats.	Stats.	Stats.	Stats	Std. Err.	Stats.	Std. Err
Knowledge delivery time	41	3.78	1.037	-.100	.369	-.709	.724
If knowledge is defined in process	41	4.68	1.312	-.002	.369	-.703	.724
If knowledge is easily accessed	41	5.32	1.234	-.311	.369	-.730	.724
Organization size	41	2.88	1.503	.450	.369	-1.309	.724
Knowledge Worker's exp.	41	5.10	1.357	-.059	.369	-.769	.724
Productivity	41	2.56	0.730	-.158	.369	-.682	.724
Valid N (listwise)	41						

Table 2 presents the Pearson Correlations Coefficients for the numeric variables. The data information in Table 2 indicates that organization size and knowledge worker's experience are strongly correlated with knowledge delivery time. The two independent variables strongly correlated with each other. The other two variables - knowledge delivery approaches and knowledge delivery forms are measured on a nominal scale.

Table 2. Pearson Correlation Coefficients for Variables

	Org. Size	Experience	Knowledge Delivery Time (H2)	If knowledge is defined in process (H3)	If knowledge is easily accessed (H3)	Productivity
Org Size		.006	.479**	.246	.170	-.251
Experience			-.286*	.074	.160	-.086
Knowledge Delivery Time				.039	-.237	-.086
If knowledge is defined in process					.434**	-.301*
If knowledge is easily accessed						-.057

5.1 Hypotheses Testing

The next step is to test the proposed hypotheses. A null hypothesis is provided for each hypothesis, which is rejected based on the value of probability p from hypothesis testing. If $p > .10$, the null hypothesis is valid and we believe that, the examined independent variables do not have significant effects on software development productivity.

Firstly, we examine the interactions between control variables and independent variables. If control variables and independent variables have strong interaction, control variables will be taken into account when testing the hypothesis. Otherwise, the main effects of independent variables on software development productivity will be used to test the hypothesis.   However, statistical tests show that there are no significant interactions between the control variables and the independent variables so the hypotheses are tested by looking at the effects of the independent variables.

H1:   The *null hypothesis* H_0 for H1 is that the population mean of software development productivity is the same for projects using either of the two knowledge delivery approaches (pull and push).

Table 3. Two Independent Samples t Test Results of H1

	t-value	Sig. (2-tailed)	Mean difference	Mean	
				pull	push
Full Sample (n = 41)	2.628**	.012	.58034	2.77541	2.19507
*p < 0.1, ** p < 0.05, *** p < 0.01					

Table 3 shows the result of the two independent-samples T test of H1 with $p = 0.012$. This result indicates that the null hypothesis can be rejected with $p < 0.05$.   As mean difference of productivity between projects using the pull approach and projects using the push approach is positive, we can conclude that projects using the pull approach for knowledge delivery are more productive than projects using the push approach. Therefore, H1 is supported.

Table 4. Spearman Correlation of T_{ab} & SWD

			Productivity	Time
Spearman rho	Productivity	Correlation Coefficient	1.000	-.370*
		Sig. (2-tailed)	.	.017
		N	41	41
	Time	Correlation Coefficient	-.370*	1.000
		Sig. (2-tailed)	.017	.
		N	41	41

* Correlation is significant at the .05 level (2-tailed)

H2:   Knowledge delivery time is measured by the period between the time of knowledge delivery and the time when such knowledge is needed. We first tested for linear relationship between the time knowledge is delivered and the time when such knowledge is needed. Let T_d be the time knowledge is delivered and $T_n = 4$ be the time knowledge is required (Figure 2).   If the respondent indicated 4 this means that $T_d = T_n$. Based on literature review [1], [3], [4], projects with T_d equals to 3 or 4 are considered as projects with "on-time" knowledge delivery. To get a better result from the hypothesis test we introduce a measure of distance (T_{ab}) of T_d from the ideal value of knowledge delivery time and we use the median value (3.5) between 3 and 4 as the indicator for measuring T_{ab}. Thus $T_{ab} = |T_d - 3.5|$. As a result, H2 can be tested by examine if T_{ab} is negatively correlated with software development productivity. Testing results (Table 4) indicates that T_{ab} is significantly ($p<0.05$) correlated with software development productivity at hypothesized sign, so H2 is accepted. To confirm the result, H2 is further tested using quadratic regression.

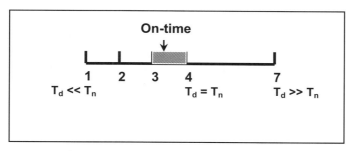

Figure 2. Measurement of Knowledge Delivery Time

H3: Table 1 shows that the two variables (if knowledge is defined in the process and if knowledge is easily accessed) have normal distribution. The correlation testing results (Table 2) indicate that neither of the two independent variables used to measure embedded-ness of knowledge delivery in SWD processes is positively correlated with software development productivity (Person correlation is -0.301 and -0.057 respectively). Therefore, there is no evidence in the data to support H3. Thus, H3 is rejected.

H4: Respondents were asked to identify which form of knowledge delivery is more often used in their projects. In about two-third (27/41) of the sampled projects, reading documents is the major form and one-third (14/41) of the projects are using inter-personal communication. Similar to H1, *two independent-samples T test* is used to test H4. The null hypothesis (H_0) for H4 is that the population mean of software development productivity is the same for projects using inter-personal communication and projects using documents as the form of knowledge delivery. The results show that there are no significant differences between the two forms of knowledge delivery. Thus, H4 is rejected.

5.2 The effects of Company size and Knowledge Workers' Experience on Knowledge delivery Factors

This section discusses the effects of company size and workers' experience on knowledge delivery factors. We summarize below the results obtained from the testing:

(1) Compared to large-sized organizations (1000 employees or more), small/medium-sized organizations prefer to use pull approach for knowledge delivery (*chi*-value = 2.753, $p < 0.1$).

(2) Small/medium sized organizations have earlier knowledge delivery time (*t*-value = 2.80, $p < 0.01$) compared to large-sized organizations.

(3) High-experienced development teams are more likely to use reading document as form of knowledge delivery (*chi*-value = 3.873, $p < 0.05$) than low-experienced teams.

(4) Knowledge delivery in low-experienced teams is more deeply embedded in development process (*t*-value = -0.149, $p < 0.05$).

6   Conclusions

In this research work, we have identified four key knowledge delivery factors that affect software development efficiency and have proposed four hypotheses by reviewing literature on knowledge management and software engineering. The proposed hypotheses were tested against a data sample collected through questionnaires returned by 41 software development companies with headquarters in North America (the US and Canada). The results of this study suggest that:

(1) Software development projects using pull approach for knowledge delivery is more efficient than projects using push approach. This leads us to believe that the software development team using pull approach of knowledge delivery may be more productive.

(2) Compared to large-sized companies, small/medium-sized software development companies prefer to use pull approach rather than push approach for knowledge delivery. This result suggests two things, One, it might be that small/medium-sized companies do not have enough resources to use push approach (e.g. traditional class-room training) to deliver knowledge. Two, knowledge workers with more experience would probably know where and from whom to obtain the knowledge they needed, thus it would be easier and more effective for them to search for knowledge by themselves.

(3) Software development will be more efficient if knowledge required is delivered close to the time such knowledge is needed. This result is consistent with concept of just-in-time knowledge delivery advocated by Kevin Cole [4].

(4) Software development efficiency is not affected by how deeply knowledge delivery is embedded in software development process.

(5) Software development teams with low-level experience have stronger needs for deeper embedded-ness of knowledge delivery in software development process. This result suggests that knowledge workers with low-experience might not have strong capability for searching necessary knowledge by themselves thus they may have stronger needs for knowledge delivery embedded-ness in development processes.

(6) Two forms of knowledge delivery, inter-personal communication or reading document, do not have statistically significant differences vis-à-vis their impacts on software development effectiveness.

(7) High-experienced software development teams tend to use reading document as form of knowledge delivery; while low-experienced development teams tend to use inter-personal communication as a form of knowledge delivery.

6.1 Limitations and Future Work

First of all, the sample data used in this research was collected from software development organizations headquartered in North America. Therefore, a larger sample that cuts across continents and comprises of more software development companies will better validate the result obtained. Secondly, this research is only focused on the knowledge delivery phase of the knowledge management life cycle. It does not cover how knowledge is created and preserved. Thirdly, this research did not investigate how characteristics of knowledge itself, like content of knowledge, or structure of knowledge, affect software development efficiency. Additional research is needed in order to investigate these characteristics. This will enable us to figure out which delivery method is better for different type of knowledge in software development. Fourthly, software development involves different types of knowledge workers, who play different roles in software development. They have different expectations on how knowledge is delivered to them. Therefore, we need to investigate if it helps to deliver knowledge in different formats or views to better meet these expectations. Lastly, further research is needed on the impact of other organizational and human factors on the knowledge delivery in software development, like what kind of process is applied in software development, whether knowledge workers are co-located in the same place or distributed over different locations, the attitude of knowledge workers toward knowledge delivery and sharing, etc.

References

1. Abecker, A., *et al.* (2001), Business-Process Oriented- Delivery of Knowledge through Domain Ontology, *Second International Workshop on Theory and Applications of Knowledge Management*, Munich, 3-7 September 2001.
2. Basili, V. R., Caldiera, G., and Rombach, H. D, Experience Factory. *In Encyclopedia of Software Engineering*, (J. J. Marciniak, ed.), vol. 1, John Wiley Sons, 1994.
3. Birk, A., Surmann, D., and Althoff, K.D., (1999), Applications of Knowledge Acquisition in Experimental Software Engineering, *11th European Workshop on Knowledge Acquisition, Modelling, and Management*, 1999, pp. 67-84.
4. Cole, K., Fischer, O., Saltzman, P. (1997), Just-in-time knowledge delivery, *Communications of the ACM.* Vol.40, Issue.7, July 1997. pp. 49 – 53.
5. Cooper, L.P. (2003). A research agenda to reduce risk in new product development through knowledge management: a practitioner perspective, *Journal of Engineering and Technology Management*, 20(2003) pp.117-140.
6. Cross, R. and Baird, L. (2000). Technology is not enough: improving performance by building organizational memory. *MIT Sloan Management Review,* Vol.41, No.3, Spring 2000, pp. 69-78.
7. Cummings, J.L. and Teng, B.S. (2003) Transferring R&D knowledge: the key factors affecting knowledge transfer success, *Journal of Engineering and Technology Management*, 20 (2003), pp.39–68.
8. Davenport, T.H., and Prusak, L. (1998), Working Knowledge, how organizations manage what they know. *Harvard Business School Press*, 1998.
9. Davenport, T.H., Long, D. W. D. and Beers, M. C. (1998). Successful knowledge management projects, *Sloan Management Review Winter*, 1998, pp. 43-57.

10. Johansson, C., Hall, P. and M. Coquard. (1999), "Talk to Paula and Peter - They are experienced" - The experience engine in a nutshell, *Proc. 11th Int. Conf. on Software Engineering and Knowledge Engineering, SEKE '99*, Kaiserslautern, Germany, June 16-19, 1999, pp. 171-186.

11. Leenders, A.J., *et al.* (2003), Virtuality, communication, and new product team creativity: a social network perspective, *Journal of Engineering and Technology Management*. 20(2003) pp. 69–92.

12. Mahé, S. and Rieu, C. (1998), A pull approach to knowledge management: Using IS as a knowledge indicator to help people know when to look for knowledge reuse, In *PAKM-98: Proc. of the Second Int. Conference*, Oct. 1998.

13. Maurer, F. and Dellen, B. (1998), An Internet Based Software Process Management Environment, In *ICSE 98 Workshop on Software Engineering over the Internet*. 1998.

14. Mohrman, S.A., *et al.* (2003), An empirical model of the organization knowledge system in new product development firms, *Journal of Engineering and Technology Management*. 20 (2003) pp. 7–38

15. Nonaka, I. And Takeuchi, H. (1995) "The Knowledge Creating Company", *Oxford University Press*, 1995, p.8

16. O'Leary, D.E. (1998), Knowledge-Management Systems: Converting and Connecting. *Intelligent Systems, IEEE*, Vol. 13, Issue. 3. May/June 1998, pp. 30 –33.

17. O'Sullivan, A. (2003), Dispersed collaboration in a multi-firm, multi-team product-development project, *Journal of Engineering and Technology Management*. 20(2003) pp.93-116

18. Rus, I. and Lindvall, M. (2002), Knowledge Management in Software Engineering. *IEEE Software*, Vol. 19, Issue. 3. May/June 2002, pp.26-38.

19. Szulanski, G. (1996), Exploring internal stickiness: impediments to the transfer of best practice within the firm. *Strategic Management Journal*, Vol.17, Winter 1996, pp.27–43.

DEVELOPING KNOWLEDGE IN "NETWORKS OF PRACTICE"

PIERPAOLO ANDRIANI, GARY ATKINSON, ALISTAIR BOWDEN & RICHARD HALL

Durham Business School, Mill Hill Lane,
Durham, DH1 3LB, United Kingdom

Much of the knowledge management literature, e.g. (Nonaka and Takeuchi 1995; Boisot 1998), concerns "Communities of practice". Brown & Duguid (2000) suggest that a "Community of practice" may be a single organisation, or it may be a tight knit inter-organisational community, whereas a "Network of practice" is a loose knit network of physically dispersed agents. This paper proposes a model for conceptualising the knowledge development process in "Networks of practice". We will suggest that "Networks of practice" require projects with a modular architecture and that the development of knowledge in these dispersed networks involves not only the process of combination (Nonaka, Reinmoeller, & Senoo; 1998) but also the iterative processes of recombination facilitated by an integrating network centre. The theoretical considerations presented in this paper were occasioned by two case studies examined by two of the authors (Atkinson & Bowden) in part fulfillment of their MBA degrees at the University of Durham. The paper uses ideas from complexity theory to analyse the issue of knowledge creation and recombination in distributed networks.

1   INTRODUCTION

Brown & Duguid (2000) identify two types of knowledge developing groupings: "Communities of practice" and "Networks of practice" (NoP). They distinguish between these groupings as follows:

"Networks of practice ... people in such networks have practice and knowledge in common. Nevertheless, most of the members are unknown to one other. Indeed, the links between the members of such networks are usually more indirect than direct ... members coordinate and communicate through third parties, or indirectly. Coordination and communication are, as a result, quite explicit" (p.142)

"Communities of practice are relatively tight-knit groups of people who know each other and work together directly" (p. 143)

The two case studies which occasioned the theoretical considerations presented in this paper both concerned "Networks of practice" (NoP) and both addressed projects with a modular architecture. Our theoretical considerations suggest the following (tentative) propositions:

- Networks of practice (as opposed to Communities of practice) require projects with a modular architecture.
- The knowledge development processes of combination and recombination require networks with integrating centres.

21

2   THE TWO CASE STUDIES

2.1 The Durham "MINER" Project

County Durham, in the North of England, is the location of one of the earliest coal mining industries in the world and the history of this industry arouses considerable interest in the region. This case study, the Durham Mining InterNet Education Resource (MINER) was a Durham County Council led project giving digital access to the many heritage resources of County Durham. These resources (typically maps, old photographs, company archives etc. stored in museums and libraries) have always been available for research. However the rapid evolution of I.C.T. technology and the level of I.C.T. skills in the community created a new opportunity to make these resources available over the Internet. The MINER project reverses the traditional direction of flow of knowledge in a museum. Normally, it is the heritage professional who decides which heritage items go onto the web and sets the methods by which items can be explored. Durham Miner puts people in the community in charge. It is these people who decide which heritage items are interesting and which will go onto the web; more importantly, rather than the cold search facilities normally offered to search for heritage items, the people in the community create their own rich sets of heritage resources and give an interpretation and context which is normally lacking. The research carried out by the people in the mining villages can focus on any mining related topic, from a pit disaster to 'washing day'. This research project is then put onto the web, either by the person that did the course or by one of the Durham MINER staff.

2.2 The MADIC Experiment

This case study examined an initiative by the UK based telecommunications company mmO^2. The advent of General Packet Radio Switching (GPRS), often called 2.5G, and 3G networks has had a significant impact on the whole of the telecommunications industry. The high bandwidth employed by GPRS and 3G suggested that the networks should be "data driven", substantially different from the traditional mmO^2 voice driven network. In addition, unlike the traditional (2G and GSM) networks, these newer networks need more than just voice traffic and high service levels to generate profitable revenue streams; they required exponential rise in network traffic to utilise the increased bandwidth. This had to come from data intensive applications. mmO^2 recognised that to increase data traffic the network must host a selection of high bandwidth digital applications with an assortment of interesting and engaging content. Furthermore as a market leading operator mmO^2 were expected to provide this catalogue at or near to launch of GPRS and 3G. Yet they had (relatively) little resource to assign to developing applications and furthermore the development of digital content was not a core skill of mmO^2.

When considered alongside the technical complexity of the networks, the monumental changes needed to their network infrastructure and the huge cost of 3G licenses it would have been easy for mmO^2 to focus on their existing strengths and leave the provision of content to others. Bravely they decided on a different path and, drawing on ideas from the new product development style typical of Open Source projects, network economics and complexity theory, they created a stand alone facility within their own organisation aimed specifically at supporting the (*external*) development of mobile applications. This facility was the Mobile Application Development and Integrations Centre (MADIC).

2.3 The Characteristics of the Case Studies

In terms of modularity and locus of knowledge creation, Durham MINER clearly fits the 'Network of Practice' mould. A few points are critical: first, the people taking part in Durham MINER are completely self-organising, as is their research; second, none of these people communicate together, so the resulting research projects are an eclectic mix, which is partly a result of a lack of 'socialisation' amongst those taking part; thirdly, the role of the integrative centre is to provide coherence, direction and motivation to the network of volunteer researchers. The integrative centre assumes many different aspects. The first and most straightforward is provided by the core team in setting up the communication/electronic infrastructure of the website and project that constitutes the basic constraint around which the contribution will be organised. The second is emergent: once a basic website and content structure is in place, volunteers (with some IT capabilities) decide how and where to post their own contributions and what type of links to establish with other parts. Finally, the core team organises the rest of the contributions and provides basic coherence and continuity to the whole of the project.

MADIC became the centre of a network of developers that were offered legal, technical and business support to develop 3G content together with mmO^2. The attractions for the developers were the revenue sharing model taken by mmO^2 and the facilities offered in one of mmO^2's premises. The structure of MADIC was a series of parallel partnerships, each one dealing with a specific 3G content development project. By being one of the partners in all of the projects, mmO^2 played the role of the integrative centre, by, first, integrating and making compatible the projects with their platform; and second, building on the projects' complementarities (which were invisible to the single developers) in order to blend several projects into higher level projects.

The MADIC initiative also fits the "Network of practice" model. Socialisation was largely absent, except in the case of mmO^2 integrating single projects into bigger ones. The role of the centre was to recombine the results of the parallel partnerships into a coherent 3G offering, compatible on the supply side with the evolving technological platform and on the demand side with the assumed customers' behaviour.

Consideration of these case study characteristics, particularly: the physical dispersion of the agents, the modular architecture of the projects, the role of the integrating centre and the self organization which was witnessed, led to the theoretical considerations presented in the next section.

3   THEORETICAL CONSIDERATIONS

3.1 *Diversity, growing complexity and the network society*

Ashby's law of Requisite Variety is described by Stacey (1993) as follows: *"According to cybernetics, an organisation must achieve the goal of continuing adaptation to its environment if it is to survive and succeed. In order to so adapt, it has to employ a control system or regulator. It will successfully adapt when the complexity and speed of the responses enabled by its regulator match the complexity and speed of the changes occurring in its environment; that is when it controls its business according to the law of Requisite Variety."* (p. 125)

The internal variety, or complexity, of a system, e.g. a firm, must match the variety of the environment within which the system (the firm) needs to survive. The recent tendency for firms to limit in house activities to those associated with distinctive capabilities, and to outsource non-distinctive functions, fosters an imbalance between the firm's reduced internal variety and the increasing variety of its external environment; this imbalance may result in some firms becoming non viable. Paradoxically, the trend toward internal simplification has happened as a reaction to the growing complexity of the environment.

What are the main features of the long-term trend toward a networked society? Castells (2000) identifies five critical elements of the paradigm underlying the *network society*.

First, the *network society* uses information as its *raw material* and contrarily to the past technological and industrial revolutions (starting from the agricultural revolution of the Neolithic (Cipolla, 1970; Diamond, 1997) innovations are not simply *"tools to be applied but processes to be developed"*. The traditional boundary between users of innovations and producers of technology becomes blurred as users *"take control of technology, as in the case of the Internet. For the first time in history, the human mind is a direct productive force, not just a decisive element of the production system"* (Castells, 2000). The changes are profound: it seems we are on the eve of a *fourth discontinuity* (Mazlish, 1993) between humans and machines. Functions that used to be typical of the human mind have been transferred to 'intelligent' machines, so that we can talk of machines as not only an extension of the human arm but also of the human mind. In Arthur's words (1966), products in the network economy are *"congealed knowledge with a little resource"* whereas they used to be *"congealed resources with a little knowledge"*.

Secondly, this revolution is probably more pervasive than the previous Shumpeterian long waves of creative destruction. The information revolution is structurally different as it not only affects the processes by which new products and services are developed, but also directly acts on the knowledge used to produce those processes. This double feature of the information communication technology (ICT) revolution ensures the pervasiveness of the current wave of change.

The third feature encompasses the networking aspect of the ICT revolution. The dominant logic of the ICT revolution features the capability to act on information by connecting users and producers of information into networks. At the same time this apparently shapeless and anarchic structure, born at the interface between two unlikely cultures, the military environment of Advance Research Project Agency (Waldrop, 2001) and the hackers' rebellious culture, is supremely able to adapt and grow at a rate never seen before in the history of technology.

Fourthly, networks in the information age are highly flexible and capable of swift reconfiguration. This has to do with the fact that the speed of exchange of information is nearly instantaneous and distance-independent. Additionally, the clean architecture of networks makes the cost of reconfiguration of networks very low. Plug-and-play modules can easily be added and removed. New networks can be connected around universal standards, thereby making the growth of the Internet not subject to the traditional growth constraints of other types of networks (Shapiro, 1999). At the same time, the capability to adapt openly to new situations makes networks capable to pursue flexibility and specialisation in a non-conflicting way.

Finally, the fifth feature focuses on the convergence of the main technological platforms into a common macro-technological trajectory. The boundaries between the once separated sectors of computers, opto-electronics, carriers of digitised information, telecommunication producers and providers, music, media and more are becoming blurred and new groupings are forming.

The features of the network society paradigm identified by Castells (2000) define a new type of society, characterised by increasing diffusion and availability of information across networks. Consequently, decision-making becomes more decentralised resulting in integrated systems disintegrating into networks of autonomous units due in large part to the drastic reduction in transaction costs.

How does this happen? We think that three factors are extremely important. Organisations are structures devoted to coordinating the flow of information across internal boundaries (groups, departments, divisions) and external boundaries (suppliers, partners, customers, stakeholders). Management can be described as the set of activities aiming at governing the processes associated with the informational flow, knowledge coordination and integration of specialisation. As Evans and Wurster (1997) claim: *"information is the glue that holds together the structure of all businesses"*. The structure, hierarchy and boundary of an organisation have the function of protecting and maintaining the information asymmetry that constitutes the *raison d'être* of the organisation. If the informational glue that keep organisations together disappears, because information is spread wide open in the society across the Internet, then the result will be the blowing apart (unbundling) of the organisation into its constituent functions. Interestingly, all else being equal, the first elements to dissolve will be the centralised coordination of the different functions that make up the organisation. This will leave a network composed of the functional parts of the disaggregated organisation. But this is not all. The deconstruction of organisations generates new business niches at the interfaces between the newly interdependent companies. These opportunities are quickly occupied by new organisations, thereby reinforcing the tendency towards more and more complex networks.

The second factor is uncertainty. It is widely accepted that one of the effects of the ICT revolution of the 1990's, coupled with the forces of globalisation and liberalisation, has been an increase in environmental risk and uncertainty that organisations have to face. The reaction has been the disintegration into networks. The increase in complexity of value chains has forced organisations to limit exposure to risk and uncertainty by adopting a simultaneous strategy consisting of, on the one hand, specialising in core competencies and, on the other hand, increasing the number of links with suppliers, customers, partners, etc. When the transformation rate accelerates toward turbulence and instability, organisations accelerate their transformation toward the network form. Radical uncertainty affects the way organisations construct mental models of the future. The activity of strategy turns from a rational positioning process based on eco-systems thinking into a decentralised model of distributed intelligence strategising, where each node of the network acts on the basis of simple rules and relative autonomy. The net result of these processes is the formation of networks within and across organisations.

The third factor is the rate of change caused by innovation. Together with the transformation brought by increased uncertainty and informational change, the faster rate of technological innovation appears to be causing tectonic shift in the structure of industries. Traditional boundaries between sectors are being redefined (witness for example the convergence between the television, telecom, information technologies and entertainment industries). On the one hand, convergence reinforces the effects of uncertainty, but it also generates the explosive diversification of the players around (1) the newly created interfaces between once independent sectors and (2) the new radical innovations that have generated convergence in the first place. The effect of these two forces is an enlarged technological and business opportunities landscape that organisations can pursue.

The three factors mentioned above are diversity-increasing mechanisms. The same mechanisms that enhance network formation and expansion also act to increase diversity. Networks are the emergent result of the self-organisation of their inner diversity.

The trend from integration to decentralisation causes a problem in the analysis of organisational change. The focus on single organisations as the correct unit of analysis looks at the trees but misses the forest. As survival and success depend often critically on the success of the business eco-system of which the organisation is part, it follows that the imbalance between internal and external diversity may be corrected by changing the unit of operational and theoretical analysis from the firm to the firm's network or, depending on the context, to the network of firms. If this is the case then the development of knowledge in a "Network of practice", i.e. a network of loose knit physically dispersed agents, becomes an important issue.

4 DISCUSSION

4.1 Knowledge processes in NoP

Nonaka, Reinmoeller *et al.* (1998) propose a SECI model of knowledge development, where SECI represents:

- Socialisation: the process of sharing and developing tacit knowledge by means of shared experience.
- Externalisation: the articulation of tacit knowledge and its translation into forms that can be understood by others.
- Combination: the conversion of explicit knowledge into more complex sets of explicit knowledge.
- Internalisation: the conversion of newly created explicit into tacit knowledge of individuals.

In a "Network of practice" the SECI model cannot apply across the network because the opportunity for socialisation, across the network, is severely limited due to the network's loose knit and dispersed character. We suggest that the SECI model breaks down in networks of practice and fails to fully explain the dynamic of knowledge creation in radically dispersed networks. In fact the only process, which may apply *across* the network, is that of "Combination". The reason why is hidden in the dynamic of the most successful example of a virtual network: the Open Source Linux project..

The Open Source (OS) approach was introduced in the 70s by Richard Stalman (Raymonds, 1999). An OS project consists of a global network of volunteers who freely maintain and develop sophisticated software, which can be modified and used by anyone. Although unusual the approach is very effective. Linux, for instance, is widely recognised as the most reliable, stable and flexible operating system, to the point that Linux has become the most effective competitor of Microsoft. The reasons behind OS success are based on a) the access of a very large base of developers, b) knowledge-sharing mechanisms that favour transparency and effective peer review, and c) effective mechanisms for reward and recognition of successful work. A further mechanism, self-organising allocation of work will be mentioned later. All mechanisms are informal but strictly adhered to. The other fundamental aspect of Linux is its intellectual property (IP) strategy. The source code is released under the GPL (GNU Public License) (Weber, 2003) that allows anyone to download, use and modify the source code. The way the 'organisation' works is unique: developers (who share a common goal) gather around a website where all contributions are posted on the bulletin board and discussions take place in a virtual environment. The role of the project owner, the *benevolent dictator* (Raymond, 1999), is a filtering one. The project owner accepts or rejects contributions (bug fixes or enhancements) but usually doesn't intervene directly in the software writing activity. The project owner therefore influences the final specification but does not pre-determine it.

The way in which knowledge is created and assembled in OS networks is significantly different from organisations, which are, in one form or another, based on a mix of virtual and face-to-face interactions. The complete absence of physical interaction in the OS case makes the sharing of contextual knowledge, with its highly tacit content, difficult. In the OS case, the unit of analysis for the knowledge creation process is not the group but rather the individual, often working in complete isolation from the other developers, except of course through the tenuous strand of the bulletin board. In contrast to the common situation where socialisation takes place among individuals who interact with one another in the context and constraints set by a group and a place, in the OS case, the process of socialisation is limited to the written communication form, taking place among individuals, who in most cases have never met one another. Most of the codified communication is of the one-to-many form, directed toward the collective group of developers. What developers exchange and discuss are lines of codes, that is, a form of communication which is amenable to an abstract and explicit form. The often excruciating process of knowledge creation that requires the continuous interactions between individuals, group and context, characterised by the slow conversion of the tacit intuitions of individuals into more general and group-based knowledge does not take place in the OS projects. In other words, the conversion from tacit to explicit takes place predominantly at the individual level. What is exchanged is codified knowledge, which is combined in an emergent architecture, enabled by the strictly respected ethical rules of the network. The processes of socialisation, as described by the current KM literature, are largely absent. The knowledge creation process is divided into two main phases: at the individual level, developers solve self-allocated tasks by externalisation and internalisation without relying on socialisation and combination. The second phase is introduced in the next section.

4.2 Modularity and NoP

We argue that whilst "Communities of practice" can address projects with either independent or modular architecture, "Networks of practice" require projects with modular architecture. Shilling (2000) describes modularity as: *"... continuum describing the degree to which a system's components can be separated and recombined, and it refers both to the tightness of coupling between component and the degree to which the "rules" of the system architecture enable (or prohibit) the mixing and matching of components"* An architecture is defined as "modular" when the subsystems that compose the functional units are connected via standardised interfaces (Sanchez and Collins 2001). Standardisation allows the emergence of nested levels (Simon 1962), whereby innovation at the subsystem level can take place without affecting the general architecture of the system. Moreover, the loose coupling among subsystems in a modular architecture creates partial independence between the modules. This implies that changes in one module do not affect other modules. The general effect is the emergence of *semi decomposable* or *hierarchical* systems (Simon 1962). In Simon's words *"interactions among the subsystems are weak, but not negligible...(a) in a nearly decomposable system, the short-run behavior of each of the component subsystems is approximately independent of the short-run behavior of the other components; (b) in the long run, the behavior of any one of the components depends in only an aggregate way on the behavior of the other components."*

The modularisation of products/services is accompanied and enabled by the modularisation of industry structure, capabilities and specialisation (Baldwin and Clark 2000). We argue that the degree of decomposability is correlated with the practice and routines of the management of knowledge. In particular, modularity affects the locus of knowledge creation. In the previous section we have argued that the traditional KM cycle does not fully apply in a context where tacit to explicit conversion of knowledge occurs purely at the individual level, and that the cycle is subdivided into two nested phases: the individual and the collective. Developers select in autonomy the part of the project they want to engage with. The result of their work is selected by the project owner and, if accepted, is added to the project. This is an important point, for it shows two things. First, the process of allocation of modules to developers is self-organising. Self-allocation of task allows massive parallelisation to occur. This means that multiple and different attempts directed at different parts of the projects will be made in the quest to find working solutions that can be solved by individual developers. The swarm of developers gathering around a project carry with them a highly competitive, individualistic and strongly meritocratic working ethic, which tends to make the project advance along a modular route, simply because the network approach cannot work in any other way. Second, the Darwinian approach of solution finding plus selection and accretion can only work given that the "goods" that developers exchange over the virtual network of the Internet is codified knowledge and that the context of the game is evolutionary, that is, one in which the specifications of the project emerge and evolve with the project itself. The secret of modularity is then two-fold. On the one hand the parallel evolutionary approach tends to generate modular architectures, and, on the other hand, the codification/abstraction inherent in software code and the tools of exchange (the Internet) favour distributed approaches to problem solving.

A third aspect concerns recombination: radical decomposability allows self-organisation to take place in the phases of module identification and recombination. The former arises when developers self-select the module they want to work on. By doing so, they implicitly (and collectively) define the evolution of the system's architecture. In the second phase (recombination), the newly created knowledge is recombined in an emergent architecture, often under the supervisory control of the project owner. We see again that the evolutionary/distributed aspects of the OS projects changes the SECI model by introducing nested sequences of externalisation/internalisation at the individual level followed by recombination at the group/project owner integrative centre. Socialisation takes place at both the level of discussion of solution proposed (if there is such discussion) and when the new version is released. As recombination is a part of the accretion approach, that is, the project grows by progressive addition and/or modification of single parts, the direction of evolution is emergent.

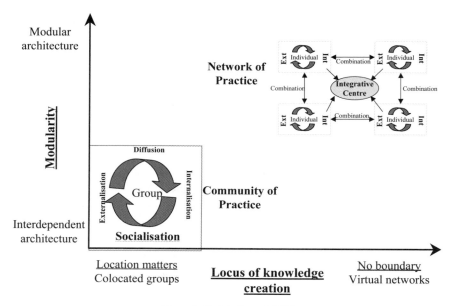

Figure 1. Modularity and SECI

In conclusion we claim that, in the case of a partial modular architecture, the inter-dependence between modules requires central control in the definition of modules' boundaries and a continuous effort in the integration of the new knowledge, which has been created. Moreover, the tacit aspects related to the unknown interdependences demand the physical collocation of groups of knowledge-creation agents (for instance geographic clusters represent a perfect case of this type of community of practice).

In the case of radical decomposability, the locus of knowledge creation becomes the individual. This allows massive parallelism and forces a redefinition of the SECI model (see Figure 1). Socialisation ceases to be determinant; integration of modules becomes an emergent property, and recombination becomes the most important feature.

The proposition we advance is that modularity is an essential enabling factor in the definition of *community vs network of practice* discussion. Whereas communities of practice can cope with independent as well as modular projects, networks of practice require modular architecture.

5   CONCLUSIONS

This paper has made the following propositions:

- Networks of practice (as opposed to Communities of practice) require projects with a modular architecture.

- The knowledge development processes of combination and recombination require networks with integrating centres.

More work is required to test these propositions, particularly with respect to the importance of: the degree to which agents join and leave the NoP voluntarily, the degree to which a network of volunteers is self organising, and the operation of different types of integrating centre.

REFERENCES

Arthur, W. B. (1996) *Increasing Returns and the new World of Business Harvard Business Review* July-August,.

Baldwin, C. Y. and K. B. Clark (2000). *Design rules: volume 1. the power of modularity.* Cambridge, MA, The MIT Press.

Boisot, M. (1998). *Knowledge Assets: securing competitive advantage in the information economy.* Oxford, Oxford University Press.

Brown, J. S. & Duguid , P. (2000). *The Social Life of Information*. Boston, Harvard Business School Press.

Castells, M. *The rise of the network society*. (Blackwell, Oxford, 2000).

Cipolla, C. M. *An economic history of world population*. (Penguin, London, 1970).

Diamond, J. *Guns, Germs and Steel. The Fates of Human Societies*. (W.W. Norton and Company, New York, 1997).

Evans, P. and Wurster T. S. *Blown to bits* (Harvard Business School Press, 1999).

Mazlish, B. *The Fourth Discontinuity: the Co-evolution of Humans and Machines* (Yale University Press, New Haven, CT, 1993).

Nonaka, I., P. Reinmoeller, *et al.* (1998). "The 'ART' of Knowledge: Systems to Capitalize on Market Knowledge." *European Management Journal* 16: 673-684.

Nonaka, I. and H. Takeuchi (1995). *The knowledge-creating company : how Japanese companies create the dynamics of innovation*. Oxford, Oxford University Press.

Raymond, E. S. (1999). *The cathedral and the bazaar: musing on Linux and open source by an accidental revolutionary*. Cambridge, MA, O'Reilly.

Sanchez, R. and R. P. Collins (2001). "Competing - and Learning - in Modular Markets." *Long Range Planning* 34: 645-667.

Shapiro, C. and Varian *H. R. Information rules a strategic guide to the network economy* (Harvard Business School Press, Boston, MA., 1999).

Shilling, M. (2000). "Toward a general modular systems theory and its application to interfirm product modularity." *Academy of Management Review* 25(2): 312-34.

Simon, H. (1962). "The architecture of complexity." *Proceeding of the American Philosophical Society* 106: 467-82.

Stacey, R. D. (1993). *Strategic Management and Organisational Dynamics*. London, Pitman Publishing.

Waldrop, M. M. *Scientific American,* December, (2001).

Weber, S. (2003). *The Success of Linux and Open Source*. Cambridge, MA, Harvard University Press.

DEMONSTRATING THE EFFECTIVENESS AND EFFICIENCY OF KNOWLEDGE HALLWAYS WITHIN PRICEWATERHOUSECOOPERS

GERARD BREDENOORD

PricewaterhouseCoopers
137 H. F. Orbanlaan, Ghent, Belgium, B-9000
gerard.bredenoord@be.pwc.com

PricewaterhouseCoopers' internal strategy for Knowledge Management represents a consolidation of external best practices and internal experiences. This strategy focuses on the development and implementation of an environment which facilitates, supports and increases the codification and sharing of explicit and tacit knowledge. The author's research examines how PwC's KM activities can ensure that the aspects of knowledge "Hallways," as defined by Nancy Dixon, will increase the collective knowledge within the firm.

1 Introduction

PricewaterhouseCoopers (PwC) has created an internal strategy for Knowledge Management (KM) that was articulated in its Knowledge Management "Blueprint."

This strategy represents the consolidation of external best practices and internal experiences, and it focuses on the development and implementation of an environment which continuously facilitates supports and increases the codification and sharing of both explicit and tacit knowledge among professional staff throughout the firm.

A large part of this strategy deals with the challenge of creating a sustainable and focused environment where practitioners feel comfortable and encouraged to share their experiences. PwC recognises that this change is largely behavioural, and as such created a specific role called the "Knowledge Broker" to assist in the long-term process of change. The objective of the author's research is to see if the content of "The Blueprint," and specifically the Knowledge Broker role, will increase the likelihood of practitioners sharing their experiences within PwC. This research focuses on the strategy and the specific aspects of the strategy, which will increase the likelihood of success.

The research draws heavily on the concepts defined in Nancy Dixon's book *The Organisational Learning Cycle*. In this work Dixon (Dixon 1999) defined "Hallways" and the characteristics that need to be present to enable hallway conversation and sharing to be focused and intentional. The moving of private knowledge to more collective knowledge must be seen as a continuous process rather than an end-state. The author's research focuses on the presence and the depth of the presence of these characteristics in the PwC Knowledge Management strategy and the day-to-day activities of practitioners within PwC that will increase the collective knowledge within the firm.

The results of this internal research have shown that "The Blueprint," and the application of specific sections of "The Blueprint" – such as the Knowledge Broker role as a way to effectively capture and share tacit knowledge – is to a large extent supportive of Dixon's characteristics. However, the research and related interviews demonstrate that there are a number of key challenges that need to be pro-actively addressed to ensure that the implementation and the sustainability of the implementation can be achieved.

In order to obtain an objective and balanced view of the current best practices regarding "Hallways" within the professional services industry, the research systematically compared PwC's current strategy to that of the framework provided by Dixon. This comparison was supported and enhanced through the research of sources that have written about "Hallways" within the professional service industry. In order to achieve this objective, information was drawn from the following sources:

(1) Literature Research, including that of professional research firms, and the relevant industry press;
(2) The current PwC KM strategy (i.e., "The Blueprint"); and
(3) Current PwC points of view that are based on structured interviews with PwC leaders, practitioners and KM professionals.

2   Approaches to Knowledge Management

One of the largest influences on a firm's KM environment is the approach that an organisation takes to the implementation of a knowledge management solution. Although there are many ways to implement a solution, until recently the best solution has always been viewed as top down, and globally uniform.

However research presented regarding industry and business level differences, and the greater impact of tacit versus explicit knowledge within the professional services industry, makes this top-down approach to knowledge management less applicable to the professional services industry than might be the case for other, more structured, industry sectors.

With the increase in globalisation, there has been an increased realisation that global knowledge is not the same as local knowledge. Research by Marcus Birkenkrahe, Auckland Business School, (Lelic 2002) points out that, "Many failures of KM implementations go back to management not understanding the difference between global and local best practices." He notes that our view of "best practice" is often automatically understood to be universal. But this is not necessarily true. Local best practices may be global worst practices, such as when the mechanism to motivate people in a local context is indeed very local, based on rewards that are not understood or appreciated outside of that context. His research indicates that more often than not, global best practices are often only successful if they refer directly to the globalised situation. Finally he reminds us that, "Ignorance of local knowledge is what leads to disaster."

In many business level strategies, the top down approach to "doing business" and KM is no longer the only solution, and that we must find solutions that work and fit the local markets. This challenge is increasing as globalisation of the professional service firms increase in-line with the increased globalisation of the professional service firm's client base. For the global professional service industry this is the challenge of moving towards a more "inside-out" approach and away from the "outside-in" approach. This approach is also in-line with research and models presented by Bob de Wit and Ron Meyer (Wit & Meyer 2002) into the relevance of specific strategies to specific industries.

One new way of looking at the workplace is presented through research conducted by MIT and Gartner (Bell & Joroff 2001). Their research suggests that we should look at the workplace as a new ecosystem within which new synergies can be achieved through the greater understanding and relationships between the various components within the ecosystem.

The new synergy is founded on an integrated perspective toward leadership, purpose, people, systems and settings. In other words, through a clear sense of purpose, leaders build a culture. Culture attracts a community of people. Those people use systems and tools to support and drive that purpose, and the workspace provides the setting in which leadership, purpose, people and systems play out.

The relationship between the workplace and the way it is changing in the face of globalisation are important factors to be incorporated into any KM solution, which is trying to increase the leverage of the firm's tacit knowledge. This relates both to the increased codification of "not yet expressed knowledge" and the increased usage and transfer of inexpressible knowledge. The transformation of tacit into explicit knowledge and vice versa makes the creation of knowledge possible (Nonaka 1991). The assumption that knowledge is created through the interaction between tacit and explicit knowledge allows us to establish four modes of knowledge conversion.

- From tacit knowledge to tacit knowledge, which is called socialization;
- From tacit knowledge to explicit knowledge, or externalization;
- From explicit knowledge to explicit knowledge, or combination;
- From explicit knowledge to tacit knowledge, or internalization.

In the knowledge-creating company, all four of these patterns should exist in dynamic interaction, like a spiral of knowledge. From the research done by Nonaka, it is important to note that in the "Third Generation of KM" we cannot forget the experiences of the past generations (i.e., the focus on explicit knowledge). His research shows that solutions should be integrated ones, covering both tacit and explicit knowledge.

3   Background to PwC's KM programme

Since the merger between Coopers & Lybrand and Price Waterhouse, PwC has tried a number of different solutions focused on getting its people to use and share knowledge within the firm. From a review of the past five years, it is possible to identify two specific phases (generations), which PwC has gone through. The first approach to increased knowledge usage and sharing was driven by the e-business era (also referred to as the "technology approach" to KM). This approach is still a significant part of the firm's environment. However PwC has come to the realisation that this approach has some key deficiencies, including:

- Without the supporting processes to create and maintain content, the system quickly loses its attractiveness, and it is impossible to maintain all the global content from one central organisation.
- Significant behavioural changes are required before people would trust these repositories above the personal networks that they had been relying on to date.
- A technological solution has limited value in increasing the codification of tacit knowledge or the increased leverage of tacit knowledge.
- This solution does not help the disconnected user (i.e., the user that does not have continuous access to the firm's network), or the cultural and language issues of the globally distributed territories.

The second approach that was applied by PwC was the increased use of online education and computer-based training. The belief was that the solutions were already available and practitioners just need to be better educated. The objective was to increase the practitioner's awareness of knowledge solutions and tools that are available, and to focus on the increased use of these offerings. Much emphasis was placed on increased productivity through the use of these learning methods, and the wider audiences that could be reached with these solutions. However as with the above approach, this approach also had a number of deficiencies:

- It was difficult to tailor the online learning to the specific education, language and cultural differences of the participants.
- It was very difficult to cater for the various territory and industry specific requirements of the practitioners.
- And as with the first solution, it had limited value in the increased codification of tacit knowledge or the increased leverage of tacit knowledge.

In 2001, PwC reviewed its various approaches to KM, and the investment versus returns that it was achieving for those investments. In some online learning courses the net cost had been $800 per seat. At the time, PwC decided to have a back-to-basics approach to KM. This approach can be thought of as the 'goal-oriented' approach (Baldacchino, Armistead & Parker 2002). Whether this approach is put forth in terms of strategic goals, competencies, or knowledge maps, the ideas are similar. The intention of this approach was to focus the firm's energy on those competencies and resource areas expected to lead to success.

It was decided that each industry sector within the firm would develop and implement a content strategy (industry sectors are PwC's go-to-market theme). The content strategy is a consolidation of the various factors / business issues that make up the business-level environment. This makes it possible to prioritise the efforts that need to be applied in order to achieve these objectives, and to identify the supporting environments that need to be established for these objectives to be met.

Further, this approach helps PwC achieve a strategic position where it can focus on achieving an acceptable level of codification and leverage of tacit knowledge. As it is impossible or unaffordable to codify all knowledge, it is important to focus on the correct level of codification required to achieve the firm's business objectives. (Figure 1 below portrays the principle drivers of PwC's internal KM strategy.)

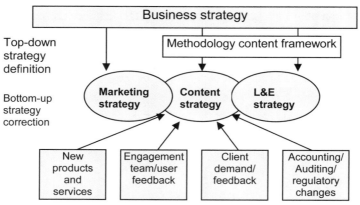

Source: PricewaterhouseCoopers "The Blueprint" 2003

Figure 1. Prinicpal Drivers of PwC's Internal KM Strategy

By focusing on the content strategy, and having the flexibility to apply the correct focus, methods and tools to specific types of knowledge has given PwC a KM strategy which can be applied in different ways at different level of maturity, while still maintaining the focus on specific objectives and increased knowledge usage and sharing.

4   Implementation of the Knowledge Broker role at PwC

The Knowledge Broker (KB) is the focal point for an engagement team's KM activities. This person adds value by championing knowledge sharing on the team, and by encouraging and reminding engagement team members to document and share their knowledge with others. The KB also liaises with the KM resources within the industry sector or lines of service within the firm.

Typically, at least one KB will be appointed for each significant or strategic engagement. Large, geographically dispersed teams may require one KB per territory or client subsidiary. The individual identified to play the Knowledge Broker role should have sufficient influence and reach within the engagement team, and must be close enough to the team's activities to spot opportunities, gaps and blockages in the flow of knowledge. It is recommended that someone at the manager level (with a minimum of four to five years of experience) assume this role. Today, PwC has more than 1,000 knowledge brokers active around the world.

The KB has a number of predefined responsibilities, which include:

- Participate in knowledge sharing with the rest of PwC by providing content, insights and expertise from their engagement team;
- Interact and network with other KBs within the local Knowledge Community; and
- Provide the respective territory- and theatre-based Knowledge Managers with input on the knowledge needs of the engagement team, and with feedback regarding the Knowledge Community's KM programmes.

The KB also plays a key role in the establishment and maintenance of focus groups and communities of practices within PwC, so as to keep up to date about specific research topics relevant to the engagement team.

These objectives may be tailored and supplemented by the engagement team leadership as needed to form part of the performance objectives for the individual assuming the role. Pilot studies within PwC have shown that this role can take up between 5% – 20% of an individual's time for a large team within one territory. The initial research showed that the role would not have an adverse impact on engagement team economics, as this role is typically a re-alignment of activities previously carried out, in a fragmented way, by several other team members. The success of the KB can be measured by the effectiveness of the knowledge-seeking and knowledge-sharing behaviour of the engagement team as a whole, as well as by the Broker's interaction with both the full community of KBs within an industry practice, and with the KM networks within the territory or industry sector.

The KB is a key link in the establishment of a bottom-up approach to the understanding and application of knowledge within the firm. The KB plays a significant role in achieving the sustainable behavioural changes that are required to increase the leveraging and sharing of tacit knowledge within the firm on an on-going basis.

5   Why do we need "Hallways"? – The business objectives

"Hallways" literally have a different feel from typical meeting rooms and offices. There is less sense of hierarchy in "Hallways" where everyone seems to be an equal participant. Hallway conversations often involve multiple perspectives, because anyone who wanders by can join in, adding their ideas to the mix. By the same token, people feel free to walk away if the subject proves uninteresting because the organisational norms that require we feign interest in the topic, are not applicable in "Hallways."

"Hallways" are places where ideas are tested against the thinking of others. As long as meaning is held privately by an individual, it is protected from the discovery that it may be wrong or limited in perspective. When it is made accessible to others, then the data in which it is based can be challenged, and the reasoning and logic that led to the conclusions can be examined.

"Hallways" are also places where collective meaning is made. In other words, meaning is not just exchanged; it is constructed in the discussions between the organisational members. In the process of each person articulating his own meaning and of the comprehending how it differs from that which others have constructed, individuals alter the meaning they hold. The act of articulating the meaning each has constructed serves to clarify it to the speaker as well as the listener. The meaning each organisational member articulates influences the others. Influence does not necessarily imply agreement, but it does suggest recognition. Out of these ideas new meaning develops, meaning that no one individual brought into the hallway. It is this group construction of meaning that is the basis of organisational learning.

"Hallways" are constructed as part of the day-to-day activities of each employee of an organisation. It is important that "Hallways" primarily focus on the tacit knowledge that an organisational member might be exposed to, but does not ignore the fact that in the normal day-to-day activities people work interactively with both. Additionally, "Hallways" should be considered an integrated part of the daily working environment, where employees shift continuously between tacit and explicit knowledge and from the routine to the unpredictable.

From the above information we can conclude that "Hallways" play a significant part in the creation of an environment where tacit knowledge can be shared. We can also conclude that the tacit knowledge holders themselves must drive these "Hallways." Lastly we can conclude that tacit knowledge transfer is an integrated part of every employee's daily activities, rather than a separately identifiable section, which can be targeted for individual improvement.

6   What are "Hallways"? – The Characteristics

Organisations need to develop processes, which have the positive characteristics of real hallways, yet are more focussed and intentional. In The Organisational Learning Cycle, Dixon suggests "Hallways" require organisational members to interact with each other, exchanging their data, conclusions, reasoning and questions with others, rather than listening to speeches or presentations.

Collective learning is more effective when organisational members talk to each other as equals rather than as disparate members of a hierarchy. "Hallways" should be where people leave their positions at the door and where ideas are judged on their worth, not on who put them forward.

This is a key factor in global organisations such as PwC, whose activities are globally distributed. To ensure that distance workers do not start to feel like second-class citizens, consultant Shannon Bradford (Guterman 2002) suggests that managers assign specific individuals to give distance workers "the big picture" as well as the daily news. Bradford says managers have to understand that people in branch offices or remote locations can easily be cut off from resources and opportunities and feel less important than those who work at the main office. "When they are not getting regular news about the office activities, workers might assume that something negative is happening," she says. "Because distance workers are disconnected from the everyday operations and conversations, it is also more difficult for them to gauge how they are performing in relation to the business."

There is a need to invite multiple perspectives into the hallway, and moreover to tolerate the tension that results from the ensuing differences long enough that new meaning can be generated from them. Dixon believes that the longer the tension is tolerated the more possible ideas will emerge. For this reason "Hallways" must intentionally invite multiple perspectives, actively encourage those perspectives to challenge accepted practices and maintain the ensuing tension while new learning emerges.

Additionally, research performed by Gartner (Gomolski 2001) points out that if an organisation is serious about building a culture that fosters learning, they must allow people within the organisation to feel that they can make mistakes without being reprimanded. Mistakes are part of the learning process and should be viewed as such. Publicly discussing lessons learned is a way of creating an atmosphere where people feel they are allowed to fumble.

Dixon points out that there are two fundamental assumptions that underlie "Hallways":

- Ordinary people, thinking together, have the capability to generate workable answers to problems of the organisation, and
- There is not just one solution to most organisational problems. In fact there are many potential solutions, which if agreed upon would be effective.

Her research also points out that because of the assumptions above, it is less critical that the organisation comes to the right answer and more critical that the collective meaning is made, so that those who must act upon the meaning can support their actions with their own reasoning.

"Hallways" should bring together the primary source of the data, allowing the "sense-making" process to be less inferential and more data based. However the focus is not the data, but the public availability and discussion that reference the data. The process of making available is a key distinction from traditional methods of communication in which learning is equated to sharing or the making public of information. The key is that the participants of the hallway, rather than a separate group within the organization, should drive this process.

Shared experiences are powerful sources of shared meaning, because it is possible to reference the experience and thus to bring to mind for everyone a meaningful image. In large organisations there are surprisingly few shared experiences. Organisations tend to hold meetings, training, and retreats by organisational unit or staff level. "Hallways" and the members of the "Hallways" need to focus on the sharing of experiences and the knowledge gained from those experiences rather than just theoretical data.

7   Challenges to Implementing "Hallways"

It is generally acknowledged that most knowledge stays embodied, that is to say that experiences, insights, memories and judgments cannot be easily extracted from the bearer. Thus most knowledge is uncodifiable, only pertinent at a given moment in time and remains tacit. This presents organisations with a major challenge. The normal official languages of the organisation (rules, manuals, processes, planning papers, reports, and so on) cannot serve to make the invisible visible.

Excluding the above inherent limitation there are a number of environmental and organisational challenges, which need to be identified and addressed in order to have a successful implementation of KM and in specific "Hallways" within any firm. Gartner research (Jacobs 2000) regarding the top ten ways for a KM implementation to fail within an organisation identifies the failure to secure an executive sponsor as number one. KM must involve cultural and process elements as well as the supporting technologies. Because of this, and the fundamental changes that a shift to explicitly managing knowledge involves, senior management must be involved in a sponsorship role. While many successful pilot programs have been started without such senior support, they almost inevitably fail to effect sustained change, and they have short-term, limited success at best.

In The Knowledge Creating Company, Ikujiro Nonaka identified that one of the key challenges for KM implementation is that deeply ingrained in the traditions of Western management, from Frederick Taylor to Herbert Simon, is a view of the organisation as a machine for "information processing." According to this view, the only useful knowledge is formal and systematic – hard (i.e., quantifiable) data, codified procedures, and universal principles. And the key metrics for measuring the value of new knowledge are similarly hard and quantifiable – increased efficiency, lower costs, and improved return on investment. This barrier limits the ability of leadership to support more people-oriented efforts, which focus on the sharing of tacit knowledge rather than the codification of all knowledge.

8   Conclusions

The ability of organisational members (practitioners) to be able to discuss challenges or new developments in an open and easily accessible environment is critical to the success of the professional service firms. Our research allows us to conclude that the Knowledge Broker role and the way that it is being implemented in PwC through "The Blueprint" is supportive of the "Hallway" characteristics described by Dixon. This research has drawn heavily on the concepts of Dixon, Snowden, Nonaka, McElroy and others who refer to the focus on the people side of knowledge management as the "Third Generation" of knowledge management. They believe that we are entering uncharted waters and that this implies that there is not one correct answer and only a few best practices to rely upon. But they emphasize that we should not forget what we have learnt about our first generation (process) and second generation (technology).

During the past 12 months, PwC has spent a significant amount of effort to collect, document and pilot KM best practices. This approach has resulted in the creation of the KM strategy called "The Blueprint." The key lesson that PwC have taken away from this exercise is that in PwC the "top-down model" for building strategy does not work. The fact is that the strategy needs to be relevant. It is not possible to take generic industry neutral best practices and try and apply them. It is critical that the KM strategy be designed to take into account the specific characteristics of the professional services industry.

PwC found that through engaging the industry sectors and the territories and drawing from them their best practices and showing them what is already working in other territories and industry sectors it has achieved a significant amount of goodwill and support. Our research and interviews allow us to conclude that "The Blueprint" contains many of the components required to encourage participation and sharing of knowledge. Specifically the elements that focus on the encouragement of the increased codification of tacit knowledge and the increased sharing of tacit knowledge seems to compare favourably to the industry best practices and the suggestions from the research communities. Our review of the "Hallways" characteristics show that many of the characteristics are present in "The Blueprint" and are being encouraged by the practitioners.

9   Challenges and Next Steps

However the implementation of these characteristics requires significant behavioural changes.

The PwC practitioner receives on average 60 e-mails every day. He has access to online resources, offline resources, professional resources, and his personal network of colleagues. What PwC has found is that most people rely on their personal network of colleagues. Thus the implementation of the KB role is specifically focused to enhance the personal network at the engagement level.

Interviews done during this research and prior interviews that have been done with Knowledge Brokers show that the non-intrusive nature of this role and that fact that it is specifically focussed on being non-hierarchical has resulted in a significant increase in sharing within the team, awareness of expertise that is available within the firm and the increase in the levels of interactions among practitioners from various engagement teams.

9.1 Adoption Rate

It is clear that the implementation of "The Blueprint" and more specifically roles such as the Knowledge Broker will allow entirely new work practices to emerge from the workplace, work technology will develop and worker value synergies will increase and we will be creating enterprise value through increased productivity and innovation, and a reduced enterprise total cost of ownership. However, the research demonstrates that we currently have, what Gartner refers to as "early adopters," among the majority of participants in the firm's KM and Knowledge Broker activities.

While the vast majority may be reluctant to adapt to the change, they will eventually do so once they accept its inevitability. A third group will strongly resist the change and never successfully adapt. Explicit strategies (to engage, leverage, contain or outplace) for dealing with each of these behaviours over time can and should be built into any change management plan. One of the key next steps that PwC should be adopting is to use the insights and experiences of the early adopters, who in part are still enthusiastic about the project, to play a significant role to influence the "reluctant majority."

By approaching those influential adopters with special incentives to participate and cooperate in the plan, they create a "leverage" strategy. Those early adopters can, in turn, work within their own peer groups to build greater awareness and interest, creating an opportunity for the project team to more deeply "engage" a broader audience in the transformation process.

Over time a critical mass of support will develop, facilitating the transformation's building momentum and eventual institutionalisation. These two behaviour patterns can be overlaid on the workplace's transformation project plan to anticipate the likely timing and form of negative organisational responses to specific project actions, phases and milestones.

9.2 *Communication, Education and Remuneration*

The research shows that one of the key success factors will be to build and enhance the integration of KM as an integral part of the communication, education and remuneration programs of the firm. This challenge is not unique to PwC.

The challenges identified during this research relate to the behavioural aspects of the firm. They specifically challenge firms such as PwC to look for new ways to encourage the desired behaviour through better reward structures and metrics systems. PwC must focus on the identified challenges and plot them against the workplace transformation plans and change strategies that are appropriate. This will ensure that it can be more proactive in the deployment of solutions.

9.3 *Leadership*

The challenge for the leadership of PwC is to not present a single point of authority on this matter but rather the visual strength and conviction that the organisational leadership is focussed on searching for the best practices and will enhance its current structures to enable and support the behavioural activities desired

References

Baldacchino, K. & Armistead, C. & Parker, D. 2002. "Information overload: It's time to face the problem." Management Services. 46 (4): 18-21

Bell, M. A., & Joroff, M. 2001. The Agile Workforce: Supporting People and Their Work. Stanford: Gartner Group Inc. & Massachusetts Institute of Technology's (MIT's) School of Architecture and Planning

Dixon, N.M. 1999. The Organizational Learning Cycle – 2nd edition. Aldershot, UK: Gower Publishing Ltd

Gomolski, B. 2001. Redefining Learning for the Knowledge Workplace. Tech. Rep. No. COM-12-6718. Gartner Group Inc., RAS Services

Guterman, J. 2002. "Out of Sight, Out of Mind?" Harvard Management Communication Letter, 5 (9)

Jacobs, J. 2000. KM 101: 10 Ways to Fail. Tech. Rep. No. TU-12-5303. Gartner Group Inc., RAS Services

Lelic, S. 2002. "It's a Small World: The Effects of Globalisation on Knowledge Management." Knowledge Management, 5 (9): 8-10

Nonaka, I. 1991. "The Knowledge Creating Company", Harvard Business Review, 69: 96-104

PricewaterhouseCoopers. 2003. The PricewaterhouseCoopers Next Generation Knowledge Management Blueprint Vr3. London, UK: PricewaterhouseCoopers

Wit de, B., & Meyer, R. 2002. Strategy Synthesis: Resolving Strategy Paradoxes to Create Competitive Advantage. London, UK: Thompson Learning

DYNAMICS IN TECHNOLOGY-ENHANCED TEAMS: TRANSACTIVE MEMORY IN TRUST NETWORKS

KLARISSA TING-TING CHANG

Carnegie Mellon University, Tepper School of Business
Pittsburgh, PA, U.S.A

The development of transactive memory facilitated by trust relationships and social exchanges is of emerging importance in distributed environments characterized by a lack of rich social presence. Situated at the nexus of research on technology-enhanced teams, this study examined the effects of trust networks and social presence on transactive memory in an experimental setting. 240 participants were randomly assigned to 3-member teams. The results indicated that dense trust networks helped to develop greater transactive memory than sparse trust networks. Participants in dense trust networks developed greater transactive memory when social presence was low than when social presence was high. Conversely, participants in sparse trust networks developed better transactive memory when social presence was high than when social presence was low. Teams with dense trust networks also had greater reciprocal exchanges, whereas teams with sparse trust networks had greater negotiated exchanges. Implications for enhancing transactive memory from a social exchange perspective were discussed.

1   Introduction

Distributed teams, characterized by geographically dispersed work where coordination and communication takes place via technologies (Ahuja & Carley, 1999; Townsend *et al.*, 1998), has become an increasingly popular and prevalent structural form in organizations (Armstrong & Cole, 2002). A significant portion of one's knowledge is derived from the relationships one has access to. This relates to the research on *transactive memory*, which analyzes how group members share task knowledge with one another via a shared system for encoding, storing, and retrieving information (Wegner, 1987). The pool of knowledge may liberate organizations from the fear of losing critical intellectual assets when employees leave.

Technology-enhanced teams require a high degree of communication governed by trust and social norms due to the lack of rich social cues. This raises the question about how social relations in such networks affect information exchange. The phenomenal increase in studies investigating *trust* indicates the belief that problems regarding motivation to share knowledge can be overcome by entrusting knowledge sharing activities to social relationships. In the context of knowledge sharing, trust refers to the willingness of a member to be vulnerable to actions of another party based on the expectation that the other will perform a particular information-sharing action important to the trustor, regardless of the ability to monitor or control the other party. The social network perspective is increasingly adopted in recent studies, but little research has examined the role of trust networks. Trust relationships among dyads in teams can be built into a network of trusting ties affecting coordination of knowledge. However, it is not clear how trusting ties in such social networks underlie the development of transactive memory. This study examines the influence of trust network density, which reflects the presence of third party trusting ties around a relationship.

In addition, media characteristics such as social presence may be significant factors in improving knowledge sharing in a computer-mediated workplace. *Social presence* refers to "the degree to which the medium facilitates awareness of the other person and interpersonal relationships during the interaction" (Fulk *et al.*, 1990). It is interesting to observe how social presence affects the influence of trusting ties on transactive memory. Hence, this paper aims to address three main research questions: (1) What are the effects of trust networks on transactive memory in technology-enhanced teams? (2) How does the degree of social presence influence the impacts of trust networks on transactive memory? (3) Does transactive memory improve as a result of the form of social exchange in different trust networks?

2 Theory

2.1 Transactive Memory

The concept of distributed cognition in the field of organizational studies (e.g., Faraj & Sproull, 2000) has created a number of research corollaries on transactive memory (Hollingshead, 1998; Moreland, 1999), collective mind, and collaborative learning (Dillenbourg *et al.*, 1996). Distributed cognition refers to the division of cognitive labor (Hutchins, 1991) that enables groups and organizations to reach cognitive goals that would be more difficult to reach individually. Team members act autonomously with an understanding of their interdependence (Boland *et al.*, 1994), but the collective knowledge links individual knowledge repositories to the larger knowledge network. Knowledge networks help to explain the diffusion of knowledge across a network of individuals (Contractor *et al.*, 1998), and represent "who knows what" in an organization. Cognitive knowledge networks are similar to the concept of *transactive memory*, which describes a specialized division of cognitive roles with respect to the encoding, storage, and retrieval of information from different knowledge domains that develop during the course of relationships (Hollingshead, 1998). Transactive memory systems are developed through four interrelated processes: expertise recognition, retrieval coordination, directory updating, and information allocation (Moreland, 1999).

2.2 Trust Networks

Trusting ties involve perception of the trustor on the attributes of trustee. A trustor may trust the trustee based on (1) competence – group of skills that enable a trustee to be perceived competent within some specific domain, (2) integrity – adherence to a set of principles (work habits) thought to make the trustee dependable and reliable; and (3) benevolence – extent to which a trustee is believed to feel interpersonal care and concern, and willingness to do good to the trustor beyond egocentric profit motive (Jarvenpaa *et al.*, 1998). A trusting tie is established when one member believes in the competence, integrity, and benevolence of another member in exchanging information. A set of such trusting ties thus builds up a network of trust relationships. Examining trust relationships around a focal actor helps to determine network density of trusting ties in a team. A dense network of trusting relationships among individuals may facilitate information exchange better than a stand-alone trusting tie between two people. One possible explanation of why trust networks may develop such transactive memory is to examine the underlying social exchanges between members.

2.3 Theory of Social Exchange

Social exchange theory explains how people obtain valued resources through their interactions with others (Homans, 1958). There are several forms of social exchange, including *reciprocal exchange* (Emerson, 1976), and *negotiated exchange* (Molm *et al.*, 1999). Reciprocal exchange is characterized by direct reciprocation that does not involve explicit bargaining about the nature and timing of reciprocation. On the other hand, negotiated exchange is characterized by an open discussion of the benefits of receiving or giving. Some theorists have used social exchange theory as a starting point for examining related areas such as trust and affective ties (Nooteboom, 1996; Molm *et al.*, 1999). For instance, an individual embedded in a dense network of trust relationships is likely to exchange information reciprocally as strong implicit trusting ties have been established. On the other hand, an individual in a sparse network of trust relationships may require explicit and openly negotiated exchanges due to the nature of the weak trusting ties. The form of social exchange may provide a reason for why trust networks facilitate specialization of expertise and coordination of information.

3   Research Hypotheses

3.1 Effects of Trust Networks

One critical aspect of social relationships is the network of trusting ties that may be developed over the course of work. In a seminal study, Granovetter (1973) seeded an interest for the role of weak ties in enhancing dissemination and exchange of information. Using a network study of product development teams, Hansen (1999) highlighted the role of weak ties in searching for useful knowledge. The flow of resources from and to members of the network is revealed from the relationships built into social networks (Granovetter, 1973; Burt, 1992). Information flows and trust are increased in networks that are dense and consist of strong ties (Coleman, 1990). An employee can trust that a coworker knows the information that the employee needs (competence), but may not trust that he will be forthcoming at the time when the information is needed (benevolence). Conversely, the employee can be confident that there may be other people who are willing to assist the employee (benevolence), but these people might not possess the knowledge or skills required (competence). Previous results reveal that knowledge exchange is more effective when the knowledge recipient views the knowledge source as being both benevolent and competent. Given the evidence of previous studies, it is likely that teams with dense networks are more willing to share knowledge among trusted others than those networks that are less dense. Hence, transactive memory is hypothesized a function of the density of trust networks, with dense networks of trusting ties leading to greater transactive memory than sparse networks of trusting ties.

Hypothesis 1: Technology-enhanced teams with denser networks of trusting ties will have greater transactive memory than those with less dense networks of trusting ties.

3.2 Effects of Social Presence

An extensive literature on technology-enhanced teams examined the role of technology in supporting remote communication and distributed work (e.g., Alavi & Yoo, 1997; Jarvenpaa & Leidner, 1999; Robey, Khoo, & Powers, 2000; Townsend *et al.*, 1998). Dispersed teams with similar backgrounds were found to lack 'mutual knowledge' of each other's local context and constraints, which hindered their ability to work effectively as teams (Cramton, 2001). It is generally more difficult for communication to take place in dispersed settings. The removal of visual cues, for example, might have reduced social presence sufficiently to cause group members to pursue self rather than group interests (Sia *et al.*, 2001). A reduction in social presence might cause difficulties in arriving at mutually agreeable communication (Lewicki & Litterer, 1985), decreasing effective social construction in the learning process (Carlson & Zmud, 1999). This calls for the development of a sense of social presence relating to the technologies in use. Evidently, trust networks are expected to enhance the development of transactive memory when teams are supported by high degree of social presence among members, regardless of density of trust networks.

Hypothesis 2: The degree of social presence will moderate the impact of trust network density on transactive memory.

3.3 Effects of Reciprocal Exchange

Social exchange can be circumscribed by the voluntary actions of individuals who are motivated by the returns these actions are expected to bring. Dense networks of trusting relationships may inculcate a norm of reciprocal exchange that facilitates development of transactive memory. Reciprocal exchanges involve intrinsic obligations and indirect exchanges. In a reciprocal exchange, members' contributions to the exchange of informational resources are performed separately and non-negotiated (Molm *et al.*, 1999). A member may make an offer (e.g., providing a piece of critical information) without knowing when, whether, or to what extent the other members will reciprocate. A reciprocal exchange takes places over time when an individual performs sequential and contingent acts that vary in timing and reciprocity. Conventional studies usually investigate such reciprocal exchange relations in social settings (e.g., Blau, 1964; Homans, 1958). Hence, it is predicted that networks consisting of denser trusting ties are likely to improve transactive memory by facilitating more reciprocal exchanges which lead to greater transactive memory developed in the team.

Hypothesis 3: The amount of reciprocal exchange among members will mediate the relationship of trust network density and transactive memory.

3.4 Effects of Negotiated Exchange

Negotiated exchanges involve extrinsic obligations and direct exchanges. In a negotiated exchange, members are usually involved in a joint decision process to determine the terms of exchange (Cook, 1987; Molm *et al.*, 1999). These terms are agreed at the same time even though the 'transactions' of information do not occur simultaneously. Although socially close relationships may encourage greater information exchange, dense trusting ties may inhibit the development of transactive memory because of the taken-for-granted nature of the interaction. Socially-isolated members have been found to participate more in discussion and emphasize more of their unique knowledge than socially-connected members (Thomas-Hunt *et al.*, 2003). Sparse trusting networks, characterized by weak trusting ties, may cause members to deliberately and explicitly state the terms of exchange. This form of negotiated exchange as a result of sparse trusting networks may still facilitate coordination of information. Despite the benefits of dense trusting networks, sparse networks are predicted to improve transactive memory by creating more negotiated exchanges among team members.

Hypothesis 4: The amount of negotiated exchange among members will mediate the relationship of trust network density and transactive memory.

The research model and the hypotheses are shown in Figure 1.

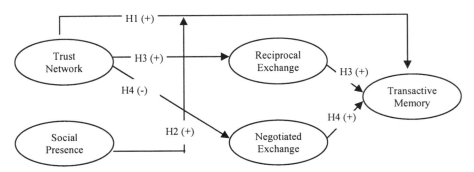

Figure 1. Research Model

4   Methods

The experiment used a 2 x 2 factorial design with two independent variables - "trust networks" and "social presence". There were two types of trust networks: "dense networks", in which a large number or all of the possible relationships in a team were trusting ties, and "sparse networks", in which only a few or no trusting ties existed between members. Social presence was operationalized as either "high" or "low". Participants in high social presence teams communicated face-to-face while working on their own computer systems, and those in low social presence teams communicated via technological networks without physical contact. There were four treatment conditions: (1) teams with dense networks of trusting ties supported with high degree of social presence, (2) teams with dense networks of trusting ties supported with low degree of social presence, (3) teams with sparse networks of trusting ties supported with high degree of social presence, and (4) teams with sparse networks of trusting ties supported with low degree of social presence. A trust-building exercise (Jarvenpaa *et al.*, 1998) was first conducted to develop trusting ties within the teams. A social network analysis (Burt, 1992) was then applied to determine the density of trusting ties. Members remained in the same team over four weeks. Each team member played a functional role that existed in a business company. Members were given a hidden profile task (i.e., each member possessed different elements of information essential to the team), and were required to make managerial decisions every week. Every session was videotaped and computerized messages were archived. Questionnaires were administered at the end of each week.

5   Results

Descriptive statistics are summarized in Table 1. ANOVA test on transactive memory is depicted in Table 2. Main effects of trust networks were found on transactive memory, supporting Hypothesis 1. Dense networks of trusting ties were associated with greater transactive memory than sparse networks of trusting ties. The results also showed significant interaction effects involving trust networks and social presence on transactive memory (see Figure 1). Hypothesis 2 was partially supported.

Table 1. Means (Standard Deviations) of Measures

	N	M (SD)
Dense Trust Network and High Social Presence		
Transactive Memory (TM)	60	6.15 (.68)
Reciprocal Exchange (RE)	60	5.48 (.81)
Negotiated Exchange (NE)	60	1.51 (.70)
Sparse Trust Network and High Social Presence		
Transactive Memory (TM)	56	2.53 (.65)
Reciprocal Exchange (RE)	56	1.68 (.60)
Negotiated Exchange (NE)	56	5.52 (.65)
Dense Trust Network and Low Social Presence		
Transactive Memory (TM)	56	6.57 (.67)
Reciprocal Exchange (RE)	56	5.50 (.65)
Negotiated Exchange (NE)	56	1.69 (.60)
Sparse Trust Network and Low Social Presence		
Transactive Memory (TM)	60	1.73 (.78)
Reciprocal Exchange (RE)	60	1.52 (.70)
Negotiated Exchange (NE)	60	5.44 (.81)

Table 2. ANOVA on Transactive Memory

Variation	SS	DF	MS	F-ratio	P
Trust Density	20.79	1	20.79	62.41	<.01
Social Presence	194.48	1	194.48	583.74	<.01
Trust Density x Social Presence	.84	1	.84	2.51	<.02
Error	72.30	217	.33		

6   Discussion

6.1 Trust Networks

Transactive memory is an important vehicle for leveraging knowledge networks, as well as a shared resource for gaining access to more knowledge that any individual could possibly possess alone (Hollingshead, 1998). Knowledge hoarding due to the nature of distributed teams and knowledge loss caused by members' departure can be prevented with an effective system of transactive memory. From a relational perspective, recent research has found optimal mixture of strong and weak ties beneficial (Hansen, 1999), but it does not specifically explain why relational networks enhance knowledge sharing.

The data analysis supports the first hypothesis that dense trust networks foster greater transactive memory than sparse trust networks. Previous studies have identified that social networks between distributed and co-located sites differed in communication network size and frequency (Herbsleb & Mockus, 2003). Distant colleagues may understand less about who has expertise in what area as a result of restricted information flow across sites and the lack of rapport (Kiesler & Cummings, 2002). However, this study suggests that developing trust relationships may help to alleviate problems arising from restricted information flow. Similar to social network analysis, the trusted third party behaves as information gate keepers (Constant *et al.*, 1996) occupying distinctive positions to pass on their knowledge.

6.2 Social Presence

The results from the study provide support for the hypothesis that sparse networks of trusting ties have greater transactive memory when social presence is high. In this case, a high degree of social presence may overcome the lack of trust relationships within the team. While sparse trust networks inhibit transactive memory development and this can be improved by increasing social presence, the results also indicate that social presence may plague the effectiveness of teams whose members have dense trusting ties. Close physical proximity and spontaneous communication may privilege interaction with people, but they may not be the right colleagues to communicate with to support productive collaboration (Kraut *et al.*, 2002). Hence, the finding may provide some evidence that trust and social presence are conceptually and empirically distinct.

Research has shown that electronic teams can develop trust over time (Iacono & Weisband, 1997). In this study, trust is found to improve over time, and its impact on transactive memory is significant in all three phases. However, social presence appears to influence transactive memory only in the beginning phase, suggesting that trust plays a stronger role over time (see Figure 2). Whether face-to-face interaction is required for transactive memory thus becomes an empirical question. Despite these inconsistent answers, an alternative perspective of trust networks and transactive memory is to view the social exchanges inherent in the teams.

6.3 Social Exchanges

The third research question examines the effects of social exchange on the relationships of trust networks and transactive memory. The findings suggest that dense trust networks encourage reciprocal exchanges, while sparse trust networks encourage negotiated exchanges. In a social exchange transaction, enticing people to share knowledge involves creating an incentive structure that persuades them to enter into the transaction in exchange for other resources. Assuming that knowledge is a private good, Coleman (1990) visualizes a repayment system where obligations are represented as credits to be traded between people. Explicit forms of rewards include access to information in cases such as availability of production-related knowledge to any member of the network (Dyer & Nobeoka, 2000), and anticipation of help (Wasko & Faraj, 2000). There is expectation of getting valuable knowledge in return for giving it, and this generates a need to contribute own knowledge to become part of the knowledge network which success depends on (Cohen, 1998). In previous work, the informal information accessed in such as way is regarded as superior in quality (Hall, 1994), and valuable in the generation of research ideas (Cronin, 1995). Forms of rewards for social exchange include enhanced reputation such as acknowledgement from peers (Berry, 2000), and personal satisfaction such as pleasure gained from demonstrating prosocial behavior (Wasko & Faraj, 2000).

A preliminary analysis of the data over three time phases shows that social exchange not only requires trust in others to discharge their obligations, but also develops trust in the process of exchange. More reciprocal exchanges in the first phase are associated with denser trust networks in the second phase ($r = 0.44$, $p < 0.05$). More reciprocal exchanges in the second phase are associated with denser trust networks in the third phase ($r = 0.36$, $p < 0.05$). Contrary to pure economic exchanges, social exchange may engender feelings of obligation and trust. Exchange relations may begin with minor transactions requiring little trust when risk involved is small. For example, one member may help another a few times. If the recipient fails to reciprocate, the member may cease further assistance or provision of information. Reciprocation helps to prove one's trustworthiness of continued favors and exchanges. By discharging their obligations for information rendered and demonstrating trustworthiness, individuals may induce mutual trust and expansion of future information supply. The processes of reciprocal exchange may generate trust in social relations recurrently. In the context of knowledge-intensive work such as software development, the results may imply that teams with sparse trust networks should work on cohesive modules (e.g. sequentially cohesive modules) so as to promote negotiated exchanges whereas loosely coupled modules (e.g. different classes) are more appropriate for teams with dense trust networks. The unifying theme is the premise that understanding social cognition is a critical component to performance. These findings set the stage for future directions in research efforts.

7   Future Work

What has emerged in this study is a new way of looking at distributed cognition in technology-enhanced teams. A culture of reciprocal exchange emerge in a dense network of trusting ties, in which social presence plays an important role in increasing transactive memory. A field study in a real distributed environment could help corroborate the experimental findings. Moreover, manipulations of trust networks involve the investigation of third party trust relationships. In a three-member group, this inevitably examines reciprocal ties between dyads. An interesting question for future research is to extend the study to teams with more members and larger social networks, and determine whether occupying strategic positions in the teams could affect knowledge flow within and outside the team. As transactive memory is a group-level construct (Moreland, 1999), investigating a collective measure of transactive memory as well as objective measures such as performance of the team could also bring insights into the dynamics of trust networks and social presence.

This study provides some evidence that social behaviors play a major role in motivating knowledge-building effort. Past studies typically focus on barriers to knowledge sharing rather than enabling factors (Homburg & Meijer, 2001). In conclusion, this study suggests that transactive memory can be increased by developing networks of trust relationships supported by appropriate degree of social presence. Underscoring the differences between dense and sparse networks of trusting ties, this study contributes empirically to the efforts in understanding cognitive and relational aspects highlighting the dynamics of technology-enhanced teams. Future research should continue to address the changes that dispersed work environments bring to organizations, and how distributed cognition can be enhanced with growing prevalence of knowledge-intensive activities.

References

Ahuja, M. K. & Carley, K. M. (1999). Network structure in virtual organizations. *Organization Science*, 10(6), 741-757.

Alavi, M. & Yoo, Y. (1997). *Is learning in virtual teams real?* Boston, MA: Harvard Business School.

Armstrong, D.J. and Cole, P. (2002). Managing distances and differences in geographically distributed work groups. In P. J. Hinds & S. Kiesler (Eds.), *Distributed work.* Cambridge, MA: The MIT Press.

Berry, J. (2000). Employees cash in on KM. *Internet Week,* May 22, 45-46.

Blau, P. M. (1964). Exchange and Power in Social Life. New York: Wiley.

Boland, R. J., Tenkasi, R. V. & Te'eni, D. (1994). Designing Information Technology to Support Distributed Cognition, *Organization Science,* 5, 456-75.

Burt, R.S. (1992). *Structural Holes*. Cambridge, MA: Harvard University Press.

Carlson, J. R., & Zmud, R. W. (1999). Channel expansion theory and the experiential nature of media perceptions. *Academy of Management Journal*, 42, 153–170.

Cohen, D. (1998). Towards a knowledge context: Report on the first annual U.C. Berkeley forum on knowledge and the firm. *California Management Review*, 40(3), 22-39.

Coleman, J. (1990). *Foundations of social theory*. Cambridge, MA: Harvard University Press.

Constant, D., Kiesler, S., & Sproull, L. (1994). What's mine is ours, or is it? A study of attitudes about information sharing. Information *Systems Research*, 5, 400–421.

Cook, K. S. (1987). *Social exchange theory*. Newbury Park, CA: Sage.

Cramton, C. D. (2001). The mutual knowledge problem and its consequences for Dispersed Collaboration. *Organization Science*, 12(3), 346-371.

Dyer, J. H. & Nobeoka, K. (2000). Creating and managing a high-performance knowledge-sharing network: The Toyota case. *Strategic Management Journal*, 21(3), 345-367.

Emerson, R. M. (1976). Social exchange theory. *American Sociological Review*, 35, 335-362.

Faraj, S. and Sproull, L. (2000). Coordinating Expertise in Software Development Teams. *Management Science*, 46(12), 1554-1568.

Granovetter, M. (1973). The Strength of Weak Ties. *American Journal of Sociology*, 78, 1360-1380.

Hall, H. (1994). Information strategy and manufacturing industry – case studies in the Scottish textile industry. *International Journal of Information Management*, 14(4), 281-294.

Hansen, M. (1999). The search-transfer problem: The role of weak ties in sharing knowledge across organization subunits. *Administrative Science Quarterly*, 44, 82-111.

Herbsleb, J.D. & Mockus, A. (2003). An Empirical Study of Speed and Communication in Globally-Distributed Software Development. *IEEE Transactions on Software Engineering*, 29(3), 1-14.

Hollingshead, A.B. (1998). Distributed knowledge and transactive processes in groups. In M. A. Neale, E. A. Mannix, and D. H. Gruenfeld (Eds.), *Research on managing groups and teams* (Vol. 1). Greenwich, CT: JAI Press.

Homans, G. C. (1958). Social behavior as exchange. *American Journal of Sociology*, 63(6), 597-606.

Jarvenpaa, S. & Leidner, D. (1999). Communication and Trust in Global Virtual Teams. *Organization Science*, 10(6), 791-815.

Jarvenpaa, S., Knoll, K., & Leidner, D. (1998). Is Anybody Out There? Antecedents of Trust in Global Virtual Teams. *Journal of Management Information Systems*, 14(4), 29-64.

Kiesler, S. and Cummings, J.C. (2002). What do we know about proximity and distance in work groups? A legacy of research. In P. J. Hinds & S. Kiesler, (Eds.), *Distributed Work.*. Cambridge, MA: MIT Press.

Lewis, K. (2003). Measuring transactive memory in the field: Scale development and validation. *Journal of Applied Psychology*, 88(4), 587-604.

Molm, L. D., Peterson, G., & Takahashi, N. (1999). Power in Negotiated and Reciprocal Exchange. *American Sociological Review*, 64, 876-890.

Moreland, R. (1999). Transactive memory: learning who knows what in work groups and organizations. In L. Thompson, J. Levine, & D. Messick (Eds.), *Shared cognition on organizations*. Lawrence Erlbaum.

Robey, D., Khoo, H. M. and Powers, C. (2000). Situated learning in cross-functional virtual teams. *IEEE Transactions on Professional Communication*, 43(1), 51-66.

Short, J., Williams E., and Christie B. (1976). *The Social psychology of telecommunications*. London: John Wiley & Sons.

Sia, C. L., Tan, B. C. Y., and Wei, K. K. (2002). Group Polarization and Computer-Mediated Communication: Effects of Communication Cues, Social Presence, and Anonymity. *Information Systems Res,* 13(1), 70-90.

Thomas-Hunt M., Ogden T. and Neale M. (2003). Who's Really Sharing? Effects of Social and Expert Status on Knowledge Exchange Within Groups. *Management Science,* 49(4), 464-477.

Townsend, A. M., DeMarie, S. M. and Hendrickson, A. R. (1998). Virtual teams: Technology and the workplace of the future. *Academy of Management Executive,* 12(3), 17-29.

Wasko, M. & Faraj, S. (2000). "It is what one does"; Why people participate and help others in electronic communities of practice. *Journal of Strategic Information Systems,* 9(2), 155-173.

Wegner, D. (1987). Transactive memory: a contemporary analysis of the group mind. In B. Mullen & G. Goethals (Eds.), *Theories of group behavior* (pp. 185-208). New York: Springer-Verlag.

APPLYING SENSE-MAKING METHODOLOGY TO ESTABLISH COMMUNITIES OF PRACTICE: EXAMPLES FROM THE BRITISH COUNCIL

BONNIE CHEUK

British Council, 10 Spring Gardens
London SW1A 2BN, United Kingdom

This paper introduces readers to Dervin's Sense-Making Methodology and demonstrates how the British Council has applied it to build communities of practice. Sense-Making is based on a set of assumptions which challenge some fundamental knowledge management thinking. The Sense-Making assumptions imply the need for alternative procedures to be implemented to build and nurture communities of practice. Three primary applications are discussed: (a) conducting interviews to understand user needs; (b) managing best practices and worst practices; (c) designing face-to-face or online discussions. They are followed by four actual applications of Sense-Making Methodology in designing a Knowledge and Learning Community within the British Council in the areas of: (a) conducting user studies; (b) designing site navigation; (c) determining what documents members should share on the community intranet site; and (d) justifying the ROI of community building activities. This paper aims at stimulating further thinking and debate in adopting theoretically informed approaches to implement knowledge management.

1 Background

1.1 Introduction to the British Council

The British Council is the United Kingdom's international organisation for educational opportunities and cultural relations. Our purpose is to build mutually beneficial relationships between people in the UK and other countries and to increase appreciation of the UK's creative ideas and achievements. Currently we have 7,000 staff in 110 countries worldwide. Our primary target audience is young people aged between 18 and 35.

We operate in three broad areas. Our aim in Learning is to increase international recognition of the range and quality of learning opportunities from the UK, to promote the learning of English, and to strengthen educational co-operation between the UK and other countries. Our aim in Creativity is to build appreciation of the UK's creativity and scientific innovation among people overseas and to strengthen their engagement with the diversity of UK culture.

Our aim in Society is to enhance awareness of the UK's democratic values and processes and work in partnership with other countries to strengthen good governance and human rights.

1.2 Why Communities of Practice?

Communities of practice, in this paper, are defined as a group of named individuals who interact both in the face to face and virtual environment to exchange experience; share learning and build their knowledge and expertise (and that of the organisation). They may work together to further specific objectives; and benefit by their association with each other.

The British Council knowledge management vision, which is recognised as an enabler of the organisation overall strategy for 2010, is to deliver world-class products and services to our customers by enabling effective sharing and utilisation of our collective knowledge. We will achieve this by finding smart ways to connect people and with relevant documents. Building and nurturing communities of practice is seen within the British Council as a means to support new ways of working, and contribute towards and support the broader cultural-change initiative.

Between January and December 2004, the British Council has been piloting an approach to build and nurture six communities to test the readiness of the organisation for knowledge management. Each of the pilot communities is supported by a new kind of intranet with collaborative functions. In addition, other channels of communications (e.g. teleconference, videoconference and face-to-face meetings) as well as alternative approaches to capture and disseminate knowledge (e.g. applying narrative techniques to conduct a project debrief) are also introduced.

In May 2004, we have launched a directory of existing communities; about 160 communities have been identified, although we believe this is the tip of the iceberg. Already in place within the British Council, and supported by the knowledge management team, is a seven-phase guide to implementing communities of practice (Cheuk, 2004). The methodology was originally introduced to 40 knowledge managers in an internal knowledge-management conference and workshop held in November 2003, and has since become the *de facto* blueprint for community development within the organisation.

2   Sense-Making Methodology as an Emerging Approach to Establish Communities of Practice

2.1 *Introduction to Emerging Approaches to Establish Communities of Practice*

A literature review of Communities of Practice (COP) shows that in the past 10 years, many companies support COP by appointing community managers to design and implement communication and information systems (e.g. discussion forums, intranet sites, database, expert database), to manage internal and external content and resources, to organise face-to-face events and to facilitate discussions amongst community members.

In most cases, the community sponsor and manager aims at providing members with easy access to corporate instructions and guidelines, internal and external best practices and expert lists. In addition, experienced colleagues and subject experts are invited to share their authoritative insights with the members. Community members are expected to benefit as they can then apply, re-use or re-purpose these best practices and expertise for their own work.

Beginning in 1996, led by David Snowden and his colleagues, there was a call for a shift away from defining 'knowledge as a thing' (usually in terms of good things such as 'best practices' and 'expertise') which can be transferred from one place to another, from one person to another. Practitioners were asked to recognise the limitation of this traditional approach and accept that 'best practices' may actually be 'worst practices' if they are applied in an inappropriate context (Snowden, 2002).

In this paper, we will share an alternative approach that the British Council has taken to build and nurture a number of communities of practice during 2004. Our approach is influenced by Dervin's Sense-Making Methodology (Dervin *et al.*, 2003). Similar to Snowden's work, Dervin belongs to the emerging school which calls for paying attention to diversity. They both challenge the transmission model of information. As Snowden's work is widely known in the knowledge management space, the theoretical assumptions of narrative techniques will not be repeated here.

In the next section, a summary of Dervin's Sense-Making theory is presented. As limited examples can be found in the literature on how companies adopt the emerging approach in the real-working context, this paper – which is not positioned as a best practice example - aims at stimulating further thinking and debate in the practicalities in adopting the emerging approach to implement knowledge management in a multinational organisation.

2.2 *Introduction to Dervin's Sense-Making Methodology*

The Sense-Making Methodology incorporates meta-theoretic assumptions, a foundation of methodological guidance, specific research methods (both for data collection and for question framing and analysis), and a set of communication practices. All of these elements are generated from a philosophical perspective that regards information as a human tool designed for making sense of a reality that is both chaotic and orderly (Dervin, 1992)

Sense-Making is based on the central metaphor of a person walking through time-space, facing a gap, bridging the gap to make sense and moving on to the next moment in time-space. This metaphor is referred to as the Sense-Making Triangle. Its central meta-theoretic concepts include: time, space, horizon, movement, gap and power. Its central operational concepts include: situation, history, gap, barrier, constraint, force, bridge, sense-making strategies, outcomes, helps and hurts.

It is important to note that Sense-Making makes no distinction between knowledge and information. Knowledge is the sense made at a particular point in time-space by an individual. As Dervin says, sometimes it is shared and codified; sometimes a number of people agree upon it; sometimes it is entered into a formalised discourse and gets published; sometimes it gets tested in other times and spaces and takes on the status of facts; sometimes it is fleeting and unexpressed; sometimes it is hidden and suppressed; sometimes it gets imprimatured and becomes unjust law; sometimes it takes on the status of dogma.

Sense-Making challenges a number of fundamental assumptions which informed the development of knowledge management practice. The key challenges of interests to knowledge management practitioners include:

(1) Sense-Making challenges the assumption that knowledge is a commodity that can be captured, stored, retrieved, used; and that knowledge can be transferred from person to person and time-space to time-space (as water can be poured from one bucket to another) without interrogation and interpretation. As a result, we believe that once we have easy access to knowledge, we know what we should (or should not) do in a certain situation (Dervin, 1999).

(2) Sense-Making challenges the assumption that knowledge presents us with 'facts' to describe the 'complete reality'. Sense-Making assumes that reality is sometimes orderly and sometimes chaotic. While no one would argue that the creation, retrieval and application of facts (what Sense-Making refers to as 'factizing') is not a worthwhile goal for knowledge management, Dervin argues that people seek not only 'facts' but also direction, ideas, support, confirmation and connection with other people etc. A knowledge management system which does not cater for the latter requirements cannot fully satisfy a living, breathing user.

(3) Sense-making challenges the assumption that knowledge should flow from the experts to the novice. Instead, it is important to promote and invite two-way sharing and negotiating of meanings (Dervin & Frenette, 2001).

(4) Sense-Making challenges the assumption that knowledge management systems/processes should be designed from the experts' perspectives. Instead, we must look for differences in how people see their worlds (e.g. information that is presented to them), and also the differences in how they 'make the worlds' (i.e. construct a sense of the world in their subject domain and how it works). For if we conceptualise the human condition as a struggle through an incomplete reality, then the similar struggles of others may well be informative for our own efforts.

2.3 Sense-Making Methodology and alternative intervention procedures to Design Communities of Practice

Each of the above assumptions implies potential alternative procedures to be implemented to design communities of practice. There are three primary applications that will be discussed here: (a) conducting interviews to understand user needs; (b) managing best practices and worst practices; (c) designing face-to-face or online discussions.

When applying Sense-Making to design a community of practice, it is helpful to use the metaphor of a community member walking down a road. At some point in time, she enters a Sense-Making situation: she encounters a gap (eg a member faces an unusual problem). To continue the journey, she has to get help to bridge the gap in order to continue her journey towards the final destination. To design support or interventions to community members, it is crucial that the members get help to bridge the gap. This may take the form of getting answers to their questions (whether in the form of best practices, previous reports, past experiences), reducing barriers, getting other types of help (e.g. the need to be connected to others to share the emotions, feel supported etc) as well as getting accidental or unexpected help. Therefore, in understanding members' knowledge needs, the Sense-Making community designer focuses not only on asking 'what information or knowledge do you need?' but instead focus on specific time-space moment, and ask members 'what gaps do they see?', 'what got in the way?', 'what has been helpful?' and 'what are the barriers?' The findings present new insights that will not come out in standard user study.

In addition, from a content management perspective, Sense-Making asks the community designer not to solely focus on providing corporate guidelines and policies, best practices (or even worse practices) to the members. This is because they represent the authoritative voices of the experts. Instead, we should find ways to allow diverse practices to be captured and shared without pre-judgement. This is based on the assumption that a shared practice may be extremely relevant to some members at some point in time, but at another times, they can be totally irrelevant. Sense-Making trusts that each member can make the relevance judgement only when she is in a particular situation. To push it even further, if we can index a piece of content by the gap that a member self-reports she face, a search which allows people to see what content another members find helpful in face of similar gap is a better search criteria than a list of pre-defined subject categories.

Last, but not least, Sense-Making asks the community designer to pay attention to the fact that knowledge can be biased by power. For example, the experts are always allowed more time to voice their opinion and they tend to (unintentionally) dominate discussions, to the extent that other members do not have the chance to share their experience, and do not feel they can contribute or are being valued. Eventually, they become 'lurkers' or they 'drop out'. Sense-Making aims at intentionally finding ways to allow diverse perspectives to surface. This can be applied to face-to-face as well as online events. One example is Snowden's anecdote circle techniques which force people to move from one discussion group to another so that diverse perspectives can emerge, and no one can dominate the discussion. Other examples include allowing all participants to share their experience anonymously, and have them all posted on a wall, and then the members vote which viewpoints they would like to hear. Another example is that when a keynote speaker shares the best practices (for example, in managing change projects), all participants take notes using a form which allow them to share whether the best practice is relevant to their projects, which aspects of the best practice has been helpful, which can hinder success, and what other good practices are not mentioned by the speaker but in fact work for the participants. The findings are then consolidated and shared with all audiences. A sample note taking form that the British Council has utilised in our internal KM conference is presented in Appendix 1. Four Applications of Sense-Making Methodology to Establish the Knowledge and Learning Community in the British Council

2.4 Conducting user studies

The Knowledge and Learning Programme aims to deliver a network of centres offering a combination of physical and virtual knowledge and learning services to our customers. In 2004, Knowledge and Learning Centres (KLC) have been established in six offices - Delhi, Belgrade, Kuala Lumpur, Paris, Cairo, Accra and Ankara. Over the next stages of the programme, the number of centres will increase significantly. It is imperative that the lessons learnt from introducing the above can be replicated in the new KLCs. Looking to the future, it is also vital that KLC managers communicate with each other so that they can work together on developing new projects. The programme director as well as the KLC managers has turned to the knowledge management team for assistance to set up the KLC community to link up 50 KLC managers worldwide to share ideas and experiences.

As part of the community building exercise, the community knowledge manager is required to conduct user studies to understand the needs of the community members. This example shows how she has adopted Sense-Making Methodology and use Micro-moment timeline interview technique to in-depth interview members to understand the knowledge needs in setting up a new KLC. The respondents were first asked to share the business processes they need to go through to set up a KLC, the interviewer than focused on picking some specific time-space moments – this would benefit from further definition as per 2.2-, and repeated ask these questions:

- What were your questions at this stage?
- How did you get the answers?
- What tools/resources did you use?
- Did you get the answers?
- Did you face any difficulties finding out the answers?
- If you could wave a magic wand, what would you like to see happen?

Sense-Making methodology has helped the community knowledge manager to get in-depth insight on the knowledge gaps which do not surface in a typical structured interview or survey. The interview proved to be very effective, because colleagues find it easy to talk about their work and the questions they have in specific context. A qualitative analysis showed that there were three main stages in a KLC manager's lifetime where they needed distinctive types of content. This is followed by a knowledge audit of all the content that was made available to members at the time. A clear list of gaps then began to emerge and we allocated responsibility for writing or gathering the content or developing plans for future knowledge exchange events.

2.5 Designing Community Site Navigation

Armed with a list of frequently asked questions in setting up a new KLC or in managing an established KLC, we conducted a one day workshop to confirm the findings, and finally we grouped the key content into 4 categories which in turn informed the navigation design of the site. Informed by Sense-Making methodology, we perceive the users as having a need to bridge a gap when they log onto the site, we therefore decided to label the navigation using verbs rather than nouns. Four labels form the main navigation:

- I want to set up a KLC
- I want ideas for content (i.e. digital resources to serve customers)
- I want to ask a question
- I want to join the KLC community

The verbs present the gaps through the KLC managers' eyes. As a result, the site naturally answers the questions that the members frequently ask and the situation that members perceive they are in whenever they log onto the site.

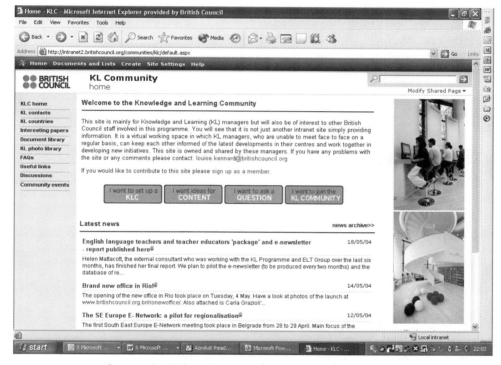

Screen grab 1: Using verbs to label the four main navigation buttons

2.6 Determining what documents members should contribute to the site

In the process of setting up a document repository, there has been endless debate on what documents should be put up on the site, and who should decide what is considered best practice. The results from the user studies show that members do not only want corporate guidelines or best practices, they also want to know what others have done, they want to view other examples (good or bad), and they like to talk to colleagues (and not necessarily experts). They also want to find out who is interested to develop joint products through internal partnerships. They want to share and talk to colleagues who have experience, they want to get emotional support from other members. They want to know what has been going on – not necessarily in areas directly related to their work. Informed by Sense-Making Methodology, one message is clear – the community members are looking not only for knowledge and information (from the corporate or best practice perspective). They want more. They want diverse perspectives, and they want to decide what suits them best in different situations.

As a result, we allowed two types of content to be shared on the site: corporate content developed in the headquarters (i.e. corporate guidelines, instructions and best practices) as well sample documents developed by colleagues working in different countries. They include any documents or examples that any KLC members would like to share. They are all listed in a document library, and all members can easily decide what they want using the filter function. (See Screen Grab 2 below)

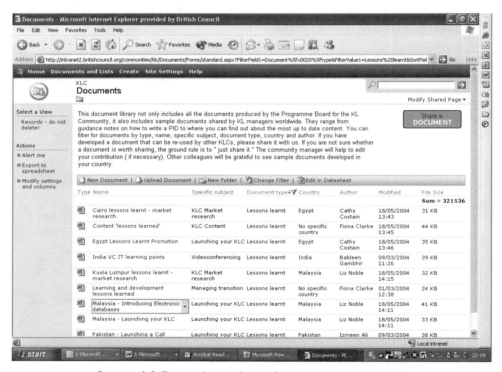

Screen grab 2: Encouraging members to share examples and experiences

To cater for members' need to get connected with one another, to share resources as well as anxiety, a discussion forum has been set up to complement face-to-face meetings, and to allow KLC members to continue their physical discussions online. The discussions can be initiated by any members without any moderation from the headquarters.

2.7 Justifying the Return-on-Investment of Communities of Practice

Like many organisations which are rolling out communities, we are constantly asked to justify the return on investment (ROI) of our community building activities. Sense-Making Methodology helps us to face up to the reality, and admit that no matter how hard we try, we cannot dictate the outcomes of having a group of community members coming together and sharing their ideas and experience.

Sense-Making Methodology challenges the traditional assumption that information is seen as inherently beneficial, that it instructs members about their work, possible actions (best practices) and the potential consequences of these actions. Very often, we assume the higher the input, the more benefits members are going to get.

Informed by Sense-Making, we recognise the limitation of measuring the ROI of community by input (e.g. number of members, number of members participating in community events, number of best practices documents shared, number of discussion threads, number of hits to the intranet etc.) and weight these benefits against the cost of setting up, creating content and maintaining a community.

If knowledge is defined as the sense made at a particular point in time-space by an individual, we need to accept that sometimes no new discoveries are made, sometimes you create a new million-dollar idea accidentally, and sometimes you make a discovery because of a document you read or a person you speak to. The value of community building is to provide that nurturing environment – or simply speaker, to deliberately design the water-cooler environment – for ideas exchange to take place even though the members are located in different countries. You can choose to leave these internal networking to chances, but if you want it to happen, it has to be designed.

The ROI of a community is in effect the potential for innovations and creative ideas to happen, to avoid reinventing the wheel and to increase staff confidence and job satisfaction. Community building activities should be seen as an investment that learning organisations should make in order to allow their staff to learn on-the-job and to grow with the organisation. This explains why demonstrating the success of communities of practice through powerful real-life case studies is still one of the most effective techniques to be widely adopted.

3   Conclusion

The British Council is committed to creating opportunities for our customers worldwide. Internally, we are very proud that we are applying the same philosophy by investing in communities of practice to create opportunities for our employees. In 2004-2005, it is our knowledge management strategy to continue to build and nurture communities of practice which are central to support our corporate vision. We aim at releasing our staff's potential and creativity by giving them the opportunities to participate in different communities of practice, as and when they see it is appropriate.

In this paper, I have given an introduction to Sense-Making Methodology and demonstrated how this alternative approach has been applied to build communities of practice for the British Council. So far, the approach has served us well and our users are satisfied in our specific context.

The approaches and techniques we have taken may appear to be obvious, but they are theoretically informed and backed up by Sense-Making research conducted since 1972. We plan to continue to apply Sense-Making Methodology to other aspects of our knowledge management work. Obviously, our journey has only just started. We believe that by sharing our experience, you can pick up new insights to inform your own journey.

Acknowledgments

I would like to acknowledge Dr Brenda Dervin for opening up my mind to the Sense-Making Methodology since 1996 and for her invaluable comment on how I apply Sense-Making in the practical workplace contexts. I would also like to thank Charlotte Marling for editing this article.

Appendix A. Sense-Making Note Taking Form

This form is used in an internal Knowledge Management Conference held in November 2004 in Edinburgh which aimed at sharing experiences in building communities of practice. Participants were asked to take notes for various sessions.

Session name:
Q: What led me to come to this session? What help do I need in this area?
Q: Which of the good practices mentioned by the speaker are relevant to my work?
Q: Which are the good practices that have worked well for me (but the speaker has not mentioned)?
Q: What are the immediate action items that I can take to improve my work in this area?
Overall rating for this session: Very Good   Very Poor   1   2   3   4   5

References

Cheuk, B. (2004) "A seven-stage guide to community implementation". In Simon Lelic (Ed), *Communities of Practice: Lessons from Leading Collaborative Enterprises*: 83-91. London: Ark Group Limited.

Dervin, B. (1999) "Chaos, order and Sense-Making: A proposed theory for information design". In R. Jacobson (Ed.), *Information design*: 35-57. Cambridge, MA: MIT Press.

Dervin, B. (1992) "From the mind's eye of the user: The Sense-Making qualitative-quantitative methodology." In J. D. Glazier & R. R. Powell (Eds.), *Qualitative research in information management*: 61-84. Englewood, CO: Libraries Unlimited.

Dervin, B., Frenette, M. (2001) "Sense-Making methodology: communicating communicatively with campaign audiences." In R. E. Rice & C. K. Atkin (Eds.), *Public communication campaigns (3rd ed.)*: 69-87. Thousand Oaks, CA: Sage.

Dervin, B., Foreman-Wernet, L., Lauterbach, E. (2003) *Sense-Making Methodology Reader: selected writings of Brenda Dervin*. New Jersey: Hampton Press.

Snowden, D. (2002) "Complex acts of knowing: paradox and descriptive self-awareness." *Journal of Knowledge Management*, 66(2), 100-111.

SOCIAL NETWORK ANALYSIS IN CONTEXT: FROM A RESEARCH METHODOLOGY TO A BUSINESS TOOL

KIMIZ DALKIR & MICHELE ANN JENKINS

GLIS, McGill University
Montreal, Quebec H3A 1Y1, Canada

An overview of the field of social network analysis (SNA) is presented with a view to improving accessibility of SNA processes and tools for both academic and business users. A brief history of the multidisciplinary origins of the discipline is provided followed by a characterization of the current state of affairs in SNA. Key issues are discussed with respect to data collection, visualization and analysis as well as the lack of standards for tools and technologies for SNA processes, weak links to business goals addressed by SNA, community of practice for SNA professionals, and ethics and incentives for non-academic participants. A number of recommendations are suggested as fruitful avenues to pursue in the near future to help others who, like the authors, embarked upon SNA solutions for the first time.

1 Introduction

This paper presents an overview of the field of social network analysis (SNA). This overview grew out of two research projects, one in an academic setting and another in a private sector organization, where social network analysis was selected as a useful approach. However, in setting out to apply SNA in these two settings, a number of key hurdles were encountered rather quickly. The literature on SNA, while abundant, is neither necessarily accessible nor easy to assimilate and apply. There appear to be two SNA "camps" – one stemming from the academic research community and the other represented by Knowledge Management (KM) practitioners and business applications. A critical overview of the SNA field that touches on its roots, its current usage and some of the key issues that need to be addressed would be helpful for both the academic and business communities. This paper is not an exhaustive survey of the field of SNAs, but rather a preliminary documentation of the obstacles encountered by our research team that appear to be readily generalizable or comparable to experiences that others have had in trying to understand, find and make use of SNAs to solve real-world business problems.

2 Brief History and Definition of Key Terms

Social network analysis, like many aspects of knowledge management, has existed for many years under different monikers: sociometry, homophily, interpersonal linkages, social network research, organizational network analysis, and others (Freeman, 1994). Moreno (1953) is most commonly cited in the literature as the father of SNA and the first to use the term "sociometry" in the 1930s to describe his study of social interactions at a New York girls' school. In its infancy, SNA was developed as a research tool for sociologists, but even then there was a multi-disciplinary aura surrounding the process. Moreno himself defined SNA in terms of sociology, mathematics and psychology.

It took another 10 years for algebraic modeling and graph theory to catch up with the possibilities of sociometry (e.g. Scott 1991). In his book, *Social Network Analysis: A Handbook,* Scott (1991), discusses how these "parallel innovations" led researchers to develop a mathematical concept of the role of the individual within his or her social network. Since then, the SNA methodology has been used by a wide variety of social sciences and in disciplines as diverse as genetics, biology and artificial intelligence (AI). Most recently, SNA has been taken up by knowledge managers and business management practitioners as a tool for intellectual capital research and modeling (e.g. Mead, 2001).

2.1 SNA Business Applications

SNA in a business context has evolved from a collection of quantitative research methods (Kilduff &Tsai, 2003) to a diagnostic tool and a catalyst for organizational change (Cross *et al.*, 2002). SNA appears to be slowly evolving from a purely research tool to a business application or solution. The following three domains of SNA business applications have been identified by Cross *et al.* (2003):

(1) Assessing individual and organizational social capital;
(2) Ensuring effective knowledge creation and sharing;
(3) Analyzing the extent to which an organization's informal structure supports strategic objectives.

These clearly stated objectives indicate that SNA has emerged as a strategic tool for knowledge management. Over the last decade, this strategic SNA has evolved into a distinct conceptual tool with distinct goals and challenges differing from traditional network analysis in its prescriptive nature, ethical issues and relationship with participants.

3   Characteristics of the SNA Landscape

Although the SNA technique itself can prove to be quite powerful, it is vital to not lose track of the fact that the entire approach consists of data collection, analysis and interpretation. One of the current shortcomings of this field is the lack of integration across the complete set of tools needed to study social interactions: beginning with best practices for data collection and including guidelines for valid interpretation of the results that are obtained.

3.1 Data Collection

As with any research design, the definition of the variables and the identification of a data collection methodology represent critical decisions. In the SNA process, data collection almost always uses multiple methods focusing on a variety of sources. This can create a greater challenge to the practitioner than the subsequent analysis of the data. It is critical to define the boundaries of the network, scope the data collection activities and above all, link the SNA to a set of business objectives. The later is often the missing link in SNA applications: a clear definition of the business problem(s) to be solved with an SNA solution.

Traditional research SNA is based on a data collection methodology involving a combination of observation, interviews and paper-based surveys that differ little from the ethnographic studies of the 1930s and 40s (Freeman, 1996). Practitioners may observe or videotape a specific area such as the lunchroom or a high-traffic hallway, making tallies of interactions. Subjects may be asked to fill out daily checklists of interactions or keep detailed diaries of their contacts.

Checklists usually involve lists of names for the user to check off to indicate a general connection or a specific interaction on a specific day. These checklists and surveys must be carefully designed whether they are paper-based or electronic. Issues such as neutrality and clarity of questions, privacy and other ethical issues and validity of responses (Zink, 1998, Yang and Tang 2004) must all be taken into account. Other information collected can investigate meeting space, company free time or the use of available communication tools or other organizational knowledge-sharing projects.

A newer approach to data collection is automated data-mining, a technique which is quickly transforming the way SNA is done. The basic premise is easy to grasp: significant untapped value exists in data assets and this value can be unlocked through a "knowledge discovery" process that identifies patterns that would be otherwise impossible to detect though conventional, deterministic (non-statistical) approaches (Grimes, 2004). (Krebs, 2004a; Schwartz & Wood, 1993; Jensen & Neville, 2002).

Email analysis has ethical and technical constraints and only focuses on one form of communication. In many organizations email may only be used for "official" communication, or to communicate with employees who do not make themselves available for other forms of communication. Adamic & Adar (2003) refer to this style of data-collection as "information side effects." However these applications do have potential as an internal organizational tool for larger companies. Unlike traditional paper-based SNA surveys or questionnaires, employees receive an instant return on their time investment – they can be creating new social networks while providing data for real-time ongoing social network analysis.

3.2 Network Visualization

Visit any web page on SNA and one thing you will always see is an image of a network. Visualization is the unofficial mascot of the SNA process. Network visualization is perhaps the most formalized aspect of the SNA process, drawing upon methodologies from algebraic modeling and statistical analysis. The greatest strength of this approach lies in the fact that it exploits the strengths of human visualization; we can grasp interesting patterns much more quickly when we view them in a graphic rather than a list or as text (Tufte, 2001).

Visualization tools for networks have come a long way with the development of graphic software and advancements in browser support for Java applets and other multimedia tools. In many cases, software developed for other networks can be applied to social networks: once the data has been collected and digitized, it can be dealt with as any data set and manipulated using a number of mathematical formulas. This is the stage of the SNA process with the most cross-disciplinary work being done.

Network diagrams are often quite successful in helping executives to focus their attention and to more easily grasp how organizational design decisions and leadership behaviors affect the relationships and information flows that lie at the core of how the work is accomplished (Cross *et al.*, 2003). On the other hand, these diagrams typically reduce the data, including employees and their relationships, to simple lines and dots which is really quite a distance from the reality being modeled. Unfortunately, in many cases, this is considered the end of the process – you have your data, it's been crunched, and now it can be displayed in a nice multi-colored, 3-D image that you can manipulate this way and that. However, what is left to do is to reconnect the dots and lines with the employees and business goals in order to gain business value out of the SNA endeavor.

3.3 Network Analysis

A number of different types of analyses may be used to study social networks. For example, the network properties of symmetry, centrality, direction, reciprocity and multiplexity may be measured (Monge & Eisenberg, 1987); the downward, upward and horizontal information flows within a given organization may be measured (Goldhaber, 1986); and role articulation that defines the participant components of any communication network may be also be identified (Mead, 2001). There is certainly no lack of measures.

In our review, we found that typical business practitioner becomes quickly mired in a wide range of sophisticated mathematical and statistical measures when analyzing SNAs – this embarrassment of riches is not only overwhelming but also quite confusing. While there is some recent literature (Cross 2003, Krackhardt & Hanson 1993, 2003) which begins the work of explicitly linking network analysis to business goals, the leap from network analysis to social capital management is still a long one.

4   Some Key Issues

While this developing field draws many of its strengths from its multidisciplinary roots, the last decade of fragmented development has also produced a detrimental tendency to emphasize complicated renderings of data that are more often than not unsuited to real-world business problems. The reason SNA has not caught on to the same extent as other KM practices is likely due to the simple reason that instead of providing clarity, it often adds another layer of abstraction. KM practitioners in business settings need a well-developed toolbox of processes and technologies that go beyond research methodologies to link directly with business goals and support business applications.

There are a number of key issues that must be addressed if SNA is to provide the potential business value that is currently under-exploited. Again, while not an exhaustive list, it includes issues that have been encountered in our own research and those that have been widely expressed by others in the field.

4.1 Tools and Technologies

Social network analysis has multiple roots that span the academic, commercial and popular or public domains. The tools and technologies used may be quite similar but it is important to underscore the fact that the goals of each of these different sectors may diverge considerably. For example, in the academic sector, we find a focus on the optimization of tools whereas in the commercial sector, the 80/20 rule may be more readily adopted. Other factors such as usability, availability and support offered may carry different weights in the different sectors. The increasing popularity of SNA is attested to by the fact that such a diverse group of users are making use of the approach.

The current popularity of SNA would not be possible without modern computing power and the advanced mathematical tools available today. Furthermore, it would not reach a fraction of its current users if it were not for the development of web application technology. The Web allows cross-platform, geographically dispersed users access to both data collection mechanisms and analyzed results. Unfortunately users must overcome non-standard user interfaces and complicated scripts for organizing and presenting information that are often poorly or incompletely adapted from other disciplines. Different tools and a more widely accepted business-process model are clearly needed in order to move the field forward in this sector.

There is not a lack of network analysis tools as such. A recent posting to the SocNET mailing list sums things up pretty well: "Can someone point me to something useful and free. I don't have time to evaluate all of the software..." One of the most commonly referred to evaluations of SNA software is on the International Network for Social Network Analysis site, http://www.sfu.ca/%7Einsna/INSNA/soft_inf.html. Of the almost 50 descriptions of software tools, only two describe themselves as "business-oriented." Although this is just a sampling of the software available and the majority of the other tools listed can and have been used for SNA in the business context, the lack of openly available, holistic tool sets for the KM practitioner can easily alienate potential users.

Even if a practitioner overcomes the terminology boundaries and recognizes the possibilities in repurposing statistical graphing tools, the available software has little in the way of a track record to refer to beyond case studies published by its developers. There are few cohesive reviews of the tools and their uses (e.g. Carrington *et al.*, 2004). The proprietary nature of the few business-specific tool creates little in the way of transparency (Jonathon N. Cummings' NetVis Module is a promising exception to this trend), an issue when one considers the sensitive nature of much of the data collected (see the section on Ethics below). A more Open Source development model would allow customization and localization of user interfaces while establishing a standard framework for the creation of new tools and the exchange of existing data.

4.2 Processes

All too often, social networking projects within organizations are developed in order to meet the needs of a research tool instead of the other way around. This over-reliance on advanced mathematical tools and graphing software can distract practitioners from the strategic business goals these tools are meant to facilitate. An example is the use of data-mining where interviews and workshops would be more appropriate. There is often a feeling that a source of information flow should be mapped simply because it can, without thought to the possible backlash that may occur when employees recognize that their informal interactions are being analyzed. As a result, at present, data collection processes are not standardized.

The form of data collection, analysis and dissemination of the resulting recommendations should all arise from the business goals and the particular business context, instead of being dictated by the availability of software. In many cases there is more need for a "processes" than a "product." The technology should support the methodology, not the other way around.

4.3 Business Goals

One of the few definitive works on the subject of SNA in a business context is Cross *et al.* (2002). Through the process of several real-world SNA projects, the authors were able to apply a SNA methodology to the following business goals:

(1) Promoting effective collaboration within a strategically important group;
(2) Supporting critical junctures in networks that cross functional, hierarchical or geographic boundaries;
(3) Identifying points where collaborative activity is not occurring due to organizational boundaries;
(4) Gaining insight into where management should target efforts to promote collaboration that will provide strategic benefit;
(5) Assessing the health of informal structure after a change has been implemented such as an internal restructuring or acquisition.

As observed by Cross *et al.* (2002, 2003) SNA is not an end unto itself, but a step in a larger process. In their case studies they consistently find the results of their analysis a useful starting point for group discussion and a tool for introspection. This often results in a common awareness of problems, helps define solutions and gain consensus on the need to bring about the desired organizational change. This crucial link back to the KM process and business goals appears to be lacking in much of the literature.

To help facilitate this link, there is a strong and immediate need for the development of a business-specific taxonomy for the SNA process. The language of the academic literature on SNA lacks immediate appeal to managers and HR staff interested in using social networking as a practical tool for social capital management in their organizations (Cross *et al.*, 2003). A sample of articles retrieved using the search phrase "social network analysis" includes titles such as "Hyper-edges and multidimensional centrality" (Bonacich *et al.* 2004), "Generalized blockmodeling of two-mode network data" (Doreian *et al.* 2004), and "Social-network analysis of Mycobacterium bovis transmission among captive brushtail possums (Trichosurus vulpecula)" (Corner *et al.* 2003).

4.4 *Ethics*

As far back as 1994, there is mention of concern over the use of data mining for SNA (Rice, 1994), but it is only recently that the literature and SNA associations have begun to address those concerns. Borgatti and Molina (2003) discuss the specific needs of SNA used in different contexts – the research and the managerial – and the threats posed not just to the subjects of analysis, but to the integrity of the results of those analyses. The authors are somewhat unique in their recognition of the different challenges of SNA in the business context. They go on to point out that the most difficult ethical challenges are for those projects that blur the line between research and business development. This is an excellent illustration of how the two fields, as they become more and more distinct, can result in a direct conflict between descriptive and prescriptive contexts. This conflict can become a minefield for practitioners who are not prepared for the possible responses to their findings.

Both Borgatti and Molina (2003) and Kadushin (2003) refer to the results of a recent Sunbelt conference which highlighted the dangers of failing to engage in ethical issues within this still emerging field. Missteps at this juncture could easily lead to a backlash resulting in future problems in collecting valid data. These authors and others readily acknowledge the need for a code of conduct. While individual SNA practitioners have made statements to the effect that they would avoid projects that might result in "resource actions" (e.g. the Krebs interview in Udell, 2004), there is no single code to which practitioners or researchers can refer. Even more disturbing is the lack of awareness of many of the potentially difficult ethical issues surrounding the fuzzy area between a company's need to "manage" their employees, including their social networks, and the privacy of those employees.

4.5 *Incentives for Organizational Participants*

Unlike a research setting where participants are typically attracted and motivated using monetary incentives to participate in the research study, there is a very problematic issue regarding incentives for those who are employees in an organization. Once an SNA has been extracted and made available, incentives are easier to articulate. For example, the benefits of being "linked in" on your first day of a new job is easy to understand and is almost immediate (a ready-made network of contacts to help you with your job, mentoring, picking up of the organizational culture such as do's and don'ts and so on). However, it is more difficult to envisage incentives for people to participate in the initial elicitation of a social network. While organizational benefits abound, it is not as easy to answer the "What is in it for me?" question of a potential participant.

5   Discussion

This paper has briefly summarized the key milestones in the history of SNA, as well as comparing and contrasting between the research and business perspectives on SNA in order to draw attention to some of the key issues facing the field today. In order to address the key issues surrounding SNAs today, the following recommendations are proposed:

1. There is a need for a one-stop shop of SNA resources (both learners and doers have expressed this particular need), for example:
    a)   Introductory book (academic and business practitioners);
    b)   Web site (similar to Brint.com for KM);
    c)   Business training courses and academic curriculum.
2. There is a need for a user-friendly interface for end-to-end SNA:
    a)   Analogous to data marts for data mining that can be used by business users without statistical/mathematical backgrounds;
    b)   A structured, guided approach to learning about SNAs and putting them into practice (e.g. a task support system with tutorials, examples, demos, templates on data collection, data visualization and data analysis complete).
3. A community of practice around the profession:
    a)   Community modeling CoP;
    b)   Standards for technology and SNA processes;
    c)   Norms for professional practice including code of ethics.
4. Conceptual clarification of the field:
    a)   A discipline or field of practice by a specific technique (i.e. SNA);
    b)   Should not define SNA technique by specific technologies;
    c)   Should define by targeted end result – suggestion: Social Capital Modeling.

These and other issues are being faced by SNA practitioners and the next step in the evolution of SNAs as an academic discipline and as an area of professional practice will parallel their resolution.

References

Adamic, L., & Adar, E. (2003). "Friends and neighbors on the Web." *Social Networks. 3.*
Baker, W., & Schumm, L. (1992). "Introduction to network analysis for management." *Connections, 15*(1-2), 29-48.
Baker, W., & Faulkne, R. (2004). "Social networks and loss of capital." *Social Networks, 26*(2), 91-111.
Batagelj, A. (1998). "Pajek - program for large network analysis." *Connections* 2(2), 47-5.

Beidernikl, G. (June 26, 2004). "Multi-lingual SNA business tools." Message posted to SOCNET.

Borgatti, S., & Molina , J. (2003). "Ethical and strategic issues in organizational social network analysis." *The Journal of Applied Behavioral Science, 39*(3), 337.

Carrington, P.J., Scott, J., and Wasserman, S. (in press). *Models and methods in social network analysis.* Cambridge, UK: Cambridge University Press

Cohen, D., & Prusak, L. (2001). *In good company: how social capital makes organizations work.* Boston, MA: Harvard Business School Press.

Contractor N., Zink, D., & Chan, M. (1998). "IKNOW: a tool to assist and study the creation, maintenance, and dissolution of knowledge networks." In Toru Ishida (Ed.), *Community computing and support systems, lecture notes in computer science.* (pp. 201-217). Berlin: Springer-Verlag.

Corner, L. A. L., D. U. Pfeiffer and R. S. Morris. "Social-network analysis of Mycobacterium bovis transmission among captive brushtail possums (Trichosurus vulpecula)" *Preventive Veterinary Medicine*, Volume 59, Issue 3, 12 June 2003, Pages 147-167

Cross,R., Parker, A., & Sasson. (). *Networks in the Knowledge Economy.* Oxford: Oxford University Press

Cross, R., Parker, A., Prusak, L., & Borgatti, S. (2001). "Knowing what we know: supporting knowledge creation and sharing in social networks." *Organizational Dynamics, 3*(2), 100-120.

Cross, R., & Prusak, L. (2002). "The people that make organizations stop – or go." *Harvard Business School Review, 80*(6), 104-112.

Cross, R., Borgatti, S., & Parker, A. (2002). "Making invisible work visible: using social network analysis to support human networks." *California Management Review, 44*(2), 25-46.

Cross, Rob, Parker, A, & Sasson. (2003). *Networks in the knowledge economy.* Oxford University Press.

Cross, R., & Parker, A. (2004). *The hidden power of social networks: understanding how work really gets done in organizations.* Boston, MA: Harvard Business School Press.

Droege, S., & Jenny M. (2003). "Employee turnover and tacit knowledge diffusion: a network perspective." *Journal of Managerial Issues, 15*(1), 50.

Freeman, L.. (1996). "Some antecedents of social network analysis." *Connections, 19*(1), 1-42.

Grimes, S. (2004). "Data mining for the masses." *Intelligent Enterprise, 7*(10), 14.

Hansen, M. (1999). "The search-transfer problem: the role of weak ties in sharing knowledge across organization subunits". *Administrative Science Quarterly, 44,* 82-111.

Hoffman, C. (2001). "Introduction to sociometry." Retrieved on June 30, 2004 from: http://www.hoopandtree.org/sociometry.htm.2001.

Jensen, D., & Neville, J. (2002). "Data mining in social network." Retrieved on June 30, 2004 from: http://kdl.cs.umass.edu/papers/jensen-neville-nas2002.pdf.

Kadushin, C., & session participants. (2003). "Ethics of Network Data Collection: A Report on the Sunbelt Session." Accessed on June 30, 2004 from: home.earthlink.net/~ckadushin/Texts/Ethics.pdf /

Kilduff, Martin & Wenpin Tsai. (2003). *Social networks and organizations.* London: Sage Publications.

Krebs, V. (2004a). "Data mining email to discover social networks and communities of practice." Retrieved on June 30, 2004 from: http://www.orgnet.com/email.html.

Krebs, V. (2004b). An introduction to social network analysis. Retrieved on June 30, 2004 from: http://www.orgnet.com/sna.html.

Lesser, E. L., & Prusak, L. (2000). "Communities of practice, social capital and organizational knowledge." In E. Lesser, M. Fontaine & J. Slusher (Eds.). *Knowledge and communities* (123-131). Boston: Butterworth Heinemann.

Mead, S. (2001). "Using social network analysis to visualize project teams." *Project Management Journal, 32*(4), 32.

Molina, J. (2001)."The informal organizational chart in organizations: an approach from the social network analysis." *Connections, 24*(1), 78-91.

Moreno, J. (1934). *Who shall survive?* Washington, DC: Nervous and Mental Disorders Publishing Co.

Nahapiet, J., & Ghoshal, S. (1998). "Social capital, intellectual capital and the organizational advantage." *Academy of Management Review, 23*(2), 242-267.

Parker, A., Cross, R. & Walsh, D. (2001). "Improving collaboration with social network analysis." *Knowledge Management Review, 4*(2), 24-30.

Rice, R. (1994). "Network analysis and computer mediated communication systems." In S. Wasserman & J. Galaskiewicz (Eds.), *Perspectives on social network research* (pp. 119-136). New York: Academic Press.

Rowley, Timothy J. (1997). "Moving beyond dyadic ties: A network theory of stakeholder influences." *Academy of Management Review, 22*: 887-910.

Scott, John. (1991). *Social Network analysis: a handbook.* London, UK: Sage Publications.

Tenkasi, R., & Chesmore, M. (2003). "Social networks and planned organizational change: the impact of strong network ties on effective change implementation and use." *The Journal of Applied Behavioral Science, 39*(3), 281.

Tufte, E. (2001). *The visual display of quantitative information* (2nd Ed). Cheshire, CT: Graphics Press.

Udell, J. (2004a). "The new social enterprise." *InfoWorld, 26*(13), 47.

Udell, J. (2004b). "Capitalizing on communication." *InfoWorld, 26*(13), 50-52.

Wasserman, S., & Faust, K. (1994). *Social network analysis: methods and applications.* Oxford, UK: Cambridge University Press.

Watts, D.J. (2003). *Six degrees: the science of a connected age.* New York, Norton.

Wellman, B. (1988). "The community question re-evaluated." In MP Smith (Ed.) *Power, Community and the City.* (pp. 81-107). New Brunswick, NJ: Transaction Books.

Wellman, B., & Tindall, D. (2001). "Canada as social structure: social network analysis and Canadian sociology." *Canadian Journal of Sociology, 26*(3), 265.

Yang, H-L., & Tang, J-H. (2004). "Team structure and team performance in IS development: a social network perspective." *Information & Management, 41*(3), 335-349.

COLLABORATIVE FACTORS AFFECTING KM PROCESSES

MIGUEL ANGEL MORALES ARROYO & YUN-KE CHANG

KM Program, College of Arts and Sciences, University of Oklahoma, 4502 E. 41st Street
Tulsa, Oklahoma 74135, United States of America

A central part of KM is to encourage collaborative practices. Human and social factors play an important role in the creation, sharing, and use of knowledge. There is a need to closely investigate some of the human and social factors that are involved in KM processes. This is an exploratory study in which twenty-five granted projects were studied, employing an online questionnaire. The operationalization of human and social factors was studied utilizing Ward's method of hierarchical cluster analysis. Snowball sampling was employed, and fifty people participated in this study.

1   Introduction

Organizations are faced with many challenges, such as producing the desired objectives, solving the right problems, and using the minimal quantity of resources in a competitive and complex environment. Among other necessities, organizations have to identify knowledge sources and assess their value when possible. They need to be proactive and/or to adapt to the rapid pace of change. They should be able to recognize the needs of their customers or users and be able to develop or adapt mechanisms that permit them to measure their intellectual capital and build the technological infrastructure that would facilitate knowledge sharing and utilization.

Technological changes and economic factors are forcing museums and libraries to collaborate in order to insure people access to their rich cultural heritage. The advent of the Internet has opened the possibility for many to have access to information, knowledge, and art works from reliable, qualified, and authoritative sources.

There are few alternatives for these institutions because electronic documents and digital representations of objects will be more frequently used in the future. In order to take advantage of the technology, they will require human, technological, economic resources, skills and knowledge to achieve this objective. Adapting to the technological change, providing accessibility to their resources, creating awareness of their roles in a lifelong learning process, providing access to the technology, and teaching the basic skills needed to access information and knowledge are some of the challenges that museums and libraries face.

In the adoption of the Internet as a mechanism for propagation of information, knowledge, and culture, some factors negatively affect museums and libraries. For example, the lack of specialists that have both knowledge about digitalization and the collections, lack of personnel to manage the digitalization projects and general lack of funding for increasing staff resources are major problems.

An alternative for reducing the negative effects of these problems is to collaborate with other organizations that have the technical capacity to digitalize. As federal agencies and some private organizations are providing funds for digitalization projects only when partnerships and collaboration occur, universities have begun to make such arrangements.

The central idea around collaboration between museums and libraries is to increase accessibility to cultural and educational resources and the integration of those resources. Collaboration between museums and libraries helps to create flexible learning systems, to assemble more dynamic learning frameworks, and to build infrastructures that bring together content and systems that supply knowledge. In this study, several collaborative projects between museums and libraries, therefore, provided opportunities for investigating the collaborative factors affecting knowledge sharing and transfer processes.

2   Literature Review

There is not accepted definition of Knowledge Management (KM). Different disciplines have been associated with KM – information technology and telecommunications, information management specialties, social psychology, cognitive science, communication, social sciences, management, and others. Also, in the KM literature, we find the following concepts: intellectual capital, knowledge creation, transfer, sharing, and dissemination, organizational learning, organizational culture, and communities of practice.

Thomas, Kellogg, and Erickson (2001) define a knowledge community as a trusted environment in which people may create, discover, use, manipulate, transfer, share, interact, and learn. In these communities, people know each other, share professional interests, socialize, and understand the context in which this exchange takes place. The community should also be able to support innovative ways for group interaction, thereby increasing creativity, and support communication, collaboration, *etc*. The challenge is how to integrate and balance a collaborative environment in a competitive arena.

Tacit knowledge is embedded in people and is thus problematic to identify, transfer, and share outside the close circumstances in which experiences occur. Within the organization, as well, sometimes knowledge sharing and transfer is hard to accomplish. The organizational resistance to share is one of the obstacles to the implementation of KM (Sveiby and Simons, 2002).

A central part of KM is to promote collaborative practices. A knowledge community encourages people to share knowledge with their peers. Trust and a sharing culture are needed to promote the use and progress of Knowledge Management practices in an organization (Moffett, McAdam, and Parkinson, 2002).

A collaborative environment is one of the most important elements in producing effective knowledge work (Sveiby and Simons, 2002). The collaborative processes are dynamic, multi-disciplinary and multi-dimensional. The variables that affect collaboration projects change over time. For example, the level of trustworthiness among the organizations initially may be low, but over time may increase (Doz & Hamel, 1998;

Blau, 1964). However, other factors may reduce their value over time, such as uncertainty related to the partner or complexity linked to the common task.

Human and social factors play an important role in the creation, sharing, and use of knowledge. There is a need to investigate closely some of the human and social factors that are involved in KM processes. Human factors affect actors' behavior and the roles they play. They also influence the social interactions in which knowledge management evolves in each organization, and affect the implementation of technologies that sustain collaboration (Thomas, Kellogg, Erickson, 2001).

Variables derived from the literature review are defined operatively as trustworthiness, commitment, competence, uncertainty, risk, interdependence, coordination, complexity, integration, expectations, and conflict.

At the beginning, the creation of a relationship is usually a slow process and commences with small transactions in which little trust is needed because little risk is implicated (Blau, 1964). Trust, an indispensable component in a relationship, increases as the relationship evolves (Chisholm, 1989). Initially, exchanges are based on the 'norm of reciprocity' (p. 114) that expresses that people should help and not harm those who have helped them. The norm of reciprocity is a foundation of virtually every society and is accepted universally in moral systems (Chisholm, 1989).

Many of the exchanges are informal, which provides flexibility and allows going beyond the constraints of formal agreements (Chisholm, 1989). Frequent and constructive contacts promote the incremental development of trust (Axelrod, 1984), consideration, and respect, and they are important to the growth of the relationship (Chisholm, 1989). The function of the exchange appears to be the creation of trust (Blau, 1964).

Commitment is defined as compromise, obligation or responsibility, and the ability to stick to the objective or course. Members' commitment has been identified as an element that affects collaborative effort (D'Aunno *et al.*, 1987; Clark & Morton, 1997; Castell, 1988; Kaplan, 1998; Winer *et al.*, 1994; Doz, 1987/1988; Browning, 1995).

Organizational commitment has been studied in different ways, involving organizational structure and its consequences, as well as performance aspects such as productivity and turnover. Organizational structure has been connected to organizational commitment using variables, such as decentralization of decision-making, formalization of procedures and processes, functional dependence, and job level (Brooks, 2002).

Competence can be understood as effectiveness. Blake & Mouton (1964) established that effectiveness depends on the manager's leadership style having two dimensions: concern for people and concern for results. Similar dimensions are used in some constructs in communication style and cultural differentiation. For example, gender orientation style has masculinity (instrumental) and femininity (expressive) components (Wheeless & Lashbrook, 1987), the masculinity dimension is also part of cultural differentiation (Hofstede, 1980); social style has assertiveness, responsiveness, and versatility elements (Wheeless *et al.*, 1987; Merril & Reid, 1981).

Spitzberg and Cupach (1984) define fundamental competence as people's ability to adapt, interact, and even alter their changing environment in order to survive, mature, flourish, and achieve goals over time. In order to adapt and modify to the changing environment, people develop context awareness—that is, the ability to identify, discriminate between, and adjust to their environment. People require two types of knowledge: knowing what to adjust and knowing how to modify their environment. Fundamental competence includes the cognitive capacity to (a) manipulate significant information from the context, (b) choose the most significant information to perform a specific activity, and (c) create new patterns by reframing known precedents to satisfy changing requirements (Spitzberg & Cupach, 1984).

Thompson (1967) provides three levels of interdependence inside organizations. The first is pooled interdependence, in which each part supplies the totality, and the totality sustains each part. The second is sequential interdependence, a consecutive arrangement where the outcomes of one part are the raw materials of another. When sequential interdependence is present, pooled interdependence is present, too. Third, reciprocal interdependence occurs when parts interchange resources and services reciprocally. The more interdependence there is among partners, the more difficult it is to coordinate activities among them. The level of contingency increases when the level of coordination and interdependence needed is high.

Kumar *et al.* (1996) extends and modifies the pooled interdependence definition in the following way: parts share and use common resources, but are independent in other aspects. In reciprocal dependency, parts provide their work from side to side among them. The level of interdependence is a significant factor, related to the extent in which one part can damage the other. Similar concern is expressed by Doz (1996); integrative tasks create a high level of interdependence, which makes the learning process difficult.

Thomson (1967) defines three levels of coordination: coordination by standardization, coordination by plan, and coordination by mutual adjustment. He also establishes relationships between the levels of coordination and the levels of interdependence. Standardization necessitates a smaller amount of decisions and a less-frequent interchange of information than coordination by planning, and planning requires fewer decisions and a less frequent interchange of information than mutual adjustment. Coordination by mutual adjustment is the most expensive because it involves more decision-making, and more interchange of information than the other types of coordination (Thompson, 1967). The level of contingency is the highest with reciprocal interdependence because activities of every party must be adapted to the activities done by others. Finally, coordination is an essential factor for managing knowledge processes within organizations, and we need more knowledge about coordination (Soares-Correa da Silva and Agusti-Cullel., 2003).

Finally, a common element in any social interaction, conflict, is defined as disagreement about one of several of the following aspects: values, status, power, needs, goals, or the way partners may use their resources (Isenhart *et al.*, 2000). Constant interaction increases the probability of misunderstandings between interrelated parties, intensifying the risk of conflict (Kumar *et al.*, 1996).

3   Method and Data

The following operatively defines each of the variables derived from the literature review, which includes trustworthiness, commitment, competence, uncertainty, risk, interdependence, coordination, complexity, integration, expectations, and conflict.

Trustworthiness has been defined as competence (Nock, 1993; Govier, 1997), openness, supportiveness, the ability to explore differences constructively , acceptance, tolerance for disagreement, and constructive use of people's openness (Zand, 1997), prediction of behavior, surveillance (Nock, 1993), fair reward system/*norm of reciprocity* (Chisholm, 1989), and expectation of benevolent and harmless behavior (Govier, 1997). In this research, trustworthiness is characterized as reciprocity, reliability, and competence.

Table 1. Operationalization of Variables

+ Trustworthiness	R14F	- Partner's reciprocity
	R14G	- Partner's reliability
+ Interdependence	R12A	- Dependency on partner's skills
	R12B	- Dependency on partner's knowledge
	R12C	- Dependency on partner's resources
	R12D	- Dependency on partner's work
+ Complexity	R1	- Impact of technology in the collaborative project
	R2	- Level of difficulty in the collaborative project
+ Integration	R5	- Level of integration achieved
+ Commitment	R3	- Project's goals match organizational goals
	R7	- Personal level of involvement
	R9A	- Support from the staff in the organization
	R9B	- Support from partner organization
+ Performance	R8	- Project results match original expectations
+ Coordination	R4	- Difficulty to obtain information
	R6	- Freedom to try new things
	R13A	- Coordination by a set routines
	R13B	- Coordination using of standard procedures defined by agreement
	R13C	- Coordination by revising the planning mechanisms
	R13D	- Coordination by mutual agreements
+ Conflict	R11A	- Different points of view
	R11C	- Different expectations
	R11D	- Different needs
	R11B	- Different interests
+ Competence	R14A	- Partners' expertise
	R14B	- Partners' creativity to find new solutions
	R14C	- Partners' ability to solve unpredicted problems
	R14D	- Partners' capacity for good inter-organizational relationships
	R14E	- Partners' adaptability

Given its importance, competence is used as a different variable. Competence is a concept used in communication and is operationalized as adaptability, knowledge, responsiveness, assertiveness, and versatility (Wheeless & Lashbrook, 1987; Merrill *et al.*, 1981). An individual is considered competent when they own significant knowledge, skills, and aptitudes that enable them to carry out a specific work (Barge, 1994).

Interdependence is typified as dependency on a partner's skills, knowledge, resources, work (Thompson, 1967), and the level of coordination (Meyer, 1993). Complexity is described as impact of technology, and level of difficulty of the collaborative project.

Commitment is expressed as the importance of the collaborative goals with respect to the organizational goals, top management support or staff support, and availability of resources (see Table 1). Morrow (1993) gives some characteristics of commitment: Self-regulation, tenure, job satisfaction, organization climate, level of stress, role overload, resource inadequacy, hours worked, formalization, routinization, formalization, and role ambiguity. Cook and Wall (1986) perceive commitment as identification, involvement, and loyalty to the organization. Mowday and Steers (1986) view commitment as affinity with organizational goals and the inclination to maintain membership in order to achieve those goals.

Multiple projects were studied using an online questionnaire to gather data for this study. To increase content validity, the study questions were developed based on the literature review, particularly on previous studies that used similar constructs. This study is exploratory; consequently, causality is not one of the goals of this research. Given the restrictions for this research, sampling, and the nature of the problem, external validity was difficult to claim. Finally, internal consistency was calculated for each one of the operationalized concepts.

The population of this study is a subset of collaborative projects funded by the Institute of Museums and Library Services (IMLS), an American federal agency. There were two criteria used to select the projects: (a) accessibility, and (b) funded partnership by IMLS. Final data collected for this study include 25 projects, and fifty participants.

The method of snowball sampling was used in this study to find members of organizations that have collaborative projects funded by IMLS. The researcher invited all the project directors of collaborative projects granted by IMLS at that moment to participate, and asked them to contact people participating in their collaborative projects.

Considering that there were 128 potential participants contacted, the rate of return for the total number of participants was 39% for the questionnaires. One of the participants asked for mailed questionnaire, and 1.3% of the questions were not answered. The roles of the participants in their projects were the following: project director 26%, project coordinator 42%, and others 32%. The status of their projects were: finished 54%, finishing 18%, more than half 6%, middle or less 20%, and starting project 2%.

According to Aldenderfer & Blashfield (1984), cluster analysis is a name given to a set of noninferential statistics procedures allowing one to group empirical data based on similarity measures. "A clustering method is a multivariate statistical procedure that starts with a data set containing information about a sample of entities and attempts to reorganize these entities into relatively homogeneous groups" (Everitt, 1980, p.7). In this case, a hierarchical cluster analysis was used to identify how well the operationalization of variables was done, using the Ward's method

4   Results and Discussion

The first cluster is formed by R14B, R14C, R14D, R14E, and R14A. They represent the concept of competence, and they have the minimal sum of squares. These variables, then, form a bigger cluster with R14F and R14G, which put all the variables related with trustworthiness together.

   The second group of variables, R12A, R12B, R12C, and R12D, represents interdependence. The following cluster is associated with commitment, performance, and coordination variables – R3, R8, R9B, R5, R6, R13D, and R7. Three variables are orphans: one is related to commitment (R9A), and two with mechanisms of coordination (R13A, R13B).

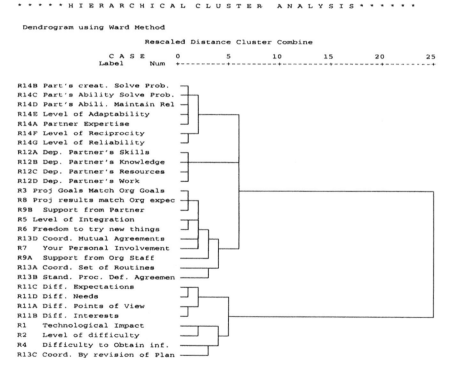

Figure 1. Cluster Analysis

The last cluster is integrated by conflict variables (R11C, R11D, R11A, and R11B). Variables linked to complexity are loosely associated (R1 and R2), and R4 and R13C, mechanisms of coordination, are orphan variables.

The operationalization of trustworthiness, competence, dependency, and conflict was very positive. Variables associated with complexity behaved as predicted and clustered, but its similarity is low (see Figure 1).

The order in which variables were clustered followed the next sequence of concepts (see Figure 1): competence, trustworthiness, interdependence, some of the variables related to commitment, objectives, integration, coordination, conflict, complexity, and possibly lack of coordination. Although the results of this study were exploratory, it is important to recognize that the sequence in which the variables clustered may have a relationship with the order in which the variables on those projects evolved. For instance, in these projects competence was the most relevant factor in the decision-making process, and also was the first factor to cluster. It will be interesting to do further research in this direction.

Variables related to competence were the first to cluster in the dendrogram, which means these variables were the most similar and their distance among themselves was the closest. It was expected that potential collaborators look for partners who have specific skills, problem-solving abilities, capacities, the creativity to confront new situations, and the resources to achieve common objectives. Zand (1997) establishes that leaders are not going to leave their future opportunities in the hands of people who are incompetent or who lack a reputable record of competence. In general, people do not put the care of their health in the hands of a professional without the credentials and the experience needed. In the same way, potential partner organizations are not going to join with an organization lacking recognized levels of competence.

Trustworthiness was defined as competence plus the levels of reliability and reciprocity. Reciprocity is an important component of trustworthiness in a relationship (Zand, 1997). Partners have to have an impression of sharing a common future (Kouzes & Posner, 2002), also known as the "shadow of the future" (Sydow, 1988, p. 50). A collaborative relationship is not likely to last if a partner is not reliable and/or is unable to reciprocate. In other words, the fact that all these variables have clustered means that the participants perceived them as closely related, and this gave support to the conceptualization of trustworthiness. Also, the participants considered the variables associated with this concept as characteristics that apply to their partners. However, these results should be considered carefully. Trustworthiness is a very complex concept, and this research did not make a differentiation among different levels of trustworthiness (Bachmann, 1988) or the conceptualizations and measurement of many others.

The findings show that the participants in this study perceived their dependency on their partners' skills, knowledge, resources, and work as a homogenous set, and they accepted their dependency on their partners. For Kouzes *et al.* (2002), interdependence is a condition in which "the success of one depends on the success of the other" (p. 251). In a collaborative effort, the success of the project was based on an acceptable degree of success by each one of the partners, and also meant that partners depended on each other. Curtis (2001) addresses the fact that participants have to recognize their dependency on the others in order to achieve a common goal.

Achieving the expected results is clustered initially with the commitment from the partner(s), and the commitment to the project's goals. Joined to the same cluster are: the level of integration, the freedom to try new things, coordination by mutual agreements, and the personal participant's involvement. A possible interpretation could be that in order to achieve the expected results, commitment is needed as well as coordination of activities and a certain level of integration among the partners. This relationship is not direct. A cluster analysis simply tells us that the variables are closely related and have the minimal variance. Johnson, Zorn, Tam, Lamontagne, & Johnson (2003) found that "strong leadership, commitment, communication, understanding different cultures, pre-planning, providing adequate resources, and minimizing territorial aspects" (p. 201) were the most important factors that contributed to the success of a collaborative effort. Their definition of strong leadership in the context of this research is essentially commitment. Commitment, in this context, means not giving up easily.

There were factors that did cluster separately: commitment, coordination, and mechanism of coordination. The last one did cluster separately, probably, because some mechanisms were not used as frequently as others.

In the case of some of the commitment variables, one possible explanation for not having a close relationship among those variables is that they are not related to the concept. Another possible explanation is that commitment has different components, and that the concept needs to be studied in more detail. Another possibility is that a variable or a set of them may be absent in the collaborative relationship. The same arguments can explain the dispersion of coordination variables.

Finally, at the bottom of the dendrogram, there are the variables that are associated negatively with collaboration. Conflict and complexity are two factors that are considered negative in collaborative efforts. Ohlinger, Brown, Laudert, Swanson, & Fofah (2003) recognize that unmanaged conflict can sabotage team progress and increase tensions and disagreements. Also, conflict is not an isolated variable. Smith (1998) declares that when there is not enough trust among collaborators, the possibility to express differences depends on the degree of trust among them. Conflict and differences can only be expressed when there is an environment and level of trust that allow disclosing them (Smith, 1998). There are different types of complexity: complexity of the project, that can include complexity of the task, but also difficulties with the relationship, and complexities associated with the environment in which the project is executed. In this study, the complexity variables studied for the variables are related to the difficulty of the project, and in that sense are considered a negative factor.

5   Conclusions

KM process such as knowledge sharing and dissemination require collaborative practices. The collaborative process is complex and dynamic, and some human and social factors benefit and harm collaboration. One way in which KM practices can be improved is to know more about underlying phenomena like collaboration. The results of this study are positive, but they should be considered preliminary. The operationalization of trustworthiness, competence, dependency, and conflict goes in the correct direction, but complexity, commitment, and mechanism of coordination should be studied in more detail. There are many issues that we need to understand about collaboration, including the stages of the collaborative process, the different levels of collaboration, and their influence in KM processes.

References

Aldenderfer, M. S., & Blashfield, R. K. (1984). *Cluster Analysis* (First printing ed.). Beverly Hills: Sage Publications, Inc.

Axelrod, R. M. (1984). *The Evolution of Cooperation.* Basic Books

Bachmann, R. (1988). Conclusion: Trust - Conceptual aspects of a complex phenomenon. In C. Lane & R. Bachmann (Eds.), *Trust Within and Between Organizations.* New York: Oxford University Press.

Barge, J. K. (1994). *Leadership: Communication Skills for Organizations and Groups.* New York: St. Martin's Press.

Blake, R. R., & Mouton, J. S. (1964). *The Managerial Grid.* Houston, TX: Gulf Pub. Co.

Blau, P. M. (1964). *Exchange and Power in Social Life.* New York: John Wiley & Sons.

Brooks, G., (2002) Knowledge-based structures and organizational commitment, *Management Decision,* 40(5/6), 566-573.

Browning, L. D. (1995). Building cooperation in a competitive industry: Sematech and the semiconductor industry. *Academy of Management Journal,* 38(1), 113-151.

Castell, A. B. (1988). Gateway to better health. *Business & Health,* 6(1), 16-17.

Chisholm, D. W. (1989). *Coordination without hierarchy: Informal structures in multiorganizational systems.* Berkeley and Los Angeles, CA: University of California Press.

Clark, D., & Morton, D. (1997). Quality as a common cause. *Journal for Quality & Participation,* 20(5), 54-55.

Cook, J., & Wall, T. (1986). New measures of trust, organizational commitment and personal need of nonfulfillment. In J. L. Price & C. W. Mueller (Eds.), *Handbook of Organizational Measurement .* White Plains, N.Y.

Curtis, R. S. (2001). Successful collaboration between hospitals and physicians: Process or structure? *Hospital Topics: Research and Perspectives on Healthcare,* 79(2), 7-13.

D'Aunno, T. A., & Zuckerman, H. S. (1987). A life-cycle model of organizational federations: The case of hospitals. *Academy of Management Review,* 12(3), 534-545.

Doz, Y. L. (1987/1988). Technology partnerships between larger and smaller firms: Some critical issues. *International Studies of Management & Organization.* 17(4): 31-57. 1987/1988, 17(4), 31-57.

Doz, Y. L., & Hamel, G. (1998). *Alliance Advantage - The Art of Creating Value Through Partnering.* Boston, Massachusetts: Harvard Business School Press.

Everitt, B. (1980). *Cluster Analysis* (Second Edition ed.). London

Govier, T. (1997). *Social Trust and Human Communities.* Montreal: McGill-Queen's University Press.

Hofstede, G. (1980). *Culture's Consequences.* Beverly Hills: Sage Publications.

Isenhart, M. W., & Spangle, M. (2000). *Collaborative Approaches to Resolving Conflict.* Thousand Oaks, CA: Sage Publications, Inc.

Johnson, L. J., Zorn, D., Tam, B. K. Y., Lamontagne, M., & Johnson, S. A. (2003). Stakeholders' views of factors that impact successful interagency collaboration. *Exceptional Children,* 69(2), 195-209.

Kaplan, B. (1998). Willow Clinic: Recipe for successful collaboration. *Healthcare Forum Journal,* 41(3), 48-51.

Kouzes, J. M., & Posner, B. Z. (2002). *Leadership the Challenge* (Third Edition ed.). San Francisco, CA: Jossey-Bass.

Kumar, K., & van Dissel, H. G. (1996). Sustainable collaboration: Managing conflict and cooperation in interorganizational systems. *MIS Quarterly,* 20(3), 279-300.

Merril, D. W., & Reid, R. H. (1981). *Personal Styles and Effective Performance.* Radnor, Pennsylvania: Chilton Book Company.

Meyer, H.-D. (1993). The cultural gap in long-term international work groups: A German - American case study. *European Management Journal,* 11(1), 93-101.

Moffett, S. McAdam, R., Parkinson, S., (2002) Developing a model for technology and cultural factors in knowledge management. *Knowledge and Process Management,* 237-255.

Morrow, P. C. (1993). *The Theory and Measurement of Work Commitment.* Greenwich, CT.: JAI Press.

Mowday, R., & Steers, R. M. (1986). The measurement of organizational commitment. In J. L. Price & C. W. Mueller (Eds.), *Handbook of Organizational Measurement .* White Plains, N.Y.

Nock, S. L. (1993). *The Costs of Privacy - Surveillance and Reputation in America.* New York: Walter de Gruyter, Inc.

Ohlinger, J., Brown, M. S., Laudert, S., Swanson, S., & Fofah, S. (2003). Development of potentially better practices for the Neonatal Intensive Care Unit as a culture of collaboration: Communication, accountability, respect, and empowerment. *Pediatrics,* 111(4), 471-481.

Smith, P. (1998). Conflict can lead to success. *Trustee,* 57(7), 26-27.

Soares-Correa da Silva, F., Agusti-Cullel, J., (2003) Issues on knowledge coordination. *Knowledge and Process Management,* 10(1), 37-59.

Spitzberg, B. H., & Cupach, W. R. (1984). *Interpersonal Communication Competence.* Beverly Hills: Sage Publications.

Sveiby, K. E., Simons, R., (2002) Collaborative climate and effectiveness of knowledge work - an empirical study. *Journal of Knowledge Management,* 6(5), 420-433.

Sydow, J. (1988). Understanding the constitution of interorganizational trust. In C. Lane & R. Bachmann (Eds.), *Trust Within and Between Organizations .* New York: Oxford University Press.

Thomas, J. C., Kellogg, W. A., Erickson, T., (2001) The knowledge management puzzle: Human and social factors in knowledge management. *IBM Systems Journal,* 40(4), 863-885.

Thompson, J. D. (1967). *Organizations in Action : Social Science Bases of Administrative Theory.* New York.

Wheeless, V. E., & Lashbrook, W. B. (1987). Style. In J. C. McCroskey & J. A. Daly (Eds.), *Personality and Interpersonal Communication* (pp. 243-272). Newbury Park, Calif.: Sage Publications.

Winer, M., & Ray, K. (1994). *Collaboration Handbook* (Fourth Printing, October 1997 ed.). Saint Paul, Minnesota: Amherst H. Wilder Foundation.

Zand, D. E. (1997). *The Leadership Triad - Knowledge, Trust, and Power.* New York: Oxford University Press.

COLLABORATIVE LEARNING BEHAVIOUR IN SOFTWARE DEVELOPMENT TEAMS

SOURAV MUKHERJI & ABHOY K. OJHA

Indian Institute of Management Bangalore
Bangalore- 560076, India

Software development is a knowledge intensive activity. Commercial production of software is carried out in teams where the collective knowledge of team members is harnessed to create a solution for a business problem. The abstract nature of software makes it imperative for team members to continuously share tacit knowledge and engage in collaborative learning. Based on analysis of data collected from 588 software developers working in 83 teams, this research identifies the factors that influence collaborative learning in software development teams and the impact of such learning on team effectiveness. The results indicate that teams that are managed by following open and transparent processes and inculcating relationships based on trust have high degree of collaborative learning among team members. However, collaborative learning behaviour does not benefit all kinds of teams. While it benefits teams involved in software product development, its impact on teams involved in support and maintenance of software solutions is insignificant. The implications of these findings for organizational knowledge management initiatives are discussed.

1   Introduction

Knowledge is the raw material for software development. In a very abstract sense, a piece of software is codification of a developer's knowledge about an information technology based solution to a real life business problem. However, given today's business requirements of shorter time to deliver and increasing scales of projects, developing a software solution almost invariably exceeds the capacity of an individual software developer. Software development is hence carried out in teams, where collective knowledge is the critical input for understanding business problems and developing software solutions Most commercial software solutions need to conform to several technical and human interfaces, many of which change continuously enhancing the need for constant learning. Moreover, the essence and complexity of the internal functioning of software solutions are rarely amenable to visual representation (Brooks, 1987). As a result, much of the knowledge that is critical for successful development of software remains tacit. In order to perform effectively in such a context, team members iteratively engage in experimentation, reflective communication and knowledge codification – all of which constitute collaborative learning behaviour (Gibson & Vermeulen, 2003).

The software industry recognizes the criticality of knowledge and learning for improving productivity. However, the dominant focus of the industry has been on the implementation of information technology based knowledge management systems to enhance inter-team and inter-divisional knowledge capture and learning. This research draws attention to the need to understand non-technology based intra-team knowledge sharing due to two prime reasons. Firstly, given that a significant amount of knowledge essential for software development is tacit, information technology based knowledge management systems are unlikely to enhance sharing of such knowledge. Hence, it is essential to understand team-based processes that may facilitate tacit knowledge sharing. Secondly, in knowledge intensive context of the software industry, the process of learning is as critical as the stock of knowledge in order to reduce the "knowing-doing gap" (Pfeffer and Sutton, 1999).

The study reported in this paper examined two primary questions (i) What are the factors that influence collaborative learning behaviour among members of software development teams? (ii) Does collaborative learning lead to greater effectiveness of software development teams? Based on data collected from 588 software developers working in 20 software organizations, it identifies the factors that lead to collaborative learning behaviour among team members and the impact of collaborative learning on the effectiveness of software developing teams. The results indicate that teams that are managed by following open and transparent processes and inculcating relationships based on trust have high degree of collaborative learning among team members. However, collaborative learning behaviour does not benefit all kinds of teams. While it benefits teams involved in software product development, its impact on teams involved in support and maintenance of software solutions is insignificant.

2   Social Nature of Collaborative Learning

Much of the knowledge essential for software development cannot be codified into explicit knowledge. Thus, knowledge that is exchanged among team members, due to its complexity and context sensitivity, is largely tacit in nature. The ease with which tacit and complex knowledge is exchanged is dependent upon the interpersonal relationships that develop among the team members. A two way interaction afforded by a strong relationship is important for assimilating tacit or non-codified knowledge because strong ties help in developing relationship specific heuristics necessary for processing complex tacit knowledge (Hansen, 1999). Thus, collaborative learning within the context of software development teams is social, personal and subjective in nature.

In this study, two sets of factors, intrinsic and extrinsic that influence collaborative learning were examined. Intrinsic factors relate to those that are embedded within the team, pertaining to individual traits, interpersonal relationships and team dynamics. Extrinsic factors are those organizational factors that are outside the boundaries of the team, but have an impact on the behavior of team members. The propensity of individuals to share knowledge, the facilitative role played by the team leader, the trust and intimacy of relationship developed among team members and the process of decision making and problem solving followed by the team can create the impetus for a team to engage in collaborative behaviour. Likewise, the knowledge management systems and processes adopted at an organization level, the attitude of senior management towards collaboration and learning and overall cultural orientation of the organization are some of the extrinsic factors that are likely to influence collaborative learning.

3   Intrinsic Factors Influencing Collaborative Learning

Individuals differ in their propensity to participate in collaborative learning. Wageman (1995) defined autonomy preference as the extent to which individuals like to work independently. Individuals high on autonomy preference are less likely to contribute to or benefit from knowledge of team members, because of their inability to collaborate with others.

Hypothesis 1: Autonomy preference will be negatively related to collaborative learning

High performance teams are found to have highly involved project managers (Guinan and Cooprider, 1998). Project managers act as conduits of knowledge by structuring and organizing information (Gibson, 2001). Such managers follow an open leadership style, provide autonomy to team members and motivate them by recognizing their individual competencies, which encourages collaboration among team members:

Hypothesis 2: Open leadership style will be positively related to collaborative learning.

Trust in relationship is a crucial factor affecting knowledge sharing, especially when knowledge is tacit and complex. When relationships are high in trust, individuals are more willing to engage in cooperative interactions and knowledge sharing (Szulanski, 1996) that would result in higher levels of collaborative learning:

Hypothesis 3: Trust will be positively related to collaborative learning.

When it comes to solving novel problems, teams that give due importance to inputs of individual members are found to perform well. Members of teams that are non-hierarchical and decentralized get greater opportunity for knowledge and information sharing (Rulke and Galaskeiwicz, 2000). Teams that overcome conflicts through consensus building among its members are better disposed towards generating knowledge (Gibson, 2001). Specifically in the context of software development, it has been found that in high performing teams, decision-making is participative and knowledge is exchanged in a classic dialectic process. Thus, there are greater possibilities for collaborative learning in teams that follow participating decision-making.

Hypothesis 4: Participative decision-making will be positively related to collaborative learning.

4   Extrinsic Factors Influencing Collaborative Learning

Features of the organization to which the team belongs can stimulate or impede collaborative learning. Organizational support creates an atmosphere of psychological safety and efficacy fostering collaborating learning in teams (Edmondson, 1999). Three factors that are likely to influence collaborative learning are the nature of knowledge management initiatives, the orientation of senior management towards learning and knowledge sharing, and existence of organizational policies that encourage knowledge absorbing behaviour (Cohen & Levinthal, 1990).

Knowledge management initiatives in organizations are primarily in two dimensions. The first comprise instituting systems and processes for capturing knowledge and learning of employees, identification of knowledge gaps, and transfer of best practices. The second dimension comprises an organization wide incentive mechanism for motivating employees to contribute to and learn from organizational knowledge management systems. Knowledge management initiatives undertaken at an organization level provide the right kind of tools and physical infrastructure for capture, storage and dissemination of knowledge. Over and above that, such initiatives provide the necessary context and motivation for team members to learn from one another.

Hypothesis 5a: The presence of a knowledge management system will be positively related to collaborative learning.

Hypothesis 5b: Incentives for knowledge sharing will be positively related to collaborative learning.

When knowledge that is critical for an organization is largely tacit, the challenge of knowledge management is to have team members engage in social processes that motivate them to think and work together and learn from one another. This requires a certain cultural orientation and two elements are necessary for creating the necessary context. The first is sustained and powerful advocacy by senior management towards learning and knowledge sharing. By assigning strategic importance to knowledge management and constantly advocating its necessity for developing sustainable competitiveness, senior management can energize the entire organization towards learning and knowledge sharing (Davenport and Prusak, 1998):

Hypothesis 6a: Advocacy by senior management will be positively related to collaborative learning.

The second necessary element for creating the right context is absorptive capacity - organizational policies and procedures that encourage active knowledge absorbing behaviour (Soo *et al.*, 2002). Processes that encourage free flow of information and knowledge, both within and across the organizational boundary, create an environment where members realize the positive effect of leveraging internal and external knowledge networks.

Hypothesis 6b: Absorptive capacity will be positively related to collaborative learning.

5   Collaborative Learning and Team Effectiveness

In section 2 it was argued that collaborative learning is critical for successful software development.   In sections 4 and 5, we hypothesized that positive interpersonal relationship and facilitative team processes would lead to collaborative learning. Synthesizing these, we argue that in software development environment, positive interpersonal relationships and facilitative team processes lead to high performance if and only if they can bring about high degree of collaborative learning among team members. In other words, in a knowledge intensive environment, extent of collaborative learning will provide the causal explanation for the positive influence of interpersonal relationship and team dynamics on team effectiveness.

Hypothesis 7: Collaborative learning will be positively related to team effectiveness.

The following figure depicts the model of collaborative learning with its antecedents and impact, as was hypothesized above.

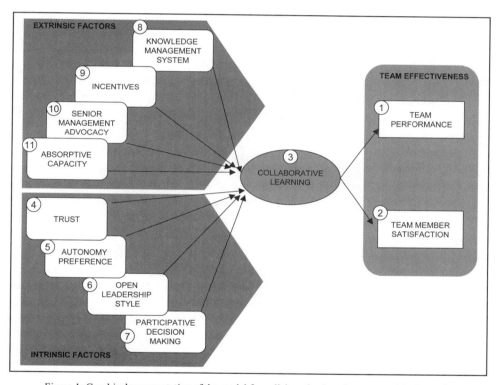

Figure 1: Graphical representation of the model for collaborative learning proposed in the study

6   Nature of Tasks in Software Development

Software development organizations engage with broadly three kinds of projects namely product development, maintenance and support, and customized solutions. The sequential life cycle model of software development comprises stages such as feasibility study, requirement analysis, detailed design, coding, unit testing, system integration and postproduction support. While projects involving product development comprise most of the mentioned stages, support and maintenance projects are largely confined to the downstream processes of testing and postproduction support. Customized solutions that are developed for specific clients might involve the upstream processes of requirement analysis and high-level design, depending upon the specificity of client's requirement.

Downstream activities of software development are largely routine in nature while upstream activities like requirement analysis and high level design, due to their unstructured and iterative nature, are non-routine. Thus, the dominant nature of tasks for team members involved in product development is non-routine while those involved in maintenance and support is routine. The dominant nature of tasks for team involved in developing customized applications varies between routine and non-routine, depending on their involvement in upstream processes. Gladstein (1984) noted that the relationship between team processes and team effectiveness was moderated by the nature of tasks. More specifically, Mohrman *et al.* (1995) found that for teams involved in routine tasks, learning behaviour might not be critical for performance:

Hypothesis 8: Nature of projects will moderate influence of collaborative learning on team effectiveness, such that the positive influence will be maximum on product development, moderate on customized solution and minimum on support and maintenance.

7   Methodology

Questionnaires were sent to 1219 software developers working in 142 teams in 26 organizations, located in Bangalore, Hyderabad and Delhi. All teams considered were physically located in one place, were involved in 'live' projects that had started at least six months earlier, and had between 5 to 15 members. Valid responses were obtained from 588 individuals working in 83 different teams from 20 organizations, giving a response rate of 48%. The mean age of the respondents was 26 years, 84% of them were male and 75% were unmarried. 83% of respondents had degree in engineering or computer science. The hypotheses were empirically tested by employing the statistical technique of Structured Equation Modeling (SEM). Team effectiveness was conceptualized to be a composite of team performance and team member satisfaction. 'Collaborative learning' was measured from the perception of team members about improvement in their decision-making and problem solving abilities as a consequence of their mutual interactions.

In order to isolate the impact of task characteristics on collaborative learning, the data was segregated into three categories. 29 teams comprising 232 individuals featured in the category of 'product development', 23 teams with 180 individuals in the category of 'customized solution development' and 29 teams with 174 individuals in the category 'support and maintenance'. Each of the categories was separately analyzed for testing the fitment of proposed model.

8 Results

The results of the analysis are provided in Table 1, below. For 'product development' teams, the chi-square value had a statistical significance level of greater than 5%, indicating satisfactory fitment. All global fit indices were above limits of acceptance. Among team level variables, 'trust' and 'participative decision making' were found to positively influence collaborative learning, while 'autonomy preference' had a negative influence on the same. 'Open leadership style' positively influenced both 'trust' and 'participative decision making', though its positive relationship with collaborative learning was not statistically significant. Among extrinsic variables, only 'absorptive capacity' and 'incentives' were found to have positive influence on team member collaborative learning. 'Collaborative learning' positively influenced both 'team performance' and 'team member satisfaction' while 'trust' had a direct positive influence on 'team member satisfaction'.

Table 1: Fit Indices and Path Coefficients

		Product Development	Custom Application	Support & Maintenance
Fit Indices				
	Chi Square	52.12	63.33	109.47
	GFI	0.96	0.94	0.91
	CFI	0.99	0.97	0.94
Path Coefficients				
Dependent variables	3,1	0.28	0.24	0.23
	3,2	0.24	0.44	0.03*
Intrinsic variables	4,3	0.27	0.42	0.60
	5,3	-0.16	-0.09*	0.06*
	6,3	0.00*	0.00*	0.00*
	7,3	0.27	0.11*	0.02*
Extrinsic variables	8,3	0.01*	0.05*	0.19
	9,3	0.26	0.11*	0.12*
	10,3	0.28	0.05*	0.17*
	11,3	0.15	0.09*	0.01*
* p > 0.05				

For teams involved in 'support and maintenance' activities, the chi-square had a statistical significance of less than 5%. Among the global fit indices, only the GFI and CFI values were above the acceptable limits. 'Trust' and 'knowledge management initiatives' positively influenced collaborative learning, which had a weak positive influence on team performance. 'Trust' also had a weak positive relationship with 'team member satisfaction'. All other team level variables directly influenced team effectiveness measures, without being mediated by 'collaborative learning'. Thus it can be concluded that for teams involved in support and maintenance of software products, collaborative learning is not a critical determinant of team effectiveness. Team level factors like 'participative decision making', 'open leadership style', 'trust' and lack of 'autonomy preference' positively contribute to team effectiveness even if they do not bring about high degree of collaborative learning behaviour among team members.

The fitment of model for teams involved in developing customized solutions was partial. While chi-square value had a significance level of less than 5%, other fitment measures like normed chi-square, GFI, CFI and Tucker Lewis were all above their recommended levels of 0.9. Trust among team members appeared to be the most critical determinant of collaborative learning among team members, which in turn had a positive influence on team effectiveness. 'Trust' also showed a direct positive relationship with team member satisfaction. All other intrinsic variables affected collaborative learning behaviour indirectly through their influence on team member trust. None of the extrinsic variables were found to have any significant effect on team member collaborative learning.

9   Discussion

The main thesis of our research was that collaborative learning among team members leads to greater effectiveness of software development teams. The results of the analysis indicate that the importance of collaborative learning for team effectiveness is contingent upon the dominant nature of tasks. Team members who are involved in product development are likely to gain a lot more by sharing knowledge and learning from one another than their counterparts who are involved in developing customized solutions. Teams involved in support and maintenance of software solutions may not derive any significant benefit from collaborative learning behaviour.

For teams involved in product development, neither the software solution, nor the process to design or develop the same is fully defined at the outset. Because the nature of the problem facing the team is ambiguous, members collectively evolve a shared mental model that necessitates extensive mutual learning and knowledge sharing. Compared to them, the nature of problems faced by teams involved in software support and maintenance is well defined and structured. Team members, more often than not, are seeking solutions to standardized problems through a well-defined process resulting in lesser needs of collaborative learning and knowledge sharing. Teams involved in developing customized solutions fall somewhere in between. While the initial phase of problem definition and solution design would require knowledge intensive collaboration, the downstream processes are likely to be much more standardized, minimizing the need for collaborative learning.

These results have important implications for leaders and managers of software development teams. The knowledge that the positive impact of collaborative learning on team effectiveness is critically dependent upon the nature of tasks the team is involved with should help team leaders and managers to decide the amount of conscious effort they exert to bring about collaborative learning behaviour within team members. As was hypothesized, the results of analysis show that factors intrinsic to the team are greater determinants of collaborative learning than are extrinsic (organizational level) factors. Teams high on trust scored higher in their ability to share knowledge and learn from one another. This led to better performance of the team and greater satisfaction of team members. Results also indicate that in order to build such levels of trust, teams must be managed by following an open leadership style, decision-making should be participative, and members should be low on autonomy preference. Ultimately, the focus of these group processes should be to increase knowledge flows and enhance collaborative learning, because on their own, such processes do not guarantee team effectiveness. Thus, the role played by the team leader in defining the correct team and people processes and facilitating knowledge intensive interactions assume significant importance.

10   Conclusion

The increasing dependence of modern industries on software systems and applications have led to the so called 'software bottleneck'. This has led the software industry to make efforts for improving their productivity. Focus on software engineering principles and knowledge management practices, a dominant characteristics of the Indian software industry, is a consequence of such efforts. The results of this research suggest that there is another way of improving performance of teams involved in software development, which is by promoting collaborative learning among team members. While software engineering principles and knowledge management practices have caused managers to focus on systems and processes at an organizational level, they need to look inwards within their teams to create facilitative conditions for collaborative learning. Managers in software developing organizations need to strike a dynamic balance between their efforts to promote collective learning at team level and managing knowledge at an organizational level. As the results of this research indicate, these are often complementary and any kind of prioritization should be contingent upon the dominant nature of tasks. We, however, do not believe that they can be substitutes for one another.

Our research makes several important contributions. First of all, it affirms the importance of learning behaviour for collaborative and knowledge intensive tasks and identifies antecedents for collaborative learning behaviour. Secondly, it points out that benefits of collaborative learning are contingent upon the nature of knowledge intensive tasks. This, we believe, will lead to a richer understanding of the phenomenon of collaborative learning in the context of software development. It also addresses a gap in knowledge management research, where the dominant focus has been on inter-unit and inter-organizational learning and not so much on knowledge creation and sharing among team members.

References

Brooks, F. P (1987). "No Silver Bullet: Essence and Accidents of Software Engineering." *Computer*. April. 10-19.

Cohen W L & D A Levinthal (1990) " Absorptive Capacity: A New Perspective on Learning and Innovation", *Administrative Science Quarterly*, 35:128-152

Davenport, T. H. & L. Prusak (1998). *Working Knowledge*. Harvard Business Press. Boston.

Edmondson, A (1999) "Psychological Safety and Learning Behaviour in Work Teams". *Administrative Science Quarterly*, 44:350-383

Gibson. C. B. (2001). "From Knowledge Accumulation to Accommodation: Cycles of Collective Cognition in Work Groups." *Journal of Organizational Behavior*, 22, 121-134

Gibson C & F Vermeulen (2003) "A Healthy Divide: Subgroup as Stimulus for Team Behaviour", *Administrative Science Quarterly*, 48:202-239

Gladstein, D. L. (1984). "Groups in Context: A Model of Task Group Effectiveness". *Administrative Science Quarterly*. 29: 499-517.

Guinan, P. J. & J. G. Cooprider (1998). "Enabling Software Development Team Performance during Requirement Definition: A Behavioral vs. Technical Approach." *Information Systems Research*. 9:2. 101-125

Hansen, M. T. (1999). "The Search-Transfer Problem: The Role of Weak Ties in Sharing Knowledge across Organizational Subunits". *Administrative Science Quarterly*, 44: 82-111

Mohrman S A, S G Cohen & A M Mohrman (1995) *Designing Team Based Organizations*. San Fransisco: Jossey Bass

Pfeffer, J. & R I Sutton (1999) " Knowing 'What' to do is Not Enough: Turning Knoweldge into Action", *California Management Review*, 42 (1): 83-108

Rulke D L & J Galaskiewicz (2000) . " Distribution of Knowledge, Group Network Structure and Group Performance" . *Management Science*. 46(5) , 612-625

Soo C, T Devinney, D Midgley & A Deering (2002) " Knowledge Management: Philosophy, Processes & Pitfalls", *California Management Review*, 44(4): 129-150

Szulanski G. (1996) . "Exploring Internal Stickiness: Impediments to the Transfer of Best Practice within the Firm", *Strategic Management Journal*, 17 (Winter Special. Issue), 27-43

Wageman R. (1995). "Interdependence and Group Effectiveness". *Administrative Science Quarterly*, 40(1), 145-180

CULTIVATING A COMMUNITY OF PRACTICE IN A SMALL RESEARCH ORGANIZATION

SAMO PAVLIN

Faculty of Social Sciences, University of Ljubljana, Kardeljeva ploscad 5
SI-1000 Ljubljana, Slovenia

The paper starts out by defining Communities of Practice (CoP), i.e. groups of practitioners working on the same topic but (not necessarily) on the same project, placing them into a broader context of knowledge society where the speed and quality of knowledge creation, dissemination and utilization assure the vital competitive advantage to an organization. Based on Etienne Wenger's CoP model the case of a community of a small research organization is considered and compared with CoPs in large organizations that are broadly described in the literature of knowledge management. By analyzing domain, practice, collaboration, roles, type and strategic purposes of the case community, a critical conceptualization of the CoP launched by a small organization is made.

1 Introduction

People and organizations in the knowledge society are learning to manage paradoxes; body and mind, flexibility and identity, innovation and tradition, top-down and bottom up approaches, specialization and collaboration, local and global, etc. These dualities are not alien to knowledge, since knowledge itself is made up of two seemingly opposite components – namely, explicit knowledge and tacit knowledge (Nonaka and Takeuchi, 2004: p.3, 4). The paper relates to another organizational dichotomy: informal social networks and formal organizational structures. Formal departments, operational and project teams within an organization seem to become insufficient for prosperous creation, dissemination and utilization of knowledge. They require the support of less formal communities. One of the most reputable types is coined as a Community of Practice (CoP), and is referred to as a group of practitioners working on the same topic but (not necessarily) on the same project. The literature presents numerous cases of CoPs in large international corporations such as Ford, IBM, Airbus, British Petroleum, Cap Gemini, Ernst & Young, Clarica, Hewlett Packard, McKinsey, Mercedes-Benz, Shell Oil, Siemens, Chevron, Xerox, etc., while the importance of CoPs in the networks of small organizations seems to be overlooked. The paper tries to fill in the gap, and stresses the role and potential importance that an emerging CoP can have for a small organization by discussing a community's key issues such as domain, practice, alignment with strategic purpose, membership, collaboration, roles and type.

A comparison between the CoP in a small organization and the CoP in large corporations is made. The argumentation includes a case study of a small research organization, which performs the CoP related activity. For that purpose three community meetings were attended in the period of four months (attendance with observation). Several informal contacts with the community members were conducted "on the spot".

Five more formal in-depth interviews with the organizational staff (mostly with the CoP's coordinator) have been conducted, and three of them tape-recorded. A considerable amount of time was spent to explain to the community coordinator the concept of CoP as defined by Wenger. Questions were related to the formation of discussion topics and knowledge domain of a community, formal and informal collaboration between members, identification of member attendance and assessment (one by one) of their contribution to the discussion and other issues presented in the paper. Apart from the interviews, other sources such as relevant project reports, the web site of the institute, and additional internal documents have been reviewed. Knowledge creation and dissemination has also been addressed several times directly at the community's forum (participation with observation). Observations are based on the recent knowledge management literature, mainly Etienne Wenger's CoP model.

2   Defining Community of Practice

People in the organizational units run the organization: they perform their jobs in teams. In networks they form relationships, and in CoP they create and disseminate the knowledge that their work is based on (Wenger, 1998). Wenger *et al.* (2002, p.4) defined CoPs as groups of people who share a concern, a set of problems, or a passion about a topic, and who deepen their knowledge and expertise in this area by interacting on an ongoing basis. Some claim that a CoP is a precondition for knowledge creation in organization (see Bettoni *et al.*, 2004). Interaction in such a community is based on collaborative tools such as face-to-face meetings, web-enabled tools or a combination of both. Frequency and formalization of collaboration vary substantially – from meetings organized only a few times per year with occasional collaboration in between, up to the regular interaction on a daily basis.

There are several CoPs within the organization and most people belong to many of them. CoPs are supported by the formal organization, and they are both self-governed and self-managed. They embody the ability to learn, and are particularly effective at turning information into knowledge because they deal with information on the basis of experience (Saint-Onge, Wallace, 2003: p. 66) or as Nonaka and Takeuchi would argue, they internalise explicit knowledge into implicit knowledge. Many claim that informal learning from others at work (and after work) is of greater importance than formal learning (see Garvin, 2000; Boud, Middleton, 2003). That is why CoPs are one of the most popular concepts in the knowledge management initiatives in times when social capital is becoming a core concept in business and other sciences.

Concepts, CoP and social capital, can be easily connected serving as catalysts to each other. However, a CoP is categorized by its primary business intents (APQC, 2001: p.8); namely to provide a forum for community members to help each other in solving everyday problems in employment, to develop and disseminate best practice, guidelines, and procedures for their members to use, to organize, manage and steward a body of knowledge from which the community members can benefit, to innovate and create ideas, knowledge and practices. In this manner the human capital, is seen as an organizations workforce and its knowledge of the business (Reinhardt, 2003, p.796), is effectively supported.

Nowadays, most large organizations use CoP as a tool for managing knowledge (see the introduction). These organizations have sufficient resources for assuring proper information support, enough human capital within widespread organizational structures that can support and benefit from knowledge cycle. They have superiors that can provide mentorship for numerous practitioners and tools for measuring the benefits of CoP. In comparison to large organizations the role of millions of small organizations as knowledge creators, disseminators and users is not at all marginal. Only the principles of their knowledge management are a bit different as the organizational structure is usually based on different types of more or less formal networks (an example of the former is Network of Excellence in the 6th European Framework program). The boundaries of such networks are difficult to define. This is also almost always the case within small research organizations at Universities. Many of them function within a number of different networks. One of these types of organization is presented in the next chapter.

3 Description of the Case Organization and its Community

The environment of the organization in our case study is in the capital of a tiny transition country in Central Europe, which is known as a place where "everybody knows everybody else". Our organization is a small research Institute in the field of education (social sciences) connected to the neighboring faculty. With six employees (three professors, two researchers and one coordinator), including part-time and full-time employees, the Institute is operating for its fourth year. Based on preexisting networks of the three funding professors, the organization has succeeded in building an extensive network of top researchers, professors, high government officials, journalists and even interested individuals who share the passion or are differently influenced by the common knowledge domain. The total number of network members exceeds one hundred. Most of them collaborate in different domestic and international projects that are financed by the public and private sectors. Members of the Institute's network are involved in different ongoing projects or other forms of cooperation although employed at various organizations. The network of the Institute can therefore be seen as a complex formation based on more or less formal networks and communities.

For three years the members of the Institute's network have gathered informally once or twice per month. Out of a hundred Institute members about one third of them participate in a forum, depending upon the theme to be discussed and time available. These events start at 7 pm, and usually last until at least 10 pm . Every community forum starts with 30 minutes presentation supported by PowerPoint graphics. All materials are published on an Institute's web page a week in advance, while every member gets invitation by e-mail. After the presentation the coordinator facilitates an emotional debate that supports knowledge creation and dissemination. Apart from the creation and sharing of knowledge domain, members informally exchange information about projects and investigate potential possibilities for cooperation. Generated and disseminated knowledge is successfully used in the member's professional working activities. Additionally the members of this community contact each other by e-mail and also phone during the forums events: *"This is the fastest way to get proper information or assistance."*[*]

The question arising at this point is, whether this community can be described as a CoP, since the participating members are employed in different organizations such as governmental, educational and even in the private sector working as academic staff, researchers and as government officials. Members are tracing common knowledge domains at their jobs, whilst the practice development varies between them. Some are preparing research programs and policies, some are executing them, others are reporting about them and finally some are teaching them, at the University. *"Despite different backgrounds of our members it is quite obvious that we share common interest for the knowledge domain although sometimes from different perspectives."* The Institute's network can therefore be called a community.

4   Identifying Domain, Community and Practice

The structure of the CoP is based on three components: the domain as the area of knowledge that brings the community together, the community as the group of people for whom the domain is relevant, and the practice as a body of knowledge, methods, tools and stories that members share and develop together. The CoP unifies three components, namely: knowledge, people and experience (Wenger, 1999). Therefore the members of CoP should have sufficient opportunities to interact, while their engagement, practices and domain should derive from common experiences at work (although performed in different organizations) that are resulting in a common identity (Kahan, 2004). Only the members of such a CoP are able to fully benefit from learning and creating knowledge in a community; master organizational processes at their jobs, negotiate political issues, and deal with different situations (Boud, Middleton, 2003). In this chapter the comparison of three fundamental components of CoP are made.

A domain is the basis of common topics, key issues, problems and issues that members share at their daily work. It is an expertise that brings people together with passion, evokes the questions they ask, and guides the way they organize their knowledge, and more over, creates a sense of accountability to the development of a practice. Without a commitment to a domain, a community is just a group of friends (Wenger *et al.*, 2002, p.29). The domain answers to 'know-what'. Regarding the domain of knowledge there seems to be no differences between CoP launched by a network of small organizations or by a single large organization. The number of qualified experts (managers, scientists, ICT personnel, etc.) in a single (large) organization may be insufficient to support the knowledge of certain domain. That is not usually the case in a

---

[*] Quotations in italics are taken from the interviews with two members of the studied Institute.

well-established network that associates the members from different organizations. The founding members of the Institute define the framework for discussion topics and knowledge domain for the community events at the beginning of the year. *"There is always an open space for a suggestion by any of the members. The domain topics of our community cover the needs of the host Institute. At the same time they also cover the needs of the organizations where the members come from."*

The *community* consists of the personal and institutional relationships between the members, interactions, atmosphere, and the evolution of individual and collective identities and, last but not least, spaces (physical or virtual) for meeting. The members of a community share profession, discipline, job role or deal with the same clients. The *practice* describes frameworks, ideas, stories, experiences, lessons learned and documents that community members share at their work. It denotes a specific, collectively elaborated know how about ways of doing tasks in a specific domain (Wenger *et al.*, 2002, p.29, 33).

Acting within the same knowledge domain but from different perspective can be an advantage. The members of our community are filling the holes in social structure between certain organizations (in which members are employed). Networking across structural holes is clearly a form of social capital (Burt, 2000, p.372). In such a manner the competitive advantage is created for the members of community and also for the organizations where they work.   The theory of social capital emphasizes that the difference (as for example in education, occupation, employee organization) is the precondition for creativity and informal learning (see for example Burt, 2000, p.362). "It is hardly possible to overrate the value ... of placing human beings in contact with persons dissimilar to themselves, and with modes of thought and action unlike those with which they are familiar... Such communication has always been, and is peculiarly in the present age, one of the primary sources of progress" (Mills, 1848. ibid, p.363). We are not arguing that in the professional network the common experiences are not important, but that 'a bit of difference in parity' is crucial. As a member of our case community explained: *"What we present is only a half open circle of people who have certain expertise. Sometimes the discussion is so specific that even some of the Institute's staff has difficulty to follow. If the number of people of the community forum would increase, the quality of discussion would decrease. That's why we are very careful about inviting new members. For now there is no reason to expand membership of the forum. We have already included most of the people we wanted and these are qualified experts that can qualitatively contribute to the discussion."*

5   Collaboration and Roles

When people participate in a community they occupy various roles. Saint-Onge and Wallence (2003, p.43) describe sparkers or debate triggers, synthesizers or summarizers, sole contributors who contribute from their own perspective, witnesses who support a position with their own point of view or experience, champions who are the most powerful members of a community and 'lurkers' – people who do not contribute to the community but who take from it what they can. Therefore, every single member can be characterized in accordance with his or her participation.

Individuals who attend the community meetings regularly form the core group. This group is usually composed of coordinator(s) and the founder(s). The next is associate member group, and finally there is a peripheral group. For example, the principle is similar to the externalization of organizational functions of knowledge-oriented organization as described by Burton-Jones (1999). Obviously, the coordinator occupies the crucial role in a community. He plans the activities, balances and energizes community events, and facilitates discussion and knowledge sharing.

In a large organization, on the other side of CoP structure there are sponsors, who are disconnected members of a community. Usually, they are the top managers who are not directly involved in a community but who support community activities. They navigate and initiate the very existence of a community towards strategic goals of the organization by providing necessary resources such as time, basic funding and legitimacy within organization. They do not manage community's knowledge, but they indirectly manage, facilitate and sometimes even create CoP.

By comparing our case organization to the CoP in large organizations described in literature we found certain similarities but also some differences. The structure of participation and attendance of our case community is simple. There is a core group of ten to fifteen people. They attend forums regularly and also contribute substantially to the discussion. The peripheral group is fluid, and depends on the discussion topics. We have noticed a strong connection between participation in the discussion and attendance; people who substantially contribute to the discussion are also regular guests and vice versa. This finding was noticed at all the three meetings that were attended for the purpose of this paper and also confirmed through assessment of particular community members that was done by the coordinator of the community. However, apart from the guests, there are individuals who do not attend community events regularly but substantially contribute to the discussion. These individuals occupy prominent positions in other networks or formal organization. *"When a minister comes, he will not pass by unnoticed."* The forum events are organized once or twice per month: *"It seems that this period of meeting just suits the needs of our members. If the dates of forums are too frequent the attendance goes down. This is our experience. In any case our Institute by now does not have enough resources to organize community events more often."*

The head of the Institute almost always occupies the role of the coordinator or chair of the community forum. Thus, unlike the CoP within a large organization where different people perform different roles of the leader, our case community has the founder, sponsor and coordinator in one person. For several reasons this can be considered as an advantage. Firstly, this person manages the financial means and has the power to provide all resources needed, including proper space for meetings, materials/information, human resources and advertisements in the public media if required. Secondly, the leader is a strong motivator for others to join (e.g. for employees at junior and senior positions to attend various meetings) and thirdly, he has the power to apply the knowledge created in the community directly in the working practices of the two organizations, where he is employed (the institute and the faculty). Finally, he has the authority to manipulate, stimulate, and unify the event with diverse membership. *"Sometimes it is difficult to coordinate discussion or problems presented by government officials versus professors, researcher or practitioners. Our members have different backgrounds and tackle to the problems from different perspectives."* As mentioned earlier after a PowerPoint presentation the discussion takes place. The coordinator invites individual participants to the discussion. The mode is friendly and informal. Loose atmosphere is very important for knowledge creation. *"If conversation would be more formal or the people would not know each other, the forum would lose its meaning. Such a forum we conduct now, allows us to take part in a spontaneous brain-storming and in a productive idea development."*

It seems obvious that for knowledge creation and dissemination social connections are more important than belonging to a formal organization. The fact that the community members are employed in different organizations and occupy different professions is not a barrier for this kind of collaboration. Overall face-to-face collaboration tools are the most important: *"We are very sceptical about spreading our discussions to the internet or to extend our membership by other means. For professional needs we do contact each other, but we prefer to keep this discussions close, so we use phone or e-mail. Also the resources for keeping our debates in larger circles are limited."*

6   The Type of CoP

There are many different types of CoPs. We have already distinguished web based and face-to-face communities, while Saint-Onge and Wallence (2003, p.36) present another important classification of CoPs. They distinguish between informal, supported and structured type. The *informal community* of practice is self-joining, without organizational sponsor, very organic, and so natural that it may not even be noticed. Still this type of community is based on the discussion forums for knowledge creation and sharing. The members would use the knowledge later at work. Therefore the informal type of community should not be mixed up with a group of friends or peers who join just to pass the time.

Supported and *structured communities* of practice are characterized by more intense involvement of the host organization. The competency building of such a CoP is aligned with the strategic purpose of host organization and monitoring of the management is present. In addition to this classification Wenger *et al.* (2002, p.24-27) present the following community categorizations: big and small, long and short lived, collocated and distributed, homogeneous and heterogeneous, within and across boundaries, spontaneous and intentional, unrecognized and institutionalized. As we can see there are numerous ways to explain a community.

Taking into account the proportions of the small transition state where the number of experts in the certain field is limited, our case community is not a small one. The number of experts and strength of their pre-existing cooperation determine the size of the community in our case. Our community can be marked both as collocated and distributed as it was based on the pre-existing network: interactions of heterogeneous membership crossed organizational *'before there was an organization'*. However, this type of community, launched from a small organization and with heterogeneous membership, can be quite beneficial for individual experts involved.

Start up of the Institute's community event was intentional and the community forum was institutionalized from the very beginning. A substantial effort has to be made for every community activity, as the number of personnel and other resources in a small organization are scarce. Organisers do invest more energy because the potential members are spread in different organizations. They do not meet on a regular basis as in the case of employees in a large organization, who meet regularly in the canteen or at the water cooler.

So far we have identified some specifics comparing CoP launched by the small organization network in comparison with a large organization. Some characteristics are self-evident such as the crossing of organizational boundaries, intentional start-up or institutionalized form. Different stages of development as potential, coalescing, maturing, stewardship and transformation (see Wenger *et al.*, 2002) could not be identified in our case since the community was developed on the basis of a pre-existing network that will probably neither start nor finish with this Institute's community. Regarding other criteria, the small organization should know how to balance many polarities examples include collocation and distribution, homogeneity and heterogeneity, big and, small organizing regular or irregular events.

7   Strategic Purpose of CoP

The main purpose of CoP is creating a platform, for supporting a structure for running the knowledge cycle (as described for example by Nonaka, Takeuchi, 1995; Di Bella, Nevis, 1998; Bhatt, 2001; Lundvall, 2001) within, among and between organizations. The community helps to disseminate and create knowledge, whilst the use (and also further creation and dissemination) of knowledge belongs to other more formal organizational structures like project groups and teams. Allee (2000) and Wenger (2002, p.16) see many synergetic effects when CoP activities are aligned with the strategy of formal organization. *Organization* benefits by faster problem solving, developing, recruiting and retaining talents, establishment of core capabilities and knowledge competencies. The development of practices for operational excellence and innovation generation is also faster, cost are reduced, quality is improved, and technological developments can be foreseen. Moreover the advantages of emerging market opportunities are better used, and necessary knowledge resources for implementing and executing strategy are provided.

When the community activities are aligned with the strategy of the organization the *community* also benefits. It is faster, and more successfully builds common language, methods and models around specific competencies, embedded knowledge and expertise in a larger population, and retains knowledge when employees leave the organization. It increases access to expertise across the company and provides the means to share power and influence with the formal parts of the organization. Finally, there are *individuals* who can perform their jobs better. They foster internal networks within the company, fulfill their social needs, and develop a professional identity as well as their skills and competencies.

Therefore the CoP aligned with a strategic purpose of host organization usually comprehend all characteristics of formal, highly structured community. It is supported by corporate resources, encouraged by the sponsors through the recognition of the members' efforts, promoted to the organization and valued by management. There are numerous ways that illustrate how a CoP is connected with the organizational strategy. The CoP can link members to the strategic knowledge domain of organization, develop core organizational competency through collaboration and learning, provide common development needs, distribute functional expertise, facilitate cross-generational and cross functional exchange of knowledge (Saint-Onge and Wallence, 2003, p.36, 91). CoP can present a toll for alignment in organization, forum for problem solving, center for knowledge creation, type of organizational infrastructure (ibid, p.71) or more of the same. In addition Wenger *et al.* (2002, p.76) classify CoPs by their strategic intent to the organization. Four types would include helping communities, best-practice communities, knowledge-stewarding communities and innovation communities.

It would be quite difficult to identify a single strategic purpose of the Institute's community as purpose of the knowledge domain varies. The aim of the Institute's community can be 'merely' sharing results of certain research, but quite often the related problems are also solved. New ideas can be developed and best practice shared. However, the main purpose of the Institute's community is not different to the goal of any other CoP; sharing and creating knowledge domain of the members. The coordinator of the Institute explained the function of a community quite broadly: *"Supporting and speeding up the research with a multidisciplinary approach is our main purpose. This is also achieved by sharing knowledge and presenting our endeavors to a wider public."*

We could find out that the purpose of the case community is in accordance with the strategy of the host Institute, but also with the strategies of organizations and professional interest of members. However, the focus is on the strategic goals of the Institute which are the following: research in the scope of knowledge domain involving faculty (research projects) and students, strengthening the status of knowledge domain as a scientific discipline and developing study programs. The Institute's community also promotes international cooperation with partner institutions and strengthens the exchange of teachers, researchers and students from various countries, particularly from the South East and Central Europe, helps to connect domestic and foreign experts, and performing other research and consultative activities. A strategic purpose of the Institute's community is also the regular meetings of its members: *"It is important that our members preserve regular contacts and conduct informal conversation before and after the event. People share ideas, plan project cooperation and search for solutions of certain problems that may not have direct connection with discussion topic. We think that some people also come to the forum for social reasons: to see colleagues even if they are not very interested in discussion topic in the first place. From time to time one has to make face-to-face contact to keep social networks alive, regular contacts with e-mail and phone are insufficient."* This is the point where identity development takes place. It is difficult for high quality expert to identify only with the organization where they are employed. There are communities that give them a sense of belonging.

8   Conclusion

Individuals who share common practices at a job, or job related activities, could be connected to the CoP. This type of community is different from the community of interest, community of purpose or learning community as practitioners themselves are creating and disseminating knowledge of working practices. They use different collaboration tools such as face-to-face exchanges or web-enabled tools. Knowledge creation and dissemination in CoP is based on common experiences in work related situations. Management cannot manage the knowledge, but it can cultivate, support or direct a community's activities towards the organizational strategy.

There are many different types of CoPs serving different purposes such as problem solving, knowledge creation, sharing best practice, and so forth but our thesis was that one of the important determinants of the community is its host organization. It makes a difference if the CoP dwells in a small or in a large organization. Higher degree of community engagement, overlapping of organizational roles such as sponsor and coordinator, scare resources, more dispersed and heterogeneous membership, and community and practice are just a few aspects that characterize a community based on the social network of small organizations.

Finally, there is a conceptual question as to whether a community based on a network created in a small organization can be considered a community of practice at all. The question is even more relevant if we take into account the fact that community members are employed in different organizations developing working practices around common knowledge domain from different perspectives as government officials, professors and researchers as in our case. We have discussed our case of a living community where common engagement of government officials, professors, researches and students can substantially enhance a knowledge domain (education in our case) with the experience of related practices. The primary element that keeps the community together that was launched by a small organization, is certainly their passion to improve, and to speed up a knowledge cycle of evolving knowledge domain. It is debatable whether such a community is mainly based on interest, learning, purpose or practice.

References

Allee, V. (2000) "Knowledge Networks and Community of practice." *Journal of organizational development networks*, 32(4). Internet: http://www.odnetwork.org/

APQC (American Productivity & Quality Center) (2001) "Building and Sustaining Communities of Practice: Continuing Success in Knowledge Management." Executive Summary Report. Internet: http://www.apqc.org/portal

Bettoni, M., Clases, C. and Wehner, T. (2004) "Communities of practice as a way to a more human-oriented knowledge management." *International conference on Human Resource Management in a Knowledge-based economy*. Ljubljana, Faculty of Social Sciences.

Bhatt, D.G. (2001) "Knowledge Management in Organizations: examining the interaction between technologies, techniques and people." *Journal of Knowledge Management*, 5(1): 68–75.

Boud, D. and Middleton, H. (2003) "Learning from others at work: communities of practice and informal learning." *Journal of Workplace Learning*, 15(5): 194–202.

Burt, S.R. (2000) "The network structure of social capital." *Research in Organisational Behavior*, 22: 345–423.

Burton, J.A. (1999) *Knowledge Capitalism*. Oxford University Press.

DiBella, A.J., Edwin N.C., (1998) *How Organizations Learn: An Integrated Strategy for Building Learning Capacity*. Jossey-Bass Publishers.

Garvin, D.A. (2000) *Learning in action: a guide to putting the learning organization to work*. Harvard Business School Press, Boston.

Kahan, S. (2004) "Etienne Wenger on Communities of Practice: Engagement, Identity & Innovation." *The Journal of Association Leadership*, 2(3).

Lundvall, B.Å. (2001) "The Learning Economy: Some Implications for the Knowledge Base of Health and Education Systems." In OECD, Knowledge Management in the Learning Society, OECD, Paris.

Mills, J.S. ([1848] 1987) Principles of Political Economy. In Burt, S.R. 2000 "The network structure of social capital." *Research in Organisational Behavior*, 22: 345–423.

Nonaka, I. and Takeuchi, H. (1995) *The Knowledge–Creating Company: How Japanese Companies Create the Dynamics of Innovation*. Oxford University Press.

Nonaka, I. and Takeuchi, H. (2004) *Hitotsubashi on knowledge management*. John Wiley & Sons (Asia), Singapore.

Reinhardt R., *et al.* (2003) Intellectual Capital and Knowledge Management: Perspectives on Measuring Knowledge: 764–820. In Dierkes, M., *et al.*, Handbook of organizational learning and knowledge, *Oxford: Oxford University Press*.

Saint-Onge, H. and Debra, W. (2003) *Leveraging communities of practice for strategic advantage*. Amsterdam: Butterworth-Heinemann.

Wenger, E. (1999) "Communities of practice the key to a knowledge strategy." *Knowledge Directions*, 1(2): 48–63.

Wenger, E. (2004) "Knowledge management is a donut shaping your knowledge strategy through communities of practice." *Ivey Business Journal*, January-February.

Wenger, E., McDermott, R.A., Snyder, W. (2002) *Cultivating communities of practice: a guide to managing knowledge*. Harvard Business School Press, Boston.

THE ROLE OF MEDIATORS IN CREATING STRATEGIC KNOWLEDGE COMMUNITES (SKC) AND PROMOTING COOPERATION BETWEEN SCIENTIFC AND LOCAL COMMUNITIES: A CASE STUDY FROM THAILAND

NUTA SUPAKATA & PIERRE FAYARD

LABCIS (LABoratoire de recherché en Communication & Information Scientifique et technique), ICOMTEC, University of Poitiers, France

In Thailand, it has now been gradually discovered that local knowledge has been neglected. Subsequently, the project called "One Tambon[1], One Product" (OTOP) has been developed by the government to make the communities in each sub-district, especially in the rural areas, self-reliant by using their own resources and wisdom, then standardizing, and finally merchandizing their products to the market. This research was conducted in Mahanam Village, Ang Thong Province, in the central part of Thailand. This village is currently participating in the OTOP project by producing fabricated handicrafts from weaving dried water hyacinth stems. To make Mahanam Village handicrafts acceptable to the international market, a mediator organizes the creation of *SKCs* for the villagers, allowing them to develop their OTOP production in cooperation with scientific scholars.

1   Introduction

During the post-war period, science and technology has played an increasing role in economic growth. However, the progress of science and technology led to a gradually emerging tension between science and technology on one hand, and people and society on the other.   This tension is a situation in which science is distant to the public. According to Pierre Fayard, the eventuality of scientific and technological developments makes economics, society and culture imbalanced. Since the late 20th Century, an international network dedicated to the public communication of science and technology (PCST) has emerged. It has three essential ambitions: firstly, a '*political ambition*' aimed to symphonize science and the public as a whole; secondly a '*cognitive ambition*' aimed to make science more understandable to the public; and last but not least a '*creative ambition*' aimed to enable the public to utilize science for the improvement of their daily lives (Fayard 2002). Thus, it is considered to be 'a good thing' to bring the two together.

At a two-day workshop in Cape Town (South Africa) in December 2002, which was a section of the 7th conference of the International Network on PCST, participants from different parts of the world jointly shared their experiences and defined a new paradigm of PCST for the *developing world*, in which the public understanding of science involves knowledge that meets the needs of people and societies in the developing world, especially in rural areas (Lewenstein 2003). Consequently, to find ways to eliminate tension and make science communication beneficial for the public, particularly for the

---

[1] Tambon is a group of villages or a sub-district.

local people in the developing world, Strategic Knowledge Communities (SKCs) may be a promising new strategy of PCST, enabling efficient interactions and collaboration between local people and scientists.

1.1 What is a "SKC"?

Strategic Knowledge Communities were first conceptualized by *Prof. Pierre Fayard* who originally founded PCST in 1987 (Fayard 2002 and Fayard 2003).

This Western hypothesis is the counterpart of the Japanese concept of 'Ba' which roughly means 'place' in English. Based on a concept that was further developed by the Japanese scholar Ikujiro Nonaka, "*a 'ba' can be thought as a shared space for emerging relationships? This space can be physical (e.g. office, dispersed business space), mental (e.g. shared experiences, ideas, ideals) or any combinations of them. What differentiates ba from any ordinary human interactions is the concept of knowledge creation. Ba provides a platform where a transcendental perspective integrates all transformations needed. Ba may also be thought of as the recognition of the self in all. According to the theory of existentialism, ba is a context which harbors meaning. Thus, we consider ba to be shared space that serves as a foundation for knowledge creation*" (Nonaka 1998 cited in Fayard 2003).

1.2 What is 'SKC' in this research?

The people of Thailand, and especially the Thai government, are gradually discovering that we have been pursuing western ways of development and have entirely neglected our own local knowledge, a splendid treasure of our nation. It is time for us to turn back to our roots, culture, and local knowledge which will be referred to as "Thai Local Wisdom". One strategy in helping the Thai people strive to rely less on borrowing from abroad and on imports is the OTOP project launched in 1999 by the government of Thailand. This project emulates the "One Village, One Product" model which originated in the Japanese town of Oita in 1979. In Thai the project is called "One Tambon, One Product (OTOP)" and its major aims are to generate sustainable income via self-reliance and to empower local villages with the capacity to develop their village's characteristic products[2] by relying primarily on local natural resources, wisdom, as well as their creativity and innovation. The government and the private sector afford assistance in developing the products and exploring the markets.   Since this project has been launched, 7,394 districts have attended this program; 15,133 OTOP products have been produced under this project. To make our wisdom more globalized, we need science to support and strengthen the areas in which local wisdom is insufficient. Unfortunately, the colossal gap between local and science knowledge and their holders parallels the lack of space for them to reach mutual understanding and cooperation.

---

[2] The government of Thailand defines "*product*" in this project as a dynamic process that includes services, value-added, environmental protection, traditional knowledge, tourism, cultures, exchanges of experiences and learning.

Therefore, the researchers in the role of mediators need to create a *'SKC'*, a *space* that opens the boundaries and allows for interactions between *local people* and *scientists* (Figure 1). By sharing and integrating their knowledge, innovative new solutions become possible.

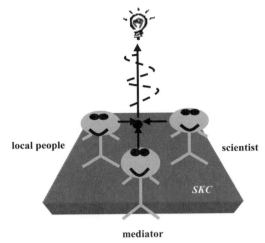

Figure 1. Model of 'SKC' research

2   Objective

The objective of this study is to understand the role and actions of mediators as they link local knowledge and local people on the one hand and scientific knowledge and scientists on the other. How do they succeed in increasing the quality of OTOP products to international standards so as to successfully face market competition and enhance the self-reliance of local communities?

3   The processes in creating a 'SKC' to link scientific and local communities

These processes adapted from the SECI model (Nonaka and Hirotaka 1995) can be detailed in four phases as follows:

Phase I: Creating Partnerships for Enhancing Collaboration for Action

Frequently, mediators are "outsiders" (for example, urban professionals: scientists, researchers) working across cultures. In order for mediators to achieve a common understanding of the characteristics at the grassroots level as well as to direct a successful SKC process and to obtain community support of their activities, partnerships between local people in the community and mediators are crucial.

To develop a positive interaction between the mediators and the creators of local knowledge, collaboration must take place between equal partners based on trust (care + love + mutual respect) and understanding built by initially *getting to know the community 'leader'*. In a local community, a leader plays a significant role in influencing community activities. Mediators have to introduce themselves and their objectives to the leader. This step is the meaningful starting point for mediators to launch the project. Second is *getting to know the 'community'*. To achieve confidence and involvement from the community, mediators must enrich their understanding of the grassroots by conducting structured observations and in-depth interviews to gather data and behavioral information which covers all aspects of the community – their social and cultural values, spirituality, learning systems, communication traditions, local resources and environment, educational and economic status, interests, problems, needs, and wants. This phase will lead to *coordination* between mediators and the community, making them work in a more *collaborative* way. It will energize them to *cooperate* in project activities and increase their interest in *communicating* through sharing and exchanging feelings, information, and ideas. All of which will help them to fulfill each other's goals better.

Akin to the "socialization" process in the SECI model, mediators and a community can capture and create common tacit knowledge – such as mutual trust and understanding – through physical proximity, that is, by mediators spending time and living in the community family.

Phase II: Crystallizing and systematizing local knowledge
In this phase, mediators will start with *studying local knowledge and its practice* by collecting information both through *direct approaches* that involve local people directly by using semi-structured interviews and observation of individuals and groups, and through *indirect approaches* like collecting information about the community from secondary sources such as government and non-government reports.

This is followed by *analyzing local knowledge*. Mediators will analyze local knowledge, its practice, and its problems in the community by involving local people through interaction. This consists of two processes: *SWOT analysis* and related *scientific analysis*. The role of mediators is to facilitate participatory actions during these processes.

Ending this phase is *documenting local knowledge*, which is important due to the nature of local knowledge. It is mostly tacit knowledge stored in people's memories and embedded in their practices and experiences, and its transmission is usually based on oral rather than in written means. This makes local knowledge gradually extinct as its system goes out of use. Therefore, mediators will set up a database in order to document, preserve and promote local knowledge.

Our knowledge collection constitutes the baseline information for us to manage a 'SKC' or 'ba': a meeting place (physical, virtual, mental) for the community and scientists to prepare operational plans and to derive indicators for monitoring and assessing the outcomes of the coming phases.

This phase is similar to the "externalization" process in the SECI model, in the sense that mediators will articulate and translate local knowledge from its owners (local people) into readily understandable forms to be shared by others.

Phase III: Assembling local knowledge and scientific knowledge in creating new solutions

In this phase, mediators will begin *searching for scientists or specialists related to local knowledge* and they *get to know the scientists or specialists* by introducing themselves and their objectives to them based on mutual respect, understanding, and transparency. Next, they cooperate with scientists/specialists to identify possible solutions based on the knowledge collected in Phase II. Then in the step of *operating experiments together with group leaders and scientists*, the role of the mediator is to conduct participatory actions between the two. The last step involves *monitoring and evaluating* new solutions to improve them.

The "Combination" process in the SECI model is equivalent to this phase in which local knowledge and scientific knowledge is captured and integrated to solve problems, leading to the discovery of new solutions. The new solution will then be applied by an experimental group. Finally, to make the new solution more useful, it will be monitored and evaluated by all stakeholders.

Phase IV: Disseminating the new solution

Mediators start Phase IV by *conducting a communication process* to disseminate the new solution to community members. This phase is closely related to "learning-by-doing" which allows each member in the community by means of action and practice to access new knowledge regarding methods or solutions about strategy, innovation, or improvement.

This phase is similar to "Internalization" in the SECI process; new knowledge that has been created is shared throughout the community by training and exercise.

4 Results

This research was conducted in Mahanam Village, Ang Thong Province (108 kilometers from Bangkok) in the central part of Thailand. Most of the villagers are farmers. Unfortunately, rapidly increasing construction of housing estates or industrial sectors means the villagers face difficulty and are unable to become self-reliant. The new generation also tends to abandon their village to work in factories or in the city which offers them better income. To survive in the face of these various challenges, Mrs. Prasit Taptimsri considered in 1989 an alternative way to provide supplementary income for her family and community by regaining her local wisdom in handicraft skills and producing utensils using local materials such as bamboo and water hyacinth. To improve her ability, she attended a handicraft training program organized by Angthong Agricultural Extension Office. After joining this course, she gradually brought and introduced this new technique to the women in the village. In 1993, the women in this village came together to found the group called "Mahanam Village Agricultural Women Group". This group was designed to (1) increase the women's traditional craft skill in weaving products such as bags, baskets, vases from water hyacinth; (2) to generate income for themselves; and (3) to bring their new generation back home. Until now there are sixty members in this group which has Mrs. Prasit Taptimsri as their leader, and the group is currently participating in the government project called "One Tambon, One Product" (OTOP).

Table 1. Four phases in linking LK and SK

Case study: Mahanam Village Agricultural Women Group
Local Knowledge (LK): the women's traditional craft skill in weaving products from water hyacinth
Local Knowledge Problem: product defect from fungi
Scientific Knowledge (SK): new solution in preventing handicraft product from fungi

Phase	Actors	Knowledge	Activities	Outputs
I. Creating partnership for enhancing collaboration for action	Mediator (M) Group leader (Gl) Group members (Gm)	tacit ➡ tacit	M gets to know Gl. M gets to know Gm.	Coordination and collaboration among actors
II. Crystallizing and systematizing local knowledge	Mediator (M) Group leader (Gl) Group members (Gm)	tacit ➡ explicit	M studies LK and its practice from Gl and Gm. M facilitates participatory actions for Gl and Gm to analyze their LK. M documents LK.	LK problems Report and database of LK
III. Assembling local and scientific knowledge and their holders in creating new solution/innovation	Mediator (M) Scientist (S) Group leader (Gl)	explicit ➡ explicit	M researches for scientists related to LK. M operates experiments together with Gl and S. All actors monitor and evaluate new solution.	Coordination and collaboration among actors New solution
IV. Disseminating new solution	Mediator (M) Group leader (Gl) Group members (Gm)	explicit ➡ tacit	M conducts a communication process to disseminate new solution to Gm.	Comprehension in applying new solution

As mentioned, Mahanam Village Agricultural Women Group produces handicrafts from weaving dried water hyacinth stems. After operating participatory actions in Phase I and

Phase II, the group and mediator found that the defects of water hyacinth stems caused by fungi was their first priority problem to be solved and the group needed the methodology to protect their products from this microorganism. In consequence, the mediator began Phase III by asking for advice from researchers at the Thailand Institute of Scientific and Technological Research (TISTR) and getting the cooperation from Alphani International CO., LTD in providing a fungicide sample (a liquid biocide formulated to combat fungi) for experimenting. After to doing experiments with the support of the group leader, the result of this experiment was satisfactory. However, because of the high cost of this fungicide, the group chose not to use this alternative. To find a lower cost solution, the mediator went again through Phase III by joining forces with Dr. Srisook Poonpholkul, plant pathologist at the Plant Protection Research and Development Office, Department of Agriculture of Thailand and Mr. Winai Rushtapakornchai from Thepwatana Chemical CO., LTD. Although the experiment was a failure the first time, the good collaboration among the stakeholders made the experiment successful eventually. Then the mediator started Phase IV by conducting a communication process to disseminate the new solution to group members. This phase is closely related to "learning-by-doing" which allows each member to access the new solution (see Table 1).

In this participatory action research, partnerships among the community, scientists, and the mediator have been successfully established and the identified problem has eventually been solved. However, the process of creating harmony between science and the public, particularly in rural areas, requires time to be nurtured.

Acknowledgments

The authors truly appreciate the help and assistance of the following people: Mrs. Prasit Taptimsri and all villagers of Mahanam Village Agricultural Women Group; Alphani International CO., LTD as a fungicide example provider; Dr. Srisook Poonpholkul, plant pathologist at the Plant Protection Research and Development Office, Department of Agriculture of Thailand; and Mr.Winai Rushtapakornchai from Thepwatana Chemical CO., LTD for collaboration in solving a local problem: Dr. Nanthaporn Viravathana, and Dr. Pinsuda Viravathana for their valuable advice and suggestions; and last but not least the Supakatas (Mrs. Nipa, Mr. Montri, and Mr. Kris) for all their support.

References

Fayard, P. (2002) "Issues for Public Communication of Science and Technologies In the Knowledge Society". Seoul:Korea.

Fayard, P. (2003) "Strategic Knowledge Communities: a Western proposal for the Japanese concept of Ba". Poitiers: France.

Lewenstein, B. (2003) "A developing-world take on science communication". Retrieved January 13,2003 from www.SciDev.Net.

Nonaka, I., Takeuchi, H. (1995). *The Knowledge-Creating Company:how Japanese companies create the dynamics of innovation*. New York :Oxford University Press.

TRUST, COHESION, AND IDENTIFICATION AS DRIVERS OF COP PERFORMANCE: THE MODERATING EFFECT OF KNOWLEDGE TYPE

KATJA ZBORALSKI & HANS GEORG GEMÜNDEN

Institute for Technology and Management, Technical University of Berlin,
Str. des 17. Juni 135, H 71, Berlin, Germany

The concept of communities of practice (CoPs) is widely recognized as a means to foster knowledge sharing and learning in organizations. Even though the number of CoPs has grown significantly, the performance impact of community characteristics – especially social features like trust, cohesion, and identification – still demands conceptual and empirical research. In this paper we analyse their impact on community performance taking into account the moderating effect of the degree of knowledge implicitness. We use data from 222 community members from different CoPs of a large German multinational company. Our research shows that communities have the potential to improve organizational performance. Trust and cohesion have an indirect performance effect mediated through the identification of CoP members with their community. The positive relationship of identification and CoP performance is not influenced by the degree to which the knowledge handled in the community is implicit.

1 Introduction

Most companies have to cope with the challenge of a knowledge-based economy. Hence, an organization's competitiveness mainly depends on its ability to acquire, develop, and strategically leverage knowledge (Kogut and Zander 1992; Nonaka and Takeuchi 1995). As a consequence, a growing number of organizations have introduced knowledge management systems into their organizations. In this context, *'communities of practice'* (CoPs) are increasingly seen as central means to foster and enhance knowledge sharing and learning in organizations (Brown and Duguid 1991; Lesser and Storck 2001).

The term 'community of practice' (CoP) has been introduced in Lave and Wenger's 'social theory of learning' (Lave and Wenger 1991). It can be defined as a group of people in an organization who interact with each other across organizational units or even across organization boundaries due to a common interest or field of application. Their objective is to learn and support one another in order to create, spread, retain, and use knowledge relevant to the organization. Initially, CoPs were understood as self-emerging and self-organizing networks in which everyone can participate (Wenger 1998). Current practice, however, shows that organizations strategically support existing networks and deliberately establish CoPs with managed memberships (Storck and Hill 2000).

Research investigating CoPs is so far mostly based on qualitative case studies (Dyer and Nobeoka 2000; Gongla and Rizzuto 2001; Sawhney and Prandelli 2000). Even though the number of CoPs in organizations has grown significantly over the last years, little is known about the performance impact of community characteristics, especially social features of the communities, like trust, cohesion, and identification.

By investigating the performance impact of these specific CoP characteristics we intend to contribute to the literature in the following ways: (1) we address the challenge of measuring the value of CoPs. (2) Based on literature from other research streams, particularly team research, we choose to focus on social features as central characteristics of CoPs and distinguish between the intensity of trust, cohesion, and identification with the community. The perception of these CoP characteristics by the individual CoP member is then investigated with respect to their direct and indirect relationship with performance. (3) We expect the relationship of CoP characteristics and performance to be moderated by the type of knowledge. We distinguish specifically between implicit and explicit knowledge handled in the CoP. Figure 1 summarizes our research framework.

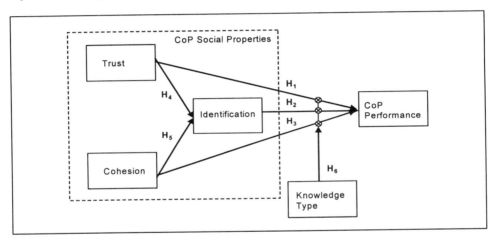

Figure 1. Research Framework

2   Social Features of a Community as Predictors of Community Performance

Implementing knowledge management systems, organizations realised very soon that an appropriate technical infrastructure provides the foundation but does not guarantee success (Barret *et al.* 2004; Jarvenpaa and Staples 2000; Pan and Leidner 2003). The 'human factor' is seen as an important success factor (Szulanski 1996; Mertins *et al.* 2003). Thus, in order to overcome barriers of knowledge sharing the influence of a community's social features has to be better understood (Ardichvili *et al.* 2003).

Although CoPs are not similar to teams (Smith and McKeen 2003), these networks can be understood as a special form of 'virtual teams' with specific community characteristics. Hence, research on team and work group performance can be applied as a basis for identifying the critical role of social relationships within a group. Several authors emphasize the importance of cohesion in terms of mutual support, the internal collaboration, etc. for the group outcome (Guzzo and Shea 1992; Hoegl and Gemuenden 2001; Mullen and Cooper 1994). Besides this, identification with the group is an important antecedent for successful team work (Scott 1997). As research results on virtual teams and intra-organizational networks show, trust is an essence of interpersonal relationships (Abrams *et al.* 2003; Jarvenpaa and Leidner 1999). This is especially important in new organizational arrangements and work forms (Jarvenpaa *et al.* 1998) which CoPs represent. As CoPs are semi-formal entities, which members are often geographically dispersed, we argue that trust is a necessary prerequisite for all community activities.

On the basis of the reviewed literature, we propose that trust, identification, and cohesion are important drivers of CoP performance.

Hypothesis H1. Trust has a direct positive impact on CoP performance.
Hypothesis H2. Identification has a direct positive impact on CoP performance.
Hypothesis H3. Cohesion has a direct positive impact on CoP performance.

Analysing the motivations of members to participate in a CoP, we propose that, above all, members need to identify themselves with the CoP. Thereby, members' identification with the CoP is effected, on the one hand, by mutual trust between the members. On the other hand, existing cohesion and mutual support will influence members' identification. Hence, we conclude:

Hypothesis H4. Trust has a direct positive influence on identification.
Hypothesis H5. Cohesion has a direct positive influence on identification.

3   Knowledge Characteristics as a Moderator for the CoP Social Features Performance Relationship

As the main objective of CoPs is to create, spread, retain, and use knowledge, we suppose that the characteristics of this knowledge may influence CoP processes and CoP performance. Regarding the knowledge handled in the CoP explicit and implicit knowledge can be distinguished. Tacit knowledge, or implicit knowledge as opposite to explicit knowledge, is considered as a key prerequisite for an organization's long-term competitiveness as this type of knowledge can hardly be imitated (Howells 1996; von Krogh *et al.* 2000). In contrast to explicit knowledge, tacit knowledge can hardly be formalized, as it is not codified, and is bound to people (Ambrosini and Bowman 2001; Berman *et al.* 2002; Hall and Andriani 2002). Hence, the knowledge type effects community processes, e.g. the communication intensity and the instrument used as the transfer of implicit knowledge requires intense interactions on a face-to-face basis (Gassmann and von Zedtwitz 2003; Leonard and Sensiper 1998). Intense interactions of people in turn require certain social features of a community. Thus, a certain level of 'personal intimacy' has to be established to communicate tacit knowledge (Seidler-de Alwis *et al.* 2003). Handling implicit knowledge implies strong uncertainties about the content and quality of information. Furthermore, transferring implicit knowledge requires stronger efforts. Ambiguities inherent in implicit knowledge may also require strong group cohesion and trust in order to apply the knowledge. Hence, the relevance of social features of a CoP for community performance increases when handling mainly implicit knowledge. Therefore, we postulate:

Hypothesis H6. Knowledge type has a moderating effect on the relationship of CoP characteristics and CoP performance.

4   Research Design

4.1 Sample and data collection procedures

To answer our research questions we conducted an empirical study in a major German multinational company which is regarded as a pioneer in knowledge management. After several qualitative interviews with experts a questionnaire was developed and successfully pre-tested with fifteen community members of a single community. We contacted 220 community brokers of the company from which 59 brokers agreed to participate in our study. The brokers were asked to distribute the questionnaire to the members of their community. As we can not control to what extent the questionnaire was sent to all community members by the brokers an adequate assessment of the response rate is difficult. The main data collection took place between July and November 2003. Finally, 222 member questionnaires from 36 communities were returned. Hence, we are able to cover about 31% of all active community members. Due to the semi-formal and dynamic character of CoPs which makes the assessment of the overall number of CoP members difficult, this sample can be considered as a very good representation of the overall population. The respondents have been community members for an average of 22.5 months and spent on average 1 to 2 hours per week on their community activities. Average tenure of the respondents with the company is 11.5 years. The average age of the community is 15.2 months, with an average of 73 members.

4.2 Measures

To develop the items for our constructs we applied previously used scales as far as possible. Besides adapting existing items, own measures were developed by taking into account the specifics of communities of practice. The members were asked to rate their agreement or disagreement with the statements on a 7-point Likert-type scale from 1 ("not true at all") to 7 ("completely true").

Following our conceptual model we distinguish between three dimensions of *social features of CoPs* covering trust, cohesion and identification with the community. Overall we use 12 items to measure the members' perception of these social features. The items finally used in our measurement model are displayed in Table 1.

Knowledge type in terms whether the knowledge exchanged in the community is of explicit or implicit nature is measured by three items – covering the difficulty to formalize the knowledge, the necessity for personal transmission of knowledge, and the possibility to systematically capture the knowledge in categories. The last item is reverse-coded.

Members are asked to assess *CoP performance* effects along ten items: increased company's competences, improved transparency of existing knowledge, improved use of existing knowledge, documentation of knowledge and experiences, distribution of Best-Practices, reduced duplicate work, increased productivity, increased number of innovations, increased intra-organizational co-operation, and higher mutual trust.

4.3 Method

Generally, the level of analysis for testing our proposed hypotheses is the individual community member. Thus, all measures reflect the members' perception on community performance and its antecedents. Our analysis follows a three step procedure: First, the developed groups of items were explored using principal component factor analysis. Items not loading strongly on the constructs as hypothesized or displaying an item-to-total correlation less 0.4 were eliminated. Second, we estimate a measurement model and a path model simultaneously using LISREL 8.5. For the CoP performance measurement we use the first order factors which were calculated as the mean over their items. Third, in order to test our moderation hypothesis we use moderated multiple regression analysis as suggest by Aiken and West (1991).

5   Results

Table 1 presents the results of the confirmatory factor analyses from the LISREL measurement model. Cronbach's Alpha and the variance explained by the variables are also reported for each construct. The items used to measure the knowledge type were also subject to similar assessment of reliability, validity and unidimensionality. Knowledge type is measured by the three items mentioned above. Cronbach's Alpha is .67 and 61.45% of the variance is explained by the construct. Alpha coefficients for our constructs range from .67 to .94 which we consider to be very satisfying as some of our constructs are comprised of only three items (Hair *et al.* 1998).

Social features of a CoP are measured along the following three dimensions: (1) Identification, (2) Trust, and (3) Cohesion. With respect to community performance three dimensions can be distinguished: (1) innovativeness (Innovation), (2) the development of competences (Competence), and (3) improved efficiency of processes (Efficiency). Knowledge type is a one-dimensional constructs.

Table 2 presents the means, standard deviations, and bivariate correlations among the variables of the developed research framework.

Table 1. Items and Constructs from the LISREL Measurement-Model.

Constructs/Dimensions/Items	Lambda-X standardized loadings	t-Values
Trust (Cronbach's Alpha .87 / Expl. Variance 71.86%)		
I trust the other members completely.	.85	14.91
I am convinced of the skills and expertise of the other members.	.85	14.53
I can rely on the knowledge of the other members.	.89	15.85
The community handles confidential knowledge responsibly.	.71	11.31
Cohesion (.85 / 69.73%)		
The members are willing to invest their time and knowledge in the work of the community.	.58	8.54
The community members mutually support each other in their tasks.	.82	12.80
The community members are particularly cooperative and friendly with each other.	.79	12.80
Our community is characterized by a strong team spirit.	.86	14.70
Identification (.86 / 71.18%)		
I feel very attached to the community.	.90	0.00
I am happy to tell my colleagues at my workplace about my activities in the community.	.77	12.92
I tell my supervisors about interesting results from our community.	.72	11.72
I view the success of the community as my own personal success as well.	.69	11.10
CoP Performance		
Innovation *(.90 / 78.15 / no. of items = 4)*	.84	0.00
Competence *(.91 / 85.06 / no. of items = 3)*	.87	14.61
Efficiency *(.79 / 70.16 / no. of items = 3)*	.88	14.83

Table 2. Sample Descriptive Statistics and Correlations.

Variable	Mean	S.D.	1	2	3	4	5
1. Knowledge Type	3.20	1.19					
2. Identification	4.64	1.53	-.10				
3. Trust	5.37	1.09	-.18*	.50**			
4. Cohesion	4.70	1.17	-.04	.50**	.58**		
5. CoP Performance	4.81	1.10	-.13	.54**	.44**	.52**	

*p < .05; **p < .01

In order to asses our hypothesized main effects between trust, cohesion, identification, and CoP performance we performed a structural equation model using LISREL 8.5. Table 3 reports the results from our path model. For the evaluation of model fit we followed a two-index presentation strategy reflecting recent research by Hu and Bentler (1998, 1999). Both the CFI (.93) and SRMR (.062) values we obtain are within the critical range recommended by Hu and Bentler, thus allowing interpretation of our results.

Table 3. Standardized Path Coefficients and Fit Statistics: LISREL Analysis.

Dependent Variable	Predictor	H	Coefficient	Conclusion
CoP Performance	Trust	H1	n.s.	H1 rejected
CoP Performance	Identification	H2	0.60	H2 confirmed
CoP Performance	Cohesion	H3	0.25	H3 confirmed
Identification	Trust	H4	0.38	H4 confirmed
Identification	Cohesion	H5	0.35	H5 confirmed

Of the hypothesized three direct performance effects of the different social features of the community, only identification and to a lesser extent cohesion show significant and positive path coefficients. Trust is not significantly directly related to CoP performance from the communities. Hence, H1 is rejected, H2 and H3 are confirmed. Our hypotheses H4 and H5 suggesting positive effects of trust and cohesion on identification of members with their community are supported by the data.

Table 4. Results of Hierarchical Moderated Regression – CoP Performance.

	CoP Performance		
	Model 1	Model 2	Model 3
Main Effects			
Identification	.42***	.42***	.42***
Trust	.30***	.31***	.30***
Cohesion	.37***	.38***	.36***
Moderator			
Knowledge Type		.01	-.01
Interaction Terms			
Knowledge Type * Identification			.05
Knowledge Type * Trust			.03
Knowledge Type * Cohesion			-.01
R^2	.43	.43	.43
Adjusted R^2	.42	.42	.41
ΔR^2	.43	.00	.00
F	41.57***	30.99***	17.61***

We report standardized beta values; *** $p < .001$

In order to assess the moderating effect of knowledge type on the relationship of social features and performance we performed moderated multiple regression analysis. Results of this analysis are presented in Table 4.

In consistency with the results of our path model the main effects regression show significant F-Values and consequently allow interpretation. Overall, the three different social features of CoPs explain 42% of the performance variance. However, neither the knowledge type in terms of the intensity of implicit knowledge handled in the community itself nor the three interaction terms have a significant effect on performance. Thus, our results do not lend support to our Hypothesis H6.

6   Discussion

This research's objective is to enhance the understanding of CoPs and the value they deliver. Building on existing research on CoPs, teams, and knowledge management the primary objective is to analyse social features of communities and to test their potential direct and indirect effects on community performance. Further, we intend to investigate to what degree the CoP social features performance relationship is moderated by the type of knowledge handled in the CoP. In order to test our hypotheses we use data from 222 members of 36 communities in one multinational corporation.

As research on CoPs is generally scarce and mainly focused on qualitative case study research it is necessary to develop valid and reliable scales for relevant constructs in the CoP context. As far as possible we build upon existing scales mainly from team research and adapt these scales for the specific situation of CoPs. Our results suggest that social features of a CoP can be measured along three dimensions: trust, cohesion, and identification. Also, we are able to present a measurement of community performance capturing organizational benefits. These benefits include improvements of the organization's ability to innovate, a general competence enhancing effect and improvements of process efficiency. Our scales allow a rigorous test of our hypothesis and may also serve as a basis for future research.

As communities of practice can be understood as a special form of a 'virtual team' with specific characteristics, we build our theoretical framework mainly upon team research. Hence, the perception of social features of the CoP in terms of experienced trust and cohesion as well as the strength of identification with the CoP are identified as potentially important drivers of CoP performance. While team research suggests that especially trust and cohesion should have a direct and positive effect on performance, our results suggest that identification is the main predictor of CoP performance. Trust and cohesion as important characteristics of the CoP show only to a limited extend direct performance effects. However, they are both positively and strongly related to identification with the CoP, i.e. their performance effect is mediated by identification. This mediated relationship may be partly explained by our measurement approach and more importantly by the specifics of CoPs: (1) we deviate from most team research and test simultaneously for direct and indirect effects of social features on performance.

When using multiple regression analysis, trust and cohesion seem to exert a direct effect on performance. However, our structural path model lends support to the notion that this effect is rather due to an indirect relationship through identification of CoP members with their community. (2) Contrary to most other teams studied, CoPs are semi-formal organizational entities, for which participation is more or less voluntary. The individual objective of participation is generally to deliver the means to improve the main organizational task of each member. Hence, CoP related activities have a support objective, are only a small fraction of the overall individual task, and are to some degree often perceived as a secondary task with much lesser priority. In addition, individual contributions to the CoP activities may not be followed by individual benefits immediately. For organizational benefits to emerge, it is required that a larger number of CoP members interact and, thereby, contribute to the common knowledge sharing and learning as the main tasks of CoP. In sum, CoPs can be understood as rather loosely coupled networks of individuals of one organization. Collaboration in terms of close team work is not the main feature of activities performed in CoPs. Thus, trust and cohesion as drivers of successful collaboration will not have the same strong relationship with performance as experienced with e.g. new product development teams. On the contrary, identification of individual team members with their CoP is an important feature, which will favour individual contributions to the CoP work. Identification with the CoP manifests itself in CoP members perceiving themselves as a part of this loosely coupled network, where overall community performance is appreciated by individual members although individual contributions may not lead to immediate personal performance improvement. Identification with the CoP is not self-evident, as the lack of collocation, the semi-formal character, and the comparatively low priority of the CoP task do not favour strong identification. Hence, variance in this important social construct can be expected. But CoPs with members identifying themselves strongly with the community should venture better as identification may motivate members to contribute to the central knowledge sharing and learning activities without assessing the immediate personal benefit for every interaction. Thus, identification enables performance driving network effects of participation in CoPs. However, trust and cohesion are still important social features of CoPs. They may not promote the intensity and quality of member interactions directly as it is the case with closely connected teams. But, trust and cohesion are necessary prerequisites for identification and, thereby, for improved organizational CoP performance.

Contrary to our hypothesis the results do not indicate a moderating effect of knowledge type on the relationship of CoP social features and CoP performance. The knowledge type in terms of the intensity of implicit knowledge handled in the CoP itself has no significant effect on performance, too. These insignificant findings may be due to the fact that the influence of social features on CoP performance is independent from the knowledge type. Also, social features have a strong direct performance enhancing effect; their importance does not vary with the degree to which the knowledge handled in the community is implicit.

With regard to further research, our results emphasize the importance of community characteristics which need to be accounted for when studying performance drivers of CoPs. It is important to assess the interaction of social features as specifically trust and cohesion seem to be antecedents of other social constructs rather than having a direct performance relationship. Additionally, as this analysis is based on community members' perceptions, further studies should include objective community performance data.

In sum, our results suggest, that CoPs have the potential to support the development, exchange, and application of knowledge in an organization. Hence, management should actively support community work by providing required resources and by establishing the necessary prerequisites on the organization. Furthermore, an appropriate community management needs to create opportunities for developing the means for identification with the CoP by trust- and cohesion-building events and by an improved internal marketing of CoPs which recognizes and acknowledges CoP participation.

References

Abrams, L. C., Cross, R., Lesser, E. and Levin, D. Z. (2003). Nurturing Interpersonal Trust in Knowledge-Sharing Networks. *Academy of Management Executive, 17*(4), 64-77.

Aiken, M. and West, S. G. (1991). *Multiple Regression: Testing and Interpreting Interactions*. Newbury Park (CA): Sage.

Ambrosini, V. and Bowman, C. (2001). Tacit Knowledge: Some Suggestions for Operationalization. *Journal of Management Studies, 38*(6), 811-829.

Ardichvili, A., Page, V. and Wentling, T. (2003). Motivation and Barriers to Participation in Virtual Knowledge-Sharing Communities of Practice. *Journal of Knowledge Management, 7*(1), 64-77.

Barret, M., Cappleman, S., Shoib, G. and Walsham, G. (2004). Learning in Knowledge Communities: Managing Technology and Context. *European Management Journal, 22*(1), 1-11.

Berman, S. L., Down, J. and Hill, C. W. L. (2002). Tacit Knowledge as a Source of Competitive Advantage in the National Basketball Association. *Academy of Management Journal, 45*(1), 13-31.

Brown, J. S. and Duguid, P. (1991). Organizational Learning and Communities-of-Practice: Toward a Unified View of Working, Learning, and Innovation. *Organization Science, 2*(1), 40-57.

Dyer, J. H. and Nobeoka, K. (2000). Creating and Managing a High-Performance Knowledge-Sharing Network: The Toyota Case. *Strategic Management Journal, 21*(3), 345-367.

Gassmann, O. and von Zedtwitz, M. (2003). Trends and Determinants of Managing Virtual R&D Teams. *R&D Management, 33*(3), 243-262.

Gongla, P. and Rizzuto, C. R. (2001). Evolving Communities of Practice: IBM Global Services Experience. *IBM systems journal, 40*(4), 842-862.

Guzzo, R. A. and Shea, G. (1992). Group Performance and Intergroup Relations in Organizations. In L. M. Hough (Ed.), *Handbook of Industrial and Organizational Psychology* (2 ed., Vol. 3, pp. 269-313). Palo Alto, CA: Consulting Psychologists Press.

Hair, J. F., Anderson, R. E., Tatham, R. L. and Black, W. C. (1998). *Multivariate Data Analysis*. Upper Saddle River (NJ): Prentice-Hall.

Hall, R. and Andriani, P. (2002). Managing Knowledge for Innovation. *Long Range Planning, 35*, 29-48.

Hoegl, M. and Gemuenden, H. G. (2001). Teamwork Quality and the Success of Innovative Projects: A Theoretical Concept and Empirical Evidence. *Organization Science, 12*(4), 435-449.

Howells, J. (1996). Tacit Knowledge, Innovation and Technology Transfer. *Technology Analysis & Strategic Management, 8*(2), 91-106.

Hu, L. and Bentler, P. M. (1998). Fit Indices in Covariance Structure Modeling: Sensitivity to Underparameterized Model Misspecificaitons. *Psychological Methods, 3*, 424-453.

Hu, L. and Bentler, P. M. (1999). Cutoff Criteria for Fit Indices in Covariance Structure Analysis: Convential Criteria Versus New Alternatives. *Structural Equation Modeling, 6*, 1-55.

Jarvenpaa, S. L., Knoll, K. and Leidner, D. E. (1998). Is Anybody out There? Antecedents of Trust in Global Virtual Teams. *Journal of Management Information Systems, 14*(4), 29-64.

Jarvenpaa, S. L. and Leidner, D. E. (1999). Communication and Trust in Global Virtual Teams. *Organization Science, 10*(6), 791-815.

Jarvenpaa, S. L. and Staples, D. (2000). The Use of Electronic Media for Information Sharing: An Exploratory Study. *Journal of Strategic Information Systems, 9*(2-3), 129-154.

Kogut, B. and Zander, U. (1992). Knowledge of the Firm, Combinative Capabilities and the Replication of Technology. *Organization Science, 3*(3), 383-397.

Lave, J. and Wenger, E. (1991). *Situated Learning: Legitimate Peripheral Participation.* Cambridge, UK: Cambridge University Press.

Leonard, D. and Sensiper, S. (1998). The Role of Tacit Knowledge on Group Innovation. *California Management Review, 40*(4), 112-132.

Lesser, E. L. and Storck, J. (2001). Communities of Practice and Organizational Performance. *IBM Systems Journal, 40*(4), 831-841.

Mertins, K., Heisig, P. and Vorbeck, J. (2003). *Knowledge Management: Concepts and Best Practices* (2 ed.). Berlin: Springer.

Mullen, B. and Cooper, C. (1994). The Relation between Group Cohesiveness and Performance. *Psychological Bulletin, 115*(2), 210-227.

Nonaka, I. and Takeuchi, H. (1995). *The Knowledge-Creating Company: How Japanese Companies Create the Dynamics of Innovation*: Oxford University Press.

Pan, S. L. and Leidner, D. E. (2003). Bridging Communities of Practice with Information Technology in Pursuit of Global Knowledge Sharing. *Journal of Strategic Information Systems, 12*, 71-88.

Sawhney, M. and Prandelli, E. (2000). Communities of Creation: Managing Distributed Innovation in Turbulent Markets. *California Management Review, 42*(4), 24-54.

Scott, S. G. (1997). Social Identification Effects in Product and Process Development Teams. *Journal of Engineering and Technology Management JET-M, 14*(2), 97-127.

Seidler-de Alwis, R., Hartmann, E. and Gemuenden, H. G. (2003). *The Role of Tacit Knowledge in Innovation Management.* Paper presented at the 19th IMP Conference, Lugano.

Smith, H. A. and McKeen, J. D. (2003). Creating and Facilitating Communities of Practice. In C. W. Holsapple (Ed.), *Handbook on Knowledge Management: Knowledge Matters* (Vol. 1, pp. 393-407). Berlin, Heidelberg, New York: Springer.

Storck, J. and Hill, P. A. (2000). Knowledge Diffusion Trough 'Strategic Communities'. *Sloan Management Review, 41*(2), 63-74.

Szulanski, G. (1996). Exploring Internal Stickiness: Impediments to the Transfer of Best Practice within the Firm. *Strategic Management Journal, 17*(Winter Special Issue), 27-43.

von Krogh, G., Ichijo, K. and Nonaka, I. (2000). *Enabling Knowledge Creation: How to Unlock the Mystery of Tacit Knowledge and Release the Power of Innovation.* New York: Oxford University Press.

Wenger, E. C. (1998). *Communities of Practice: Learning, Meaning and Identity.* Cambridge, UK: Cambridge University Press.

PART III

Knowledge Sharing

KNOWLEDGE SHARING IN RESPONSE TO A SUPPORTIVE WORK ENVIRONMENT: EVIDENCE FROM AN AUSTRALIAN ENGINEERING FIRM

PRASHANT BORDIA, BERND E. IRMER, MARY-ANN GARDEN,
KATE PHAIR & DAVID ABUSAH

*School of Psychology, University of Queensland,
Brisbane, QLD 4072, Australia*

Employee willingness to share knowledge is vital for successful knowledge management. In this paper, we propose that employees are more likely to engage in knowledge sharing if they feel supported by their organization and co-workers. On the other hand, if employees feel that the organization has failed in its obligations (i.e., a violation of psychological contract), they will withhold knowledge. We test these ideas with empirical data from an Australian engineering firm. Knowledge sharing was measured by employee self-report and supervisor ratings. Our results show that perceived organizational support was related to knowledge sharing with the organization (e.g., codifying knowledge into databases) and perceived co-worker support was related to knowledge sharing with individuals at work (e.g., sharing personal expertise with a co-worker). Further, as predicted, psychological contract violation was negatively related to knowledge sharing. These findings have important implications for initiatives to enhance knowledge sharing, as managers need to adopt differing strategies to promote different types of knowledge sharing.

1 Introduction

Organizations are expending large amounts of capital resources on knowledge management enabling technologies, such as groupware and intranets. It is estimated that the world market for knowledge management software will be worth $3.5 billion in 2004 (Bahra 2001). However, while technology enables knowledge management, it is ultimately the employee's choice to share his or her tacit knowledge that permits a KM initiative to realize the anticipated returns. Indeed, research on "communities of practices" and "knowledge networks" have emphasized the importance of interpersonal communication in knowledge transfer and recognize that technology is best viewed as a KM facilitator (Davenport and Prusak, 1998; McDermott 1999). Knowledge management initiatives that do not address the motivations of individual employees and provide them an incentive to share are likely to fail (Meso and Smith 2000).

Although much research has been conducted on the positive impact of knowledge sharing in organizations, studies to date have tended to focus on operational level issues such as design of knowledge management enabling technologies and organizational levels issues such as culture (Bussing and Herbig 2003; McDermott and O'Dell 2001). There is a limited but rapidly growing literature examining interpersonal factors that encourage or discourage individual employees to share their knowledge (e.g., Constant *et al.* 1994; Jarvenpaa and Staples 2001). In this literature, knowledge sharing has been conceptualized as the discretionary behavior of making knowledge available to others when one does not have to pass it on (Davenport 1994; Jarvenpaa and Staples 2001). Anecdotal evidence from case studies suggests that employees often resist sharing their knowledge (Ardichvill *et al.* 2003; Ciborra and Patriota 1998). Accordingly, there is a greater need for understanding the human and social aspects of knowledge sharing (e.g., Cross and Barid 2000; Davenport and Prusak 1998).

In the research reported here, we investigate the determinants of knowledge sharing in organizations. In particular, we were interested in voluntary and discretionary knowledge sharing. Borrowing from the field of organizational behavior, we classify knowledge sharing as an organizational citizenship behavior and argue that knowledge sharing is more likely to occur when employees feel that the organization looks after and takes care of employee needs. When employees feel supported and cared for, they are more likely to reciprocate by engaging in discretionary knowledge sharing. These ideas are tested with empirical data from an Australian engineering firm. In the next section, we define knowledge sharing as an OCB and note how different types of knowledge sharing (i.e., organizational and interpersonal) are influenced by different sources of support (i.e., organization and co-worker). We then detail the methodology we used to test our hypotheses and present our findings. We conclude by discussing the implications of our findings and directions for future research.

1.1 Knowledge sharing as an organizational citizenship behavior

Knowledge sharing can be a voluntary or discretionary behavior of making knowledge available to others when one does not have to (Davenport 1994; Jarvenpaa and Staples 2001). This definition of knowledge sharing contains the essential elements that define organizational citizenship behaviors (OCB). Organ (1988) defined OCB as "individual behavior that is discretionary, not directly or explicitly recognized by the formal reward system, and that in the aggregate promotes the effective functioning of the organization" (p.4). It would therefore seem that, in general, knowledge sharing can be defined as a type of OCB, as knowledge sharing is discretionary, not formally rewarded and in the aggregate increases organizational effectiveness. Further support for defining knowledge sharing as an OCB can be drawn from Podsakoff and MacKenzie's (1997) work on the impact of OCBs on organizational performance. Podsakoff and MacKenzie (1997) identified seven ways in which OCBs impact on work unit and organizational effectiveness. Examples for five of the seven reasons provided included knowledge sharing behaviors, such as spreading best practice, touching base and coordinating with other team members or members from other functional groups, providing feedback on changes in the marketplace and offering suggestions on how to respond, and disseminating information throughout the organization.

OCBs can be directed at different targets, such as the organization, co-worker or supervisors (Williams and Anderson 1991). Williams and Anderson (1991) differentiate between relationships that employees have with their organizations (as entities) and with their co-workers. Specifically, employees engage in interpersonally focused (OCBI) and organizationally focused (OCBO) OCBs. This two-factor classification of OCBs into organizational and individual focused behaviors has received substantial empirical support (e.g., Kaufman *et al*. 2001; Rousseau 1990). Similarly, we argue that knowledge sharing can also be directed at the organization (i.e., knowledge sharing-organization or KSO, such as codifying knowledge into a database) or at an interpersonal level (i.e., knowledge sharing-interpersonal or KSI, sharing client information with co-workers to bring them up to speed on a project).

1.2 Perceived organizational and co-worker support as antecedents of OCB

Social exchange theory (Blau 1964) has been the primary theoretical framework to account for the occurrence of OCB (Rhoades and Eisenberger 2002). An important variable in exchange accounts of OCB is perceived organizational support (POS). POS is "the global belief held by an employee that the organization values her or his contributions and cares about their well-being" (Eisenberger *et al*. 1986; p. 501). Employees develop global beliefs about POS in order to meet socio-emotional needs and to determine the organization's response to increased work effort (Eisenberger *et al*. 1986; Rhoades and Eisenberger 2002). When employees feel that their organization cares for their well-being it may create a sense of obligation to reciprocate, and one way to do this is by engaging in OCBs that benefit the organization (Eisenberger *et al*. 2001).

Employees not only receive and perceive support from the organization but also from other sources, such as supervisor and co-worker (Eisenberger *et al*. 2002). Further, it is proposed that employees do not only differentiate between sources of support but also engage in different behaviors to reciprocate different sources of support. This is in line with the two-factor classification of OCBs into organizational (OCBO) and individual (OCBI) focused. Accordingly, Ladd and Henry (2000) found that POS was associated with OCBOs and that perceived co-worker support (PCS) was associated with OCBIs

Based on the OCB and POS literature, we argue that knowledge sharing can be conceptualized as an OCB and that it can be classified as knowledge sharing directed towards the organization (KSO) or directed at other individuals (KSI). Further, KSO and KSI will be associated with different sources of support. Specifically, we predicted that:

Hypothesis 1:   *POS will be positively associated with knowledge sharing directed at the organization (KSO).*

Hypothesis 2:   *PCS will be positively associated with knowledge sharing directed at other employees (KSI).*

1.3 The role of obligation as a mediator

Social exchange theory is based on Gouldner's (1960) norm of reciprocity, which postulates that if support is received from others then they must be compensated, and that the greater the support received the greater the subsequent compensation. Several authors have noted that this need to reciprocate is like a moral obligation (Greenberg 1980).

Paese and Gilin (2000) noted that "the reciprocity rule exerts its influence via feelings of obligations to return another's favor, and these feelings occur almost automatically, regardless of whether the former is requested or uninvited" (p.82). Eisenberger *et al.* (2001) provided empirical support for felt obligation as a mediator of the POS-outcome relationships by finding that the effect of POS on outcome variables (i.e., affective commitment, organizational spontaneity and in-role performance) was mediated by felt obligation. Based on this literature, we predicted that:

Hypothesis 3: *The relationship between POS and KSO would be mediated by feelings of obligation to the organization.*

Hypothesis 4: *The relationship between PCS and KSI would be mediated by feelings of obligation to co-workers.*

1.4 Perceived contract violation

An alternative way of conceptualizing supportive organizational practices is in the form of psychological contracts. A psychological contract is a perceived arrangement between an employee and employer regarding their mutual obligations to each other in terms of an exchange agreement (Rousseau 1990). The psychological contract focuses on the reciprocal obligations of both the employee and the employer (Robinson and Morrison 1995). Employees reciprocate what they receive from the organization (e.g., job security, support, salary) with their contributions (e.g., job performance and commitment), depending on how well they perceive the organization as meeting its contractual obligations to them (Robinson and Morrison 1995). Robinson and Rousseau (1994) found that over 50% of the managers they sampled felt that their organization had failed to meet all its promised obligations. These perceptions of unfulfilled psychological contract have been linked with reduced in-role performance, OCB, trust, satisfaction and intentions to stay with the organization (Robinson 1996; Robinson and Morrison 2000). Thus, when an employee feels that the organization has failed to meet its obligations to him or her, the employee experiences a violation of the psychological contract. This feeling of violation of psychological contract may lead the employee to withhold his or her knowledge and not engage in knowledge sharing.

Hypothesis 5: *Psychological contract violation will be negatively associated with KSO.*

Hypothesis 6: *Psychological contract violation will be negatively associated with KSI.*

2 Method

2.1 Participants

One hundred and fifty permanent full-time employees of a medium sized engineering firm were distributed questionnaires at their place of work. All divisions (workshop, maintenance, projects, electrical and administration) and levels (non-supervisory, supervisory, middle management and senior management) of the organization were represented in the sample, which comprised of all employees with the exception of those working off-site at the time the questionnaire was distributed (approximately 50 employees). Seventy-one employees responded to the questionnaire, providing response rate of 48%, of this 16 were female, 52 were male, and 3 did not indicate gender. Supervisor ratings of 63 participants' knowledge sharing were also obtained. The average age of the sample was 36.04 years with a majority of the participants reporting their highest achieved education level as trade-level qualifications. The average organizational tenure was two and a half years.

2.2 Procedure

Two weeks prior to the distribution of the questionnaire a memo from the CEO of the company to all employees introduced the research. The questionnaires were accompanied by letters of introduction from the research team and self-addressed reply paid envelopes. The employees were requested to return the questionnaires within two weeks. Reminders to complete and return the questionnaire were emailed to all employees a week and a fortnight after the questionnaires were distributed. The questionnaire was pilot-tested to ensure applicability of the items in the organization's work environment.

2.3 Measures

All measures used a 7-point scale of agreement (1 = 'strongly disagree' and 7 = 'strongly agree'). The shortened POS scale (Eisenberger *et al.* 2001) was used to measure *perceived organizational support*. An example was "My organization is supportive of my goals and values." The 9-items were combined to form a single measure of POS ($\alpha=.88$). The PCS scale was identical to the POS scale except that the referent of the items was changed to co-workers rather than organization, as per Ladd and Henry (2000). An example item was "My co-workers are supportive of my goals and values". The 9-items were combined to form a single measure of PCS ($\alpha=.91$). Eisenberger *et al.*'s (2001) seven-item scale was used to measure *feelings of obligation to the organization*. An example item was "I feel a personal obligation to do whatever I can to help the organization achieve its goals". The 7-items were combined to form a single measure of felt obligations to the organization ($\alpha=.80$). The feelings of obligation to co-workers scale was identical to the feelings of obligations to the organization scale except that the referent of the items was changed to co-workers rather than organization. An example item was "I feel a personal obligation to do whatever can to help my co-workers achieve their goals". The 7-items were combined to form a single measure of feelings of obligation to co-workers ($\alpha=.83$). Robinson and Morrison's (2000) four-item measure of *perceived psychological contract violation* was used. An example item was "I feel that my organization has violated the contract between us". The 4 items were combined to form a single measure of PCV ($\alpha=.80$).

The five-item measure of *KSI* conceptualized as an OCB was developed by Abusah (2002). Example items were 'I go out of my way to help my co-workers perform their work role, by passing on useful information to them' and 'I voluntarily share my ideas, experiences, and knowledge with my co-workers in order to facilitate their work performance'. The five-items were combined into a single measure of KSI (α=.88). The six-item measure of *KSO* was adapted from the Abusah (2002) KS-I measure. Example items were 'I go out of my way to share my knowledge in the development of training manuals and other company documentation' and 'I would contribute my knowledge, information and expertise to a formal knowledge sharing system in the organization'. The six-items were combined into a single measure of KSI (α=.88). The items used above to measure self-report knowledge sharing were adapted to develop a *supervisor rating of knowledge sharing*. The supervisor ratings of KSO and KSI were highly correlated (r=.92, p<.001) and therefore combined into a single measure of knowledge sharing (α=.96).

3   Results

3.1 *Knowledge sharing – organization*

3.1.1 *POS and obligation*

To test hypotheses 1 and 3, three separate regression analyses were conducted, in line with Kenny *et al.*'s (1998) guidelines for mediation analysis. First, the relationship between POS (IV) and KSO (DV) was tested controlling for the demographic variables. POS was positively related to KSO (β = .28, p<.05), supporting hypothesis 1. Second, another regression analysis was conducted to test for the relationship between POS (IV) and obligation to the organization (mediator). POS was positively related to obligation to the organization (β = .32, p<.01), meeting the second requirement for mediation. The third regression analysis was conducted to test for the effect of POS (IV) and obligation to the organization (mediator) on KS-O (DV) (see Table 1). The relationship between POS and KSO was weakened, such that it was no longer significant, by the inclusion of obligation to organization into the regression.

Table 1. Regression analysis of POS and obligation to organization predicting KSO.

Predictor Variable	Knowledge Sharing - Organization		
	Step 1	Step 2	Step 3
Gender	.11	.14	.11
Tenure in organization	.20	.20	.20
POS		.28*	.10
Obligation to the organization			.56**
Change in R^2		.08	.28**
Adjusted R^2	.04	.10	.39**

n=71, *p<.05, **p<.01

Next, the indirect effect path coefficients were calculated by multiplying the unstandardised regression coefficient of the association between POS and obligation to the organization with the unstandardised regression coefficient for the association between obligation to the organization and knowledge sharing. The standard error for these coefficients was calculated using the formula provided by Kenny *et al.* (1998, p.260). The indirect regression coefficient divided by the standard error yielded a test statistic approximately distributed as a Z distribution. POS had a significant indirect effect on knowledge sharing (β = .18, Z = 2.18, p < .05). Since all of the requirements for mediation prescribed by Kenny *et al.* (1998) were met, obligation to the organization had a mediating effect on the relationship between POS and KSO, providing support for hypothesis 3.

3.1.2 PCV and KSO

PCV (β =.-.28, p < .05) explained additional variance above the effect of gender and organizational tenure for self-report knowledge sharing with the organization (R^2_{change} = .07, F_{change} = 5.53, p < .05), supporting hypothesis 5.

3.2 Knowledge sharing – co-workers

3.2.1 PCS and obligation

To test for hypotheses 2 and 4, three separate regression equations were conducted. First, the relationship between PCS and KSI was established (β = .41, p<.001), supporting hypothesis 2. Second, PCS was marginally related with obligation to co-workers (β = .22, p<.10). Finally, we tested the effect of PCS and obligation to co-workers on KSI (see Table 2). The relationship between PCS and KSI was weakened but remained significant, by the inclusion of obligation to co-workers. Further, in line with Kenny *et al.* (1998) PCS had significant indirect effect on knowledge sharing (β = .09, Z = 2.58, p < .05). Obligation to co-workers partially mediated the effect of PCS on KSI, providing tentative support for hypothesis 4.

Table 2. Regression analysis of PCS and Obligation to co-workers predicting KSI.

Predictor Variable	Knowledge Sharing - Individual		
	Step 1	Step 2	Step 3
Gender	-.05	-.02	-.07
Tenure in organization	.27*	.34*	.32**
PCS		.41**	.32*
Obligation to co-workers			.47**
Change in R^2		.17	.21**
Adjusted R^2	.04	.20	.40**

n=71, *p<.05, **p<.01

3.2.2 PCV and KSI

Tenure in the organization (β = .27, p < .05) was a significant predictor of self-report KSI. PCV (β =.-.11, p = .39) did not explain additional variance above the effect of gender and organizational tenure for self-report knowledge sharing with co-workers (R^2_{change} = .01, F_{change} = .74, ns), failing to support hypothesis 6.

3.3 *Supervisor ratings of knowledge sharing*

We also conducted regression analyses on the supervisor rating of knowledge sharing. The demographic variables of gender (β = .32, p < .05) and organization tenure (β = .-.18, ns) explained a marginally significant amount of variance in supervisor ratings of knowledge sharing (p < .08). POS, PCS, obligations to coworkers and obligations to the organization did not explain additional variance above the effect of demographic variables, (R^2_{change} = .09, F_{change} = 1.21, ns). However, PCV significantly predicted supervisor ratings of knowledge sharing (β = -.34, p < .01) above the effect of demographic variables, (R^2_{change} = .11, F_{change} = 7.75, p <.01).

4   Discussion

The current research provides further support for the utility of using social exchange theory as a framework to study employee motivations of knowledge sharing. Knowledge exchange can be conceptualized as a type of social exchange occurring within knowledge markets (Davenport and Prusak 1998). The conceptualization of knowledge as a valued commodity traded between individuals has its basis in social exchange theory. We drew on the wider social exchange literature in organizational behavior to re-define knowledge sharing as an OCB. We found that employees were more likely to engage in knowledge sharing when they perceived they were receiving support. Importantly, different sources of support were associated with different types of knowledge sharing. Employees who felt the organization was supportive were more likely to reciprocate or engage in knowledge sharing behavior targeted towards the organization, such as codifying their knowledge into databases. Similarly, perceived support from co-workers was associated with higher levels of knowledge sharing behavior targeted at co-workers. This has important implications for strategies to enhance knowledge sharing, as organizations who want to increase either codification or personalization strategies need to adopt differing strategies (see practical recommendations section).

Organizational practices cannot only promote knowledge sharing but can also inhibit it. Employees' perceptions that the organization is not providing adequate support or meeting its obligations to them may result in feelings of violation which in turn has an impact on knowledge sharing behavior. We found that employees' perceptions of contract violations had a detrimental effect on knowledge sharing with the organization but not on knowledge sharing with co-workers. This relationship was found for both self-ratings of KSO and supervisor ratings of the combined measure of knowledge sharing. This provides further support for employees differentiating between sources of support. PCV is about the exchange relationship between an employee and the organization. Therefore, it should primarily impact on behaviors that are aimed at the organization and not affect behaviors that reciprocate co-workers.

4.1 Limitations and future directions

The primary limitation of this study is that it used a cross-sectional correlation design and therefore limits the conclusions that can be made about causal relationships. A second limitation of this study was that some of the conclusions reached were based solely on self-report measures, therefore common method variance may have potentially inflated some of the observed relationships. However, the presence of complex relationships (i.e., mediation) among the self-report variables cannot be accounted for by common method variance. Further, the relationship between PCV and knowledge sharing was also found for supervisor ratings of knowledge sharing. Future research would benefit from utilizing a longitudinal design to examine causality.

Future research may also want to examine how perceptions of support interact with other psychological determinants of knowledge sharing. For example, how does POS relate to perceptions of ownership of knowledge (Constant *et al.* 1994; Jarvenpaa and Staples 2001). Does POS increase perceptions of organizational ownership of knowledge or does organizational ownership of knowledge moderate the POS-KSO relationship?

4.2 Conclusion and practical recommendations

Encouraging employees to actively and willingly engage in knowledge sharing, whether it be codification of knowledge into a database or sharing expertise interpersonally, is a major challenge facing managers. The current paper provides further evidence that social exchange theory provides not only a framework to understand knowledge sharing but also practical guidance on how to facilitate knowledge sharing. Specifically, we found that employees were more likely to share knowledge when they felt they were supported. Interestingly, different types of support were associated with different kinds of knowledge sharing. Support from the organization was associated with knowledge sharing directed at the organization and support from co-workers was associated with knowledge sharing that more directly benefited co-workers.

Organizations initiating a knowledge management strategy need to first consider what type of knowledge sharing they are trying to promote. Is it knowledge exchange between employees (i.e. personalization) or codification of knowledge into knowledge management systems (i.e. codification) or both? The determinants of these types of knowledge sharing are different, hence the strategy to promote them need to be different. Managers wanting to increase knowledge sharing among co-workers need to increase perceptions of co-worker support. Managers can promote feelings of support from co-workers by providing opportunities to develop informal and formal networks (McDermott and O'Dell 2001). Interpersonal contact allows employees to establish a sense of reciprocity and trust with co-workers (Cross and Baird 2000) and develop an understanding of co-workers knowledge, skills and abilities (Cramton 2001).

Managers wanting to increase knowledge sharing directed towards the organization, such as contributions to databases, need to target employee's perceptions of organizational support. A recent meta-analysis of over 70 studies on POS (Rhoades and

Eisenberger 2002) found that procedural justice, supervisor support and job conditions were the primary antecedents of POS. Thus, organizations and supervisors can promote POS, and in turn KSO, by implementing policies that are fair, provide employees a voice, and treat them with dignity and respect (Rhoades and Eisenberger 2002). POS can also be influenced through instituting favorable job conditions, such as reward and recognition programmes, increasing autonomy and job security. Further, the clarification of organizational expectations, rules and policies provides increased situational cues to guide individuals to behave in a specific manner. Strong situational cues will increase knowledge sharing by making it less discretionary (Dirks and Ferrin 2001).

References

Abusah, D. (2002) "Knowledge sharing at work: The role of evaluation apprehension, perceived benefits and organizational commitment." *Unpublished Masters Thesis, University of Queensland.*

Ardichvilli, A., Page, V. and Wentling, T. (2003) "Motivation and barriers to participation in virtual knowledge-sharing communities of practice." *Journal of Knowledge Management,* 7(1): 64-77.

Bahra, N. (2001) *Competitive knowledge management.* Palgrave: Houndmills.

Blau, P.M. (1964) *Exchange and power in social life.* New York: John Wiley.

Bussing, A. and Herbig, B. (2003) "Implicit knowledge and experience in work and organizations." *International Review of Industrial and Organizational Psychology,* 18: 239-280.

Ciborra, C. U. and Patriota, G. (1998) "Groupware and teamwork in RandD: Limits to learning and innovation." *RandD Management,* 28(1): 1-10.

Constant, D., Kiesler, S. and Sproull, L. (1994) "What's mine is ours, or is it? A study of attitudes about information sharing." *Information Systems Research,* 5 (4): 400-421.

Cramton, C. D. (2001) "The mutual knowledge problem and its consequences for dispersed collaboration." *Organization Science,* 12(3): 346-371.

Cross, R. and Baird, L. (2000) "Technology is not enough: improving performance by building organizational memory." *Sloan Management Review,* Spring: 69-78.

Davenport, T. H. (1994) "Saving IT's soul: Human-centered information management." *Harvard Business Review,* 72(2): 118-126.

Davenport, T. H. and Prusak, L. (1998) *Working knowledge: how organizations manage what they know.* Boston: Harvard Business School Press.

Dirks, K. T., and Ferrin, D. (2001) "The role of trust in organizational settings." *Organization Science,* 12: 450-467.

Eisenberger, R., Armeli, S., Rexwinkel, B., Lynch, P. D. and Rhoades, L. (2001) "Reciprocation of perceived organizational support." *Journal of Applied Psychology,* 86: 42-51.

Eisenberger, R., Huntington, R., Hutchison, S. and Sowa, D. (1986) "Perceived organizational support." *Journal of Applied Psychology,* 71: 500-507.

Eisenberger, R., Singlhamber, F. Vandenberghe, C., Sucharski, I. L. and Rohades, L. (2002) "Perceived supervisor support: Contributions to perceived organizational support and employee retention." Journal *of Applied Psychology,* 87: 565-573.

Gouldner, A. W. (1960) "The norm of reciprocity: A preliminary statement." *American Sociological Review,* 25: 161-178.

Greenberg, M. S. (1980) "A theory of indebtedness." In K. S. Gergen, M. S. Greenberg and R. H. Willis (Eds.), *Social exchange: Advances in theory and research:* 3-26, New York: Plenum Press.

Jarvenpaa, S. L. and Staples, D. S. (2001) "Exploring perceptions of organizational ownership of information and expertise." *Journal of Management Information Systems*, 18(1): 151-184.

Kaufman, J. D., Stamper, C. L. and Tesluk, P. E. (2001) "Do supportive organizations make for good corporate citizens?" *Journal of Managerial Issues*, 13: 436-449.

Kenny, D. A., Kashy, D. A., and Bolger, N. (1998) "Data analysis in social psychology." In D. T. Gilbert, S. T. Fiske and G. Lindzey (Eds.), *The handbook of social psychology Vol.1, 4th ed.*: 233-265, New York: McGraw-Hill.

Ladd, D. and Henry, R. A. (2000) "Helping co-workers and helping the organization: The role of support perceptions, exchange ideology and conscientiousness." *Journal of Applied Social Psychology*, 30 (10): 2028-2049.

McDermott, R. (1999) "Why information technology inspired but cannot deliver knowledge management." *California Management Review*, 41: 103-117.

McDermott, R., and O'Dell, C. (2001) "Overcoming cultural barriers to sharing knowledge." *Journal of Knowledge Management*, 5(1): 76-85.

Meso, P., and Smith, R. (2000) "A resource-based view of organizational knowledge management systems." *Journal of Knowledge Management*, 4: 224-234.

Organ, D. W. (1988) *Organizational Citizenship Behavior: The good solider syndrome.* Leighton Books: Massachusetts.

Paese, P. W. and Gilin, D. A. (2000) "When an adversary is caught telling the truth: Reciprocal cooperation versus self-interest in distributive bargaining." *Personality and Social Psychological Bulletin*, 26(1): 79-90.

Podsakoff, P. M. and MacKenzie, S. B. (1997) "The impact of organizational citizenship behavior on organizational performance: A review and suggestions for future research." *Human Performance*, 10: 133-151.

Rhoades, L. and Eisenberger, R. (2002) "Perceived organizational support: A review of the literature." *Journal of Applied Psychology*, 87(4): 698-714.

Robinson, S. (1996) "Trust and the breach of the psychological contract." *Administrative Science Quarterly*, 41: 574-599.

Robinson, S. L. and Morrison, E. W. (1995) "Psychological contracts and OCB: The effect of unfulfilled obligations and civic virtue behavior." *Journal of Organizational Behavior*, 16: 289-298.

Robinson, S. L. and Morrison, E. W. (2000) "The development of psychological contract breach and violation: A longitudinal study." *Journal of Organizational Behavior*, 21: 525-546.

Robinson, S. L. and Rousseau, D. M. (1994) "Violating the psychological contract: Not the exception but the norm." *Journal of Organizational Behavior*, 15: 245-259.

Rousseau, D. M. (1990) "New hire perceptions of their own and their employer's obligations: A study of psychological contracts." *Journal of Organizational Behavior*, 11: 389-400.

Williams, L. J. and Anderson, S. E. (1991) "Job satisfaction and organizational commitment as predictors of organizational citizenship and in-role behaviors." *Journal of Management*, 17 (3): 601-617.

INTRAORGANIZATIONAL KNOWLEDGE SHARING IN KNOWLEDGE INTENSIVE FIRMS

AKSHEY GUPTA

Microsoft Operations Pte Ltd, Singapore
aksheyg@microsoft.com

SNEJINA MICHAILOVA

Centre for Knowledge Governance and Department of International Economics and Management,
Copenhagen Business School, Denmark
michailova@cbs.dk

This paper is a study of the knowledge-sharing difficulties experienced by three departments in a knowledge-intensive firm, a global consulting firm that has been on the forefront of knowledge management and has won several knowledge management related international acclaims. Our analysis shows that there are strong disincentives in place for departments to share knowledge. We found that the nature of the businesses of the departments was very different and so were their knowledge requirements and the preferred ways to seek knowledge. Additionally, confidentiality agreements with clients and lack of cross-departmental interaction inhibited knowledge sharing beyond departmental boundaries. Contrary to the common belief in the organization, we found that one single IT system could not satisfy the context-specific knowledge-sharing needs of the different departments. We suggest that some very recent breakthrough technologies could be applied to facilitate cross-departmental knowledge sharing provided they are implemented at the strategic organizational level.

1   Introduction

To gain sustainable competitive advantage, it is imperative for global consulting companies to be knowledge-intensive, apply reuse economics, create knowledge and deliver quality to keep pace with the change. They need to harness knowledge and learn faster than competition. In order to achieve that, they need to effectively and efficiently organize and manage the processes of knowledge sharing internally in the organization.

In the context of this paper "knowledge" will be taken to mean "a fluid mix of framed experience, values, contextual information, and expert insight that provides a framework for evaluating and incorporating new experiences and information" (Davenport & Prusak 1998: 5). We adopt the definition of 'knowledge sharing' as providing one's knowledge to others as well as receiving knowledge from others (Davenport & Prusak 1998).

Knowledge sharing among departments within the same organization is in reality not as natural as it may appear at first glance. It is an ungrounded assumption that departments will share the knowledge they possess with others or tap into the collective corporate knowledge base in order to find a solution to their problem merely because such systems have been made available to them (Sbarcea 2001). Instead, knowledge-sharing hostility is a phenomenon that widely dominates organizational reality (Husted & Michailova 2002).

There are various difficulties in the process of knowledge sharing. First, knowledge is developed from the local level, e.g. by definition, knowledge sharing is embedded in a certain cognitive and behavioral context. Without understanding the context, one cannot inquire into the reasoning and the assumptions behind the particular piece of knowledge. Second, knowledge is asymmetrically distributed in any organization (Davenport & Prusak 1998; O'Dell & Grayson 1998). Third, knowledge sharing is voluntary (Dixon 2002) and efficient knowledge sharing depends on the willingness of individuals to identify the knowledge they possess and to share knowledge when required (Nonaka 1994). Knowledge sharing involves direct commitment from both transmitter and receiver. If the potential knowledge transmitter is not aware that someone in the organization would be interested in the knowledge she/he possesses, she/he will not actively share this knowledge. As human behavior is inherently opportunistic, adverse selection and moral hazard may influence the individual's motivation to share knowledge in a negative manner. Moreover, an individual's ability to appreciate new knowledge is a function of their "absorptive capacity" (Cohen & Levinthal 1990).

The present paper focuses on the difficulties of knowledge sharing across departments within the same organization. The firm we have studied is the Copenhagen branch of a global consulting company. The rest of the paper is organized as follows. First, we introduce the studied organization. We then present and discuss our data collection methods. We introduce a few selected theoretical frameworks and utilize them in the analysis of our empirical data. We conclude the paper by summing up the key points of our analysis and by suggesting solutions to the identified knowledge-sharing challenges.

2 The studied organization and its knowledge sharing challenges

ConCop (ConsultCopenhagen) is a fictional name for the Copenhagen branch of a large global consulting company (referred to here as ConGlobal). The Copenhagen branch is a part of the Northern Europe office, which, in turn, is a part of ConGlobal. ConGlobal has been on the knowledge management (KM) forefront since the beginning of the 1990s. It has several hundred full-time employees to manage its knowledge programs and over the years, it has received a number of awards as recognition of its KM related activities.

The aim of KM as defined at ConGlobal is supporting the overall strategy of the company, becoming recognized for delivering value to clients. Proper pursuit of this vision encompasses definition and fulfillment of different roles and functions, both internally, at the established Knowledge Center, and externally, in terms of assigning knowledge managers in different business units of the company.

ConCop employs 500 people. Among other departments, in ConCop there are three departments: Finance services department (FD), Audit services department (AD) and Mentor services department (MD). FD provides Mergers and Acquisitions and other advisory services. AD provides audit and business advisory services. MD services is a relatively new department, created in 2001 to help grow starting-up companies by tapping into ConGlobal's worldwide resources. MD services could provide knowledge on venture capital markets to a client company either by stepping on its own experience or by introducing the client to AD in order to offer audit services to it. However, due to lack of formal procedures for sharing knowledge of this type, MD services often find it tough to reach out to AD and FD. AD has wider industry exposure in Denmark than FD. Due to its larger market presence AD is aware of clients or non-clients requiring FD services. It also conducts in-depth industry analyses. If AD shares their knowledge on industry and targets with FD, FD could derive more business. In turn, FD often comes across clients that can be potential targets for AD. If FD were to share their knowledge on targets with AD, AD could generate more business too.

Despite KM initiatives in ConGlobal, there is a definite disconnect in the flow of knowledge between FD, MD and AD. Each department can see tremendous benefits from potential knowledge sharing and yet, the latter does not take place. The departments recognize that their resources are often being employed on similar tasks at different points in time which leads to additional costs and lower revenues.

3   Empirical data collection

Our data collection started with getting access to and studying thoroughly sizable written material available on KM in ConCop. We have used policy statements and other documents as a starting point for understanding the current KM structure.

Individual personal interviews were the next step of the data collection. In the context of the studied organization, the choice of the word "interview" was not most appropriate: since many knowledge-sharing issues border on organization culture and strategic direction, the interviewee can be confidential or apprehensive of the questions put forward and his/her replies. Therefore, in both internal mails and phone calls we always referred to "discussions on knowledge sharing", not "interviews". The discussions were conducted by one of the authors using an interview guide. The interview guide was designed as a questionnaire which was filled during the discussion by the interviewer. After filling out the questionnaire the interviewee was asked to attest his/her replies.

We opted to have middle managers as our primary respondents for two main reasons. First, in ConCop the existing KM systems are predominantly IT systems and middle managers utilize these systems most. Second, we expected to get a more realistic picture on knowledge sharing from the middle managers rather than from top-level executives since the latter ones tend to stick to official statements and "espoused values" rather than to the actual situation and "values in use".

Two main rounds of discussions were performed. All 21 interviews were tape-recorded. In case of any additional clarifications needed, the interviewer discussed them in an informal session with the interviewee.

4 Distributed knowledge

Knowledge is created by individuals and bounded by their mental models and reality perception. Knowledge is also deeply rooted in action and in an individual's commitment to a specific context – a craft or profession, a particular technology or product market, or the activities of a work group or a team (Nonaka 2000). While working in a team, part of the knowledge gets shared and goes into forming the "collective mind" (Weick & Roberts 1993) - lies between rather than within participating individuals (Spender 1996). The collective mind is manifested in the manner in which individuals inter-relate their actions (Weick & Roberts 1993). Consequently, a firm can be considered as sum of the participating individuals' knowledge. So, if a firm is considered as a group of teams, the organizational knowledge should be located in the collective mind of these teams. Unless these teams interact, organizational knowledge will remain in the isolated pools of collective mind. Not only that, even when the teams interact, the knowledge sharing will be partial because no individuals in the teams possess all knowledge in the collective mind of their team.

Knowledge sharing involves socialization, articulation, combination and internalization (Nonaka 2000). Tacit knowledge sharing is possible only through strong ties (Hansen 1999). Assuming that a team working together has strong ties, tacit knowledge created by team members inside each one's head can be shared through the process described by Nonaka (2000) among team members. Following Hansen's (1999) argument, it cannot be shared across the organization as the team does not have strong ties within the whole organization. This knowledge will be different from knowledge created in another team and so on. Thus there will be knowledge pools in the organization. This tie in with the distributed knowledge system approach (Tsoukas 1996): a firm can be seen as a collection of teams, where knowledge systems are decentralized systems.

5 The codification personalization dilemma

The initial push for the growth of the interest in KM is associated with the development of IT (Scarbrough *et al.* 1999). Some scholars (e.g. Knights *et al.* 1993; Ruhleder 1995) view knowledge as being inseparable from the development of contemporary technologies. Others have considered technology as an important enabler in KM (Davenport 1997; Ruggles 1998; O'Dell & Grayson 1998) by focusing on sharing explicit knowledge through groupware, databases, portals and other formal knowledge repositories (Zack 1999). Zuboff (1996) argues that technologies are fully imbuing tasks of every sort and providing even more powerful opportunities for the kind of learning that translates into value creation.

A number of assumptions underlying these approaches have, however, been challenged by pointing out that KM relies heavily upon social patterns, practices and processes and goes far beyond computer-based technologies and infrastructures (Davenport & Prusak 1998; Coleman 1999; Liebowitz 1999). Empirical evidence on inhibitors to knowledge sharing stresses the importance of behavioral and cultural factors rather than to outline reasons associated with technology (Skyrme & Amidon 1997; De Long & Fahey 2000). The tension between technology dominance and interpersonal dynamics in knowledge sharing is reflected in the distinction between codification and personalization (Hansen *et al.* 1999)

Codification is based on technologies, such as intranets, electronic repositories, databases, etc. Personalization emphasizes knowledge sharing among individuals, groups and organizations through social networking and/or engaging in "communities of practice" or "epistemic communities" (Brown & Duguid 2000; Hansen *et al.* 1999; Wenger 2000). Social and interpersonal aspects seem to override technology-based and procedural mechanisms in terms of "meaningful KM" (Hansen *et al.* 1999). McDermott (1999: 104) concludes that the great trap in KM is using information management tools and concepts to design KM systems.

The above pointed distinctions are useful provided there is an unquestionable agreement regarding tacit and explicit knowledge, existing and new knowledge, and weak and strong ties: not in terms of what they mean in general, but rather what they mean where, when, and to whom.

6   Analysis

We develop the analysis of knowledge sharing in ConCop by taking FD as the knowledge recipient and AD and MD activities as knowledge transmitters to FD. Similarly, either AD or MD can be considered as a recipient and the respective analysis can be conducted.

Our analysis of the interview data suggests that the FD knowledge requirements are of two types: knowledge on targets and knowledge on industry. We have identified the following knowledge sources:

- Personal networks like counterparts in other offices, industry experts etc.
- External sources and internal sources like Knowledge Center reports etc.

The major knowledge requirements of FD are met through networks and external sources – not through internal sources like reports, documents, databases and the like. AD and MD can provide the knowledge required by FD if they can contribute either knowledge on targets or knowledge on industry through either of the channels – personal networks and external sources that FD employs. Knowledge that will help FD can be shared in one of the following ways:

- Knowledge on targets through Codification or Personalization
- Knowledge on industry through Codification or Personalization

Knowledge on targets through codification is considered in ConCop either highly inefficient or not suitable. Regarding the possibility to share knowledge on targets and industry through personalization, we have observed that FD professionals do not interact with other departments in the firm. Several AD audit professionals admitted that they "do not know anything except that there is a FD in this house". Since no systems are involved in this process, the reason for not sharing through personalization can be expected to be more that of 'intent' than lack of systems.

AD and FD provide very different services. Consequently, it would be logical to expect that their knowledge requirements will differ too. This issue was clarified in the interviews when audit professionals confirmed to using the internal sources as rarely as FD professionals. Table 1 summarizes some of the key differences in business activity between the two departments. The third column lists the implications on knowledge requirements. The table helps in establishing why sharing industry knowledge between these two departments through codification is difficult.

Table 1 : Comparison of AD and FD business and the consequences for knowledge seeking

No.	AD	FD	Implications on knowledge requirement
1	Audit is a localized business driven by local laws and regulations for local companies. ConDenmark caters to many mid-size audit clients	FD services are more often regional than local. Buyers or sellers of companies looking for M&A services could be located in any part of Europe or another part of the world	FD would require wider industry knowledge than AD
2	Audit work focuses on client operations	FD work focuses on client strategy	Knowledge required for industry or a company would be of strategic type for FD than for Audit
3	AD sells high involvement service	FD sells very high involvement services	For FD, clients always look for references – contacts in the industry
4	AD engagement lasts for a number of years	Usual engagement is short-term, at the most a few months	FD has shorter time frame to acquire wider industry, sub-sector, company knowledge than AD
5	There is considerable time lag between changes in the environment and their effect on the way audit is done	Since engagement time is shorter and the involvement is high, time is scarce	Knowledge life time is shorter for FD. FD needs a strong network that can constantly feed it the new knowledge
6	AD draws regular income from clients	FD engagement is based on success fee	There is less margin of error and shorter time to gain back lost trust in case of any issue
7	AD interacts with middle management	FD interacts with top management	This puts greater pressure on FD for delivering the right knowledge all the time

As can be seen from above, FD requires knowledge that is different from AD in at least two dimensions. First, it requires more time-dependent, complex and wider industry knowledge due to its short engagements. Second, it requires better information on its networks both due to its interaction with top management and high involvement services and due to its requirement to remain better informed of the changes in the environment.

Based on discussions with AD and FD executives as well as observations on the nature of the business of the two departments, we can conclude that FD is exposed to a much more unstable environment with many more unpredictable factors at every point. Using Malhotra's (2003) framework, we argue that FD needs a Model 2 based KMS whereas AD would profit from exercising a Model 1 based KMS. Hence, there is good justification in that maybe its not just the 'intent' but the system itself is incompetent for such dynamic and complex knowledge sharing.

On top of above, HR executives confirmed that there are no incentives to AD for sharing knowledge or for introducing clients that need Type 2 services (services sold by FD) to FD. Additionally, incorporating incentives for selling Type 2 services will be against the new corporate governance rules being adopted in international business. Discussions with interviewees have led us to conclude that this area constitutes a potential minefield. Therefore, as a background and support for further discussion, it is essential to consider the following brief from ConGlobal Knowledge Sharing Policy document: "*generally avoid entering into agreements with clients that restrict our ability to share knowledge beyond what is required to protect client-confidential information*".

AD maintains that confidentiality clause necessitates that Type 2 services not be sold to Type 1 clients (customers already being served with Type 1 services but potential clients or targets for FD); As a result AD executives protect their clients. However, FD maintains that there are certain Type 2 services that can be sold to audit clients – they maintain this as the case particularly in Denmark. Both these arguments are supported by the knowledge sharing policy document.

The policy statement in italics above on the one hand espouses knowledge sharing while simultaneously expects confidentiality to be maintained. This generates twos ets of employees – one, those who leave this potential minefield completely unexplored and the other, those who are forced to walk a very thin line. This situation leads to impasse and we can clearly see the disincentives to share knowledge are in place.

AD has the knowledge on clients as well as on industry. Since AD assumes the worst-case scenario, they refuse to share knowledge also on their industry expertise. This leads to a serious interaction gap. There can be a win-win situation provided both parties agree to share the knowledge that is present in public domain instead of choosing not to explore the minefield altogether.

FD has strong ties (Granovetter 1973) within the department that are good for problem solving and idea generation (Hansen 1999). The ties which will be established as people locate competencies in the network will be weak ties that can assist bringing non-redundant knowledge into the group. Several of our interviewees currently use lists to locate experts outside their groups within ConGlobal to share knowledge. The frequency of such interaction on an average is about once a fortnight per person interviewed. The frequency is much higher for senior than junior executives. We found no evidence relating to regular cross-department interactions. In fact, several people in AD have no information on the people in FD.

This raises two concerns. First, the frequency of interaction is highly limited and is limited to among similar groups. Second, the two departments are far from visible to each other. Littlepage (1995) found that individual perception of others' expertise is closely related to the rate of others' participation in the discussion rather than their actual expertise. Therefore, it is important that members of an organization looking for active interaction should signal their counterparts by making themselves visible.

At this point of our analysis, we bring in the third department under consideration, MD services. This is a relatively new department which aims to help grow a starting up company by tapping into worldwide resources of ConGlobal. MD services could provide knowledge on venture capital markets or introduce the client to the FD department if a need for raising capital arises or if the company wants to buy or sell a part or in full. This is a clear business opportunity that MD services can bring to FD's table. However, our discussions with FD professionals have shown that taking up business with starting up companies is not cost-effective for them. FD could maintain a database of solutions which can help FD in picking up the closest solution it has for a particular requirement at a MD company and then customize it to the client's satisfaction. But such a suggestion will take the discussion back to Malhotra's (2003) Model 1 that has already been proven less applicable in FD's case. On the other hand, FD can share knowledge on targets that might be of interest to MD. Also, FD and MD can share knowledge on industry with each other. All our informal discussions have proven this observation to be correct. FD and AD can leverage on the knowledge of relationships that MD services can provide due to its strategic position that helps it connect to the venture capital industry and private equity investment community. This is the knowledge on relationships in the market that FD will be most willing to take up.

As claimed by DiMaggio and Louch (1998), buyers tend to prefer social relations to make purchases of one-time items. According to them, within networks exchange reduces buyer risk by imposing cost on sellers who take advantage of opportunities internal to the exchange. The commercial transaction is embedded in a multiplex network of ongoing interactions, so that the actors' behavior in the commercial exchange influences the way in which he or she is treated by many different actors across a range of interactions extending well into the future. This implies that buyers are more willing to buy such services from within their network. Seen from a FD perspective, it will be easier for FD department to sell services if they have a relationship with the target. DiMaggio and Louch (1998) also state that people who transact with members of their social relations are more likely to report high levels of satisfaction with the product or service they receive. This, in turn, implies that from a sum total of such transactions, it is likely that FD departments will always end up with positive points. This will add up to both a larger network and positive future references which in turn, can potentially drive the business in an upward rising spiral.

Apart from personal networks, this analysis can be done on the basis of organizational networks. According to Uzzi (1996), organization networks operate on logic of exchange which differs from the logic of markets. He refers to this exchange logic as "embeddedness" because ongoing social ties shape actors' expectations and opportunities in ways that differ from the economic logic of market behavior. The level of embeddedness in an exchange system produces opportunities and constraints that are particular to network forms of organizations and that result in outcomes not predicted by standard economic explanations.

MD services has a vast network of angel investors, venture capital companies and private equity companies who invest in companies that may be start-ups or later stage companies. MD services can regularly draw on the networks of its investors and feed any contacts that they may have to FD and AD. If FD was to leverage this network, it is very likely that in a small economy like Denmark, they will find relationships that help them grow their business. Following Uzzi (1996), embeddedness shifts actors' motivations away from the narrow pursuit of immediate economic gains toward the enrichment of relationships through trust and reciprocity. Trust helps reduce transactional uncertainty and creates opportunities for the exchange of goods and services that are difficult to price or enforce contractually. Larson (1992) reported that "thicker information" on strategy, know-how and profit margins is transferred through embedded ties, thus promoting learning and integrated production in ways that the exchange of only price data cannot. Thus we conclude that for all 3 departments there is serious business potential in practicing relationship capital building together and in accepting knowledge on social networks from each other.

7   Conclusions and proposed solutions

Knowledge sharing among the three studied departments in ConCop is hindered by a few important factors. First it is the different nature of the everyday business activities they are engaged in. FD operates in a more unstable business environment than AD and therefore, the current IT-based KM system does not yield outcomes acceptable to FD. For its KM strategy, FD needs to differentiate between IT and KM and employ IT for sharing of explicit knowledge only.

The nature of the business of the three departments predispose different requirements to the type of knowledge sought as well as different preferences to how the needed knowledge is obtained. We have identified three clusters of people in this respect. The first group sought knowledge to speed up certain processes. The second group was looking for standard templates to be used to save time to perform well-documented tasks. The third group was not looking for knowledge on a particular topic but for a peer who possessed the needed specific knowledge. Their cost of searching the database for real nuggets of knowledge, making sense of the document and then applying it to the situation at hand far exceeded the cost of finding and contacting the expert and taking first-hand advice.

Second hindrance to cross-departmental knowledge sharing is the way codification and personalization is utilized by the different departments. Knowledge sharing on industry through codification is difficult since the knowledge requirements of the departments differ. Knowledge sharing on industry and targets through personalization is difficult because of confidentiality agreements with the clients. Knowledge sharing on targets through codification was considered unfeasible.

Last, the current KMSs in ConCop heavily rely on IT databases - they are mammoth, structured and therefore too slow to provide new knowledge required by the departments.

If it is knowledge of networks that can drive the business, then why is this knowledge not harnessed? We found a possible answer in an ongoing research project entitled "small world project" in the field of social networks by Watts *et al.* (2002). Their research shows that any individual can reach any other individual in the world in short chains of social ties.

According to Watts *et al.* (2002), despite the "it's a small world after all" phenomenon and the "six degrees" theory of social connection, people still appear largely disconnected because they only have local information on networks. People tend to limit the members in their immediate group to a number that is cognitively manageable. However lately certain break through social networking concepts have been used to create IT applications.

With support from these new IT tools, it is possible to virtually scan all the personal networks in an organization to exploit the value in relationships. This new emerging field of social network analysis and tools, also called relationship capital management, is in our view the best tool to be employed to increase knowledge sharing between the departments. The best way to share industry knowledge would be to share competencies in a network. This would enable department teams to interact outside their closed group to bring in new information not only from their own groups in other offices but also from other industry sources known to other departments. The new knowledge from this interaction will help increase the respective groups' situated expertise, which, in turn, will most likely increase group performance. It is also likely that increased group performance will make the departments more visible to each other. This can potentially build more confidence and trust among departments and will possibly in the future bring more revenues.

The IT systems we propose are related to sharing knowledge based on competencies and relationships, a kind of knowledge which is explicit and can be shared as suggested by Malhotra (2003) whereas the IT systems we discount, particularly in case of FD, are systems trying to enable sharing tacit knowledge. The knowledge is changing faster than the systems can keep up with. Therefore we need systems that can be kept locally, need no maintenance, are self-driven and are very simple to use. Social networking applications suggested by us are exactly such systems that can help all three departments leverage their explicit knowledge to the maximum and also help bring in new actors to increase tacit knowledge sharing.

References

Brown, J. S. & Duguid, P. 2000. Balancing act: How to capture knowledge without killing it. *Harvard Business Review*, May-June: 73-80.

Cohen, W. M. & Levinthal, D. A. 1990. Absorptive Capacity: A new perspective on learning and innovation, *Administrative Science Quarterly*, 35: 128-152.

Coleman, S. 1998. *Knowledge management: Linchpin of change*. London: ASLIB.

Davenport, T. H. 1997. *Some principles of knowledge management.* Working paper.

Davenport, T. H. & Prusak, L. 1998. *Working knowledge: How organizations manage what they know.* Boston, MA: Harvard Business School Press.

De Long, D. W. & Fahey, L. 2000. Diagnosing cultural barriers to knowledge management. *Academy of Management Executive.* 14(4): 113-127.

DiMaggio, P. & Louch, H. 1998. Socially embedded consumer transactions: for what kinds of purchases do people most often use networks? *American Sociological Review,* 63(5).

Dixon. N. M. 2002. *Common knowledge: How companies thrive by sharing what they know.* Boston: Harvard Business Press.

Granovetter, M. 1973. The strength of weak ties, *American Journal of Sociology,* 78: 1360-1380.

Hansen, M. T. 1999. The search transfer problem: The role of weak ties in sharing knowledge across organizational sub-units. *Administrative Science Quarterly,* 44: 82-111.

Hansen, M. T.; Nohria, N. & Tierney, T. 1999. What's your strategy for managing knowledge? *Harvard Business Review,* March-April, 106-115.

Husted, K. & Michailova, S. 2002. Diagnosing and fighting knowledge sharing hostility. *Organizational Dynamics,* 31(1): 60-73.

Knights, D.; Murray, F. & Willmott, H. 1993. Networking as knowledge work: A study of strategic inter-organizational development in the financial services industry. *Journal of Management Studies,* 30(6): 975-995.

Larson, Andrea. 1992. Network Dyads in Entrepreneurial settings: A study of the governance of exchange relationships. *Administrative Science Quarterly.* 37(1).

Liebowitz, J. (Ed.) 1999. *Knowledge management handbook.* London: CRC Press.

Littlepage, G. E., Schmidt, G. W., Eric, W. & Frost, A.G. 1995. An input-output analysis of influence and performance in problem solving groups, *Journal of Personality and Social Psychology,* 69.

Malhotra, Y. 2003. Knowledge management lessons learned: what works and what doesn't. *Information Today* Medford N.J.

McDermott, R. 1999. Why information technology inspired but cannot deliver knowledge management. *California Management Review,* 41(4): 103-117.

Nonaka, I., Ryoko, T. & Akiya, N. 2000. A firm as a knowledge creating entity: a new perspective on the theory of the firm. *Industrial and Corporate Change,* 9(1).

O'Dell, C. & Grayson, C. J. 1998. If only we knew what we know: Identification and transfer of internal best practices. *California Management Review,* 40(3): 154-174.

Ruggles, R. 1998. The state of notion: Knowledge management in practice. *California Management Review,* 40(3): 80-89.

Ruhleder, K. 1995. Computerization and changes to infrastructures for knowledge work. *The Information Society,* 11(2): 131-144.

Sbarcea, K. 2001. The mystery of knowledge management. *New Zealand Management,* 48(10).

Scarbrough, H.; Swan, J. & Preston, J. 1999. *Knowledge management: A review of the literature.* London: Institute of Personnel and Development.

Skyrme, D. J. & Amidon, D. M. 1997. *Creating the knowledge-based business.* London: Business Intelligence.

Spender, J.-C. 1996. Organizational knowledge, learning and memory: Three concepts in search of a theory. *Journal of Organizational Change Management,* 9(1): 63-78.

Tsoukas, H. 1996. The firm as a distributed knowledge system: A constructivist approach. *Strategic Management Journal,* 17: 11-25.

Uzzi, B. 1996. The sources and consequences of embedded ness for the economic performance of organizations: the network effect, *American Sociological Review,* 61(4).

Watts, D.J., Dodds, P.S., & Newman, M. E. J. 2002. Identity and search in social networks, *Science*, 29(6).

Weick, K. E. & Roberts, K. H. 1993. Collective mind in organizations: Heedful interrelating on. *Administrative Science Quarterly*. 38(3).

Wenger, E. 2000. Communities of practice and social learning systems. *Organization*, 7(2): 225-246.

Zack, M. H. 1999. Managing codified knowledge. *Sloan Management Review*, 40(4): 45-58.

Zuboff, S. 1996. The emperor's new information economy, in W. J. Orlikowski, G. Walsham, M. R. Jones & J. I. De Gross (Eds.) *Information technology and changes in organizational work.* London: Chapman & Hall.

PREDICTING KNOWLEDGE SHARING ON KNOWLEDGE MANAGEMENT SYSTEMS

SCOTT KREBS & PRASHANT BORDIA

School of Psychology, University of Queensland,
Brisbane, QLD 4072, Australia

Knowledge management systems (KMS) enable the codification and transfer of individual and organizational knowledge across a firm. Used effectively, KMS can promote organizational learning and thus develop a firm's competitive advantage. However, many KMS implementations have been unsuccessful, as important contextual factors of knowledge and its management is neglected in both research and practice. The purpose of this paper is to stimulate KMS research by proposing a theoretical model, which aims to predict knowledge sharing on to electronic databases. As knowledge sharing largely relies on employees' willingness to share, we theorize that social and organizational influences will be critical factors in employees' intention to contribute to databases. Practical implications of the model are discussed.

1   Introduction

To generate value from individual and organizational expertise, firms must develop strategies for systematically *capturing* and *sharing* the knowledge residing in the organization. Information and communication technologies, in the form of knowledge management systems (KMS), have been proposed as effective tools to support knowledge sharing (Alavi and Leidner 1999). KMS codify employees' knowledge into structural assets owned by the organization and make this knowledge available to all levels of the firm. However, many KMS implementations have been unsuccessful with failure rates above 80% reported in KM literature (Schultze and Boland 2000). Moreover, field studies in diverse settings indicate that employees frequently resist sharing their knowledge on KMS (Ciborra and Patriota 1998). There is a dearth of empirical research examining the determinants of knowledge sharing in organizations and there is a need for further understanding of the barriers and facilitators of staff contributions to KMS (Irmer *et al.* 2002).

Employee acceptance of information systems (IS) is a necessary condition for system success, and may lead to an enhanced organizational performance (Venkatesh 2000). However, staff resistance to IS is a widespread problem and can result in undesirable consequences such as financial losses and dissatisfaction among employees (Venkatesh 2000). IS research has generally focused on individuals' perception of how beneficial the system is to the individual and how easy the system is to use (Mahmood *et al.* 2001). This research places less emphasis on important social factors affecting system use, such as influences of workgroup norms, and organizational factors, such as perceptions of support from the firm. A fundamental reason why KMS implementations might fail is that system designers do not consider social and cultural dimensions of knowledge and its management (Davenport and Prusak 1998; Malhorta 2003).

The aim of this paper is to propose a theoretical model of the social and organizational predictors of knowledge sharing on KMS. The KMS we refer to in this paper are electronic databases, as they are the most widely implemented KMS (Wachter 2000). The proposed model offers a starting point for empirical research on the determinants of knowledge sharing on KMS. We seek to make several contributions to extant literature with the present paper. We begin by framing the sharing of knowledge on KMS as a voluntary contribution of knowledge directed towards and greatly benefiting the organization. The paper extends KM literature by investigating social and organizational predictors of knowledge sharing. We apply and extend recent work on technology acceptance literature by incorporating managerial endorsement and support as an important antecedent to system use. We also draw on recent conceptualizations on group normative influence and the moderating role of group identity. We begin the paper by providing a definition of knowledge sharing on KMS.

1.1 A Definition of Knowledge Sharing on KMS

Knowledge is defined as "a fluid mix of framed experience, important values, contextual information, and expert insight that provides a framework for evaluating and incorporating new experiences and information" (Davenport and Prusak 1998, p.5). The current paper conceptualizes knowledge as an object that can be collected, stored, organized, and disseminated. It is generally acknowledged that there are two forms of knowledge: *explicit* and *tacit*. Explicit knowledge is easily communicated and can be found in books, documents, databases and policy manuals, while tacit knowledge is contained in people's minds and includes specific information, experiences and memories, and is not as easily communicated (Gore and Gore 1999). Not all types of knowledge can be codified on KMS, and thus the utilization of knowledge is dependent on the individual's willingness to share, especially if the transfer requires time and personal contact (Leonard and Sensiper 1998). As tacit knowledge is most effectively transferred through collaboration, shared experience, and rich interpersonal interactions over time (Alavi 2000), KMS are designed to enable the management of explicit knowledge. Thus, we will be concerned with the sharing of explicit knowledge in our model.

Interpersonal knowledge sharing is defined as the voluntary behavior of making knowledge available to others when one does not have to (Jarvenpaa and Staples 2001). In the KMS context, knowledge sharing will be viewed as a voluntary contribution to the firms KMS – this will be operationalized in the form of a database entry. In this regard, knowledge sharing on KMS can be framed as an organizational citizenship behavior (OCB; Organ 1988). OCB is extrarole behavior that is voluntary, not formally rewarded by the organization, and contributes to the firm's effectiveness and success (Podsakoff and MacKenzie 1997). OCB literature distinguishes between OCB directed at either an individual (OCB-I) or towards the organization (OCB-O). Thus, when employees voluntarily share their knowledge on to KMS they are making a generalized exchange with their organization (an OCB-O). In summary, employees share knowledge on to KMS by making voluntarily contributions of explicit knowledge to KMS in the form of database entries. This knowledge is made available across the firm.

2   A Model of Knowledge Sharing on KMS

System characteristics (such as perceptions of usefulness and system user friendliness) are well documented in technology acceptance literature as influencing IS use (for a review see Mahamood *et al.* 2001). However, a number of barriers may constrain individuals' motivation to share knowledge. For example, a lack of monetary incentive (e.g., Alavi and Leidner 1999), insufficient time to share (e.g., Weiss 1999), a lack of recognition or praise (e.g., Weiss 1999), a poor knowledge sharing culture of the firm (e.g., McDermott and O'Dell 2001), the geographic dispersion of knowledge workers (Alavi 2000), and the fear of being evaluated by knowledge seekers (Irmer *et al.* 2002) influence knowledge sharing behavior. These motivational barriers suggest that an understanding of KMS contributions requires examination of factors additional to the system. Figure 1 presents a schematic representation of the proposed model of knowledge sharing on KMS.

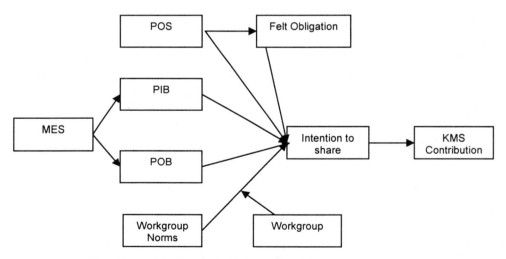

Figure 1. A model of knowledge sharing on knowledge management systems.

The proposed model consists of intentions (intention to share knowledge), system-related perceptions (i.e., perceived individual benefit; PIB) and perceived organizational benefit; POB), social influences (i.e., workgroup norms and managerial endorsement and support; MES), and organizational influences (i.e., perceived organizational support; POS). Intention to share knowledge is posited to directly influence staff contributions to

KMS. Five factors are proposed to influence employees' intention to share knowledge: PIB, POB, workgroup norms, POS and felt obligation. The relationship between POS and staff contributions to KMS will be mediated by employees' felt obligation to the firm. Managerial endorsement and support is proposed to influence both PIB and POB. Finally, the impact of workgroup norms will be moderated by employees' workgroup identification. That is, for individuals who identify weakly with their workgroup there is no relationship between workgroup norms and intention to share knowledge, and for individuals who identify strongly with their workgroup there will be a positive relationship between workgroup norms and intention to share knowledge. In the following sections, we develop propositions about these factors and their relationships with knowledge sharing on KMS.

2.1 Intentions

Individuals' intention to perform a specified behavior (such as intention to vote) is a strong predictor of their actual performance of the behavior (Armitage and Conner 2001). Intentions are assumed to summarize the motivational factors that influence performance of a behavior (Ajzen 1991). They directly indicate how hard people are willing to try or how much effort they are planning to exert to perform that behavior. According to technology acceptance literature, intention to use an IS is a strong predictor of actual system use (Legris *et al.* 2002). Thus, individuals who intended to use an IS are likely to use that system. The relationship between intentions and actual IS usage behavior is robust across technologies, settings, time and populations (Chin and Todd 1995). Consistent with extensive research linking intentions and system use, we propose that employees' intention to share knowledge on KMS will directly influence their actual contributions of knowledge.

Proposition 1: Intention to share knowledge on KMS will be positively related to individuals' actual contributions to KMS.

2.2 System-related perceptions

2.2.1 Perceived benefits

IS research generally focuses on system-related perceptions, such as an individual's perceived benefit of using a particular system. Perceived benefit refers to perceptions of the benefits derived from using an IS. Two forms of *individual* benefit may arise from contributing to a KMS. First, employees may derive financial reward or recognition and praise from making knowledge contributions. KM literature is replete with case studies and anecdotal evidence which suggest that incentive schemes to reward knowledge sharing fosters a culture of sharing (e.g., Alavi and Leidner 1999; Weiss 1999). Second, staff may receive benefits through an increased job performance. Technology acceptance literature examines the concept of perceived usefulness, which refers to the degree to which employees believe that using a system would enhance their job performance

(Davis 1986). In line with IS research we propose that PIB will influence employees' intention to share knowledge on to KMS.

Individuals' contributing knowledge to electronic databases may perceive little enhancement to their job performance – as it is other staff members who may benefit from acquiring the knowledge. The organization ultimately benefits when employees utilize knowledge on KMS through improved organizational learning. When making a voluntary contribution of knowledge to a database, staff may be more influenced by whether they believe that sharing will add value to the organization's effectiveness. Thus, we introduce a new concept for KMS researchers to consider as a driver of knowledge sharing: *perceived organizational benefit*. This concept has been neglected in IS and KM research.

Knowledge management is based on the premise that individual and work team performance will increase through the more effective utilization of organizational knowledge (Sveiby 1997). Employees may engage in OCB-O such as knowledge sharing on to KMS if they believe that it will facilitate organizational performance. The premise behind this argument is that employees will be more likely to engage in knowledge sharing if they can see the instrumentality in doing so (Van Erde and Thierry 1996). Thus, we theorize that the more a KMS is perceived to impact organizational effectives, the more likely staff will be to share knowledge on to the system.

Proposition 2: The perceived individual benefit of contributing knowledge to KMS will be positively related to individuals' intention to share knowledge on KMS.

Proposition 3: The perceived organizational benefit of contributing knowledge to KMS will be positively related to individuals' intention to share knowledge on KMS.

2.3 Social Influences

Social influences to share knowledge may arise from two sources within the organization: co-workers and management. The next section discusses the impact of employees' work peers on their knowledge contributions. The following section describes management support as a determinant of knowledge contributions.

2.3.1 Workgroup normative influences

Technology acceptance literature has received criticism because it pays little attention to social influence factors, such as workgroup norms, in its prediction of system use (Malhotra and Galletta 1999). Norms are shared beliefs about what is the appropriate behavior for group members and provide guidance for members to determine whether certain patterns of behavior are acceptable within a given context. Recent extensions to technology usage models have found that in addition to its effects on intentions, social influence has an important relationship with beliefs about the usefulness of a technology (Venkatesh and Davis 2000). However, other studies have found no relationship between social influence variables and beliefs about the usefulness of a technology (Lewis *et al.* 2003). Lewis and colleagues (2003) argued that moderator variables should be investigated to clarify the relationship between social influence variables and other constructs in IS research.

To account for these contradictory findings we draw upon developments in the literature on normative influence (Terry and Hogg 1996). Behavioral norms have recently been proposed to provide an important role in the prediction of intentions. Behavioral norms refer to the extent to which significant others are perceived to perform the behavior themselves (Nucifora *et al.* 1993). This differs from traditional conceptualizations of norms, which refers to perceptions of what people *ought* to do (e.g. Ajzen 1991). Moreover, recent literature on normative influence has interpreted the role of group influences in light of the social identity theory (SIT; Tajfel and Turner 1979). SIT proposes that normative influences will be moderated by the extent to which people identify with their group. People who strongly identify with their group are posited to comply with the norms of their group more than people who weakly identify with their group (Terry and Hogg 1996).

To summarize, individuals are more likely to engage in a particular behavior if it is in accord with the norms of a behaviorally relevant group (such as a workgroup), particularly if the individual identifies strongly with the reference group. Thus, SIT proposes that staff will be influenced by the behavioral norms of their workgroup members, and that this effect would be more pronounced for people who strongly identify with their workgroup.

Proposition 4: Behavioral workgroup norms regarding knowledge sharing on KMS will be positively related to intentions to contribute knowledge.

Proposition 5: The relationship between behavioral workgroup norms and intention to contribute knowledge will be moderated by individuals' identification with the workgroup. That is, for individuals who identify weakly with their workgroup there is no relationship between workgroup norms and intention to share knowledge, and for individuals who identify strongly with their workgroup there will be a positive relationship between workgroup norms and intention to share knowledge.

2.3.2 Managerial endorsement and support

Recently, organizational or management support has been proposed to be a critical variable for increasing technology acceptance and usage (Venkaseth and Davis 2000; Lewis *et al.* 2003). The attitudes and behaviors of management are proposed to influence the perceptions and attitudes of their staff. Organizational support is defined as the extent to which "the organization and its management support the implementation and use of IT systems" (Mahmood *et al.* 2001, p. 108). Organizational support has been operationalized in a variety of ways including managerial encouragement, educational opportunities, and the availability of user-friendly software. To account for the variety of organizational support variables in the literature, we propose a broad definition of system-related support referred to as *managerial endorsement and support*. Managerial endorsement and support is employees' overall perception of the extent to which the organization provides support for the system. It addresses factors such as employees' perceptions of the extent to which the system is 'championed' by management; perceptions of the extent that the system is advertised; training opportunities provided by management; and other implementation issues for example employee involvement in system design.

The impact of management support on IS usage is mainly derived through an individual's perception of system usefulness (Igbaria *et al.* 1997). For example, Lewis and colleagues (2003) found that top management commitment enhanced employees' usefulness beliefs. System-related support serves as an indication of how important the system is perceived to be in the organizational context. Management support influences employee's beliefs that the IS is beneficial for individual and organizational effectiveness and that its use will be normatively valued and instrumentally rewarded (Pruvis *et al.* 2000). Thus, organizations that expend great effort in providing computer and management support are sending a strong signal to employees that they are expected to use the system, and that its use will result in individual and organizational performance improvements. Therefore, managerial endorsement and support will be positively related to PIB and POB.

Proposition 6: Individuals' perception of the extent to which the organization supports the KMS will be positively related to their perception of how beneficial the system is to the individual.

Proposition 7: Individuals' perception of the extent to which the organization supports the KMS will be positively related to their perception of how beneficial the system is to the organization.

2.4 Organizational influences

2.4.1 Perceived organizational support

Perceived organizational support (POS; Eisenberger *et al.* 1986) refers to the inferences made by employees about the extent to which the firm values their contributions and cares about their well-being (Rhoades and Eisenberger 2002). Employees are proposed to reciprocate such perceived support with increased commitment, loyalty and performance (Rhoades and Eisenberger 2002). POS differs from perceptions of managerial endorsement and support discussed earlier. Managerial endorsement and support refers to system-specific support provided by management, whereas POS refers to support from the organization in any facet of the work context. Consequences of POS for employees, identified in a meta-analysis, include an obligation to care about the organization's welfare and strengthened beliefs that the organization recognizes and rewards increased performance (Rhoades and Eisenberger 2002). The concept of reciprocity is fundamental to these consequences. That is, if employees have received positive outcomes from the organization in the past, then they are more likely to help the organization with its future endeavors. Employees' perception of organizational support has not been investigated in relation to system acceptance and usage.

Employees who feel that they are supported by the organization may, over time, reciprocate and reduce the imbalance in the relationship by engaging in organizational citizenship behaviors (OCB). For example, POS is positively related to organizational spontaneity (Eisenberger *et al.* 2001), which refers to OCB such as aiding fellow employees, offering constructive suggestions, and gaining knowledge and skills beneficial to the organization. A study of both a manufacturing and service firm found that POS encourages OCB that are directed towards the organization (OCB-O) such as sharing ideas for new projects, rather than those citizenship behaviors that benefit specific individuals directly, such as coworkers and supervisors (Kaufman *et al.* 2001). As previously mentioned, sharing knowledge on KMS is an OCB directed toward the firm (OCB-O) as it is voluntary, not formally rewarded, and involves a generalized exchange with a large audience. Thus, it is predicted that employees with higher levels of POS will share more knowledge on KMS than employees with low levels of POS.

2.4.2 Felt obligation

Felt obligation, or the compulsion of individuals to care about the organization's welfare and help it reach its objectives, is a concept that has been proposed to mediate the positive relationship between POS and OCB. For example, research has found that felt obligation mediates the relationship between POS and organizational spontaneity (Eisenberger *et al.* 2001). These results support the relationship between employees' perceptions of favorable treatment and their felt obligation to aid the organization. POS may create trust that the firm will fulfill its exchange obligations by noticing and rewarding employee efforts made on its behalf (Eisenberger *et al.* 1990). Therefore this sense of obligation will result in higher intentions to share knowledge on a KMS. Based on past research, we make two predictions. First, POS is predicted to influence employees' intention to share knowledge on to KMS. Second, felt obligation is proposed to mediate the relationship between POS and intention to share knowledge.

Proposition 8: POS will be positively related to individuals' sharing their knowledge on KMS.

Proposition 9: Individuals' felt obligation to the firm will mediate the positive relationship between POS and knowledge contributions on KMS.

3 Summary and conclusions

This paper makes several contributions to extant KM literature. First, it provides theoretical development to an understudied area of KM literature. There is a paucity of research examining the determinants of staff contributions to KMS. The paper proposes a comprehensive model of factors influencing knowledge contributions. Second, the model presents a set of testable propositions from which empirical research can spawn. The propositions set forth in this paper highlight that staff contributions require an understanding of system-related perceptions, social influences, and organizational influences. Third, KM practitioners may take heed of the central tenet of this paper. A

KMS driven by technology and not by people will be doomed for failure. KMS implementations must be part of a wider KM strategy that promotes knowledge sharing. We believe that a number of the factors included in the model will positively impact knowledge sharing. For example, management has an important role in establishing some of the key conditions to facilitate knowledge sharing. They have a major influence on the organizational culture and the support conditions needed for knowledge sharing. Thus, management must be seen to endorse and support knowledge contributions to the KMS. Also, if team leaders are encouraged to participate in knowledge sharing on KMS, the powerful influence of workgroup norms may motivate team members to make contributions. Team building exercises, strengthening employees' identification with their workgroup, will enhance this relationship. At an organizational level, if employees perceive the firm to have a culture which values the contributions of its employees and cares about their well-being, then staff may seek to engage in OCB such as making knowledge contributions to KMS.

References

Ajzen, I. (1991) "The theory of planned behavior." *Organizational Behavior and Human Decision Processes, 50*: 179-211.

Alavi, M. (2000) "Managing Organizational Knowledge." In R. Zmud (Ed.), *Framing the Domains of IT Management: Projecting the Future – Through the Past*: 15-28. Pinnaflex Education Resources: Cincinnati, Ohio

Alavi, M., and Leidner, D. (1999) "Knowledge management systems: A descriptive study of key issues, challenges and benefits" *Communications of the AIS, 1,* 7.

Alavi, M., and Leidner, D. (2001) "Knowledge management and knowledge management systems: Conceptual foundations and research issues." *MIS Quarterly, 25*(1): 107-136.

Armitage, C. J. and Conner, M. (2001) "Efficacy of the theory of planned behavior: A meta-analytic review." *British Journal of Social Psychology, 40*: 471-499.

Chin, W., and Todd, P. (1995) "On the use, usefulness, and ease of use of structural equation modelling in MIS research: A note of caution." *MIS Quarterly, 19*: 237-246.

Ciborra, C., and Patriota, G. (1998) "Groupware and teamwork in R&D: Limits to learning and innovation." *R&D Management, 28*(1): 1-10.

Davenport,T. H. and Prusak, L. (1998) *Working Knowledge: How Organizations Manage what they Know.* Harvard Business School Press, Boston, MA.

Davis, F. (1986) *A technology acceptance model for empirically testing new end-user information systems: Theory and results.* Doctoral dissertation, Sloan School of Management, Massachusetts Institute of Technology.

Eisenberger, R., Huntington, R., Hutchinson, S. and Sowa, D. (1986) "Perceived organizational support." *Journal of Applied Psychology, 71,* 500-507.

Eisenberger, R., Fasolo, P., and Davis-LaMastro, V. (1990) "Perceived organizational support and employee diligence, commitment, and innovation." *Journal of Applied Psychology, 75*: 51-59.

Eisenberger, R., Armeli, S., Rexwinkel, B., Lynch, P., and Rhoades, L. (2001) "Reciprocation of Perceived Organizational Support." *Journal of Applied Psychology, 86*(1): 42-51.

Gore, C., and Gore, E. (1999) "Knowledge Management: The Way Forward." *Total Quality Management, 10*: 554-560.

Igbaria, M., Zinatelli, N. Cragg, P., and Cavaye, A. (1997) "Personal computing acceptance factors in small firms: A structural equation model." *MIS Quaterly*: 279-305.

Irmer, B., Bordia, P. and Abusah, D. (2002) "Evaluation apprehension and perceived benefits in interpersonal and database knowledge sharing." *Best Paper Proceedings of the Academy of Management Annual Conference, 2002*, Denver, CO.

Jarvenpaa, S., and Staples, D. (2000) "The use of collaborative electronic media for information sharing: An exploratory study of determinants." *Journal of Strategic Information Systems, 9*: 129-154.

Kaufman, J. D., Stamper, C. L. and Tesluk, P. E. (2001) "Do supportive organizations make for good corporate citizens?" *Journal of Managerial Issues, 13*(4): 436-449.

Kraut, R. E., Egido, J. and Galegher, J. (1990) "Patterns of contact and communication in scientific research." In R. E. Kraut, J. Egido, and J. Galegher (Eds.), *Intellectual Teamwork: Social and Technological Foundations of Cooperative Work*: 149-171, Erlbaum, Hillsdale, NJ.

Legris, P., Ingham, J. Collerette, P. (2002) "Why do people use information technology? A critical review of the technology acceptance model." *Information and Management, 1981*: 1-14.

Leonard, D., and Sensiper, S. (1998) "The role of tacit knowledge in group innovation." *California Management Review, 40*: 112-132.

Lewis, W., Agarwal, R., and Sambamurthy, V. (2003) "Sources of influence on beliefs about information technology use: An empirical study of knowledge workers." *MIS Quarterly, 27*(4): 657-678.

Mahmood, M., Hall, L. and Swanberg, D. (2001) "Factors affecting information technology usage: A meta-analysis of the empirical literature." *Journal of Organizational Computing and Electronic Commerce, 11*(2): 107-130.

Malhorta, Y. (2003) "Why knowledge management systems fail? Enablers and constraints of knowledge management in human enterprises." In K. Srikantaiah and M.E.D. Koenig (Eds.), *Knowledge Management Lessons Learned: What Works and What Doesn't*: Information Today, Medford, N.J.

Malhotra, Y., and Galletta, D. (1999) "Extending the technology acceptance model to account for social influence: Theoretical bases and empirical validation." *Proceedings of the 32nd Hawaii International Conference on System Science*.

Nucifora, J., Gallois, C., ands Kashima, Y. (1993) "Influences on condom use among undergraduates: Testing the theories of reasoned action and planned behavior." In D. Terry, C. Gallois, and M. McCamish (Eds.), *The Theory of Reasoned Action: Its Application to AIDS-preventative Behavior*: 47-64. Oxford: Pergamon.

Organ, D. W. (1988) *Organizational Citizenship Behavior: The Good Soldier Syndrome*. Lexington, MA: Lexington Books.

Podsakoff, P. M., and MacKenzie, S. B. (1997) "Impact of organizational citizenship behavior on organizational performance: A review and suggestions for future research." *Human Performance, 10*(2): 133-151.

Purvis, R. L., Sambamurthy, V., and Zmud, R. W. (2000) "The antecedents of knowledge embeddedness in CASE technologies in organizations." *IEEE Transactions on Engineering Management, 47*(2): 245-257.

Rhoades, L., and Eisenberger, R. (2002) "Perceived organizational support: A review of the literature." *Journal of Applied Psychology, 87*(4): 698-714.

Schultze, U. and Boland, R. J. (2000) "Knowledge management technology and the reproduction of knowledge work practices." *Journal of Strategic Information Systems, 9*: 193-212.

Sveiby, K. E. (1997) *The new organizational wealth: Managing and measuring knowledge-based assets.* San Francisco: Berrett-Kohler.

Tajfel, H., and Turner, J. (1979) "An integrative theory of intergroup conflict." In W. Austin and S. Worchel (Eds), *The Social Psychology of Intergroup Relations*: 33-47. Monterey, CA: Brooks-Cole.

Terry, D., and Hogg, M. (1996) "Group norms and the attitude-behavior relationship: A role for group identification." *Personality and Social Psychology Bulletin,* 22: 776-793.

Van Erde, W., and Thierry, H. (1996) "Vroom's expectancy models and work-related criteria: A meta-analysis." *Journal of Applied Psychology,* 81(5), 575-586.

Venkatesh, V. (2000)   "Determinants of perceived ease of use: Integrating control, intrinsic motivation, and emotion into the technology acceptance model." *Information Systems Research,* 11(4): 342-365.

Venkatesh, V., and Davis, F. (2000) "A theoretical Extension of the Technology Acceptance Model: Four Longitudinal Field Studies." *Management Science,* 46(2): 186-204.

Wachter, R.M. (2000) "Technology support for knowledge management." *Mid-American Journal of Business,* 14: 13-20.

Weiss, L. (1999) "Collection and connection: The anatomy of knowledge sharing in professional service firms." *Organizational Development Journal,* 17(4): 61-77.

KNOWLEDGE INTEGRATION PROBLEMS AND THEIR EFFECT ON TEAM PERFORMANCE*

BRIGITTE STEINHEIDER

*Department of Psychology, University of Oklahoma, Tulsa Graduate College,
Tulsa, OK 74135, USA*

NATALJA MENOLD

Institute for Human Factors, Ruhr-University Bochum, 44780 Bochum, Germany

The increase in product complexity, the interconnectedness of research questions, and the decrease in product development time are forcing organizations to share and integrate their diverse areas of expertise in collaborative teams. Experiences with collaborations in cross-functional and interdisciplinary teams have shown that the expected positive effects like higher productivity and better decision-making are counterbalanced by negative effects such as higher individual stress and ineffective work. In this study, we analyzed the effects of knowledge integration problems on team performance, and we identified variables facilitating or hindering knowledge integration within cross-functional teams. Ninety-seven members of German R&D teams assessed their knowledge integration problems and their subjective stress. They also evaluated the efficiency of the product development process in terms of time, costs and quality. Heterogeneity of team composition in terms of educational background increased knowledge integration problems significantly. Knowledge integration problems were significantly associated with meeting deadlines and lower product quality. At the same time, knowledge integration problems correlated with increased subjective stress, and job dissatisfaction. However, knowledge integration was not associated with cost aspects or overtime. Divergence within the team seemed to hinder knowledge integration, whereas the integration into the team and a netlike communication structure with defined communication rules facilitated knowledge integration. These results emphasize the importance of knowledge integration and the need to develop training to facilitate interdisciplinary collaboration in R&D teams.

1   Introduction

Knowledge has become the most important asset for companies, and raising its productivity is seen as the major challenge for managers (Drucker, 1991). In order to remain competitive, companies must use and integrate the knowledge of their employees as well as the knowledge of their customers and suppliers to develop innovative products and services. Most products and services are highly complex and require the collaboration of many experts in organizational research and development teams.

Knowledge sharing and conditions facilitating a knowledge sharing culture have thus become a major focus of organizational research (Dixon, 2000; Goh, 2002; Smith & McKeen, 2001). Lee and Al-Hawamdeh (2002) define knowledge sharing as the deliberate act in which knowledge is made reusable through its transfer from one party to

---

* This work is part of the Collaborative Research Center SFB 374 'Rapid Prototyping' financed by the German National Science Foundation.

another. Davenport (1998) stated that knowledge sharing involves two actions: transmission (sending or presenting knowledge to a potential recipient) and absorption by the audience. If knowledge is not absorbed, it has not been shared. Merely making knowledge available is not sharing, as studies with interdisciplinary or cross-functional teams have shown. While some studies found performance improvement and more innovation as was expected by the broader range of experience within the team (Simons, Pelled, & Smith, 1999; Drach-Zahavy & Somech, 2001), other studies have shown a negative relation between team heterogeneity and the occurrence of problems (Gladstein-Ancona & Caldwell, 1992; Bunderson & Sutcliffe, 2002). Obviously, an intermediating variable seems to be accountable for the negative or positive effects of team heterogeneity. In the following, we will argue that knowledge sharing in heterogeneous teams requires the development of a common ground (Clark, 1997) which is the basis for successful integration of team members' diverse knowledge.

1.1 Knowledge Integration in Collaborative Engineering Teams

The complexity in collaborative engineering projects stems from two sources: the amount of information the team has to process and the difficulty of integrating their diverse knowledge. Information processing refers to the current product features, the development goals, technical or organizational interfaces and the interaction with other participants, such as customers or suppliers. The processing of this information is hindered by the fact that the necessary knowledge is usually distributed across many specialists integrated through a collaborative process. In order to be effective, this specialized knowledge has to be communicated in a way that other team members, who are not familiar with it, can absorb and use it. Each team member has a very specific knowledge base, shaped individually by educational, professional and functional experiences over decades of their lives. Consequently, team members have very differing but often only implicit presumptions of definitions, interrelations, methods of implementation and goal hierarchies. This results in experts having very different opinions about what, how and by which means problems should be solved.

Knowledge integration means having a clear understanding of the team members' diverse professional areas of expertise, and acquiring a meta-knowledge connecting the different areas of needed expertise as they relate to the project they work on. Knowledge integration is achieved only slowly and step-by-step, by developing a common ground (Clark, 1997). Insufficient 'grounding' is sometimes revealed by the discovery of critical issues late in the work process, leading to additional iteration cycles and slowing down the product development process. Only after having developed a shared base of relevant knowledge, are teams able to communicate and coordinate their activities efficiently.

1.2 Model for Interdisciplinary Collaboration

We assume that collaboration processes in teams consist of three components which are equally important: communication, coordination and knowledge integration (see Figure

1; Steinheider *et al.*, 1999). Communication refers to the fast, accurate and comprehensive flow of information among team members. Coordination manages the dependencies between actors and activities; it also integrates and harmonizes the individual contributions with regard to the superordinate goal (Malone & Crowston, 1994). In addition to communication and coordination, we consider knowledge integration the crucial component for the success of interdisciplinary team interaction. Knowledge integration enables the collaboration of actors with different professional backgrounds and refers to the process of the systematical construction of meta-knowledge that connects fields of knowledge and expertise by developing shared mental models and using metaphors and analogies (Ganz & Hermann, 1999).

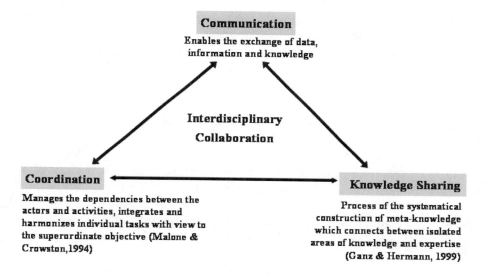

Figure 1. Model of Interdisciplinary Collaboration (Steinheider *et al.*, 1999)

This model was applied in a study with department heads of interdisciplinary research and development teams who assessed collaboration problems of their teams and evaluated their satisfaction with team performance (Steinheider & Al-Hawamdeh, 2004). Results revealed that heterogeneity of team composition in terms of educational backgrounds hinders knowledge sharing, and that problems of knowledge sharing and coordination were more frequent compared to problems of communication. Higher frequencies of collaboration problems of interdisciplinary teams were associated with significantly lower performance ratings by their department heads. Knowledge integration turned out to be the most important predictor variable for performance evaluation by explaining 30% of the outcome variance compared to 16% for communication and 19% for coordination.

1.3 Knowledge Integration Problems and their Performance Effects in Product Development Teams

The goal of this study was to examine how members of R& D teams assessed their collaborative conditions teams within engineering companies and their effect on knowledge integration. Furthermore, we wanted to analyze the relationships between communication, coordination and knowledge integration and outcome variables, such as team performance and the well-being of team members. We assumed that team characteristics, such as heterogeneity of the team in terms of educational backgrounds and the divergence of team members, hinder knowledge integration, whereas the integration of team members in the team and a net-like communication structure with defined rules facilitate knowledge integration. We predicted that knowledge integration problems are associated with problems of being on schedule and with working overtime, as well as reduced product quality and increased product development and production costs. Furthermore, we assumed that team members who complain about knowledge sharing problems estimate their workload to be higher and are less satisfied with their job.

2   Methodology

Ninety-seven members of German research and development teams took part in a survey that covered areas such as team characteristics, collaboration problems, team performance, subjective stress and job satisfaction. 70% of the participants were engineers, 13% technicians, 8% scientists, 2% computer scientists, 2% master craftsmen and 4% academics. The companies they represented were systems engineering (40%), electronics industry (24%), automobile industry (18%), and medical technology (16%). 55% of the companies were small and medium size enterprises with less than 500 employees, 43% were large enterprises with more than 500 employees.

2.1 Team Structure and Team Characteristics

Team structure was operationalized by the size of the team (one item) and the number of disciplines represented therein. As team characteristics, we assessed integration in the team (7 items, $\alpha = .79$, example 'Every team member is well integrated in the team work'), communication structure and rules (6 items, $\alpha = .68$, example 'The team consists of several subgroups which rarely communicate') and divergence (7 items, $\alpha = .74$, example 'The team has a high potential for conflicts'). The scales had a 5-point format from 0 (completely disagree) to 4 (completely agree).

2.2 Collaboration Problems

Collaboration problems were assessed by a scale based on the collaboration model of Steinheider *et al.* (1999), and described in more detail in Steinheider & Burger (2000).

The communication scale consists of 15 items ($\alpha = .85$, N=92, example 'Team members do not openly address problems') and assesses personal factors like openness, personal trust, willingness to compromise, common interests and sympathy, as well as spatial proximity, and means of technical communication. The coordination scale with 16 items ($\alpha = .87$, example 'Team members withhold information and ideas relevant for the project'), comprises factors like systematic project and time management, and team composition in respect to stability and competencies. The categories associated with knowledge integration are as follows: shared understanding of objectives and problems, shared terminology, having multiple perspectives and background knowledge of others disciplines, experience with interdisciplinarity, and motivation to work in interdisciplinary teams (17 items; $\alpha = .95$; example 'Team members are not willing to engage in viewpoints of others'). One item focused on motivation ('Team members show too little commitment'). In order to assess problems, all items were formulated negatively. The scales had a 5-point format from 0 (very low) to 4 (very high).

In a former study (Steinheider & Burger, 2000), inter correlations between the scales were low ($r < .30$), indicating that they assessed different aspects of collaboration problems. Cronbach alpha values in the range between $\alpha = .72$ and $\alpha = .95$ confirm satisfying to very good internal consistency. Concerning the external validity, knowledge integration has been a significant predictor for supervisor's satisfaction with the performance of their R&D teams, explaining about 30% of the outcome variance (Steinheider & Al-Hawamdeh, 2004).

2.3 Team Performance

Team performance was operationalized by self-assessments of time, costs and quality. The time factor was assessed by one item ('The product development process is on schedule') with a scale from 0 (completely disagree) to 4 (completely agree), and the number of hours working overtime during the last four weeks. Concerning the costs we distinguished between product development costs (five items, $\alpha = .71$, N=83, example 'The incurred labor costs are' with a scale from 0 (too low) to 4 (too high) and production costs (five items, $\alpha = .62$, N=90, example 'The estimated manufacturing costs are' with a scale from 0 (too low) to 4 (too high). Product quality was assessed by such characteristics as functionality, reliability, operability, security standards, environmental impact, accuracy and production-oriented design. Respondents assessed the accordance between the achieved and the required quality with 7 items on a scale from 0 (not in accordance) to 4 (very much in accordance; $\alpha = .74$, N=73).

2.4 Subjective Workload and Job Dissatisfaction

Individual job satisfaction was measured by means of two subscales form SBUS-S questionnaire (Weyer, Hodapp & Neuhäuser, 1980). Tested aspects were subjective workload (16 items, $\alpha = .83$, N=90; 'I don't have the feeling that I can use my full capacity in my work') and job dissatisfaction (4 items, $\alpha = .74$, N=90; 'I often have an aversion against my work').

2.5 Data Analysis

The influence of the heterogeneity of team composition on collaboration problems was tested by a multivariate analysis of variance with the number of disciplines as independent variable at three levels (single discipline, technical disciplines, and inter-disciplinary teams) and with communication, coordination and knowledge integration as dependent variables. Post-hoc tests were carried out by means of Tukey's test.

Data were analyzed by means of a linear regression analysis with performance variables as dependent and communication, coordination and knowledge integration as independent variables. We calculated separate regression analysis for the collaboration problems because of the high correlations between communication, coordination and knowledge integration ($r \geq .74$, $p < .001$). However, partial correlations between the variables were considerably lower ($.30 \leq r \leq .60$), indicating the influence of a third variable. In order to investigate the influence of team characteristics on knowledge integration, a multiple linear regression analysis was carried out with team characteristics as independent variables and knowledge integration as the dependent variable.

3   Results

Figure 2 depicts the relationship between the functional heterogeneity of teams in terms of their educational background and their communication, coordination and knowledge integration problems. The more disciplines were represented within a team and the more dissimilar these disciplines were, the more they complained about problems in integrating their knowledge ($F(2,89) = 3.12$, $p < .05$). The influence of team heterogeneity on communication ($F(2,89) = 2.53$, $p < .10$) is marginally significant, and there is no association between team composition and coordination ($F(2,89) = 0.77$, ns).

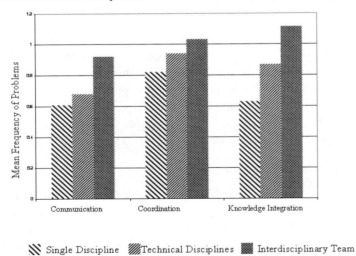

Figure 2. Mean frequency of communication, coordination and knowledge integration problems in dependence of the heterogeneity of team members' educational background.

Besides team composition, team characteristics influence knowledge integration significantly. The model with integration in the team (t = 2.41, p < .05), communication structure (t = 3.39, p < .001), divergence (t = 2.65, p = .01) and interdisciplinary team composition (t = 2.24, p < .05) is highly significant and explains about 56% of the outcome variance of knowledge sharing problems (F(4,87) = 27.25, p < .001). Integration in the team and communication structure facilitate knowledge sharing and explain about 43% and 8% of the outcome variance, divergence and an interdisciplinary team composition each explain 2.6% of the variance and are negatively correlated with knowledge sharing.

As effects of knowledge sharing, we assessed time, cost and quality factors as well as the subjective workload and job dissatisfaction. Problems in knowledge sharing were significantly associated with 'not being on schedule' (t = 3.94, p < .001, r² = 0.14). They also affected the product quality negatively (t = -3.19, p < .01, r² = 0.10), increased perceived subjective workload (t = 4.38, p < .001, r² = 0.17) and decreased job satisfaction (t = 4.35, p < .001, r² = 0.17). On the other hand, knowledge integration did not correlate with working overtime (t = 0.02, ns), product development costs (t = -0.18, ns), or production costs (t = 0.43, ns).

Communication problems were significantly associated with 'not being on schedule' (t = 3.94, p < .001, r² = 0.14), reduced product quality (t = -3.35, p < .001, r² = 0.11), higher subjective workload (t = 5.55, p < .001, r² = 0.25) and lower job satisfaction (t = 4.45, p < .001, r² = 0.17). However, communication did not correlate with working overtime (t = 0.33, ns), product development costs (t = -1.34, ns), or production costs (t = -0.09, ns).

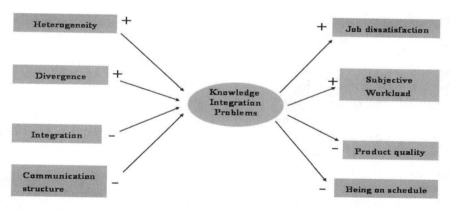

Figure 3. Significant relationships between knowledge integration problems and team heterogeneity, divergence, integration in the team and communication structure as predictor variable and job dissatisfaction, subjective workload, product quality and being on schedule as outcome variable. Facilitating respectively increasing effects are indicated by +, hindering respectively decreasing effects are indicated by -.

Coordination problems correlated significantly with more working overtime (t=2.31, p < .05, r² = 0.05), 'not being on schedule' (t = 5.42, p < .001, r² = 0.24), reduced product quality (t = -4.10, p < .001, r² = 0.15), higher subjective work load (t = 5.43, p < .001,

$r^2 = 0.24$) and lower job satisfaction ($t = 5.27$, $p < .001$, $r^2 = 0.23$). Coordination problems were not associated with product development costs ($t = -0.40$, ns), or production costs ($t = 1.05$, ns).

Figure 3 summarizes the results of knowledge integration. Integration in the team and a net-like communication structure with defined communication rules decrease the number of knowledge sharing problems, whereas divergence between team members and an interdisciplinary team composition increase the number of problems. Knowledge integration problems hinder the team from being on schedule and they impair the product quality; while team members evaluate the subjective workload to be higher and are less satisfied with their job.

4   Discussion and Conclusion

The increased complexity of products and the increasing competitive pressure forces organizations to make the best use of their knowledge and to tap unused potential in order to gain a competitive edge. Consequently, organizations are paying more attention to knowledge sharing and knowledge integration problems. The implementation of cross-functional and heterogeneous teams seems to be a promising way for organizations to speed up product development processes and reduce time-to-market. Studies on heterogeneous teams, however, have found heterogeneity to be a double-edged sword, with some studies revealing performance improvement and more innovation (Simons, Pelled, & Smith, 1999; Drach-Zahavy & Somech, 2001), others even showed negative effects on team performance (Gladstein-Ancona & Caldwell, 1992; Bunderson & Sutcliffe, 2002). We thus assumed that knowledge integration is an intervening factor between team heterogeneity and team performance.

In this study, we studied the effects of heterogeneity on collaboration problems and analyzed the relationships between communication, coordination and knowledge integration and team performance and well-being. We also identified facilitating and hindering team characteristics for knowledge integration. We also identified team characteristics that either facilitate or hinder knowledge integration.

Heterogeneous teams composed of team members with different educational backgrounds have significantly more knowledge integration problems than more homogeneous teams. However, team heterogeneity did not influence the number of communication and coordination problems.

Knowledge integration problems correlated significantly with subjective assessments of team performance, such as not being on schedule and reduced product quality. Knowledge integration, however, was not associated with working overtime, product development costs and production costs. Knowledge integration problems were also associated with reduced well-being of team members in terms of increased subjective workload and decreased job satisfaction. This is in accordance with a study by Sethi (2000) who found information integration in product development teams to have positive effects on product quality. Information integration was defined as integration of divergent perspectives and understanding of the implication of these differences for decisions.

We found similar relationships between communication and coordination with outcome variables. Contrary to our expectations, coordination problems explained more outcome variance than knowledge integration problems. In a former study, knowledge integration was the best predictor for department heads' satisfaction with the performance of their R&D teams (Steinheider & Al-Hawamdeh, 2004). Also another study comparing team members' and supervisors' evaluation of team performance revealed differing perceptions between both groups (Steinheider & Bayerl, 2003). A possible explanation for these differences is that team members and supervisors focus on different aspects in evaluating team work with team members being more aware of their coordination problems and supervisors more likely realizing team members' problems of developing a common ground. Unfortunately, sample size was rather small so that these findings have to be replicated in future studies.

We also identified team characteristics which hinder or facilitate knowledge integration in teams. Besides heterogeneity within the team, we assessed integration in the team, divergence within the team and communication structure and rules. Based on a pilot study with R&D teams, we assumed that integrating team members during the whole product development process instead of including them only in relevant phases would be beneficial for knowledge integration. Team cohesion has also been shown in other studies on R&D teams to be beneficial (Högl, 1998). We also expected a communication structure, with every team member being able to contact the others directly and defined communication rules to be positive. Even though communication nets are time-consuming and less organized, they are supposed to be advantageous for solving difficult and complex problems and increase team members' satisfaction (Wahren, 1987). Furthermore, we assumed that divergence within the team and a high potential for conflicts would hinder knowledge integration. Our findings supported these assumptions, and integration in the team turned out to be the most importance factor for knowledge integration and accounted for more than 40% of the explained variance of knowledge integration. Heterogeneity of the team composition, on the other hand, explained only about 3% of the outcome variance.

Limitations of this study are that its findings are based on self-reports by members of R&D teams. Further studies should thus try to assess heterogeneity of team composition and team performance more objectively as demonstrated in the study by Bunderson and Sutcliffe (2002). In addition to questionnaire studies, observational data might provide more insights into team processes as shown in a qualitative study analyzing video tapes of team meetings (Steinheider & Bayerl, 2003). Finally, our results emphasize the importance of knowledge integration and the need to facilitate this process by providing training. The Knowledge Integration Training for Teams (KITT; Kremer & Bienzeisler, 2004) addresses typical problems of the knowledge integration process and provides a variety of training tools for developing a common ground. Further studies and applications within organizations will determine the effectiveness of this training.

References

Bunderson, J. and Sutcliffe, K., (2002) "Comparing alternative conceptualizations of functional diversity in management teams: Process and performance effects." *Academy of Management Journal*, 45 (5), 875-893.

Clark, H. (1997) *Using language*. Cambridge: Cambridge University Press.

Davenport, T.H., and Prusak, L. (1998) *Working Knowledge: How Organizations Manage What They Know*. Boston: Harvard Business Review Press.

Dixon, N. (2000) *Common Knowledge: How Companies Thrive by Sharing What They Know*. Boston: Harvard Business Review Press.

Drach-Zahavy, A. and Somech, A. (2001) "Understanding team innovation: The role of team processes and structures." *Group Dynamics*, 5 (2), 111-123.

Drucker, P. F. (1991) "New Productivity Challenge." *Harvard Business Review* 6, 69-79.

Ganz, W. and Hermann, S. (1999) *Wissensintegrative und koordinative Dienstleistungstätigkeiten – Erfolgsfaktoren für einen nachhaltigen Wettbewerbsvorsprung*. Stuttgart: Fraunhofer IRB Verlag.

Gladstein-Ancona, D. and Caldwell, D. (1992) "Demography and design: Predictors of new product team performance." *Organization Science*, 3 (4), 321-341.

Goh, S. C. (2002) "Managing effective knowledge transfer: an integrative framework and some practice implications." *Journal of Knowledge Management*, 6 (1), 23-20.

Högl, M (1998) *Teamarbeit in innovativen Projekten: Einflussgrössen und Wirkungen*. Wiesbaden: Deutscher UniversitätsVerlag.

Kremer, D. and Bienzeisler, B. (2004) "Improving the Efficiency and Innovation Capability of Collaborative Engineering: The Knowledge Integration Training for Teams (KITT)." In: Horváth, I.; Xirouchakis, P. (Eds), *Proceedings of the TMCE 2004, Fifth International Symposium on Tools and Methods for Competitive Engineering, April 12-16, 2004, Lausanne, Switzerland*. Rotterdam: Millpress.

Lee, C. K. and Al-Hawamdeh, S. (2002) "Factors Impacting Knowledge Sharing." *Journal of Information and Knowledge Management*, 1 (1), 49-56.

Malone, T. and Crowston, K. (1994) "The interdisciplinary Study of Coordination." *ACM Computing Surveys*, 26 (1), 87-119.

Sethi, R. (2000) "New product quality and product development teams." *Journal of Marketing*, 64, 1-14.

Simons, T., Pelled, L. and Smith, K. (1999) "Making use of diversity: Diversity, debate, and decision comprehensiveness in top management teams." *Academy of Management Journal*, 42(6), 662 – 673.

Smith, H. A. and McKeen, J. D. (2001) *Instilling a Knowledge-Sharing Culture*. Ontario: Queens University School of Business.

Steinheider, B. and Al-Hawamdeh, S. (2004) "Team Coordination, Communication and Knowledge Sharing in SMEs and Large Organizations." *Journal of Information and Knowledge Management*, 3 (3), 223-232.

Steinheider, B. and Bayerl, P. S. (2003) "Wissensintegration in interdisziplinären Teams – Probleme und Lösungsansätze. " *Wirtschaftspsychologie*, 1, 26 – 29.

Steinheider, B. and Burger, E. (2000) "Kooperation in interdisziplinären Entwicklungsteams." In Gesellschaft für Arbeitswissenschaft e.V. (Ed.), *Komplexe Arbeitssysteme – Herausforderung für Analyse und Gestaltung. Bericht zum 46. Arbeitswissenschaftlichen Kongress der Gesellschaft für Arbeitswissenschaft e.V. vom 15.-18. März 2000* (pp. 553 – 557). Dortmund: GfA-Press.

Steinheider, B., Ganz, W., Nogge, W. and Warschat, J. (1999) "A model to support expert co-operation." In R. Roller (Ed.), *Automotive mechatronics design and engineering* (pp. 159 – 162). ISATA: Croydon.

Wahren, H.K, (1987) *Zwischenmenschliche Kommunikation und Interaktion in Unternehmen. Grundlagen, Problems und Ansätze zur Lösung.* Berlin: de Gruyter.

Weyer, G., Hodapp, V. and Neuhäuser, S. (1980) "Weiterentwicklung von Fragebogenskalen zur Erfassung der subjektiven Belästigung und Unzufriedenheit im beruflichen Bereich (SBUS-B). " *Psychologische Beiträge,* 22, 335-355.

KNOWLEDGE SHARING THROUGH SOCIAL NETWORKS IN PROJECT-BASED ORGANIZATIONS

WANG JIANGDIAN & YIM-TEO TIEN HUA

Technology and Enterprise Management Research Group, School of Electrical and Electronic Engineering, Nanyang Technological University, 639798 Singapore

Based on literature on knowledge management and social networks, this paper investigates the effects of four aspects, namely perceived task interdependency, hierarchical distance, historical experiences and background homophily, on the formation of mutual-choice relations for knowledge benefit in project-based organizations. In addition, this paper also finds that the strength of relations for knowledge sharing affects project members' preference of knowledge management approaches. Strong ties support the choice of Human-Centric (HC) Knowledge Management approaches, when people obtain double-loop knowledge benefits; while weak ties support a beneficial effect on the use of Technology-Centric (TC) Knowledge Management approaches, when dyads share single-loop knowledge benefits.

1 Introduction

In the last few years, knowledge is increasingly regarded as the most important resource for sustaining competitive advantage in organizations, especially in knowledge intensive organizations, such as project-based organizations (Disterer 2001; Lytras and Pouloudi 2003). In project-based organizations, people tend to participate in knowledge intensive behaviors as their daily business through which knowledge is greatly exchanged through mutual-choice relations (Kasvi *et al.* 2003), and KM is suggested to be a day-to-day practice.

Research on KM has primarily concentrated on the applications of KM systems and communities of practice. For example, many studies endeavor to investigate the intricate relationships between these two typically applied KM approaches and contextual properties (Nonaka and Takeuchi 1995; Davenport and Prusak 1998; Hansen *et al.* 1999; Alavi and Leidner 2001). However, few studies have been done on knowledge behaviors through informal social networks (Cross *et al.* 2001a; 2001b). Until recently, a new research subject emerges which emphasizes on the study of links between properties of social relations and performances of KM (Argote *et al.* 2003). In this paper, we take a modest step toward analyzing this research issue by trying to explain the role of similarities of social, organizational and background domains between two project members in the formation of a knowledge-sharing dyad, and in the preference of KM approaches. More specifically, our objectives are twofold: first, we address the influence of some important factors which are proposed to have effects on knowledge sharing within project members. This objective is in line with the findings of a literature review on social networks, which reveal that task interdependency, hierarchical distance, experiences of historical interaction and background homophily may improve or inhibit the likelihood of forming relations. The second objective is to further investigate the interaction of knowledge benefit levels and the strength of knowledge-sharing relations on the choice of technology-centric (TC) and human-centric (HC) approaches for knowledge sharing. This research may provide an alternative to the problem of how to successfully perform KM in project-based contexts.

2   Theoretical Background

2.1 Knowledge Benefits: Single and Double-loop Benefits

In general, when people turn to others for information and knowledge, they seek to achieve at least five categories of benefits (Cross *et al.* 2001a, b):

- *Direct Solution*: a specific and detailed answer that addresses a question or problem. It can be either declarative (know-what) or procedural (know-how) that enables the seeker to solve a given problem.
- *Meta-knowledge*: the direction to a source or location of relevant knowledge which may be stored in an articulated form (e.g. paper archives, databases, and various form of publications) or held by other people.
- *Problem Reformulation*: knowledge and information which lead them to rethink and reformulate their problems, and re-discover potential solutions.
- *Validation*: value may be to validate knowledge seekers' own solutions or plans, allowing them to more confidently introduce their plans or solutions to others.
- *Legitimation*: benefits by virtue of citing a respected source for reviewing one's idea can increase the credibility of the quality of the idea.

In adopting the concept of 'organizational learning' (Senge 1990), we consider the first two categories of knowledge benefits as *single-loop* benefits, which mean the 'advisers' provide knowledge which may not be challenged or questioned by the existing assumptions held by the 'consulters' on the questions asked (Cross *et al.* 2001a). The single-loop knowledge benefits may have high efficiency of knowledge sharing as the shared knowledge can be directly applied (Figure 1).

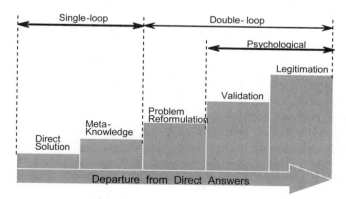

Figure 1. Knowledge Sharing Benefits

Besides single-loop benefits, knowledge seekers and providers may engage each other in re-shaping the dimensions of a problem space which may be critical to the solutions. This kind of benefits may not provide explicit solutions directly, but enlightens the knowledge seekers to comprehend the given problem from another horizon, and encourages the exploration into the problem once more. Similar with the 'problem reformulation', the last two benefits trigger knowledge seekers to re-think of problems and plans. In the last two categories of benefits, knowledge seekers may appreciate the psychological and social meanings than knowledge support. We regard the last three knowledge benefits as *double-loop* benefits, which may result in modification and validation of the problem and plan, together with restructuring the assumptions of the problem. The double-loop benefits ensure the effectiveness of knowledge sharing and facilitate knowledge creation (Cross *et al.* 2001a).

2.2 Knowledge Management Approaches

In general, KM approaches can be classified into two broad categories: technology-centric (TC) and human-centric (HC) (Hansen *et al.* 1999; Brensen *et al.* 2003). TC approaches emphasize on codifying and disseminating knowledge through extensive applications of Information-Communication Technologies (ICT). Conversely, HC approaches stress knowledge flow through enhancing person-to-person contacts and communications. Each kind of approaches has its own advantages and disadvantages.

TC approaches foster knowledge re-utilization and reduce the cost of knowledge re-use. Organizations applying TC approaches aim at offering access to codified knowledge, and avoiding time-space barriers through computer-based databases and networks. Advanced-technology machines ensure the transmission of knowledge (largely explicit knowledge) accurately and at high speeds. However, TC approaches generally demand far more investment in technology infrastructures than HC approaches. High expense involved in using TC approaches may hamper their extensiveness in most small and medium sized enterprises (Brensen *et al.* 2003). Furthermore, TC approaches are poorly equipped to transfer tacit knowledge. Because electronically mediated channels omit large part of contextual cues, tacit knowledge is greatly lost during transmission.

By contrast, HC approaches are used to transfer tacit knowledge. Tacit knowledge is naturally and effectively conveyed among individuals through personal interactions in a project group (Nonaka and Takeuchi 1995). Consequencely, collective tacit knowledge, which is important for high-order group innovation, exists in the head of each project team member. Active socialization produces communal tacit knowledge (Leonard and Sensiper 1998). Due to its intangibility, tacit knowledge is almost impossibly plagiarized by other firms. Nevertheless, as socialization is a two-way process, the success of HC approaches is largely dependent upon contextual factors, such as opportunities, space, time, socio-cultural influences, and group climates.

3   Influences on the Formation of Dyads

Taking on the cue of pioneering researchers (e.g. Louch 2000; Zeggelink 1994; Robinson and Balkwell 1995; Cross *et al.* 2001b), this research presents four independent variables to explain the variation in the incidence of personal networks. The first influence which is likely to contextualize mutual-choice dyads for knowledge sharing, is perceived task interdependency. The second factor in this study is hierarchical distance. The third predictor examines historical experiences shared by two involved persons, including friendship, co-workers in previous projects/departments and community memberships. The last predictor examines the importance of homophily between two project members.

3.1 Perceived Task Interdependency

Perceived task interdependency refers to the extent to which an individual team member believes that he or she depends on other members of the team in carrying out his or her job (Brass 1985; Kiggundu 1983; Van der Vegt *et al.* 2000, 2001). It results from how organizations divide work among project teams, and how work is further divided among individuals within their teams (Van der Vegt and Janssen 2003). Some prior studies have illustrated that knowledge providers and users who have similar tasks in organizations have a higher likelihood to share knowledge (Rice *et al.* 1999; Cross *et al.* 2001b). Task interdependency facilitates mutual-choice dyads' access to useful knowledge between members. The similar jobs necessarily involve some similar task information and knowledge, technical processes and expertise. People with greater task overlaps have greater relevant absorptive capacity and hence are more likely to learn from each other (Lane and Lubatkin 1998).

Comparing it with double-loop benefits, we propose that perceived task interdependence of two project members may support the potential relations for single-loop knowledge benefits, which include direct solutions and meta-knowledge. As people work for similar tasks, it is easy for them to provide direct solutions to problems and be quick in telling the potential sources of solutions, if they know the answers. Psychologists and managerial researchers distinguish trust as two types: competence trust and benevolent trust (Shapiro 1987; Lewicki and Bunker 1996; Levin *et al.* 2002). Competence trust describes the belief an individual has of another person as knowledgeable enough about a given area, while benevolent trust refers to the belief that "an individual will not intentionally harm another when given the opportunities to do so" (Levin *et al.* 2002:2). Benevolent trust is achieved on the basis of emotional closeness (Granovetter 1973). Single-loop benefits are more related to competence trust (than benevolent trust). Those people who work together with high task interdependency are likely to form competence trust. Therefore, when they need answers to concrete problems, they would probably turn to peers with competence trust. Hence, the task interdependency facilitates achieving single-loop benefits, for it increases task overlap and knowledge bases to seek, recognize, and assimilate knowledge that is directly related to task-related problems.

H1a: *The likelihood of forming mutual-choice relationship for single-loop knowledge benefits is higher when the dyad shares greater task interdependency.*

3.2 Hierarchical Distance

The hierarchical distance (dissimilarity of hierarchical positions) between two project members may influence the level of knowledge transfer between the dyad. Within heterogeneous groups, status differences may affect the relative participation of members (Dovidio *et al.* 1988) and task-related knowledge sharing performance of team members (Lord and Saenz 1985). A project-based organization identifies project members as project managers, senior project members and junior project members, within which hierarchy difference does not result from official status, but from the different levels of expertise. Those team members who are identified as possessing expertise are often accorded power and status (French and Raven 1959) that alters their performance within the team (Thomas-Hunt *et al.* 2003).

Two project members with large hierarchical distance are not likely to form mutual-choice relation for knowledge sharing, especially for high level knowledge benefits (e.g. legitimation and validation). Cross *et al.*'s study (2001a) on problem-solving networks found that members belonging to the same hierarchical position are likely to share similar perceptions and have similar needs in functional organizations. However, members in high hierarchical positions may not turn to those in lower positions. Two reasons can be given to explain it. First, in project teams, project members have to submit reports regularly to their managers. The formal submission reduces the inquisition to ask for extra advices. Second, research indicates that acknowledged task-related expert status may increase individual members' confidence (Trafimow and Sniezek 1994), which might stop senior members turning to peers for advice whose expert status is lower than themselves, especially for high level of knowledge benefits. For example, the legitimation benefit that requires contact with a respected person may lead to a one-side relation if the two persons have different hierarchical positions. Thus, the hierarchical distance between two project members impedes a dyad's knowledge sharing, especially for double-loop knowledge benefits.

H1b: *The likelihood of forming mutual-choice relationship for double-loop benefits is lower when the hierarchical distance between the dyad is large.*

3.3 Historical Experience

Organizational theorists propose that the search for knowledge and solutions is often influenced by a person's past experiences (Granovetter 1973). In this study, historical experiences include friendship between co-workers in their previous projects and their community memberships. Project members are likely to help each other who have historical experiences which make them relationally close (Stevenson and Gilly 1993), because they have developed a trusting relationship which allows them to exchange knowledge, seek psychological support, and emotional encouragement. We propose that historical experiences have a positive effect on the networks for knowledge sharing, especially for double-loop knowledge benefits. On one hand, project member who are seeking double-loop benefits require each other with benevolence trust as well as competence trust. On the other hand, double-loop benefits usually need dyads to spend extra time and more efforts to help each other, and people with strong ties are more willing and available than those with weak ties. Compared with those without historical experiences, people experiencing previous interactions are more likely to maintain strong ties with each other. Therefore, historical experiences between two project members improve the formation of knowledge sharing relationships, especially for double-loop benefits.

H2: *The likelihood of forming mutual-choice relationship, especially for double-loop benefits, is higher when the dyad has prior experiences as friends, co-workers in previous projects, and community membership.*

3.4 Background Homophily

In social networks literature, researchers note that personal networks tend to be homophilous (Marsden 1988). Studies find a positive relationship between homophily and similarity of attitudes and behaviors towards knowledge seeking. For example, members of the same gender possibly share similar perspectives, similar communication styles, or belong to the same communication networks (Ibarra 1992; 1993), and hence are likely to form the knowledge sharing networks (Cross *et al.* 2001b). According to Marsden (1988), we identify some important dimensions of homophily for this research: age, educational, gender, and mother tongue. They are useful dimensions for analyzing the effects of dyadic homophily (Marsden 1988; Louch 2000).

H3: *The likelihood of forming mutual-choice relationship is higher when the dyad has similar background homophily (age, educational, gender and mother tongue).*

4 Social Networks and Knowledge Management Approaches

After the formation of mutual-choice knowledge sharing relations, the next step of this study is to determine whether the single and double-loop benefits will influence the choice of KM approaches. We find that the interaction between different levels of knowledge benefits and the strength of knowledge sharing relations affect the preference of KM approaches. Strong ties constitute a base for trust that can reduce the resistance of change and provide comfort (Krackhardt 1992). A robust relationship between two members exists when three necessary and sufficient conditions are satisfied: interaction, affection and certain interaction history (Krackhardt 1992). Units within strong networks should interact with each other, and their interactions produce opportunities for the exchange of information and knowledge, some of which may be confidential and intangible (Krackhardt 1992; Hansen 1999). Strong ties also require reciprocal affection (Granovetter 1973; Krackhardt 1992), which can create motivation to treat the other in a positive way. Units with strong ties also spend sufficient time together (Granovetter 1973; Krackhardt 1992; Hansen 1999), which improves relationships and creates the experiences necessary to allow each unit to use shared knowledge (Krackhardt 1992). Strong networks produce trust, care and collective commitment, which are not only ingredients of project success, but also socio-cultural necessities of knowledge dissemination.

The strong and intimate relationships support the success of HC approaches, especially when knowledge benefits are related to double-loop (illustrated in Table 1). In this case, people need to exchange a large part of tacit knowledge, e.g. thinking styles, intuitions and cumulative expertise, which is complex, and demands extra articulating and interpreting. Therefore, double-loop benefits require people to have great enthusiasm to help peers, which strong ties provide. Although ICT can be helpful to shape a network project organization, issues of uncertainty, ambiguity, and risk are difficult to address through electronic systems. In particular, rich, multi-dimensional and robust relationships can only be developed through direct human-centric interaction (Nohria and Eccle 1992) which exchanges huge amounts of both knowledge and socio-emotional communications with other project members, especially dependent, complex knowledge and emotional support (double-loop benefits). Besides, the two-way interaction afforded by a strong tie provides the opportunity to try, err, and seek instruction and feedback in time.

H4: *Strong ties have a positive effect on the choice of HC approaches, where dyads share double-loop knowledge benefits.*

On the other hand, weak ties, which are infrequent and distant relationships, are likely to assist the success of taking TC approaches, when people share single-loop knowledge benefits. Weak ties are less costly to maintain direct relations with each other than strong ties. People with weak ties are not likely to spend much time cultivating relationships and processing the incoming information and knowledge through extra direct contacts. It is appropriate to develop weak ties to provide easily understanding and direct answers as well as the potential sources of new knowledge, which belong to single-loop benefits (Hansen 1999). In seeking single-loop benefits, knowledge seekers are certain about their questions and expected solutions, and knowledge providers are clear about the solutions. In this way, project members may not have difficulty interpreting the solutions to their problems.

However, sharing double-loop knowledge benefits in weak ties proves to be difficult (Hansen 1999; Zander and Kogut 1995). Double-loop knowledge benefits need people to spend more time and energy articulating knowledge by discussing together, because they usually contain complex knowledge. When sharing complex knowledge, knowledge recipients probably need to interpret the complex knowledge with the help from knowledge providers. Such sharing requires knowledge providers and seekers to have greater motivation to be of assistance and it involves in two-way interactions. However, weak relations of dyads determine that people are not likely to spend too much time and energy on keeping their relations, and not likely to help each other for interpreting complex and tacit knowledge. On the other hand, the knowledge for single-loop benefits is direct and concrete, and the application of TC approaches will make transfer of this kind of knowledge simple and convenient (illustrated in Table 1). When sharing single-loop knowledge benefits, project members tied with weak relations would thus prefer TC approaches.

H5: *Weak ties have a positive effect on the choice of TC approaches, where dyads share single-loop knowledge benefits.*

Table 1. Characteristic of Relationships and Knowledge Management Approaches

Strength of Ties / Knowledge Benefits	Weak	Strong
Single-loop	Technology-Centric (TC)	Human-Centric (HC)/ Technology-Centric (TC)
Double-loop	Human-Centric (HC)/ Technology-Centric (TC)	Human-Centric (HC)

5   Research Model

Based on the above discussions, we generate a research model (Figure 2) to illustrate how the various factors influence the formation of dyads for knowledge benefits, and how strengths of networks and knowledge benefits levels influence the preference of TC and HC KM approaches.

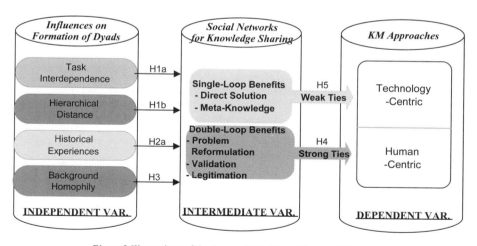

Figure 2 Illustrations of the Research Model and Research Hypotheses

6   Conclusions and Future Work

This paper contributes to theory on KM in project-based contexts by theoretically analyzing potential influences of some key factors exerting on the formation of mutual-choice knowledge-sharing networks. The paper takes into account four predictors: perceived task interdependence, hierarchical distance, historical experiences and background homophily. It then attempts to study whether and how these factors influence the preference of KM approaches. The findings of the study are: Strong ties have a positive effect on the choice of HC approaches, where dyads share double-loop knowledge benefits, while weak ties have a positive effect on the choice of TC approaches, where dyads share single-loop knowledge benefits. This paper also develops a research framework to illustrate the discussed relationships. The model suggests specific themes about project-based organizational KM that can be tested in future research. With the research model developed, an appropriate set of instruments to measure the research variables can be developed. The model can then be studied first in the case study phase where it can be refined. The refined model will serve as the model for further confirmatory study using surveys to test the hypotheses of the refined model.

References

Alavi, M. and Leidner, D. (2001) "Review: knowledge management and knowledge management systems: conceptual foundations and research issues", *MIS Quarterly,* 25(1): 107-136.

Argote, L., McEvily, B. and Reagams, R. (2003) "Managing knowledge in organizations: An integrative framework and review emerging themes", *Management Science,* 49(4): 571-582.

Bowman, B., Grupe, F.H., Lund, D. nad Moore, W. (1993) "An examination of sources of support preferred by end-user computing personnel", *Journal of End User Computing,* 5(4): 4-11.

Bresnen, M., Edelman, L., Newell, S., Scarbrough, H., and Swan, J. (2003) "Social practices and the management of knowledge in project environments", *International Journal of Project Management,* 21(3): 157-166.

Cross, R., Borgatti, S.P. and Parker, A. (2001a) "Beyond answers: dimensions of the advice networks", *Social Networks,* 23: 215-235.

Cross, R., Rice, R.E. and Parker, A. (2001b) "Information seeking in social context: Structural influences and receipt of information benefits", *IEEE Transactions on Systems, Man, and Cybernetics-Part C: Applications and Reviews,* 31(4): 438-448.

Davenport, T.H. and Prusak, L. (1998) *Working Knowledge: How Organizations Manage What They Know,* Cambridge, MA: Harvard Business School Press.

Disterer, G. (2002) "Management of Project Knowledge and Experiences", *Journal of Knowledge Management,* 6(5): 512-520.

Dovidio, J.F., Brown, C.E., Heltman, K., Ellyson, S.L. and Keating, C.F. (1988) "Power displays between women and men in discussions of gender linked tasks: A multi-channel study", *Journal of Personality and Social Psychology,* 55: 580-587.

French, R. P., Jr., & Raven, B. (1959) "The bases of social power". In Cartwright, D. (Ed.), *Studies in Social Power:* 150-167, Ann Arbor: University of Michigan Press.

Granovetter, M. (1973) "The strength of weak ties", *American Journal of Sociology,* 78: 1360-1379.

Hansen, M.T. (1999) "The search-transfer problem: The role of weak ties in sharing knowledge across organization subunits", *Administrative Science Quarterly,* 44: 82-111.

Hansen, M.T., Nohria,N. and Tierney, T. (1999) "What's your strategy for managing knowledge?", *Harvard Business Review,* 77: 106-116.

Ibarra, H. (1992) "Homophily and differential returns: Sex differences in network structure and access in an advertising firm", *Administrative Science Quarterly,* 37: 422-447.

Ibarra, H. (1993) "Personal networks of women and minorities in management: A conceptual framework", *The Academy of Management Review*, 18: 56-87.

Kasvi J.J.J. (2003) "Knowledge Support in Learning Operative Organizations", HUT Industrial Management and Work and Organizational Psychology Dissertation Series No 2.

Kiggundu, M.N. (1983) "Task interdependence and job design: Test of a theory", *Organizational Behavior and Human Performance*, 31: 145–172.

Krackhardt, D. (1992) "The Strength of Strong Ties: The Importance of *Philos* in Organizations", In: Nohria, N. and Eccles, R.G. (Eds.) *Networks and Organizations: Structure, Form, and Action*: 216-239, Boston, Mass: Harvard Business School Press.

Lane, P.J. and Lubatkin, M.H. (1998) "Relative absorptive capacity and interorganizational learning", *Strategic Management Journal*, 19(5): 461-477.

Leonard, D. and Sensiper, S. (1998) "The role of tacit knowledge in group innovation", *California Management Review*, 40(3): 112-131.

Levin, D.Z., Cross, R., Abrams, L.C. and Lesser, E.L. (2002) "Trust and knowledge sharing: A critical combination", URL: www-1.ibm.com/services/strategy/e_strategy/trust.html

Lewicki, R. J., and Bunker, B. B. (1996) "Developing and maintaining trust in work relationships", In: Kramer, R. M. and Tyler, T. R. (Eds.) *Trust in Organizations: Frontiers of Theory and Research*: 114 -139, Sage, Thousand Oaks, CA.

Lord, C.G., and Saenz, D.S. (1985) "Memory deficits and memory surfeits: Differential cognitive consequences of tokenism for tokens and observers", *Journal of Personality Social Psychology*, 10: 215-221.

Louch, H. (2000) "Personal network integration: transitivity and homophily in strong-tie relations", *Social Networks*, 22: 45-64.

Lytras M.D. and Pouloudi, A. (2003) "Project management as a knowledge management primer: the learning infrastructure in knowledge-intensive organizations: projects as knowledge transformations -and beyond", *The Learning Organization*, 10(4): 237-250.

Marsden, P. (1988) "Homogeneity in confiding relations", *Social Networks*, 10: 57-76.

Nohria, N. and Eccles, R.G. (1992) "Face-to-Face: Making Network Organizations Work", In: Nohria, N. and Eccles, R.G. (Eds.) *Networks and Organizations: Structure, Form, and Action*: 288-308, Boston, Mass: Harvard Business School Press.

Nonaka, I. and Takeuchi, H. (1995) *The knowledge-creating company: How Japanese companies create the dynamics of innovation*, New York: Oxford University Press.

Rice, R.E., Collins-Jarvis, L. and Zydney-Walker, S. (1999) "Individual and structural influences on information technology helping relationships", *Journal of Applied Communication Research*, 27(4): 285-309.

Robinson, D.T. and Balkwell, J.W. (1995) "Density, transitivity, and diffuse status in task-oriented groups", *Social Psychology Quarterly*, 58: 241-254.

Senge, P.M. (1990) *The Fifth Discipline: The Art and Practice of the Learning Organization*, London, Century Business Books.

Shapiro, S.P. (1987) "The social control of impersonal trust", *The American Journal of Sociology*, 93(3): 623 -658.

Stevenson, William B. and Mary C. Gilly. (1993) "Problem-Solving Networks in Organizations: Intentional Design and Emergent Structure", *Social Science Research*, 22: 92-113.

Thomas-Hunt, M.C, Ogden, T.Y. and Neale, M.A. (2003) "Who's really sharing? Effects of social and expert status on knowledge exchange within groups", *Management Science*, 49(4): 464-477.

Trafimow, D. and Sniezek, J.A. (1994) "Perceived expertise and its effect on confidence", *Organizational Behavior and Human Decision Processes*, 57: 290-302.

Van der Vegt, G.S. and Janssen, O. (2003) "Joint Impact of Interdependence and Group Diversity on Innovation", *Journal of Management*, 29(5): 729-751.

Van der Vegt, G. S., Emans, B.J.M. and Van de Vliert, E. (2000) "Affective responses to intragroup interdependence and job complexity", *Journal of Management*, 26: 633–655.

Van der Vegt, G.S., Emans, B.J.M. and Van de Vliert, E. (2001) "Patterns of interdependence in work teams: A two-level investigation of the relations with job and team satisfaction", *Personnel Psychology*, 54: 51–69.

Zander, U. and Kogut, B. (1995) "Knowledge and the speed of the transfer and imitation of organizational capabilities: An empirical test", *Organization Science*, 6(1), 76-92.

Zeggelink, E. (1994) "Dynamics of structure: an individual oriented approach", *Social Networks*, 16: 295-333.

PART IV

Culture as Context

TACIT KNOWLEDGE AND CULTURE

PETER BUSCH & DEBBIE RICHARDS

Department of Computing, Macquarie University,
North Ryde, N.S.W. 2109, Australia

Tacit knowledge is characteristically unwritten, but may over time become articulated or codified depending on its nature. Because of the importance of the role tacit knowledge plays in both individual and organisational success, it is important that it's transfer be unhindered from a knowledge management point of view. Culture plays a part in knowledge transfer insofar as people tend typically to associate with others of similar background. We have conducted a series of case studies in a number of IT organisations to determine the extent to which culture affects the likelihood of tacit knowledge flows. Our findings indicate that where the organisation is highly multi-cultural, the likelihood of culture affecting tacit knowledge flows is limited. Nevertheless staff, where they do share a common culture, do generally associate with one another and this in turn may impede the free-flow of soft knowledge.

1   Introduction

Tacit knowledge is obviously contextual, yet at the same time is culturally influenced. Culture in this instance need not necessarily refer to the macro/country level, rather the role of culture is important even down at the ethnic level. For example in Finland much tacit knowledge is transferred in the sauna (Koskinen 2000). Understandably this has led to present-day difficulties as women begin to participate in business to the extent that business in Finland is now moving towards western style boardrooms. The complexity for modern western organisations in particular is to integrate the tacit knowledge backgrounds of their (often) highly multicultural staff. For "cross-cultural working involves the interaction of people whose tacit knowledge has been developed in different ways, and who have learnt different approaches to sense-reading and sense-giving. A necessary first condition for trying to facilitate effective cross-cultural working is to take these cultural differences seriously" (Walsham 2001: 606). Understanding whether culture influences the existence and transference of knowledge is important, as it will impact the applicability of a particular knowledge management strategy.

2   A background to culture and tacit knowledge

The majority of references relating to tacit knowledge literature from a cultural standpoint discuss the differences between western, typically Anglo-American, and eastern, meaning Japanese points of view. Certainly the Japanese approach towards knowledge management differs from a western one, from anything as taken for granted as *nemawashi* (discussions behind the scenes) to agreement on contracts, which is typically tacit in the Japanese case, to more formally contracted in the U.S. example (Yamadori 1984).   The differences in the cultures have also meant that Japanese car

187

designers for example, but not their U.S. counterparts, were able to detect reasons why a vehicle had not been selling well because of the shape of it's grille and headlights (Leonard and Sensiper 1998). Another cultural example of tacit knowledge differences is given by way of Japanese work practices. The Japanese approach is to conduct a morning discussion session where staff are able to 'air' their viewpoints and transfer their tacit knowledge. Such an approach has often appeared to visiting U.S. staff as a waste of time (Nonaka and Takeuchi in Durrance 1998).

Japanese firms also appear to differ with respect to knowledge sharing at an intra – organisational level.   The Japanese approach is often to involve many people. The western approach tends to reflect a 'need-to-know' basis, meaning that knowledge (both codified and more particularly tacit) is not so readily transmitted (Hamel 1991 in West and Meyer 1997).   Certainly the Australian approach tends to follow the U.S. example. Meetings are conducted on the basis of only involving directly concerned personnel and information   is   typically   transferred   on   a   'need-to-know'   basis.   From   an articulate/codified knowledge point of view, this makes sense and indeed is practical given the 'information overload' of most professional personnel today.   What we do not have sitting on our desks in front of us, we can easily acquire, either through libraries or the Internet.   The disadvantage culturally within western spheres is that articulable tacit knowledge (the subset of tacit knowledge that is over time articulated, for example 'trade secrets' or 'street smarts')   is not being transferred because of the codified knowledge management 'mindset'. At this stage we are beginning to see the role the organisation plays in regard to soft knowledge.

3   Culture's Role within the many Dimensions and Definitions of Tacit Knowledge

In seeking to understand the phenomena of tacit knowledge and the work that has already been conducted in this field we used grounded theory[1] to examine 68 recently published documents, which we placed in a hermeneutic unit.[2] We found the following definitions to be the most widely cited, in descending order of groundedness, that is to say appearance in the literature. The terms given are subjectively coded 'themes' that have been derived from the literature. The codes which have a groundedness of greater than 2 instances in the literature are as follows:

> Knowledge (80); Individuals (50); Organisational domain (46); Skill (35); Non-Codification (28); Non-verbal (27); Experience (26); Context specific (24); Intuition (20); Learned (16); Know how (15); Not formal (13); Action (12); Expertise (11); Culture (10); Contingency based (9); Environment (9); Externalisation (9); Knowing (9); Not easily communicated (9); Practical (9); Sub-consciousness (9); Understanding (9); Cognitive (8), Internalisation (8); Mental models (8); Not directly taught (8); Not easily transmitted (8); Process (8); Abilities (7); Apprenticeship (7); Low environmental support (7);

---

[1] A grounded theory is a theory that is induced from the data rather than preceding them (Lincoln & Guba 1985 in Cutcliffe 2000; Partington 2000).

[2] A hermeneutic unit is an entity encompassing *documents* worked on, *codes* created out of the documents, *families* of codes that are related, and *links* or *associations* between codes.

Management (7); Practice (7); Society (7); Two dimensional (7); Behaviour (6); Beliefs (6); Conscious (6); Direct contact (6); Face to face transfer (6); Goal attainment (6); Inferences (6); Learning by doing (6); Maxims (6); Non-awareness (6); Pattern recognition (6); Perceptions (6); Procedural in nature (6); Routine (6); Subjectivity (6); Tasks (6); Technology (6); Values (6); Common sense (5); Decision making (5); Embodied (5); Implicit (5); Implied (5); Information (5); Judgement (5); No idea (5); Not easily codifiable (5); Sharing (5); Taken for granted (5); Unconscious (5); Everyday situations (4); Interaction (4); Job knowledge (4); Know more than we can tell (4); Not easily formalised (4); Not formal instruction (4); Others (4); Physical control (4); Riding a bicycle (4); Rule (4); Schema (4); Time (4); Touch sensitivity (4); Wisdom (4); Abstraction (3); Access constraints (3); Awareness (3); Communal (3); Competitive advantage (3); Embedded (3); Emotions (3); Experientially established cognitive structures (3); Focal awareness (3); Groups (3); Holism (3); Ideals (3); Importance of language (3); Information retrieval (3); Insight (3); Learning by using (3); Meaning (3); Mind (3); Motor skills (3); Observation (3); Oneself (3); Particular uses/particular situations (3); Performance (3); Practical intelligence (3); Procedures (3); Resistance to revelation (3); Rules of thumb (3); Selective comparison (3); Semantics (3); Sense perception (3); Transmission (3).

The above list is not complete, and a significant number of codes remain that contain a groundedness of 1 and 2 instances in the literature (code total 1,310), which were considered too trivial for inclusion. It can be noted from the codes above that tacit knowledge is typically individualistic (50 instances) {beliefs (6); oneself (3)}, it is heavily organisationally based (46), it is directly related at least to skill (35) and it is context specific (24). Furthermore it tends to be practically (9) rather than theoretically oriented in nature {practice (7); learning by doing (6); learning by using (3); practical intelligence (3)}, and given the nature of human competition, it is acquired in conditions of low environmental support (7) (Sternberg *et.al.* 1995), which leads to it's being used for competitive advantage (3). One other very important issue, is the need for understanding (9) {internalisation (8); others (4); awareness (3); meaning (3); oneself (3)} on the part of the receiver. Culture appears at number 15 in this ordered list of 110 frequently used notions related to tacit knowledge. Many of the concepts in the list attempt to define tacit knowledge (e.g. knowledge, not-codified, know how, experience, non verbal, etc) and relate to its nature (e.g. learned, action, behaviour, not easily communicated). Culture, on the other hand can be viewed as an influence on tacit knowledge (as with concepts such as individuals, organisational domain and environment). From a knowledge management point of view, a focus on what affects its existence and transfer, rather than a sometimes-futile discussion attempting to pin down its definition, will bring the greatest benefits.

Saint-Onge (1996) includes intuition, perspectives, beliefs, and values people form as a result of their experiences in his definition of tacit knowledge. When Saint-Onge's description of tacit knowledge at the individual level is congregated into an organisational level, it can approach the definition of culture (Schein 1985 in Brockmann and Anthony 1998).

The above quote goes beyond defining culture as an influencing factor to defining culture as a form of tacit knowledge itself. If we view tacit knowledge as a component of expertise we can appreciate that an expert in one culture is not necessarily so in another and vice versa.

4   A Study on the effect of culture on tacit knowledge flows

As our research is concerned with the measurement of tacit knowledge within the IT domain we use the following working definition of tacit knowledge as the *articulable implicit IT managerial knowledge* that IT practitioners draw upon when conducting the "management of themselves, others, and their careers" (Wagner and Sternberg 1991a; 1991b). We have conducted an in-depth study involving three IT organisations, which, while also seeking to answer a number of additional research questions, includes the following question directly related to the effect of culture.

Research Question: Do people clique with one another based on biographical factors such as ethnicity? If so, does it affect tacit knowledge transfer?

In this section we describe the design of our study and the instrument used for data collection. In the following sections we introduce the participating organisations and offer our findings related to the above research question. In the final sections we provide some discussion and our conclusions.

4.1   Design of the case studies

Due to the individual and contextual nature of tacit knowledge, each organisation formed a separate case study and involved testing along psychological lines (as developed by Sternberg at Yale) for who may be said to have more tacit knowledge than others, and also how well tacit knowledge is being transferred between individuals using Social Network Analysis (SNA) (Scott 1991). To this end an online questionnaire was developed and deployed in the three organisations of sizes small: roughly 10 IT staff and roughly 16 IT staff and large (roughly 1,400 IT staff). In total 129 IT practitioners were involved. To graphically model the survey data, and to provide a qualitative dimension to data analysis to complement quantitative statistical analysis[3] given the small sample sizes, we employed Formal Concept Analysis (FCA) (Wille 1992).

4.2 The questionnaire

The questionnaire comprised three major components. Firstly a biographical section, secondly a social network analysis section, and finally the tacit knowledge inventory itself. Let us now examine each of these three components in slightly greater detail.

4.2.1 Section A: Biographical

The first component of the questionnaire included questions relating to: gender, age, *language other than English*, occupation of employees today, 3 years ago and 6 years ago, highest formal qualification, technical qualification/certifications; whether the individual was permanent or a contractor, the number of years of IT experience, the

---

[3] In addition to analysis of descriptive statistics, a Wilcoxon test of matched pairs was conducted on the datasets. It was found there was a limited, but nevertheless statistically significant variation between how expert and non-expert respondents answered the scenarios.

number of years with the current organisation and which Australian Computer Society (ACS) level they belonged to determine their level of responsibility in the organization.

4.2.2 Section B: Social Network Analysis

We chose to measure the diffusion of articulable tacit knowledge through the adoption of SNA. Such analysis has a number of underpinnings. These include the assumption that relations among actors or people are considered as channels or thoroughfares of resources. Secondly, that the interaction among actors is directly constrained or aided by the structure of the relationships themselves. Furthermore, that relations taking place between the actors determine all economic, political and social structures (Wasserman and Faust 1994). As a result of this we consider the presence of cliques[4] or groupings of individuals to aid in tacit knowledge flow.

Scenario 3

You as a team leader are responsible for implementing a payroll system for another branch within the parent organisation. Although you are expected to do the bulk of the work (55%), you do have five other colleagues able to help as you so desire. The project should take 12 months in total to complete.

You have undertaken some of the initial systems design work largely yourself for the past couple of months, and you now require your colleagues to further help you with the next stage which is mainly that of coding.

You are comfortable with hierarchy, however some of your team members are not. You delegate some tasks to subordinates within your team. One of the team members who specialises in programming has been allocated some software specification work, but would prefer really just to be programming. This person has performed well on coding related tasks in the past, but at this point in time lacks project management skills which would prevent him from becoming an effective team leader. Nevertheless you feel that the person should at least do some of the software specification work.

Rate each of the following responses in relation to the given scenario. It is advisable to read all of the responses before replying.

2. Consider approaching a mentor within the organistion or perhaps the Human Resources section, in the expectation they might provide you with some advice as to how to handle the individual in question

ETHICAL
Choose one: ○ ○ ○ ○ ○ ○ ○
Extremely Bad — Neither Good nor Bad — Extremely Good

REALISTIC
Choose one: ○ ○ ○ ○ ○ ○ ○
Extremely Bad — Neither Good nor Bad — Extremely Good

Figure 1: Illustrating scenario 3, answer 2 of the IS articulable tacit knowledge inventory

Within this section of the questionnaire respondents were to select (a) the person with whom they networked, (b) how often, (c) the type of working relationship with the person, in other words whether the colleague was superior or subordinate to the respondent. And lastly (d) the type of meeting/communication pattern that takes place. The latter point is particularly important; as evidence would suggest that much

[4] Usually defined as a group comprised of at least 3 people.

information is transmitted face-to-face, in other words tacit knowledge is *not* communicated in electronic form.

4.2.3 Section C: Tacit Knowledge Inventory

Respondents were presented with a given number of scenarios in a random order from the bank of 16 scenarios and associated answer options we had developed based on interviews, pre-pilot and pilot studies. For each one of the answer options presented there were Likert scales of 1 to 7 in value (Extremely Bad, Very Bad, Bad, Neither Good nor Bad, Good, Very Good, Extremely Good, respectively). Participants did not see a numerical value; only the wording from *Very Bad* through to *Extremely Good* was visible. Two Likert Scales per scenario were presented, requesting both an Ethical and a Realistic value as a means of working out how much a variation there would likely be between what a person 'should' be doing, as opposed to what they would actually and sensibly do.[5] One such example of a tacit knowledge scenario with a Likert scale answer arrangement used in this research may be seen in Figure 1 above.

5   Case Study Results

5.1 Background to the organisations

The three IT organisations studied will be referred to as Organisation X (large), Organisation Y (small) and Organisation Z (also small). In keeping with the working definition of tacit knowledge used in the study, we were concerned with IT personnel *only* within these organisations. For example Organisation X is an insurance company, however what is referred to as Organisation X in this paper is in fact the IT support group for the wider organisation. Organisation Y differs insofar as it is a management consultancy with a specialisation in IT. To that end the staff under study represent the *core* of the organisation, rather than the IT support staff, as is the case in Organisation X. Organisation Z is a home and office furniture supply company. However what is referred to as Organisation Z here is the IT group providing support to the logistics of storing and selling furniture items. Thus Organisation X and Z under study are similar insofar as they provide a service role to the wider organisation. Organisation Y differs, as its mission is to deliver IT/IS managerial expertise. As we will see, the mission of the organisation appears to have influenced the degree of multiculturalism found in each organisation.

   Taking language other than English spoken as an indicator of multiculturalism, Organisation X is highly multicultural, with over 50 IT staff (out of 108 participating), speaking over 35 languages other than English. Organisation Y is almost totally the opposite, with only one staff member speaking Cantonese and Malaysian, the remainder of the staff (7) being Anglo-Celtic Australian. Organisation Z had seven IT staff (out of 13 participating) that spoke nine languages other than English. To what extent do the

---

[5] Experience from the pre-pilot showed that respondents felt they should be given the opportunity to state how they *would* answer questions in addition to how they *should* answer them.

varying levels of multiculturalism displayed in all three organisations affect the tacit knowledge flow process?

5.2 Organisation X

In Figure 2 we examine the languages other than English utilised by respondents in Organisation X using a concept lattice generated using FCA. In FCA a concept is seen as a set of objects and the set of attributes shared by those objects, thus providing the extension and intension of the concept. In the concept lattice in Figure 2 developed with Toscana[TM], labeling has been reduced using term subsumption. To find all attributes belonging to an object (in this case a participant) follow all ascending paths. The interpretation of the lattices will be discussed in the relevant subsequent section. The number attached below each node is the code of the participant. An (E) after the code indicates an expert (as identified by their peers in the survey). We note the number of Chinese speakers, whether Mandarin, Hokkien, Hakka or Cantonese. Note also the numbers of experts who speak these languages, but Cantonese primarily. The number of such experts could also imply one of two things. Firstly that Chinese speakers are in some way proportionately more expert than non-Chinese speakers. If this is the case, then it would suggest that people from these backgrounds have had to try even harder than native English speakers in gaining expertise, given the language difficulties people from such backgrounds ordinarily have to face. Or secondly that Chinese speakers are perhaps identifying other Chinese speakers as experts. As we shall later see, there is evidence of cliquing taking place among Cantonese speakers. This last point in particular has serious ramifications for likely tacit knowledge transfer.

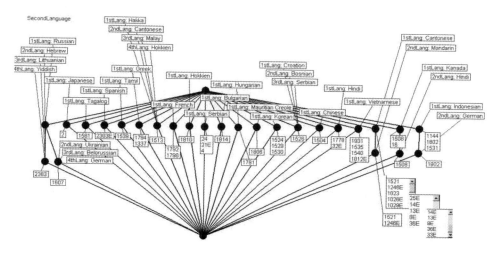

Figure 2: Concept lattice illustrating language other than English

5.3 Organisation Y

Organisation Y reveals a staff profile that is senior in terms of age and made up of very experienced staff for the size of the organisation. All of the staff are tertiary educated. The structure of the firm appears very flat and the proportion of individuals identified as experts would indicate quite a close working relationship with one another. This Organisation appears to be a professional bureaucracy along Mintzberg lines. Of interest to this particular study we note that Organisation Y is basically mono-cultural. Of the seven IT staff only one is female and she is also the only multicultural individual. She speaks Cantonese and Malay as languages other than English

5.4 Organisation Z

Languages other than English spoken by the IT staff in Organisation Z, reveals quite some degree of multiculturalism. Although one participant did not include biographical details, we still find seven out of thirteen respondents spoke a language other than English. In all, eight languages other than English were represented. They were in order of popularity {Cantonese, Mandarin}, followed by at least one instance each of {Greek, French, Hindi, Persian, Assyrian and Indonesian}. Of the experts, one spoke Hindi, the other spoke Cantonese as well as Mandarin. The remaining experts (3) spoke no language other than English. Simplifying the language groups there was again a noticeable orientation towards the east-Asian language grouping as in Organisation X.

5.5 Ethnicity and social networks

Having examined the ethnicity of the participants via FCA we wanted to determine if ethnicity had a possible impact on the diffusion of knowledge. Diffusion was mapped via the capture of the social networks within the organisations. By processing the SNA related questions in the survey we could map the frequency and nature of meetings and develop a picture for each organisation. We found that there were some people in Organisation X who met one another frequently and had an ethnic language in common.

One could reasonably conclude they met partially because of their ethnicity. Whilst it will be observed that there is some ethnic 'collaboration', in fact this is not significant for two reasons. Either the Organisations (X, Z) tend to be so diverse ethnically, that little collaboration is possible because the ethnicities tend to be disparate. Or the Organisation is largely mono-cultural (Y) in which case cliquing behaviour on the basis of ethnicity is not taking place, simply because it cannot. One instance where some cliquing on the basis of ethnicity is taking place is that in Organisation X of Cantonese speakers (Figure 3).

In terms of where these Cantonese-speaking individuals belong in the organisation, we find that they are on the same floor within the same building and also in close physical proximity in terms of multidimensional scaling[6] in the SNA diagrams. In the SNA diagrams we can also see participants tagged with the code "ENE" for "expert non experts" which identifies them as individuals not chosen by their peers as experts but exhibiting responses similar to those that were identified as experts. We used FCA for the purposes of identification but do not have space here to describe the process. A key concern in analysing the SNA data was to check whether experts or ENEs were interacting with novices or whether they were primarily unavailable.

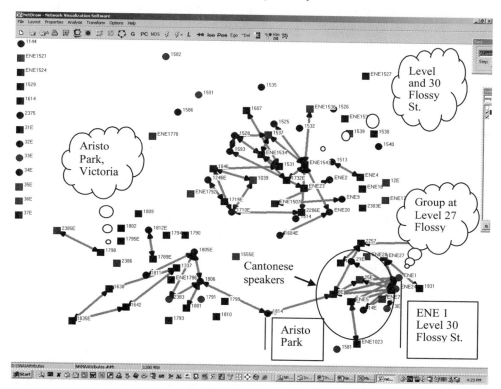

Figure 3: Illustrating physical locations of IT staff in Organisation X

The diagrams were also able to visualise the frequency and nature of the meeting. This data was captured via the questionnaire by asking respondents with whom they associated, how often (hourly through to bi-monthly), the type of meeting they had (morning tea to perhaps formal organisational meeting) and the level of importance of their contact with regard to themselves (from 'try not to see' through to 'simply have to see'). There were a trivial number of associations (groups of two only), taking place

---

[6] SNA software factors in a person's distance from someone else in terms their closeness of relationships with other individuals. In other words the closeness of dots actually has some indication of the distance the person holds with the other person in real life.

based on other ethnicities. For example two Melbourne-based Greek speakers in Organisation X met on an hourly basis, whilst two Sydney-based Japanese speakers in the same Organisation met on a daily basis. A couple of Serbian speakers met fortnightly. It is interesting that the third Serbian speaker in our sample who whilst sharing the same language (and one concludes ethnicity), did not in fact communicate with the other two Serbian speakers. No other relations between ethnic groups were distinctly identified. Again we feel this is due to the highly multicultural nature of the organisation, meaning that cliquing on the basis of ethnicity was actually limited. There was some cliquing taking place on the basis of a shared language, of which in Organisation Z, there were only the Chinese languages in common amongst three staff members.

6   Outcomes and findings

We found in our tacit knowledge research that biographical parameters did not play a *significant* role with regard to tacit knowledge utilisation and IT personnel. However there was *some* indication for a higher than average distribution in Organisation X of experts being of Chinese extraction (proportionately speaking with regard to all the ethnic groups represented).

In answer to our research question whether people clique with one another based on biographical factors such as ethnicity and if it affects tacit knowledge transfer we found:

- There was little evidence for cliquing on the basis of ethnicity.
- There was however some evidence for cliquing amongst Chinese speakers, a number of whom were considered experts.
- However the overwhelmingly multicultural nature of Organisations X and Z, meant that cliquing on the basis of ethnicity was not possible to any but a very minor degree.
- Furthermore there was found to be negligible evidence of cliquing on the basis of any of the other biographical factors.

Our literature study revealed that culture is considered to be strongly associated with tacit knowledge. Our definition of culture was restricted to the notion of shared ethnicity based on a shared language other than English. Our case studies have concentrated on the effect of culture on tacit knowledge flow and if individuals of a certain ethnic background exhibited more tacit knowledge than others. Obviously culture can be defined and measured in many other ways besides language/s spoken. Organisations themselves can be said to provide a particular cultural environment, such as supportive, creative, stagnant, dynamic, and so on, which will impact the existence and flow of tacit knowledge. Further, we did not attempt to determine how or whether tacit knowledge is different for different cultures and thus cannot enter into the western vs. eastern debate often discussed when cultural impacts are considered.

Given the contextual nature of knowledge itself and the diversity of even the companies we studied, our findings cannot be easily or confidently generalised to other organisations. Nevertheless, based on the case studies we conducted we can state that:

- some organisations will choose to be primarily multi or mono-cultural as that may be seen to fit better with organisational goals,
- some cliquing may occur based on ethnicity, but that this does not necessarily result in bottlenecking of tacit knowledge and
- some ethnic groups may exhibit more tacit knowledge either because their cultural background (including training and education) has prepared them well for the job (and are thus considered favourably when being selected for a position), or they may be more motivated to improve themselves by acquiring more experience leading to greater tacit knowledge, such as in the situation of migrant employees.

7　Final Remarks

We, in Western societies in particular, have tended to emphasise the value of what Sternberg (1999) refers to as 'book smarts'. The consumption of codified knowledge has been commensurate with the increasing size and complexity of organisations, which in turn has led to lesser emphasis being placed on 'street smarts'. Certain cultures such as the Japanese have managed to better maintain their respect for tacit knowledge all the while modernising into the workforce they have today. They have managed to do this because they try to provide maximum opportunity for face-to-face discussion both within and external to the workplace itself. It is little coincidence that our small firm (Organisation Y) presented the best prospects for tacit knowledge transfer. We found that the parameters conducive to tacit knowledge transfer, such as intimate meetings, lack of electronic communication and repeated contact were ideal for tacit knowledge flows. Certainly it is more difficult for large organisations such as X to achieve this model. But for the sake of effective soft knowledge management, we must at least try.

References

Brockmann, E., Anthony, W., (1998) "The influence of tacit knowledge and collective mind on strategic planning" *Journal of Managerial Issues* Pittsburg Summer (electronic format)

Cutcliffe, J., (2000) "Methodological issues in grounded theory" *Journal of advanced nursing* 31(6) June :1476-1484

Durrance, B., (1998) "Some explicit thoughts on tacit learning" (Cover Story) *Training & Development* 52(12) p24(6) Dec

Koskinen, K., (2000) "Tacit knowledge as a promoter of project success" *European journal of purchasing & supply management* Vol 6 :41-47

Leonard, D., Sensiper, S., (1998) "The role of tacit knowledge in group innovation" *California Management Review* Berkeley; Spring 40(3)

Partington, D., (2000) "Building grounded theories of management action" *British journal of management* 11(2) :91-102

Scott, J., (1991) *Social Network Analysis: A handbook* Sage Publications London U.K.

Sternberg, R., Wagner, R., Williams, W., Horvath, J., (1995) "Testing common sense" *American psychologist* 50(11) November :912-927

Wagner, R., Sternberg, R., (1991a) *TKIM: The common sense manager: Tacit knowledge inventory for managers: Test Booklet* The Psychological Corporation Harcourt Brace Jovanovich San Antonio U.S.A.

Wagner, R., Sternberg, R., (1991b) *TKIM: The common sense manager: Tacit knowledge inventory for managers: User Manual* The Psychological Corporation Harcourt Brace Jovanovich San Antonio U.S.A.

Walsham, G., (2001) "Knowledge management: The benefits and limitations of computer systems" *European Management Journal* 19(6) December :599-608

Wasserman, S., Faust, K., (1994) *Social Network Analysis: Methods and Applications* Cambridge University Press Cambridge U.K.

West, G., Meyer, G., (1997) "Communicated knowledge as a learning foundation" *International Journal of Organisational Analysis* January (From ABI Proquest)

Wille, R. (1992) "Concept Lattices and Conceptual Knowledge Systems" *Computers Math. Applic.* (23) 6-9: 493-515.

Yamadori, Y., (1984) "Office automation in Japan" *Science and technology in Japan* 3(10) April/June :24-26

ORGANIZATIONAL ATMOSPHERE FOR NURTURING SOCIAL AND INTELLECTUAL CAPITAL: A CASE STUDY OF AN IT SERVICES VENDOR

N. DAYASINDHU & KRISHNAN NARAYANAN

*Software Engineering Technology Labs, Infosys Technologies Ltd.,
Electronics City, Hosur Road, Bangalore, Karnataka 560100, India
dayasindhun@infosys.com & krishnan_narayanan@infosys.com*

An organization can be viewed as a social community specializing in speed and efficiency in the creation and transfer of knowledge. Organizational advantage accrues from the particular capabilities (social capital) organizations have for creating and sharing knowledge (intellectual capital). Based on existing research on the knowledge view and resource based view of an organization and the case studies from an IT services vendor, we propose a model for nurturing social and intellectual capital based on Szulanski's (2003) framework. At the heart of the model is a five step process that leverages social capital in an organization to convert existing intellectual capital to new intellectual capital. The first step is initiation, the processes leading to the decision to transfer intellectual capital. The second step is implementation, the processes through which intellectual flows to the recipient from the source. The third step is ramp-up, the processes by which the recipient starts using transferred knowledge. The fourth step is integration, the processes by which the transferred knowledge becomes institutionalized. The process of incentivization runs across all the four processes mentioned earlier and motivates the source of intellectual capital to share it with the recipient. New intellectual capital helps organizations deliver customer value and leads to competitive advantage.

1 Introduction

A perspective of the organization is that it can be understood as a social community specializing in effectively and efficiency creating and transferring knowledge. Organizational advantage accrues from the capabilities organizations have for creating and sharing knowledge. Practitioners are increasingly looking at creating organizational advantage based on value creation i.e. invest in productivity and in new technologies to enhance functionality of products and services, and ensure their appropriateness for new situations. As organizations change focus to value creation, the practitioner's primary task is redefined from institutionalizing control to embedding trust, from maintaining the status quo to leading knowledge creation and transfer.

Knowledge can be either explicit or tacit and can be held by individuals or collectively in groups. Explicit and individual knowledge constitute technical expertise. Explicit and collective knowledge are the rules, regulations and laws. Tacit and individual knowledge constitutes intuitiveness. Tacit and collective knowledge constitute the wisdom of social practice. While studying intellectual capital creation, we focus our analysis on the social explicit and social tacit knowledge. Social capital provides ideal condition to create new intellectual capital by the combination and exchange of existing intellectual capital. Organizational advantage results from the increase in intellectual capital. Our arguments draw on the resource based view of the firm to explain the competitive advantage created.

We have studied the operations of the R&D division of an Information Technology (IT) services vendor and its relationship with other divisions that execute IT services projects for customers (Dayasindhu and Narayanan 2004). Based on the case studies and existing theory postulated by Nahapiet and Ghoshal (1998), Nonaka and Takeuchi (1995), and Szulanski (2003) we propose a model that nurtures an atmosphere to create new intellectual capital.

The model is being used by the IT services vendor in establishing and institutionalizing a mechanism for creating new intellectual capital. Though we have attempted to codify the new intellectual capital creation process, we are also aware that the implementation of the model would involve tacit knowledge of how an organization works in reality.

2   Theoretical Foundations: Social Capital, Intellectual Capital, Knowledge Transfer, and Competitive Advantage

2.1 Social Capital

Granovetter (1985) posits that social Capital is the sum of the actual and potential resources embedded within, available through, and derived from the network of relationships possessed by an organization. Social capital thus comprises both the network and the assets that may be mobilized through that network. In the context of our research, the role of social capital in the creation of intellectual capital, it is useful to consider three dimensions: the structural, the relational, and the cognitive dimensions of social capital. Social capital is owned jointly by the employees in a network of relationships, and no one player has, or is capable of having, exclusive ownership rights. Social capital cannot be traded easily and creates the conditions that create new intellectual capital. Social capital encourages cooperative behavior, thereby facilitating the development of new forms of association and innovative organization.

Structural dimension of social capital refers to the overall pattern of connections between employees in a firm that is, who you reach and how you reach them (Granovetter 1985). Among the most important facets of this dimension is the presence or absence of network ties between employees, network configuration describing the pattern of linkages in terms of such measures as density, connectivity, and hierarchy; and appropriable organization that is, the existence of networks created for one purpose that may be used for another. Relational dimension of social capital refers to the assets created and leveraged through relationships and bonds between employees (Granovetter 1985). Among the key facets in this dimension are trust, norms, obligations, and identity. Cognitive dimension of social capital refers to those resources providing shared representations, interpretations, and systems of meaning among employees (Conner and Prahalad 1996). These resources also represent facets that include shared language and shared narratives.

2.2 Intellectual Capital

Intellectual capital refers to the knowledge and knowing capability of a firm (Coleman 1988). The focus is on the social explicit knowledge and the social tacit knowledge (that which cannot be expressed) that has a predominant role in the firm's organizational advantage. Social explicit knowledge represents the shared corpus of knowledge, for example, scientific communities. A wide range of organizations, are investing in a big way in the development of such objectified knowledge as firms attempt to pool, share, and leverage their distributed knowledge. Social tacit knowledge represents the knowledge that is fundamentally embedded in the forms of social and institutional practice and that resides in the tacit experiences and collective behaviour of employees. Combination and creation of intellectual capital involves making new combinations either incrementally or radically (Nonaka and Takeuchi 1995). This happens by combining knowledge with employees who were previously unconnected or by developing novel ways of combining knowledge with employees who are already connected. Exchange and creation of intellectual capital usually occurs where knowledge held by different employees, exchange is a prerequisite for combining knowledge (Nonaka and Takeuchi 1995). Since intellectual capital generally is created through a process of combining the knowledge and experience of different employees, it is dependent upon exchange between employees.

There are four conditions that must be satisfied for exchange and combination of intellectual capital (Nahapiet and Ghoshal 1998). These are access to employees, anticipation of value, motivation and capability. The four conditions are influenced by the three dimensions of social capital viz. structural, cognitive and relationship. The first condition is that the opportunity exists to make the combination or exchange. In our context we see this condition being determined the ease of accessibility to the objectified and collective forms of social knowledge for employees. Second, in order for the employees to avail themselves of the opportunities that may exist to combine or exchange intellectual they must expect such deployment to create value. In other words, they must anticipate that interaction, exchange, and combination will prove worthwhile, even if they remain uncertain of what will be produced or how. The third condition for the creation of new resources highlights the importance of motivation. Even where opportunities for exchange exist and employees anticipate that value may be created through exchange or interaction, those involved must feel that their engagement in the knowledge exchange and combination will be worth their while. The fourth condition for the creation of new intellectual capital is combination capability. Even where the opportunities for knowledge exchange and combination exist, these opportunities are perceived as valuable, and parties are motivated to make such resource deployments or to engage in knowing activity, the capability to combine information or experience must exist among employees.

2.3 Knowledge Transfer

A related theory that is more practitioner friendly has been proposed by Szulanski (2003) where knowledge transfer or new knowledge creation by combination of existing knowledge can be understood using a four step organizational model.

(1) Initiation: The processes leading to the decision to transfer the practice such as discovery of both the need and the knowledge within the organization
(2) Implementation: The processes through which knowledge flows to the recipient from the source, the social ties between recipient and source, and the 'how' of making knowledge transfer less threatening to recipient
(3) Ramp-up: The processes by which the recipient starts using transferred knowledge, identifies and resolves unexpected problems, and improves performance
(4) Integration: The processes by which the transferred knowledge becomes routinized and institutionalized in the organization

We add a fifth step to the Szulanki's model that is Incentivization. Organizational atmosphere may or may not be conducive to knowledge transfer. The source may not be motivated to share knowledge because of a fear that they might lose their personal competitive edge. The recipient may not be motivated to use the knowledge transferred typified by the "not invented here syndrome". Incentivization refers to those processes aimed to create an environment conducive for knowledge transfer cutting across all of Szulanksi's four steps.

(5) Incentivization: The processes through which the source is motivated to share knowledge and the recipient is motivated to receive the knowledge.

2.4 Competitive Advantage and Customer Value

The new intellectual capital can be viewed as resources. These arguments are consistent with resource-based theory that highlights the sustained competitive advantage of firms as based in their unique constellation of resources: physical, human, and organizational. A firm is said to possess sustained competitive advantage only when current or potential competitors can neither simultaneously implement nor duplicate the benefits of its value creating strategy. Resources refer to resources (in a traditional context, capabilities and processes). Applying this view, intellectual capital (and social capital) are resources of the firm. Resources are found to result in sustained competitive advantage when valuable, rare, inimitable, and non-substitutable (Barney 1991; Dierickx and Cool 1985). This is commonly referred to as the VRIN condition.

(1) Valuable: Resources are useful to create some value for the firm.
(2) Rare: There is a finite amount of resources available and different firms are competing for them.
(3) Inimitable: The resources cannot be imitated easily by those firms who do not have them.

(4) Non-substitutable: Firms not having the resources cannot be substituted with other types of resources to generate value.

A conceptual model of the organizational model to nurture social and intellectual capital to create new intellectual capital is shown in Figure 1.

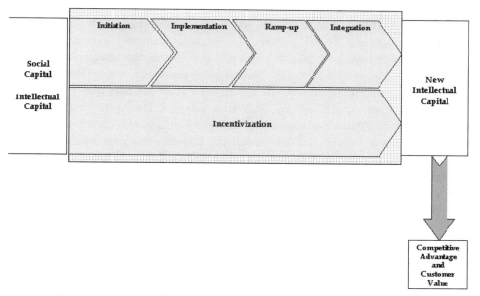

Figure 1. Nurturing Social and Intellectual Capital to create New Intellectual Capital

3   Methodology

The contemporary nature of the research and nurturing an atmosphere for creating intellectual capital in an IT services vendor and the lack of control over the events makes case study an appropriate research methodology (Yin 1994). The data for the case studies primarily came from eighteen in-depth semi structured interviews with project managers, researchers, project leads, technical architects, programmers associated with the IT project from both the R&D division and the project executing divisions of the IT services vendor. Data was also obtained from internal reports maintained by the IT services vendor. One representative case study is discussed in this paper. All names are masked due to the sensitive and confidential nature of the case studies. The dominant mode of analysis of the case study used in this research is explanation-building (Miles and Huberman 1994). The emphasis of the case study is to examine how an IT services vendor has nurtured an atmosphere that creates new intellectual capital that has led to customer value and competitive advantage.

4   Case Study: Collaboration between Project Executing Division and R&D Division in an IT Service Vendor

In early 2002, the senior management at a global logistics company was aggressively pursuing an acquisition driven growth strategy. This resulted in a plethora of disparate business processes and IT systems across the new organization. A critical requirement for a successful merger of organizations was the successful integration of the disparate business processes and IT applications. The logistics company expected their long standing IT services vendor to play an active role in achieving this integration.

The IT services vendor was successfully managing the maintenance and development of several critical software applications in the logistics firm and thus had a good knowledge of the applications. This knowledge predominantly resided with the project team in the IT services vendor that had been working with the logistics firm. In order to achieve a solution for integrating the disparate business processes and IT applications post merger, the project team felt the need for an innovative solution for business process and application rationalization. Further, there was a need to have a better methodology for requirement gathering to ensure maximum and comprehensive knowledge transfer between the different organizations of the merged company and between that company and the IT services vendor. The project team was planning to leverage the expertise in IT strategy and business process management that existed in the R&D division to achieve a suitable solution for the logistics company. The process of leveraging existing expertise across different divisions in the IT services vendor and delivering innovative IT led business transformation solutions has its roots in the atmosphere in the IT services vendor that nurtures both social and intellectual capital.

Even prior to this project there were ties that existed between members of the R&D division and the project team.

(1) The Engagement Manager of the project team and the Business Manager of the R&D division had worked together earlier and were well acquainted, both being "old timer" employees in the IT services vendor.

(2) The Deployment Manager at the R&D division and the Engagement Manager were at a common residential training program at the IT services vendor

(3) One of the Technical Architects in the R&D division was earlier part of the projects division and knew the Engagement Manager and many of the Project Managers as well.

The following excerpt from a mail from a project manager with the project team to the Deployment Manager in the R&D division illustrates how the previous connections provided a network of access to people, information and knowledge.

"We need some help going forward. We have convinced the client to use your division's expertise in a particular area. <Project Leader> would be sending you his issues etc which u can either address or point to the right person. "

In September 2002, awareness sessions on the methodologies for user process mapping and user requirement analysis developed by the R&D division were held for the project team. The intention of these sessions was to inform and educate the Project

Managers about the usefulness of the methodology and how it may help them deliver better solutions for the client. Simultaneously, the Business Manager in the R&D division established contact with the Engagement Manager of the project team. Presentations were made to explain the benefits of using the methodologies in projects in and commitment was obtained for adoption of the methodologies. The project team then started incorporating the methodologies in their ongoing projects.

The project team had been maintaining several software applications of the logistics company for over five years and was looking at ways to codify the knowledge that existed in the minds of members of the team. The codified knowledge was essential not only for creating newer opportunities for the IT services vendor but also as a knowledge base for newcomers joining the project team. The codification of knowledge involved not only capturing the specifications about the applications but also the business processes these applications supported. Process thinking came into focus with the software development team. The same process thinking was what the R&D division had worked on in creating the Business Process Management framework. In December 2002, the R&D division organized a hands-on training for the project team on process mapping and user requirement methodologies. A practice of "train-the-trainer" sessions on the methodologies was put in place.

In January 2003, the team Engagement Manager of the project team and the Deployment Manager in charge of evangelizing the methodologies developed by the R&D division made a presentation to key influencers in the logistics company. The intention was to share the initial outputs of work done by the project team to demonstrate the usefulness of the process mapping and user requirement analysis methodologies and explore further opportunities. This meet led to several other discussions with the logistics company that now expected their long standing IT services vendor, to play an active role in achieving business – IT integration apart from the ongoing maintenance of software applications. Simultaneously, the logistics company expected the IT services vendor to provide Ready for User-Acceptance-Test capability. In order to achieve these objectives, the IT services vendor felt the need for an innovative solution for business process and application rationalization. Further, there was a need to have a better methodology for requirement gathering to ensure maximum and comprehensive knowledge transfer between the multiple organizations post merger and between the logistics company and the IT services vendor.

In March 2003, the Deployment Manager met up with the Engagement Manager and finalized the collaboration initiatives between the project team and the R&D division for the year ahead. Important initiatives that emerged were globalization framework for business application rationalization and an improved system appreciation methodology. The Engagement Manager identified project leaders from the project team for each of the initiatives. A dedicated workbench development team was identified at the R&D division. The globalization framework for the logistics company used some of the methodologies developed by the R&D division. The lead for this initiative from the project team says,

"The globalization framework leveraged the application effectiveness approach we were using. The reviews by the R&D division have added a lot of value to our understanding."

The R&D division had created a methodology for evaluating the effectiveness of IT investments and tool for application portfolio analysis the previous year. The project team was clearly impressed with the successes of the engagements in assessing effectiveness of IT investments with other customers and they believed that the R&D division may be able to bring in value to their project.

Another example of sharing existing intellectual capital to create new intellectual capital was seen in the use of X-Query by the R&D division for the analysis tool in globalization framework. The methodologies group in the R&D division was experimenting with X-Query technology for XML reporting purposes. When the project team came up with a requirement for a tool for analysing the business processes and applications, the workbench team dedicated to the logistics company used X-Query to address this need. The use of a technology was extended to a new business context and an innovative solution was created. The methodologies group subsequently submitted this idea through a paper to a leading journal to illustrate a novel use of technology. The Engagement Manager recounts that,

"Thanks to the workbench team in the R&D division for including the project requirements at a great speed. This would help us take the relationship with the logistics company to the next level."

While all these activities were underway, the relationship between the project team and the R&D division was nurtured. Trust between the project team and the R&D division was built over a period of time. Adherence to timelines of deliverables, and focused attention to the project team led to creation of trust. The trust and confidence built between the two teams is illustrated in the words of the Engagement Manager when he agrees to become a R&D Division Champion.

"As discussed, please feel free to use the case study wherever you feel it could add value. Also, if you feel I or other members can help in anyway, all you need to do is "sneeze" :) I feel the R&D Division is bringing in a lot of value for us in the project - lot has already come; more to come. This is the least we can do!"

The relationships were getting strengthened in other ways as well. Obligations represent a commitment or duty to undertake some activity in the future. Clearly the R&D division wanted to highlight the initial successes achieved in collaborating with the project team to rest of the IT services organization and make the project team and the Engagement Manager champions of the R&D division's cause. The R&D division's newsletter carried this success story in July 2003 and the commitment to deliver was thus increased.

In Dec. 2003, the R&D division started working with the project team on an important engagement involving integration of applications and processes of a company that the logistics company had merged with. The knowledge from prior projects and methodologies were utilized in this project.

The intellectual capital both explicit and tacit that resided with the project team and R&D division as shown in Table 1.

Table 1. Existing Intellectual Capital.

Existing intellectual capital	Type of intellectual capital	Intellectual capital residing with
Knowledge of applications in the logistics company	Tacit	Project team
Knowledge of specific methodologies for user requirement analysis	Explicit	R&D division
System appreciation approach	Explicit	Project team
Initial ideas on a framework for business / application rationalization	Tacit	Project team / R&D division
Knowledge of X-Query	Explicit	R&D division

The main activities that created new intellectual capital from the existing intellectual capital were:

(1) Several awareness sessions about the R&D division's methodologies and tools were held for the project team (Initiate)
(2) The buy-in to this collaborative work was taken from the senior management of both the project team and R&D division and this facilitated faster and involved transfer of knowledge (Implementation)
(3) The R&D division actively participated and consulted in several projects along with the project team and brought in their expertise (Ramp-up)
(4) The Engagement Manager became a Methodologies Champion and was featured in the R&D division's newsletters (Integration)
(5) The collaboration between the project team and R&D division worked on a basis of soft mandates and annual goals (Incentivization)

A structured twenty six step approach for leveraging existing social and intellectual capital was developed and included the mechanisms shown in Table 2.

Table 2. Mechanisms for Nurturing Social and Intellectual Capital.

Process	Mechanisms
Initiation	Knowledge sharing sessions between members of R&D division and project divisions
Implementation	Create Research Champions to communicate the benefits of leveraging the R&D division
	Identify single point of contacts at the R&D division and project divisions for effective communication
Ramp Up	Active participation and observer participation of research teams in IBU projects
	R&D divisions conducting train the trainer programs at the project divisions
Integration	Make use of existing institutionalized mechanisms in the IT services vendor for effective communication
	Derive norms that guide collaboration between R&D division and project divisions
Incentivization	Goals of the collaboration synchronized with the performance metrics of the members of the R&D and project divisions

The new intellectual capital created has helped the IT services vendor in deepening and strengthening its relationship with the logistics company, and in improving delivery effectiveness and efficiency. Some of the new intellectual capital created is shown in Table 3.

Table 3. New Intellectual Capital.

New intellectual capital	Type of intellectual capital	Intellectual capital residing with
Knowledge of business processes and applications in the logistics company	Explicit	Project Team
Application of BPM methodology in large scale business context	Tacit	R&D Division
Enhanced system appreciation approach	Explicit	Project Team and R&D Division
Applying the globalization framework that included an IT effectiveness application portfolio analysis approach and application of X-Query to create a tool for the globalization framework	Explicit	Project Team and R&D Division
Application of X-Query in business analysis context; paper submitted on this subject	Explicit	R&D Division

The new intellectual capital possessed the VRIN characteristics

(1) Helped the IT services vendor to generate revenues from the logistics company and other customers
(2) Created from certain unique social capital in the IT services vendor (i.e. the network ties between the R&D division and the project divisions, the trust between team members) and existing intellectual capital like process methodologies, knowledge of applications etc.).
(3) Could not be imitated easily by competitors of the IT services vendor because of several factors – time compression diseconomies as it involved a complex web of relationships within the IT services vendor, and evolved in a context dependent environment.
(4) Could not be substituted easily by the pre-existing intellectual capital in the IT services vendor and would require large investments to procure them from outside.

5   Conclusion: Benefits to the Logistics Company and IT Services Vendor

The cycle of knowledge creation and transfer comprising the steps of initiation – implementation – ramp-up – integration (in that order) and incentivization made it easier for the IT services vendor to create new intellectual capital that was used both to provide competitive advantage and to add customer value.

The value derived by the logistics company from the engagement were:

(1) Application of proprietary business methodology to model business requirements to the customer's global processes. Reuse of these business process maps for subsequent engagements in the logistics firms have helped reduce cost.
(2) Enhancing system appreciation of the customer's IT systems and thus increasing the comprehensiveness and reliability of information captured
(3) Applying the globalization framework that included an IT effectiveness application portfolio analysis approach and application of X-Query to create a tool for the globalization framework. The framework and the tool bring in efficiency and comprehensiveness.

The IT Services vendor has derived value from the exercise as well.

(1) Increasing revenue: Developing new solutions – Globalization Framework, deepening relationships with customers, and opening new cross selling opportunities for services (several other solutions and ideas from the R&D division have been positioned with the Logistics company).
(2) Decreasing costs: Developing methodologies and frameworks that facilitate reuse (reuse of X-Query, the globalization framework plug-in reused with another client in the healthcare industry) and increasing slope of learning curve (use of process maps makes learning curve steeper for new project team members).
(3) Enhancing thought leadership: Publications for journals and conferences (the paper on X-Query submitted to the XML Journal by the R&D Division)

References

Barney, J. (1991) "Firm resources and sustained competitive advantage." *Journal of Management,* 17(1): 99-120.

Coleman, J. S. (1988) "Social capital in the creation of human capital." *American Journal of Sociology,* 94(Supplement): S95-S120.

Conner, K. R. and Prahalad, C. K. (1996) "A resource-based theory of the firm: Knowledge versus opportunism." *Organization Science,* 7(5): 477-501.

Dayasindhu, N. and Narayanan, K. (2004) "Delivering customer value by leveraging social and intellectual capital." *Cutting Edge: A Thought Communique From Infosys,* 4(4): 1-4.

Dierickx, I. and Cool, K. (1989) "Asset stock accumulation and sustainability of competitive advantage." *Management Science,* 35(12): 1504-1511.

Granovetter, M. S. (1985) "Economic action and social structure: The problem of embeddedness." *American Journal of Sociology,* 91(3): 481-510.

Miles, M. B. and Huberman, A. M. (1994) *Qualitative data analysis: An extended source book.* 2nd ed. Thousand Oaks: Sage Publications.

Nahapiet, J. and Ghoshal, S. (1998) "Social capital, intellectual capital, and the organizational advantage." *Academy of Management Review,* 23(2): 242-266.

Nonaka, I. and Takeuchi, H. (1995) *The knowledge creating company.* New York: Oxford University Press.

Szulanski, G. (2003) *Sticky knowledge: Barriers to knowing the firm.* London: Sage Publications.

Yin, R. K. (1994) *Case study research, design and methods. 2nd ed.* Thousand Oaks: Sage Publications.

THE COMMUNICATION AUDIT: TRIED AND TRUE, BUT NOW LET'S USE IT FOR SOMETHING NEW – EXAMINING ORGANISATIONAL KNOWLEDGE SHARING

CELINA PASCOE

School of Information Management and Tourism,
Division of Communication and Education
University of Canberra, ACT, 2600, Australia
Celina.Pascoe@canberra.edu.au

ELIZABETH MORE

Macquarie University, NSW, 2109, Australia
Elizabeth.More@vc.mq.edu.au

This paper reports research on the role of communication in knowledge management, examined through the lens of communication climate. The research is being undertaken in a major public sector organisation, on a longitudinal basis over 2003 and 2004. The organisation wishes to shift its culture to one characterised by internal information sharing, and to this end it has undertaken a three-year knowledge management initiative that comprises an integrated suite of formal and informal knowledge sharing activities. The present paper provides results of the first survey of the organisation's communication climate, and they suggest that communication audits can be used to gauge whether knowledge and information sharing are occurring by providing data on two antecedents to such sharing: perceptions of other organisational members' openness to the *receiving* as well as the *sending* aspects of sharing.

1   Introduction

Today we still find ongoing debate about the very definition of knowledge management and a variety of views on its utility and its link to organisational strategy, performance, and competitiveness. More recently, Wenger (2004:1-2) has emphasised the contextual nature of knowledge management:

> You need to have processes in place to coordinate the management of knowledge and integrate it into business processes such as technology for information flows, interpersonal connections, and document repositories, as well as institutional and cultural norms of paying attention to knowledge. ... Practitioners, the people who use knowledge in their activities, are in the best position to manage this knowledge.

The research reported in the present paper endorses the emphasis on intangibles Wenger mentions – the interpersonal, institutional and cultural norms and the focus on the practice of knowledge management. For whilst information technology may have inspired the vision of a perfectly managed global knowledge network, enabling staff to increase effectiveness and efficiency, technology alone cannot realise such a vision (McDermott 1999).

Consequently, the paper reports a research study which investigates the link between communication climate and the openness of organisational members' interaction, in particular their willingness to share knowledge and voice their ideas. In so doing, we are mindful that knowledge management research and that of communication scholars have much to learn from each other, and yet traditional silos remain.

2   The role of knowledge in today's organisations

There is little doubt that, for many organisations, their knowledge is the only asset they have and so their survival depends on being able to make best use of this existing knowledge and to create new knowledge. In this knowledge-based economy, the need for communication between organisational members has never been greater. This is highlighted by the description of organisations as distributed knowledge systems (Tsoukas 1996). The role of communication in the survival of today's organisations is also highlighted by the discussion of organisational knowledge as socially constructed, context specific, and ambiguous rather than being composed of objective, clearly generalisable rules that can be codified in any form (Morris 2001). For Cilliers (2000) knowledge is interpreted data, and this interpretation only comes from interaction. Further, as Nonaka (1999: 66) so aptly describes it: 'human knowledge is created and expanded through social interactions between tacit and explicit knowledge'. Since knowledge processes cannot be separated from social processes, human relationships are an integral element of knowledge management.

The distinction between explicit and tacit knowledge further highlights the vital role of communication in optimising an organisation's knowledge assets. Tacit knowledge cannot be as easily communicated and codified as explicit knowledge (Winter 1987; Quinn *et al.* 1996; Horvath 2000; Grund *et al.* 2002). As Davenport and Prusak (1998: 95) explain: explicit knowledge can be embedded in procedures or represented in documents and databases, and transferred with reasonable accuracy; however, tacit knowledge generally requires extensive personal contact – tacit knowledge cannot be transferred readily in any other way. Therefore, tacit knowledge is more difficult for competitors to 'steal', and it is in this context that some of the knowledge management literature stresses the need for organisations to capitalise on tacit knowledge as a means of achieving a competitive advantage.

If today's organisations need to capitalise on their existing knowledge and to use it as a framework for the creation of new knowledge, then high levels of organisational commitment and willingness to expend innovative effort are also vital to the survival of today's business organisations. Favourable communication climates have been related to higher levels of organisational commitment, higher levels of communication openness, and higher levels of willingness to expend innovative effort (Hosmer 1994; Hosmer 1996; Ruppel and Harrington 2000).

3   KM strategies neglect an important facet of human communication

In 1998 (p.1), Ash stated '... here's the terrible punch line for KM: we appear to be constructing KM communication networks without accessing expertise in communication strategy.' In 1999, More argued that communication in knowledge management is traditionally viewed as a conduit and a container for the storage and transmission of knowledge.

Whilst a body of literature on the role of human relationships in knowledge management has been emerging for some time, the conduit view lives on with only a few exceptions (for instance, Isaacs 1994; Horvath 2000; Empsen 2001; Jian 2001; Morris 2001). This conduit perspective is appropriate when applied to the sharing of information, but not so for the sharing of knowledge. In their discussion of organic knowledge management, Davenport and Prusak (1998) describe information as a 'message', that has a receiver and a sender; by contrast, knowledge originates and is implied in the minds of people, and can only be volunteered (not conscripted). In this sense, knowledge sharing, and creation, involves a facet of the communication process that differs from the transfer or sharing of information - knowledge sharing not only paves the way for the *creation of shared meaning* between communicators, but in doing so, also lays the foundation for the creation or generation of new knowledge.

More (1999) points out that Isaacs is one author who discusses a form of organisational learning with an emerging focus on this facet of the communication process. His discussion of triple-loop learning focuses on dialogue, which is quite different to debate (win-lose) or to discussion (consensus). Dialogue alters underlying patterns of meaning and brings to the surface the fundamental patterns leading to disagreement. In this sense, it provides an environment in which people can consciously participate in creating shared meaning (More 1999: 355). Similarly, Jian (2001) emphasises the role of organisational discourse in the constitution of knowledge, suggesting that knowledge be conceptualised as a process of 'knowledgizing' and situated in communication practices. Such a conceptualisation, he claims, enables organisational discourse to be recognised as constitutive of knowledge rather than as merely representative of it. However, our individual defensive reasoning and organisational defensive routines fly in the face of creating an environment which enables dialogue (Argyris and Schon 1996; Argyris 2000; Friedman 2001).

If we accept that knowledge management is the leveraging of an organisation's existing knowledge and creating new knowledge in the process, and that it is about a volunteer, rather than conscript, mentality in employees and managers (Davenport and Prusak 1998), then it becomes clear that fostering relationships and communication between organisational members must be integral elements of any meaningful KM program. In light of the research that links communication climate with open communication, organisational commitment, and willingness to expend innovative effort, the research reported in this paper extends discussion of human communication in knowledge processes beyond its function as a conduit. It does so by examining the role that communication climate plays in enabling knowledge sharing and creation.

4   Link between communication and knowledge

Favourable communication climates, overall, have been related to higher levels of organisational commitment (Welsch and LaVan 1981), as have higher levels of communication openness and perceived information adequacy (Trombetta and Roberts 1988), management sharing of accurate information (Guzley 1992), the clarity of information (Meyer 1968; Guzley 1992), and the supportiveness of superior-subordinate relations (Dennis 1975; Guzley 1992). Ethical work climate is characterised by 'right', 'just', and 'fair' (ethical) treatment by managers (Hosmer 1994). There is evidence that such a climate alone, and coupled with opportunities for employee communication, lead to higher levels of willingness to expend innovative effort (Hosmer 1994; Hosmer 1996; Ruppel and Harrington 2000). Furthermore, greater network participation and denser networks can be expected in organisations where the climate is perceived as open and supportive of communication (Goldhaber *et al.* 1979; Roberts and O'Reilly 1979).

Goodell (1992) claims that the common theme in definitions of climate given by Taguiri (1968: 25), Forehand and Gilmer (1964: 362), Campbell *et al.* (1970: 390), Schneider (1975: 474), Howe (1977: 106-7), and Poole (1987: 2) is that it is the experienced environment of the organisation, it has wide-spread influence, and that it is enduring over time. Goodell states that 'It is logical that the environment we experience in an organization influences – at least in some part – our behavior' (Goodell, 1992: 323). The fact that climate influences behaviour is particularly relevant when it comes to knowledge management because, in attempting to create cultures of knowledge sharing, organisations are trying to influence the communication behaviours of their members; thus, communication climate might be a variable that can be used to effect knowledge sharing behaviour.

The notion of an ideal communication climate was postulated by Redding (1972) with the dimensions of particular importance being: 1) supportiveness; 2) participative-decision making; 3) trust, confidence, and credibility; 4) openness and candour; and 5) high performance goals. Table 1 below summarises numerous factors that have been found to be components of organisational communication climate. Some instruments (for instance, the International Communication Association Communication Audit) distinguish between satisfaction with the amount/quality of information received from managers and other aspects of communication relationships such as trust of and from one's managers (and other organisational members), guidance from supervisors, involvement in decision-making, and so on. The table reveals four categories of factors: leader-member communication, other aspects of communication relationships, reliability and quality of information received from other organisational members, and use of and satisfaction with various modes of communication.

Table 1. Components of communication climate and associated surveys (italicised items are those associated with communication openness and trust)

	ICA	O'Connell 1979 / Dennis 1974	Redding 1972 / Dennis 1975	Roberts & O'Reilly / Read	Downs *et al.*
Leader-member communication (amount)	Commu'n sources *Info sending* *Info receiving*	Superior-subordinate comm'n *Opportunities for upward comm'n*	Superior-subordinate comm'n *Opportunities for upward comm'n*	Directionality-upward Directionality-downward	*Supervisor comm'n* Subordinate comm'n *Personal feedback*
Other aspects of communication relationships	Comm'n follow-up Working relations *(includes trust, satisfac'n with relationships, upward influence)* Org'l outcomes (job satisfac'n)	*Superior openness / candour*	*Participative decision-making / influence of upward comm'n* *Trust, confidence, credibility* *Supportiveness* *Openness / candour (especially superior-subordinate relationship)* High performance goals	*Influence* *Trust* *Desire for interaction* Satisfaction Mobility Directionality-lateral	*Org'l integration* *Org'l perspective* *Comm'n climate* Comm'n satisfac'n
Reliability / quality of information	*Timeliness* *Accuracy / usefulness of info*	*Reliability of info* *Quality of info*	*Perceived quality / accuracy of downward comm'n* *Perceived reliability of info from subordinates and coworkers*	*Accuracy* Summarisation Gatekeeping Overload	*Comm'n overload*
Modes of communication	Comm'n channels			Modality-written Modality-face-to-face Modality telephone Modality other	Media quality

Table 1 above reveals the extent to which openness is an integral element of communication climate. The research reported in this paper takes information and knowledge sharing to be a form of communication openness, and therefore posits that it is intrinsically tied to the data provided by communication audits. This research also takes reciprocity as a major influence on one's communication openness (Jablin 1978; Baird 1974; Stull 1975). By doing so, it attempts to establish that communication audits can be used to gauge organisational members' knowledge sharing and creation potential, by providing data on the extent to which they perceive that others openly share their knowledge and voice their ideas.

Whilst this research takes the position that the conduit perspective of communication is both inappropriate and inadequate in representing the type of communication needed in today's knowledge-based organisations, it does acknowledge that communication openness comprises two dimensions: openness in message *sending* and openness in message *receiving* (Redding 1972; Jablin 1985; Jablin 1992). Openness in message sending is the candid, but not indiscriminate, disclosure of important company facts, 'bad news', and one's feelings (Eisenberg & Witten, 1987). Openness in message receiving involves encouraging, or at least permitting, the frank expression of views divergent from one's own, as well as the willingness to listen to 'bad news' or discomforting information (Redding, 1972). Many of the components of communication climate, and the instruments used to examine it, reflect this parallel nature of openness. For instance, in Table 1, in the category 'Other aspects of communication relationships', others' openness in message receiving is reflected in participative decision-making, supportiveness, communication follow-up (following up on information received is an indication of openness to its receipt in the first place), and perceptions of overload (one who claims that they suffer from communication overload would surely not be open to further receipt). Some elements in this same category, by contrast, relate to openness in message sending. One important example is superior openness/candour; another is timeliness (since the speed with which one sends information might very well be related to their willingness to share that information). Similarly, all the elements listed under 'Reliability/quality of information' relate to openness of sending (since if the information one tends to send is neither reliable nor accurate, their communication behaviour is unlikely to be described as open).

Alongside openness of both sending and receiving, trust is another factor that is prevalent in the communication climate literature, and in most of the communication audit questionnaires there are questions that relate directly to trust for, and from, superiors, colleagues, and coworkers. There is considerable research evidence that, via trust, open employee communication and organisational communication climate influence willingness to expend innovative effort (Hosmer 1994; Hosmer 1996; Oldham and Kummings 1996; Costigan, Ilter and Berman 1998; Bokeno and Gantt 2000; Ruppel and Harrington 2000). Similarly, there is research evidence that trust is necessary for organisational knowledge creation and sharing (Davenport and Prusak 1998; Lesser

2000; Abrams *et al.* 2002; Adler 2002). The study reported in this paper brings together these two bodies of research (communication climate and trust, and organisational knowledge sharing/creation and trust). This is represented in Figure 1 below.

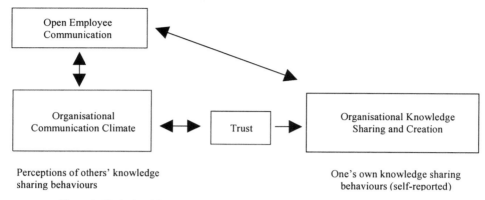

Figure 1: The Role of Communication and Climate in Knowledge Sharing and Creation

Trust links both sides of the model because:

(1) It is trust that is influenced by communication climate (Hosmer 1994; Hosmer 1996; Oldham and Kummings 1996; Bokeno and Gantt 2000; Ruppel and Harrington 2000) and actual incidents of communication between people (Costigan, Ilter and Berman 1998; Ruppel and Harrington 2000).

(2) Trust, in turn, influences preparedness to share knowledge and expend innovative effort (Hosmer 1994; Hosmer 1996; Davenport and Prusak 1998; Bokeno and Gantt 2000; Lesser 2000; Ruppel and Harrington 2000; Abrams *et al.* 2002; Adler 2002).

Data representing respondents' perceptions of organisational communication flow and others' openness (or knowledge sharing behaviours) appears on the left side of the above diagram, and can be collected using a communication audit questionnaire. The right side of the diagram represents one's own communication openness (or knowledge sharing behaviour). Since existing audit questionnaires tend to focus on perceptions of others' communication behaviours more so than on one's own, it is proposed that data on one's own communication behaviours be collected via interviews, focus groups, and participant observation. The extent of correlation between both sets of data will indicate the extent of the link between communication climate and organisational knowledge sharing and creation.

5   A rich case study

The research study reported is being undertaken in a large Australian federal government organisation, employing 1,500 staff, across every capital city in the country. The organisation has recently implemented a three-year knowledge management program and is endeavouring to shift its culture to one characterised by information sharing within and across organisational units. It is doing so with an integrated suite of formal and informal knowledge sharing initiatives supported by appropriate information management programs and technology.

As mentioned above, the questionnaire survey of communication flows and climate comprises only one method of data collection in this study. This data was collected in June 2003, via a representative sample of the organisation, of 167 employees. The communication climate survey comprised elements of the Downs-Hazen Communication Satisfaction Questionnaire (CSQ) and the International Communication Association (ICA) Communication Audit. Elements of both questionnaires were used because the ICA provides valuable data on communication flow, and satisfaction with the amount of information on various topics and from various sources, whereas the CSQ provides valuable data on the relational aspects of communication satisfaction.

An ethnographic approach was taken to collect data on one's own communication openness (or knowledge sharing behaviour). One of the authors 'worked' in the organisation for almost a year and was thereby able to conduct participant observation of key meetings, and content analysis of organisation documentation over that period. However, the size of, and geographical dispersion within, the organisation made participant observation a difficult means of collecting sufficient data on *one's own* knowledge sharing. Therefore, the next stage of the research, conducted in the second half of 2004, involved interviews and focus groups to complement the data already collected on staffs' own openness to sharing information.

'Working' in the organisation enabled that author to become involved in the design and implementation of a communication program to publicise the various elements of the newly implemented knowledge management program. This not only expedited data collection and analysis but also enabled a fuller investigation of the impact of this intervention on the organisation's knowledge sharing and creation. A second climate survey, also conducted in the second half of 2004, will complement the analysis of the impact of this intervention.

The results to date indicate relatively high levels of communication satisfaction in all areas except corporate communication issues (that is, communication at the organisation-wide level). In accordance with these results, the majority of respondents are satisfied with their jobs (78%), and with their job productivity (80%).

Very high satisfaction levels were reported on relations between staff and their immediate supervisors. The only exception relates to 'my superiors' understanding and knowing the problems that staff face. Whilst there is some discontent with the timeliness of receiving information needed to do one's job, it is not specified that this is confined to information from managers.

The highest levels of satisfaction with information shared by managers related to organisation-wide issues, and lower levels related to personal work issues and transparency of management decision-making.

Staff reported very high levels of satisfaction with the extent to which their managers are open to receiving shared information. The exceptions, again, relate to more personal work issues, namely, expressing opinions on one's job and the performance of one's immediate supervisor. High levels of satisfaction (60%-64%) were reported with the amount of action that one's immediate supervisor, or middle, senior, or executive management take on information sent to them by their staff. Very high levels of satisfaction (between 70%-89%) were reported by managers with the extent to which their staff are willing to share information with them.

The data on information sharing between coworkers indicate that sharing occurs more often within organisational units (61%) than between them (51%). Senior Executive Service staff (SES) are more likely to feel that not enough action is taken by coworkers on information sent to them, and staff at the administrative levels of 3 and 4 are more likely to feel too much action is taken. (Within the organisation staff classifications are Administrative levels 1, 2, 3, and 4, Executive levels 1 and 2, and SES levels A, B, C. The current study grouped the classifications into four categories as follows: Administrative levels 1/2, Administrative levels 3/4, Executive Level 1/2, and Senior Executive Service.)

Eighty-one percent of respondents saw the organisation's grapevine as being active, and 62% feel that informal communication in the organisation is both accurate and active. This suggests that the grapevine is seen as very active but, sometimes, inaccurate.

The channels rated as most satisfactory for receiving information are one-on-one meetings, the organisation-wide internal newsletter, and the organisation's intranet (all approximately 68%). The least satisfactory is 'special talks given by managers' (49%). There is also some dissatisfaction with the amount of information received via meetings within organisational units and sub-units. Statistical testing revealed that staff in the small organisational units are most likely to be satisfied with the amount of information they receive via the organisation's communication channels.

Perceptions of corporate communication (that is, communication at the organisation-wide level as against the group, or individual level) were found to be less positive than the other types of communication that were surveyed. Whilst the majority of respondents (57%-67%) are satisfied with organisational publications, the organisation of meetings, and written directives and reports, fewer (41%-45%) are satisfied with the channels used to handle conflicts, the inclusiveness and amount of organisational communication, and organisational members' communication abilities.

The survey revealed a very strong understanding of the purpose of the knowledge management initiative, and a less strong understanding of the specific facilities it incorporated and how they can be used in daily worklife. This is in accordance with the finding that the greatest reported barrier to using the initiative's facilities is lack of knowledge of their existence and/or how they can be used in one's work. Lack of time to use the facilities, like reading the information made available by them, is another major barrier.

Evidence, however, was found of blurring between what are considered naturally occurring information sharing activities and those that have been created under the knowledge management initiative. This suggests that information sharing behaviours are, to an extent, already embedded in the organisation's culture.

The results to date highlight the complex and extensive communication networks characteristic of large government organisations, confirming the need to pay particular attention to communication climate and its role in fostering knowledge.

6 Conclusion

This paper has focussed on outlining work in progress - a rich, longitudinal case study-based research project that touches on some of the key intangible variables involved in the crucial field of knowledge management. It has endeavoured to bring together much of the best in what remain two somewhat distinct fields of scholarly endeavour – knowledge management and communication with a special emphasis on communication climate's role in facilitating knowledge sharing and creation. A range of methodological strategies was outlined to demonstrate data collection and analysis. These have worked well so far in increasing our understanding of the interdependencies and feed into the ongoing research to be completed early next year. Nevertheless, in the midst of such research, it remains of concern that the field of organisation studies and management still largely ignore the crucial place of communication in organisational life and especially so in change and knowledge management arenas.

References

Abrams, L. C., R. Cross, E. Lesser and D. Z. Levin. (2002) "Nurturing interpersonal trust in knowledge-sharing networks." *Academy of Management Executive* 17(4): 64-77.

Adler, P. S. (2002) "Market, Hierarchy, and Trust: The Knowledge Economy and the Future of Capitalism." *The Strategic Management of Intellectual Capital and Organizational Knowledge.* C. W. Choo and N. Bontis. New York, Oxford University Press: 23-46.

Argyris, C. and D. Schon (1996) *Organizational Learning: volume 2. Theory, Method, and Practice.* Reading, MA, Addison-Wesley.

Argyris, C. (2000) "Good Communication that Blocks Learning." *Harvard Business Review on Organizational Learning.* Boston, Harvard Business School Press: 87-109.

Ash, J. (1998) Communication missing from KM's core strategies, Association of Knowledgework. http://www.kwork.org/White%20Papers/missing.html Accessed 28 February 2004.

Baird, J. W. (1974) "Analytical field study of "open communication" as perceived by supervisors, subordinates, and peers." *Dissertation Abstracts International.* 35: 562B.

Bokeno, R. M. and V. W. Gantt (2000) "Dialogic Mentoring." *Management Communication Quarterly* 14(2, November 2000): 237-270.

Campbell, J., M. Dunnette, E. Lawler and K. Weick. (1970) *Managerial behavior, performance, and effectiveness.* New York, McGraw-Hill.

Cilliers, P. (2000) "Knowledge, Complexity, and Understanding." *Emergence* 2(4): 7-13.

Costigan, R. D., S. S. Ilter and J. J. Berman (1998) "A Multi-dimensional study of trust in organizations." *Journal of Managerial Issues* 10(3): 303-317.

Davenport, T. and L. Prusak (1998) *Working Knowledge: how organisations manage what they know*. Boston, Harvard Business School Press.

Dennis, H. S. (1975) *The construction of a managerial communication climate inventory for use in complex organizations*. International Communication Association, Chicago.

Eisenberg, E. and M. G. Witten (1992) "Reconsidering Openness in Organizational Communication." *Readings in Organizational Communication*. K. L. Hutchinson. Dubuque, IA, Wm. C. Brown Publishers: 122-132.

Empsen, L. (2001) "Introduction: Knowledge management in professional service firms." *Human Relations* 54(7): 811-817.

Forehand, C. A. and B. von Haller Gilmer (1964) "Environmental variation in studies of organizational behavior." *Psychological Bulletin* 62(6): 361-82.

Goldhaber, G., H., H. Dennis, G. Richetto and O. Wiio (1979) *Information strategies: New paths to corporate power*. Englewood Cliffs, NJ, Prentice-Hall.

Goodell, A. L., Ed. (1992) "Organizational Climate: Current Thinking on an Important Issue." *Readings in Organizational Communication*. Dubuque, IA, Wm. C. Brown Publishers.

Grund, J., B., B. Hennestad, J-A. Johannesen, A. Karsson and J. Olaisen (2002) "Innovation as Knowledge Management in Corporations." European Academy of Management Conference 2002, Stockholm.

Guzley, R. M. (1992) "Organizational climate and communication climate: predictors of commitment to the organization." *Management Communication Quarterly* 5(4, May 1992): 379-402.

Howe, J. (1977) "Group climate: an exploratory analysis of construct validity." *Organizational Behavior and Human Performance* 19: 106-25.

Friedman, V. J. (2001) "The individual as agent of organizational learning." *Organizational Learning and Knowledge*. M. Dierkes, A. Berthoin Antal, J. Child and I. Nonaka. Oxford, England, Oxford University Press.

Hosmer, L. T. (1994) "Why be Moral? A Different Rationale for Managers." *Business Ethics Quarterly* 4(2): 191-204.

Hosmer, L. T. (1996) "Research Notes and Communications: Response to 'Do Good Ethics Always Make for Good Business?" *Strategic Management Journal* 15 (Special Issue): 17-34.

Isaacs, W. (1994) "Dialogue." *The fifth discipline fieldbook*. P. Senge, A. Kleiner, C. Roberts, R. Ross and B. Smith. New York, Currency Doubleday: 357-364.

Jablin, F. (1978) *Message response and "openess" in superior-subordinate communication*. New Brunswick, New Jersey, ICA/Transaction Books.

Jablin, F. M. (1985) "Task/work relationships: A life-span perspective." *Handbook of Interpersonal Communication*. M. L. Knapp and G. R. Miller. Beverly Hills, CA, Sage: pp615-54.

Jablin, F. M. (1992) "Reconsidering Openness in Organizational Communication." *Readings in Organizational Communication*. K. L. Hutchinson. Dubuque, IA, Wcm Brown: 122-132.

Jian, G. (2001) "Organizational Knowledge and Learning - A Speculation, Review, and Directions for Communication Research." *The 2001 Annual Convention of the International Communication Association*.

Lesser, E. (2000) "Leveraging Social Capital in Organizations." *Knowledge and Social Capital - Foundations and Applications*. E. Lesser. Worburn, MA, Butterworth-Heinemann: 3-16.

McDermott, E. (1999) "Why Information Technology Inspired But Cannot Deliver Knowledge Management." *California Management Review,* 41(4), 103-117.

Meyer, H. H. (1968) "Achievement Motivation and Industrial Climates." *Organization Climate: Explorations of a Concept*. R. Taguiri and G. Litwin. Cambridge, MA, Harvard Business School, Division of Research: 151-166.

More, E. (1999) "The role of communication in current debates on knowledge management." *Journal of Communication Management* **3**(4): 353-361.

Morris, T. (2001) "Asserting Property Rights: Knowledge Codification in the Professional Service Firm." *Human Relations* **54**(7): 819-838.

Nonaka, I. (1999) "The Dynamics of Knowledge Creation." *The Knowledge Advantage: 14 Visionaries Define Marketplace Success in the New Economy.* R. Ruggles and D. Holtshouse. Dover, NH, Capstone.

Oldham, G. R. and A. Kummings (1996) "Employee Creativity: Personal and Contextual Factors at Work." *Academy of Management Journal* **39**: 607-634.

Poole, M. S. (1987) *The structuring of organizational climates.* Minneapolis, MN, University of Minnesota.

Quinn, J., P., P. Anderson and S. Finkelstein (1996) "Leveraging Intellect." *Management Executive* **10**(3): 7-27.

Redding, W. C. (1972) *Communication within the organization: An interpretive review of theory and research.* New York, Industrial Communication Council.

Roberts, K. H. and C. A. O'Reilly (1979) "Some correlates of communication roles in organizations." *Academy of Management Journal* **22**: 42-57.

Ruppel, C. P. and S. J. Harrington (2000) "The relationship of Communication, Ethical Work Climate, and Trust to Commitment and Innovation." *Journal of Business Ethics* **25**(313-328).

Schneider, B. (1975) "Organizational Climates: an essay." *Personnel Psychology* **28**: 447-79.

Stull, J. B. (1975) ""Openness" in superior-subordinate communication: A quasi-experimental field study." *Dissertation Abstracts International.* **36**: 603A.

Taguiri, R. (1968) "The concept of organizational climate." *Organizational Climate: explorations of a concept.* R. Taguiri and G. Litwin. Cambridge, MA, Division of Research, Harvard Business Press.

Trombetta, J. and D. Roberts (1988) "Communication climate, job satisfaction and organizational commitment: The effects of information adequacy, communication openness and decision participation." *Management Communication Quarterly* **1**(4): 494-514.

Welsch, H. P. and H. LaVan (1981) "Inter-relationships between Organizational Commitment and Job Characteristics, Job Satisfaction, Professional Behavior, and Organizational Climate." *Human Relations* **34**: 1079-1089.

Wenger, E. (2004) "Knowledge management as a doughnut: Shaping your knowledge strategy through communities of practice." *Ivey Business Journal,* Jan-Feb, 1-8.

Winter, S. (1987) "Knowledge and Competence as Strategic Assets." *The Competitive Challenge - Strategies for Industrial Innovation and Renewal.* D. Teece. Cambridge, MA, Ballinger.

MISSING FUNDAMENTAL ILLUSION: A NEW THEORY BASED ON JAPANESE KNOWLEDGE MANAGEMENT

MARÍA SARABIA

Department of Business Administration, University of Cantabria, Avda.Los Castros, s/n, 39005 Santander, Cantabria, Spain

JUAN CORRO

Technical Telecommunications Engineer, Specialism in Electronic Systems, Avda.Los Castros, s/n, 39005 Santander, Cantabria, Spain

JOSÉ M. SARABIA

Department of Economics, University of Cantabria, Avda.Los Castros, s/n, 39005 Santander, Cantabria, Spain

We propose the *Fundamental Illusion Theory* to explain knowledge creation in the case of Japanese companies. This theory is based on an analogy with a hearing illusion which explains that when two tones occur together a third lower pitched tone is heard. However, this last perceived pitch is a frequency (fundamental) for which there is no actual source vibration. If we make an analogy between fundamental frequency and knowledge, and between tones occurring together and learning + culture + leadership, we arrive at a new management model.

1   Introduction: Japanese Knowledge Management

Japanese companies enjoy a mysterious halo which makes them especially attractive because although they are not extremely efficient or venturesome, they have improved their position in international competition. This is thanks to the creation of organizational knowledge, that is to say, thanks to the capacity of Japanese companies to generate new knowledge, diffuse it among its members and to materialize it in products, systems and services. We witness a type of company especially capable of continuous innovation (Nonaka and Takeuchi 1995).

But what is knowledge? Knowledge is conceived as very significant information (Zeleny 2000), the result of a consecutive process spanning data, information, knowledge and wisdom (Bierly *et al.* 2000). If we want to specify this concept we should not only ask ourselves what knowledge is, but also how knowledge arises. Drucker (1993) coined the term *Knowledge Society* to characterize the new prevailing economy that displaced traditional production factors, highlighting that knowledge has become an indispensable resource for survival.

The paper proceeds as follows. In section 1, we explain the Japanese knowledge creation model; in sections 2, 3 and 4, we reflect on the key elements of knowledge management (learning, culture and leadership); in section 5, we explain the analogy between Missing Fundamental Illusion and knowledge management. In the final section, we discuss how the two derived company types are related to the proposed analogy.

1.1 Japanese Knowledge Creation

The Japanese knowledge model focuses on *tacit knowledge* that possesses two dimensions: a *technical dimension,* called *know-how* (what competitors want to know but cannot buy); and a *cognitive dimension,* consisting of mental models (Johnson-Laird 1983; Senge 1990), beliefs and perceptions which subjectively define the environment that surrounds us (Nonaka and Takeuchi, 1995). In the 90's, the knowledge concept of western analysts was still focussing on the *explicit and formal* aspects of knowledge. Drucker (1993) explained how productivity began to increase when Frederick Taylor applied knowledge to the work process, but that knowledge only referred to the use of empirical data for production optimization.

Japanese knowledge creation is best understood by looking at practical examples. As, for instance, the Honda Civic project highlighted by Nonaka and Takeuchi (1995), which unveils three important characteristics of knowledge creation: First, to express the inexpressible; second, to disseminate the knowledge of an individual so that it can be shared by others; and third, the ambiguity of the corporate mission guiding management and the redundancy of work teams generating different points of view of the same circumstance. In spite of initial incredulity, western thought absorbed the Japanese knowledge philosophy and tried to apply it in western companies. However, the problem is that knowledge cannot just be learnt from others or simply be bought from outside – it needs the commitment and interaction of corporate human resources.

1.1.1 Organizational knowledge creation model

The West remains perplexed as Japan revolutionizes organizational thought. Real knowledge is neither learnt, nor can it be taught by others, knowledge has to be experienced and felt (Levitt 1991). This causes chaos in western companies, accustomed to the installation of traditional educational systems for knowledge transmission.

Nonaka and Takeuchi (1995) studied 20 Japanese companies (e.g., Honda, Kao, NEC, Fujitsu) when they enjoyed international success in the 80's. Systematic Japanese knowledge creation had allowed these companies to go on despite the economic crises suffered later. This research led to a model of five steps of organizational knowledge creation: (1) *Sharing tacit knowledge*: it is embodied in individuals; (2) *creating concepts*: from tacit to explicit; (3) *justifying the concepts*: verify their viability; (4) *building an archetype*: from a prototype to a model; and (5) *expanding the knowledge*: interactive distribution and knowledge hairspring.

A practical example of Japanese knowledge creation was the knowledge hairspring of the homemade bread-making machine of Matsushita Electronics Co. The process began with the exchange of experience among workers, which resulted in a failed prototype. In a second cycle, a software programmer, Tanaka, became an apprentice of a baker which eventually enabled her to introduce the required know-how into the dough-making mechanism ("stretch-twist"). The third cycle perfected the dough making process by reviving the traditional "Chumen" technique of fermentation. This hairspring describes the process of knowledge distribution inside the organization.

1.1.2 Knowledge interplay

Tacit knowledge and *explicit knowledge* are two faces of the same coin. However, Japanese and Westerners tend to have a single face coin: tacit and explicit, respectively. But without both faces there is no dynamic model of knowledge creation. Nonaka and Takeuchi (1995) explained the four ways of conversion or interaction of tacit and explicit knowledge (Figure 1): (1) *Socialization*: from tacit to tacit. An example is *tama dashi kai*, or brainstorming as established in Honda. This process leads to shared mental models (Cannon-Bowers *et al.* 1993) or *harmonized knowledge.* (2) *Externalization*: from tacit to explicit; it involves dialogue and collective reflection and results in *conceptual knowledge.* (3) *Combination*: from explicit to explicit; it generates *systemic knowledge*, like in the case of a prototype. (4) *Internalization*: from explicit to tacit; "learning by doing" is the essence of *operational knowledge.*

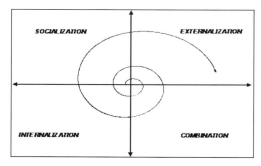

Figure 1. Knowledge Interplay (adapted from Nonaka and Takeuchi 1995).

2   Organizational Learning

An organization learns when the knowledge of each individual who is part of the group is shared beyond temporary, space or structural limits (Yeung *et al.* 1999). Thus, in the same way as individuals, the organization must face the changes of its circumstances (Cohen and Sproull 1991) and for this reason learning is presented as the key tool in the management of companies in turbulent environments. According to Huber (1991), learning can be defined as the capacity of an organization to self-adapt to changes of the environment, to be flexible and to generate actions for quick response by managing the internal change of the organization.

Argyris and Schön propose two learning types (1978): (1) *Single-loop learning* involves making continuous adaptations to keep the organization stable and within normal operating parameters; (2) *double-loop learning* involves being prepared to question the fundamental values and parameters under which the organization operates. Nonaka and Takeuchi (1995) contribute their own point of view: The creation of knowledge implies the interaction of the two types of learning of Argyris and Schön. What is the connection between knowledge and learning? Garvin (2003) was able to establish a clear relationship between both concepts: "An organization that learns is an expert organization in creating, acquiring and transmitting knowledge, and in modifying its behavior to self-adapt".

3   Culture

Organizational culture defines how individuals are identified within the organization, how they conceive its system of values, and how they relate it to their own value system. It is an accumulation of answers that the organization has learned from prior problems (Schein 1988). Or as Nonaka and Takeuchi (1995) observe: "From previous organizations we acquire knowledge in culture form". The question is based on how the culture is perceived and the consequences that it bears for the development of the organization in a turbulent environment. The survival of the organization rests on its capacity of adaptation or transformation, which in turn will depend on the organizational learning processes. In this way, looking for a conncetion between culture and organizational learning, we obtain four bonds (DeLong and Fahey 2000): (1) Culture defines what knowledge is outstanding; (2) the relationships among the levels of individual and organizational knowledge need culture for their viability; (3) the context of social interaction that learning needs is formed through culture and; (4) cultural behaviors brake the adoption of new knowledge.

4   Leadership

The characteristics of Japanese management include: managerial autonomy, consensus decision making, lifetime employment, promotion based on seniority and rigid hierarchical organizations (Chen 1995). "Within organizations, the Japanese have a characteristic management style that is credited for the worldwide success of the Japanese economy in the latter part of the twentieth century. The management system is intertwined with Japanese culture" (Francesco and Gold 1998).

Therefore, to understand the Japanese management style, we must study the Japanese intellectual tradition (Nonaka and Takeuchi 1995): (1) *Oneness of Humanity and Nature:* Japanese believe that it is very important to be flexible regarding the flow and the transition of the world; it makes them dedicate their existence to the flow of time. The plot of their novels is an example of this. The lack of a fixed temporary text is because Japanese experience time like a continuous "present" that it is updated in a constant way. (2) *Oneness of Body and Mind:* Knowledge means acquired wisdom, that is, it is not obtained from theoretical thought, but through the mind and body. Western epistemology exalts theory and abstraction, while Japanese epistemology values the incorporation of personal experience. (3) *Oneness of Self and Other:* This is a consequence of the two previous positions and echos the distinction between individualism vs. collectivism. The western individual sees concepts; the Japanese sees concepts relating them with other things and other individuals. This unity provides the basis for teamwork systems: "To work for others means to work for oneself" (Nonaka and Takeuchi 1995).

5   What is the Missing Fundamental Illusion?

"When two tones occur together, such as in a complex sound, a third lower pitched tone is often heard. This is called "Missing Fundamental Illusion" because the perceived pitch is a frequency (fundamental) for which there is no actual source vibration" (Chialvo 2003).

Musical instruments emit sounds that consist of several pure or harmonic tones whose frequencies are multiples of a given frequency (fundamental); that is to say, from a mother frequency, a group of perfectly periodic daughters are born following the expression $(f_F \cdot 2 \cdot \pi \cdot t)$, where f is the frequency of the pure tone. The frequency that each of the daughters continues, based on the mother's frequency or fundamental, f_0 , is derived from the following expression:

$$f_1 = k \cdot f_0$$
$$f_2 = (k+1) \cdot f_0$$
$$...$$
$$f_n = (k+n-1) \cdot f_0 \tag{1}$$

Consider the simple case of a complex tone composed of two pure tones of equal amplitudes and frequencies which are multiples of a third one:

$$x(t) = A_0 \cdot \sin(f_0 \cdot 2 \cdot \pi \cdot t) + A_1 \cdot \sin(f_1 \cdot 2 \cdot \pi \cdot t) + A_2 \cdot \sin(f_2 \cdot 2 \cdot \pi \cdot t) \tag{2}$$

The surprising discovery is that, if we eliminate the fundamental frequency and keep its two harmonics (expression 3), the ear continues perceiving the sound in the same way. The fundamental one is continued to be heard in spite of not being in the sound.

$$x(t) = A_1 \cdot \sin(f_1 \cdot 2 \cdot \pi \cdot t) + A_2 \cdot \sin(f_2 \cdot 2 \cdot \pi \cdot t) \tag{3}$$

5.1   Japanese Knowledge Management and Missing Fundamental Illusion

Let us suppose that knowledge is the fundamental frequency of the organization. Nonaka (1994) summarizes the current importance of the knowledge: "in an economy whose only certainty is the uncertainty, knowledge is the best source to get competitive advantage".

Therefore, if we assume that knowledge is the fundamental one, which are its harmonics, that is, what organizational elements are born from knowledge? Nonaka and Takeuchi (1995), define an analogy like a halfway between imagination and logical thought. This way, we will study the analogy that exists between knowledge and its harmonics and the fundamental frequency and its harmonics, starting from the case of the knowledge hairspring of a homemade bread-making machine.

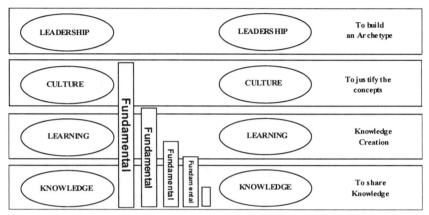

Figure 2. The knowledge hairspring on Missing Fundamental Illusion (adapted from Nonaka and Takeuchi)

Let us suppose that the fundamental frequency of knowledge has some harmonics: learning, culture and leadership (Figure 2). Each harmonic is based on the fundamental frequency, that is to say, knowledge is that which develops the successful melody listened to inside the organization and that culminates in the way its leader acts. The stack of the fundamental frequency and its harmonics, are a compilation of knowledge + learning + culture + leadership. Why are learning, culture and leadership harmonics of knowledge? In this paper we are developing these harmonics and their direct relationship with Japanese knowledge creation.

Let us introduce noise in the listened fundamental sound and its harmonics. That noise may represent a leadership change, as a consequence of generational renewal, for example, or due to the bad expectations of the company that push it to make the decision of replacing the leader of the first stack to get a second stack. We are facing a knowledge cycle change. Some authors describe this phenomenon like "to create knowledge starting from the noise" or "order starting from the chaos" (Nonaka and Takeuchi 1995).

5.2 Missing Fundamental Illusion and Company Types

The missing fundamental illusion is based on: (1) fundamental frequency (knowledge); (2) harmonics (learning, culture and leadership); (3) stack (knowledge + harmonics); and (4) noise (cycle change or stack change). These initial assumptions imply two different company behaviours, represented by the *Amplifier Company* and the *Modulator Company*.

5.2.1 Amplifier company

Let us suppose the leader, who leaves an organization, is a guitarist and when he leaves, he plays two strings of the guitar that configure the stack: learning and culture. In the vibration of both strings, one can perceive the missing fundamental sound, that is, the knowledge. The missing fundamental frequency keeps playing the successful melody of the organization; a little later, it disappears (Figure 2). Before the fundamental stops to be listened to (knowledge), the leader has to negotiate the cycle change.

The Amplifier Company (Figure 3) is characterized by the non-generation of a second stack. Once the first leader leaves the fundamental frequency sound, the second leader, simply takes up the position left by his predecessor. The new leader does not create new knowledge in order to create learning and culture. What will happen to this company type? While the fundamental frequency continues sounding, the company will survive thanks to the stack created by the first leader, but when the fundamental stops sounding, the leader will not have any base and the organization structure will tend to disappear.

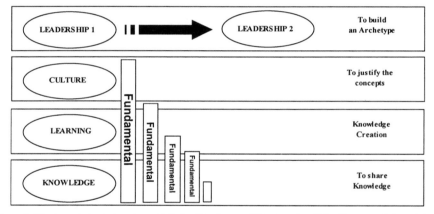

Figure 3. The knowledge hairspring of Missing Fundamental Illusion: Amplifier Company (adapted from Nonaka and Takeuchi 1995).

The Amplifier Company possesses a structure which amplifies the sound, that is to say, it tries to stretch or to amplify the duration of the fundamental frequency to survive for a period of time. But the fundamental disappears with its harmonics.

5.2.2 Modulator company

This company type modulates the knowledge (Figure 4). The substitute leader creates a second stack from the knowledge that he receives from the fundamental frequency which is still sounding. The missing fundamental illusion allows him to create knowledge again and to generate a second cycle.

We must look at the knowledge interplay to understand the stack change or cycle change (Figure 1). The hairspring is born from knowledge (Figure 5), goes to learning (tacit to tacit), from learning to culture (tacit to explicit), from culture to leadership (explicit to explicit), and when we arrive to leadership the stack culminates. We get from one stack to another by starting over with knowledge (explicit to tacit).

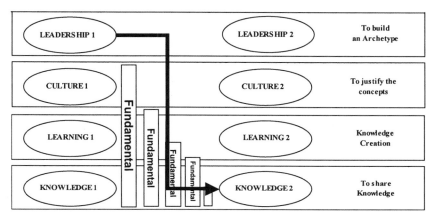

Figure 4. The knowledge hairspring of Missing Fundamental Illusion: Modulator Company (adapted from Nonaka and Takeuchi 1995).

The hairspring of knowledge interplay developed by Nonaka and Takeuchi (1995) explains how knowledge combines the tacit-explicit step so that harmonic figures of knowledge are born. In this regard, Japanese learning is characterized by its main process of acquiring tacit knowledge which is through the direct way of personal experience (Easterby-Smith 1998).

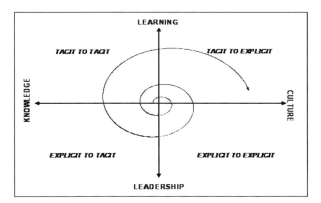

Figure 5. Knowledge interplay based on the Missing Fundamental Illusion.

From knowledge to learning is the first step of the knowledge stack. And culture? How do we take the step from tacit to explicit? Culture indicates what knowledge is outstanding (DeLong and Fahey 2000), that is to say, culture is the externalization of the tacitly extracted knowledge. The third step of the stack, from explicit to explicit, that is, from culture to learning represents "combination", a process of systematizing concepts. The leadership of a company is carried out when the firm combines a product concept with a concept of corporate vision (Nonaka and Takeuchi 1995).

What is the importance of the four steps of the stack? The four steps correspond to four phases of knowledge creation starting from the missing fundamental frequency and following Nonaka and Takeuchi (1995): (1) *share knowledge*; the organization does not create knowledge, but its individuals create it inside an atmosphere of appropriate dialogue. (2) *Create concepts*; the initial dialogue becomes an exchange of experiences. (3) *Justify the concepts*; the concepts which learning generates are selected by the culture, which justifies the viability of each. (5) *Build an archetype*; the justified concept becomes tangible and concrete, that is, the required leadership is obtained from the sum of knowledge + learning + culture.

6   Discussion

The Japanese knowledge creation model can be characterized as informal, holistic and tacit (Easterby-Smith 1998). It has been envied and imported by the West. The innovative character of Japanese companies, has given a new sense to knowledge management. In spite of the setback suffered by Japanese companies subjected to a long recession, organizational knowledge creation has been a good tool to manage the crisis, to forget the past and to find new opportunities (Nonaka and Takeuchi 1995).

We borrow the knowledge hairspring from Japanese knowledge management to generate the stack structure of each cycle. This stack is the result of compiling knowledge + learning + culture + leadership. Starting from the Fundamental Missing Illusion Theory, we define knowledge like the fundamental frequency and learning, culture and leadership as the harmonics of knowledge. The step of the fundamental and its harmonics, which build the stack, are based on the idea of knowledge conversion by Nonaka and Takeuchi (1995).

If we introduce noise inside the melody that the fundamental frequency and its harmonics generate, we suppose a crisis inside the knowledge stack that culminates in a new leader. The leadership change generates two types of firms: *amplifier* and *modulator companies*.

The *amplifier company* (Figure 6) is characterized by a person's substitution inside a leader's position, surviving while the fundamental frequency (knowledge) of the first leader's stack is sounding. The amplifier company disappears when the fundamental frequency stops sounding. The amplifier company has similarities with *Western-type organizations* that Nonaka and Takeuchi (1995) characterise as follows: explicit knowledge prevails and it could suffer "paralysis from analysis".

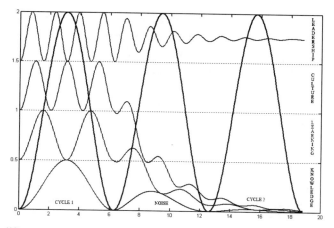

Figure 6. Amplifier company behaviour across time (cycles). Fundamental frequency is knowledge; first harmonic: learning; second harmonic: culture; third harmonic: leadership.

On the other hand, the *modulator company* (Figure 7) manages the crisis by creating a second stack of knowledge. This kind of company survives the noise because the second leader is able to generate new knowledge, affirming his own leadership. The second leader uses the fundamental frequency as a temporary survival platform while he generates a second stack.

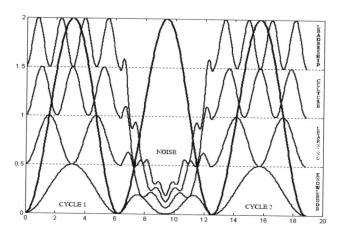

Figure 7. Modulator company behaviour across time (cycles). Fundamental frequency is knowledge; first harmonic: learning; second harmonic: culture; third harmonic: leadership.

The modulator company shares characteristics with the *Japanese organization* that Nonaka and Takeuchi (1995) characterise as follows: tacit knowledge and leadership change based on an appropriate crisis management. We can find Japanese companies that are *amplifiers* and western companies that are *modulators*, and vice versa. The cultural component is not distinctive because the import and adaptation of Japanese systems in western companies can create knowledge that changes stack or cycle. It is even possible that a Japanese company is not able to generate a second stack because its initial leader does not leave the fundamental frequency sounding or, because the second leader does not know how to create the necessary knowledge for his own leadership.

The Fundamental Missing Illusion based on Japanese knowledge management offers a new vision of knowledge creation and leads to a differentiation between two company types according to how each kind manages noise.

References

Argyris, C. and Schön, D.A. (1978). Organizational Learning. Reading, MA: Addison-Wesley.

Bierly, P.E., Kessler, E.H. and Christensen, E.W. (2000). "Organizational Learning, knowledge and wisdom". *Journal of Organisational Change Management*, 13(6), 595-618.

Cannon-Bowers, J.A., Salas, E. and Converse, S. (1993) "Shared Mental Models in Expert Team Decision Making", in NJ Castellan Jr (ed.), *Individual and Group Decision Making*, Lawrence Erlbaum Associates, Hillsdale, New Jersey, 221-246.

Chen, M. (1995) *Asian Management Systems: Chinese, Japanese and Korean Styles of Business*. NY: Routledge.

Chialvo, D.R. (2003) "How we hear what is not there: A Neural Mechanism for the Missing Fundamental Illusion", *Chaos*, 13 (4), 1226-1230.

Cohen, M.D. and Sproull, L.S. (1991) "Editor's Introduction", *Organization Science*, 2, (1).

Delong, D.W. and Fahey, L. (2000) "Diagnosing Cultural Barriers to Knowledge Management", *Academy of Management Review*, 4 (4).

Drucker, P.F. (1993) *Post-Capitalist Society*, Butterworth Heinemann, Oxford.

Easterby-Smith, M. (1998) "Organizational Learning and National Culture: Do Models of Organizational Learning Apply Outside the USA?", *Boletín de Estudios Económicos*, LIII, (164), 281-295.

Francesco, A.M. and Gold, B.A. (1998) *International Organizational Behavior: text, readings, cases and skills*. Prentice-Hall, Inc. New Jersey.

Garvin, D.A. (2003) "Crear una Organización que aprende". *Harvard Business Review: Gestión del Conocimiento*. Ediciones Deusto, 51-89. Bilbao.

Huber, G.P. (1991) "Organizational Learning: The Contributing Processes and the Literatures", *Organization Science,* 2(1), 88-115.

Johnson-Laird, J.N. (1983) *Mental Models*, Cambridge University Press, Cambridge.

Levitt, T. (1991) *Marketing Imagination*, The Free Press, New York.

Nonaka, I. (1994) *Harvard Business Review in Knowledge Management*. Harvard Business Scholl Press. Boston.

Nonaka, I. and Takeuchi, H. (1995) *The Knowledge-Creating Company*. New York, NY: OUP.

Schein, E.H. (1988) *Organizational Culture and Leadership*, Jossey-Bass, San Francisco, CA.

Senge, P.M. (1990). *The Fifth Discipline: The Art and Practice of the Learning Organization*. Doubleday, New York.

Yeung, A.K., Ulrich, D.O., Nason, S.W. and Von Glinow, M.A. (1999) *Organizational Learning Capability*. Oxford University Press, INC. NY.

Zeleny, M. (2000) "Knowledge vs. information". *The IEBM Handbook of Information Technology in Business*, 162-168. London: Thomson Learning.

ORGANIZATIONAL CULTURE, SOCIAL EMBEDDEDNESS AND KNOWLEDGE LOSS: A CASE STUDY OF CHINA CENTRAL TELEVISION (CCTV)

LINGJIE WANG[1]

*Centre for Cultural Policy Studies, University of Warwick, Coventry
CV4 7AL, UK*

Following the organic approach to knowledge management, this paper argues for a closer focus on people and organizational culture in knowledge management practice. With a case study of China Central Television (CCTV), this paper analyzes the importance and difference of knowledge management in the broadcasting industry under Chinese context. By highlighting the social embeddedness of organizational culture, the author intends to analyze how traditional hierarchical ideology and management style, guanxi oriented culture and Chinese communication styles have resulted in knowledge loss in this particular organization during its transitional period.

1   Introduction

The term knowledge management itself was introduced into popular discourse during the early 1990s, however, it is still uncertain if there is one commonly accepted definition of knowledge management. A huge amount of research has been done to disclose the essence of knowledge and knowledge management. Among them, De Long and Fahey (2000) regarded knowledge as a product of human reflection and experience which is dependent on context and a resource that is always located in an individual or a collective, or embedded in a routine or process. From these and many other similar analyses on knowledge, it is clear that two elements are highlighted to make the difference: people and context (Davenport, 1997; Blackler, 1995; De Long & Fahey, 2000; Barth, 2002).

From what we understand about organizational learning and previous experience in knowledge management, organizational culture background and social settings of an organisation seem to be the most intangible but influential factors of this process. Following organic approaches to knowledge management, this paper argues that in knowledge management practice, a focus on human connectivity is necessary in order to get an understanding of the environment and a comprehensive picture of how things are done naturally in a particular society or organization.[2] In practice, the following listed obstacles (Table 1) to knowledge management implementation provides further evidence that knowledge management practice, to a great extent, is related to organizational

---

[1] The author could like to thank Dr. Chris Bilton and two referees for their kind comment on the earlier version of this paper.
[2] Next Generation Knowledge Management: The Complexity of Humans, in *Executive Tek Report*, November 18, 2002, p.2.

culture. Most importantly, we could also find evidence that the organizational culture's role in knowledge management has been undervalued.

Table 1. Obstacles for Knowledge Management Implementation[3]

KM Implementation Obstacles	%
Employees have no time for KM	41%
Current culture does not encourage sharing	36.6%
Lack of understanding of KM and benefits	29.5%
Inability to measure financial benefits of KM	24.5%
Lack of skill in KM techniques	22.7%
Organization's processes are not designed for KM	22.2%
Lack of funding for KM	21.8%
Lack of incentives, rewards to share	19.9%
Have not yet begun implementing KM	18.7%
Lack of appropriate technology	17.4%
Lack of commitment from	3.9%
No challenges encountered	4.3%

The most cited obstacle for knowledge management implementation is that "employees have no time for knowledge management". As we have discussed previously, the most important aspect of knowledge management practice is deeply buried in the daily working routine, and human resource management practice. When people say they have no time for knowledge management, it means that they still do not know what knowledge management is really about. The second most cited obstacle is that "current culture does not encourage sharing", which directly points out the importance of culture in knowledge management practice. The third obstacle is related to the first one in terms of understanding and attitudes to knowledge management, which is also inevitably involved with organizational culture and most of the times, national culture and ideology as well. The number six most cited obstacle refers to organizational process and its influence on knowledge management. It is well accepted that organizational process as one of the important aspects of the "way things are done here" is actually a major part of the organization's culture.

To sum up, the obstacles to knowledge management implementation are very much related to organizational culture. The main aspect involves people's understanding and attitudes to knowledge management, the traditional way of daily work practice and the way people are treated in an organization. All of these will reflect on the implementation and effect of knowledge management eventually.

2   Knowledge management and CCTV Case

Just as some companies like Sun are very good in knowledge management practice, but don't think they are actually doing anything called "knowledge management", there are

---

[3] Suresh Ram, Knowledge Management – An Overview, in *KnowledgeBoard.com 13th June 2002. http://www.knowledgeboard.com.*

other companies like China Central Television who are experiencing very serious harm to knowledge management without being aware of it. Moreover, dominating position in domestic market and huge advertising profits seems to gloss over the potential problems in the CCTV.

Like argued before in this paper, organizational culture as a main influence to knowledge management practice is so intangible and embedded in the traditional management style and routine that it is always the most easily forgotten and ignored factor. Due to the mission transfer, there are a series of changes taking place in China Central Television.[4] Like many other state-owned enterprises in China, to a great extent, the challenges confronting CCTV on the way from a government ruling tool to a modern enterprise are not infrastructural or financial, but the ideological one which has influence on every aspect of the daily managerial practice. So far, infrastructural changes do not seem so painful compare to traditional management cultural and ideological changes.

According to Therivel (1995, pp.73-92.), a farming society with a stable feudal structure would be one where tradition counts more than novelty. The reform of state-owned enterprises in China was introduced from 1979. Even after more than 20 years, the current Chinese campaign for "modernization" is still not necessarily a process of change in Chinese people's fundamental mentality or behaviour. State-owned enterprises and organizations still need a break through from the passive, to-be-planned ideology. In terms of knowledge management, it is not that there is no IT platform to support it, most of the time; it is the invisible traditional culture and ideology that are the "stumbling blocks".

This paper will analyze the relationship between Knowledge loss, organizational culture and social environment. By knowledge loss, the author indicates failure or ineffectiveness in cultivating, capturing, sharing and sustaining knowledge and knowledge resources. With CCTV case, the author intends to unfurl some potential risks and difficulties a knowledge-intensive company in the Chinese context may have. In this paper, I am going to focus on the way people communicate and the way things are done in CCTV. I am also going to discuss how traditional Chinese State-owned Enterprise (SOE) management culture and ideology influence the daily managerial practices which make knowledge creation, sharing and transfer difficult if not impossible; and how the most invisible organizational culture result in knowledge loss of a Chinese broadcaster in its transitional period.

3 The CCTV Case: how culture become a problem in the CCTV

As the most protected industry in China, reform in media was delayed intentionally by the central government. China Central Television with 45 years of history, mostly supported and controlled by government, traditional ideology and managerial style are even more deeply rooted, any change takes even longer. The influence of organizational

---

[4] To summarize, main changes lie in the following three aspects: financial system changes, personnel system changes, infrastructure and contents providing changes.

culture on knowledge management can be analyzed in great detail, but in this paper I intend to focus on three dominating aspects of culture and their impact on knowledge loss. The dominating culture in this 45 years old national broadcaster could be summarized under three main headings: 1. Hierarchy and its influence on communication styles in CCTV. 2. *Guai*/to be obedient and knowledge sharing 3.*Guanxi* oriented culture and its effects.

3.1 Hierarchy and communication in CCTV

Most Asian cultures retain more hierarchical structures and traditions than those in the West. This is especially so in China, where Confucianism originated. One of the focuses of Confucianism is on the five hierarchical relationships, on which the social stability is based on. These five relationships are called *"Wulun"*, or five basic relationships.[5] The importance of an individual's place in the hierarchy of social relationships is stressed. A person's fulfillment of the responsibilities of a given role ensures the smoother functioning of society. Social hierarchy and relations of subordination and superiority are considered natural and proper. Apart from the performance of assigned duties, filial submission, loyalty, decency, or reciprocity are also required.[6]

Confucian principles provide the basis for Chinese organizational bureaucracy, respect for seniority, rituals of etiquette, ceremony, and various types of business relationships. This hierarchical tradition in Chinese society has a great impact on knowledge sharing in families, among clans, between groups and within the *danwei*/work unit.[7] Status-free communication and expressions are thus limited due to one's position in the social hierarchy. In an organizational context, work is organized through mutual understanding and acceptance of the informal cultural boundary in terms of administrative status, age difference, difference in experiences, etc.

Apart from the influence of traditional founding ethos, the hierarchical culture in China Central Television is also a direct result of its status in the Chinese *danwei*/work unit administrative system. Originally a party mouthpiece representing the central government, CCTV, under direct control of the Publicity Department and State Administration of Radio, Film and Television (SARFT) [8] of the Chinese Communist

---

[5] Five relationships refer to relationships between father and son, ruler and ruled, husband and wife, elder brother and younger brother, and friend and friend (this pair is equal in position).See Geert Hofstede, *Culture's Consequences* (Sage Publications, 1984) and others.

[6] Fan Xing, The Chinese Cultural System Implications for Cross-Cultural Management, SAM Advanced Management Journal, winter 1995 V. 60 n1 p. 17.

[7] In China, *danwei*, or work unit, refers to those urban workplaces through which the CCP-state administrates and controls economic activities and arranges the jobs and lives of people. For more information, see Qiushi Liu, *Danwei-oriented System and the Formations of Social Organizations in Urban China: An Institutional Perspective*, Fourth Annual Conference on East Asia, Harvard University, April 7th, 2001.

[8] The CCP's Publicity Department is subject to the heavy influence of the ideological group of the CCP's Politburo and is responsible for setting ideological and propaganda themes in programmes The State Administration of Radio, Film and Television (SARFT). The former deals with

Party (CCP) is ranked at the vice-ministry level in the CCP's administrative ranking system.[9] CCTV enjoyed monopoly status in mainland China for 30 years before the first provincial satellite TV channels transmitted all over the country.[10] But it is still in a dominant position in terms of coverage, advertising, and access to news resource. Moreover, government media policies and regulation continue to privilege it over other television stations in China. All these advantages make the CCTV more like a government sector and a mouthpiece than a company, especially a creative business company. Having been regarded as top level of TV stations representing the central government, bureaucracy is a dominating style, not only for content censorship, but also in daily management culture.

The hierarchical environment in CCTV is so obvious that one can easily feel it when stepping into the organization for the first time. The general way for a new member to address everybody older, higher in status or people who joined the CCTV earlier, is *"laoshi"*, means "master/teacher". And one can easily tell the status of people in an office by whether they have their own desk or they share with others; whether they make the effort to talk to other people and whether they come to the office early or late everyday. Officially, there is another important system categorizing people into different groups by their employment contract status with different coloured ID cards – white, pink or blue. People with white and pink card are the ones employed with government employment quota, those with blue cards are employed temporarily by a certain department or channel. Different colour of the ID card indicates different level of access to CCTV's resources. Due to the rapid expansion, there are still a lot of people do not have an ID card, which means they are not allowed to get into the CCTV main building, therefore have no rights to attend the monthly or weekly meetings held there. Surprisingly, many of these no ID staff have been working in the CCTV for more than a year.

The invisible cast system put people off in communicating with each other freely, let alone to share with no reservation. Junior/less experienced staff may not be willing to disagree with their *laoshi(s)*/seniors in order to keep the balance of hierarchy. This may lessen the possibility of creating positive results or innovative ideas through "creative friction." One extreme example is that the contact list of people in the production team I used to work for was listed according to administrative status, and time working in the division. In this way, the producer was listed on top, directly below them are editors in

---

regulatory, technological, and administrative affairs. See John Sinclaire, Elizabeth Jacka, and Stuart Cunningham (eds.) *New Patterns in global Television: Peripheral Vision* (Oxford: Oxford University Press, 1996), p.134.

[9] Originally, the rank system was implemented only in the army. This military rank system, accomplished with a parallel CCP rank system, had been adapted as a basic structure of rank system after 1950 and still exists nowadays. The level of administrative rank of a *danwei* usually relate to the ability of that *danwei* to obtain resources from the state, and therefore, relate to its possibility of providing benefit for its leaders and members. See Zhang Quanjing, 1996, 3-4.

[10] Guizhou, and Yunnan satellite TV are the ones who first started to transmit on satellite, Yunnan Satellite TV started from Feb 1989.

chief, and editors or researchers who joined the team earlier, with the most recent on the bottom. When having weekly group meeting, after the producer's summary and report on viewing figures, the discussion is always conducted in the order of seniority under the prompt of the producer. The sharing is therefore constrained by the producer and the mutual understanding of the invisible "order". With limited time available, people may really want to share problems and ideas but have not been given the chance and will have to save it till next time, or even forget about it.

One recent recruit complained in the interview: "Everything – visible or invisible reminds you that you are not important in this team. Therefore your ideas are not valuable. Under these circumstances, you sometimes do not want to bother". To a certain extent, "brainstorming" is never a brainstorming in its real value in the CCTV. Even though the new 16 characters guideline of the News Commentary Department highlighted innovation, it is hardly the case in its managerial practice. Like Bilton (2002, p.52) argued that the brainstorming process deliberately postpones any value judgment on the quality of ideas produced. But in this case, the value of ideas is ignored both by managers and non-managers rather unconsciously or habitually instead of deliberately. The communal space and time are artificially interfered with an invisible hand. If there is no equality in life, there is no freedom in sharing and communication.

3.2 *Guai/being obedient and knowledge sharing*

As cultural guideline accommodating hierarchy, *guai* or being obedient is regarded as the standard of a good child, student and employee in Chinese society. From a very early stage of life, Chinese people were taught to be *guai,* and listen to parents, teachers and leaders. Therefore, people are not used to say "no", let along being straightforward in saying it. More over, Chinese people are encouraged to keep a low profile in public to fulfill the Confucian guidance on maintaining good manners. Western people may see someone expressive as a sign of confidence, but Chinese people may view this as being too talkative or vain (trying to overshadow others, related to group oriented culture). Therefore, the result is an indirect, hinting, subtle and accommodating communication style. This may not be conducive to effective knowledge sharing because honesty and open discussion of ideas would facilitate the flow of knowledge as a social process.

In terms of production, one producer in CCTV's News Commentary Department mentioned the embarrassment they experienced when they had to sacrifice the creative independence to show respect to comments from their line managers.[11] What is interesting is that, on the one hand, CCTV staff are complaining about the lack of freedom for creativity, on the other hand, people who are complaining themselves have been so used to it that they have been numb and even follow suit. It is dangerous that most of people working in CCTV know the problems, but they feel that they have no say or power to change it. And this is why following the government's voice and waiting for instructions from top down, is still the dominate working culture.

---

[11] From personal interview in Beijing, Sept. 2003.

As the example above demonstrates, with people being obedient to their seniors, what senior people said was obeyed and reinforced, and what they did not know was kept away from them longer. This communication style always result in a late response to possible problems or risks, a careless environment for creative ideas, and a devastating response to the desire to raise problems, be different, or shout in different voice. It is important that decision makers have authority and decisions can be carried out to its full value. But in the artistic production process, it is also important that creativity could be respected and encouraged by authority so that it can grow and flourish to its full potential. It is doubtful that being *guai/* obedient and try to follow suit will help to achieve innovation or just make it more difficult for a healthy knowledge creating and sharing environment.

3.3 Guanxi Effect and the damage of trust among team members

It has been argued that strong ties between co-workers appear to facilitate knowledge sharing. A study by IBM Institute for Knowledge-Based Organizations shows that the "magic ingredient" that links strong ties and knowledge sharing is trust.[12] Fukuyama (1995) categorizes China into low trust countries, where it is not impossible but highly difficult to build up trust without a *guanxi*/connection. *Guanxi*/connection effect has been acknowledged by many as a vital factor in doing business successfully in China (Yeung and Tung, 1996, p.60). In the CCTV case, we will see how this penetrating *guanxi* effect in Chinese society act as a negative influence on trust building in this organization.

Due to its prominence, working in television, especially in CCTV has been a symbol of status. Given the difficulties to work in CCTV, *guanxi* or connection is proved to be a must. Many of those I interviewed at CCTV confirmed that when they start working in CCTV, one of the first questions they were asked by co-workers either directly or indirectly was "who recommended you here?". As Sun Yusheng (2003, p.61), one of the founders of the best known CCTV programme *Horizon* (Dongfang Shikong) documented in his book *Ten Years*, at the beginning of the public recruitment for this programme in 1993, many people were recommended to him by the then team members, or their friends. Sun, in his book, called the connections between his team members as "kinship by *guanxi (renji xueyuan guanxi)*".

With everybody tied up to a certain network of *guanxi,* the whole organization and work culture was obscured with layers and layers of network under the surface (Sun, 2003, p.60). When who you know matters more than what you know, it is obviously a problem to management. Sun has realized, the intangible network will bring unnecessary difficulties to management in the long term, and will distort the relationship between colleagues (Sun, 2003, p.87). Indeed, with this huge intangible network, if one connection does not work, it will influence the whole situation. According to many

---

[12] Daniel Z. Levin, Rob Cross, Lisa C. Abrams and Eric L. Lesser, *Trust and Knowledge Sharing: a Critical combination,* IBM Institute for Knowledge-Based Organizations, p. 2. From: http://www-1.ibm.com/services/strategy/e_strategy/trust.html

interviewees, the communication between colleagues is full of understatement, and the process of decision making lacks transparency. In one interview, a CCTV producer complained that it does not matter whether he really needs somebody to fill a position, if there is a strong recommendation from the top, he could not say no, due to the fear of the consequence of this refusal. Similarly when there is a need to slim down, he had to make his decision based on a comparison of each one's connection (*guanxi*) background, and the length of the time they served in the team. Most of the time, it is not the least able who get fired; it is the ones most vulnerable and new to the team who suffer the consequence.

Many interviewees have argued that they cannot feel safe and loyal to their team. The relationship between team members is very cold, and sometimes hostile, especially to new comers. Some new comers even adopt the term "three weeks silence" to describe the situation when they first started working in CCTV. They explained that during those three/four weeks, no one will talk to you actively and sociably, they felt that they were not welcomed, and people were checking them out, as if they were trying to work out their background network before they started talking to them in a friendly way. Obviously, under an atmosphere lack of transparency, it is highly difficult to promote an honest and open discussion environment for knowledge sharing with a low trust team.

4   What is vital in the transitional period?

With the launch of a new TV-magazine programme *Horizon (Dongfang Shikong)* and later *Focus (Jiaodian Fangtan)* in 1993. CCTV started the most influential reform in the Chinese television sector ever by introducing a brand new institutional system of production named "Producer Responsibility System" starting in its News Commentary Department. This new reform entitles the producers of each programme autonomy in personnel, finance and production management within their own teams. Among other policies geared to avoid red tape and inefficiency, the department may autonomously employ people on a temporary basis, without the limit of the traditional employment quota.[13] The most widely acknowledged contribution of 'Producer Responsibility System' is the break through from the traditional employment system. It would be a great step forward if the new personnel reform practice took the place of the traditional employment stereotype, and fundamentally broke the 'iron rice bowl'. However, there seems to be a double standard as a consequence of an incomplete reform. The breaking of the 'iron rice bowl' seems only for those inferior in this organization.

Ten years after the introduction of the reform in 2003, when the author visited the CCTV News Commentary Department with great anticipation of witnessing a brave new world of Chinese television, it was disheartening to see that the spirit of innovation and

---

[13] In a decision on *Unifying the State Financial and Economic Work* issued by the State Council for Political Affairs in March 1950, it was stipulated that, the numbers of personnel at all government departments, public schools and SOEs should be fixed. (See Xinhua shishi congkanshe, 1950, p4.)

creativity is fading away. The general morale and loyalty towards the organization is very low, and the reforming force is losing the battle; while the traditional SOE management culture and hierarchical style as government sector is still deeply rooted in the organization. In an online interview series commemorating the 10 year anniversary of *Horizon,* one of the program's founders admitted that there is a bottleneck in further development of *Horizon* and CCTV itself.[14]

From 1993 till now, people employed on temporary contracts or with no contract base have been dominating the Chinese television workforce. Take the News Commentary Department of CCTV as example (see Table 2): the total number of people working on a temporary contract basis increased from 0 to 50 within the first 5 years. People working with no contract have increased from 92 to 290 in the meantime. The ratio of people formally employed and informally employed was 1:2 in 1993, and 1: 10.3 in 1998. There is no access to the latest data, but with the CCTV's transition increase to 15 terrestrial channels, 270 hours daily transmission and 406 programmes,[15] it would not be an exaggeration to estimate that the number of temporarily employed people has doubled, or even tripled, compared to the 1998 numbers. One the one hand, as acknowledged by Qian (2002, p. 113), people working on temporary contract or no contract are now the founding blocks for the smooth operation of the CCTV. On the other hand, with the explosive employee increase at CCTV, it seems that people are the least valuable asset, let alone to consider what they think, how they feel, how they work. One producer said in the interview: "we never worry there is no people working for us".

Table2. CCTV News Commentary Department Employment Type 1993-1998[16]

	1993	1994	1995	1996	1997	1998
Formally employed with quota	31	24	25	30	32	33
Temporary contract based	0	8	16	28	47	50
No contract	61	108	126	225	230	290
Total	92	140	167	283	309	373

What's worse, due to their special employment status, there is less opportunity for people work with temporary contract or no contract to get promoted. According to a 1997 survey by Prof. Guoming Yu, 96.3% of the then producers in the CCTV were formally employed with quota. Only 3.7% of them were originally from public recruitment.[17] Given the fact that chances to become Producer is slim for the majority of people

---

[14] Meng Chen in *Horizon 10th Anniversary Online Interview Series,* news.tom.com, 3rd Sept. 2003.

[15] Data collected from CCTV website: www.cctv.com.

[16] Wei Qian, *Politics, Zhengzhi, Shichang Yu Dianshi Zhidu – Zhongguo Dianshi Zhidu Bianqian Yanjiu (Market and Media – A Study on Chinese Television Institutional Change)* (Zhengzhou, Henan People's Publishing House, 2002), p.113.

[17] Guoming Yu, *Survey of CCTV Producers Status, 8th Aug 1997,* Pu Wang, *Current Status of Television Producers and Prospects (Dianshi Zhipianren de Xianzhuang yu Fazhan Qianjing),*(Beijing, Chinese Broadcasting and Television Publishing House (*Zhongguo Guangbo Dianshi Chubanshe),* 1998), p.298.

working in CCTV, it is therefore a very unpredictable future and career path in front of them. Some of the very successful TV professionals left CCTV finally for *Phoenix* in Hong Kong or *Oriental TV* in Shanghai. Some are now working for their own business. Most of them are still fighting for a decent identity in CCTV, or looking for other development opportunities. To CCTV, this is a great knowledge loss.

5   Conclusion

It was argued that any discussion of knowledge in organizational settings without explicit reference to its cultural context is likely to be misleading (De Long & Fahey, 2000). We have seen in the CCTV case that knowledge and culture are inextricably linked in this organization. We could also see in the CCTV case that to some extent, a particular organization's culture is embedded in its national culture and dominant ideology, and sometimes, this embeddedness of organizational culture could be the stumbling block in change.

In this paper, by analyzing three aspects of the dominant culture, we have discussed different communication styles under the influence of organizational culture, and shown how these result in knowledge loss. Both formal brainstorming sessions and informal daily communication styles in the CCTV have been considered and it is clear that the hierarchical culture has inhibited creativity, and willingness to share ideas. The mysterious *guanxi* elements make internal relationships more obscure and therefore less transparent in facilitating an open and easy environment for daily communication in CCTV. The existing two managerial circles also serve as another intangible line separating people into different categories. I have argued that all these factors are toxic to a healthy knowledge management system. Furthermore, since these factors are so embedded in the cultural heritage and social changes of the country, it makes it harder for people to identify their importance. As we have argued in the former part of this paper, serious damage has been caused without intention or awareness. Indeed, most of the time, it is just "the way things are done" for so many years that caused the problem; it is the informal cultural boundaries that prevent knowledge transfer. It is not difficult to see how "the way we do things" is a critical success factor for organizational knowledge management (Knapp & Yu, 1999, p.16).

This paper has focused on organizational culture and the communication styles in China Central Television, and how they result in knowledge loss. The hierarchical and *guanxi* oriented culture is not unique to CCTV, but due to its position as the biggest and most important media organization in China, especially when media in general and television in particular are still under direct government control, CCTV serves as a typical case highlighting a more general problem in Chinese media organisations.

References

Bilton, Chris (2002). "What Can Managers do for creativity? Brokering Creativity in the Creative Industries" *International Journal of Cultural Policy,* Vol. 8(1), pp.49-64.

Blackler, F. (1995). "Knowledge, knowledge work, and organizations" *Organization Studies*, 16, pp. 1021-1027.

De Long, David W. & Fahey, Liam, (2000). "Diagnosing Cultural barriers to Knowledge Management" *Academy of Management Review*, Vol. 14, No. 4, pp.113-127.

Fan, Xing (1995). "The Chinese Cultural System Implications for Cross-Cultural Management" *SAM Advanced Management Journal*, Winter95, Vol. 60 Issue 1, pp.14 -20.

Fukuyama, Francis, (1995). *Trust: The Social Virtues and the Creation of Prosperity* (New York: Free Press).

Hofstede, Geert (1984) *Culture's Consequences* (Sage Publications).

Knapp, Ellen & Yu, Dorothy (1999) "Understanding Organizational Culture: How culture helps or hinders the flow of knowledge" *Knowledge Management Review*, Issue 7, March/April, pp.16-21

Qian, Wei (2002). *Politics, Zhengzhi, Shichang Yu Dianshi Zhidu – Zhongguo Dianshi Zhidu Bianqian Yanjiu (Market and Media – A Study on Chinese Television Institutional Change)* (Zhengzhou, Henan People's Publishing House).

Sinclaire, John Jacka, Elizabeth & Cunningham, Stuart (eds.) (1996).*New Patterns in global Television: Peripheral Vision* (Oxford: Oxford University Press).

Sun, Yusheng (2003). *Ten Years (Shi Nian)*, (Beijing: Shenghuo, Dushu, Xinzhi Book Store).

Therivel, W.A. (1995) 'Long-term effect of power on Creativity' in *Creativity Research Journal*, Vol. 8, Issue 2, pp.173-192.

Warner, Malcolm (2004). "Human resource management in China revisited: introduction" *International Journal of Human Resource Management*, Jun/Aug, Vol. 15 Issue 4/5.

Wen, Lu & Liu,Yangguang (1994). "Interview with *'Focus'*" *Chinese Journalists*, July.

Yeung, Irene Y.M. & Tung, Rosalie L. (1996). "Achieving Business Success in Confucian Societies: The Importance of *Guanxi* (connections)" *Organizational Dynamics*, autumn96, Vol. 25 Issue 2, pp.54-65.

PART V

Knowledge Management Strategies

MECHANISMS FOR INTEGRATING DISTRIBUTED KNOWLEDGE

WAI FONG BOH

Nanyang Business School, Nanyang Technological University
Nanyang Avenue, Singapore 369798

Organizations need to effectively combine and utilize knowledge resources that are distributed amongst the employees and groups in the firm. This paper examines the use of knowledge-sharing mechanisms to leverage on the learning, experience and expertise of employees to create capabilities that transcend beyond individuals and teams. In this paper, we specify an overall framework that provides a typology of the types of knowledge-integrating mechanisms used by project-based organizations. We build an overall picture by identifying two important dimensions of knowledge-sharing mechanisms and the key knowledge-sharing mechanisms illustrating each quadrant in the framework. The first dimension is personalization vs. codification. If knowledge is shared through a codification strategy, knowledge is carefully codified and stored in databases and documents. If knowledge is shared through a personalization strategy, it will be closely tied to the person who developed it and shared mainly through direct person-to-person contacts. The second key dimension in our typology is whether the mechanisms facilitate knowledge sharing through integration processes at the individual and group levels, or whether the mechanisms facilitate knowledge sharing through processes institutionalized in various organizational routines, artifacts, or organizational structure. The interaction of these two dimensions provides a typology of knowledge-sharing mechanisms used by project-based organizations. To examine the usefulness of the typology, we conducted empirical studies in two project-based organizations. We observe that the organization that is smaller in size and less mature makes use of predominantly integration and personalization knowledge-sharing mechanisms, while the organization that is bigger in size and more mature makes use of predominantly institutionalized knowledge-sharing mechanisms. This typology highlights that organizations can institutionalize both codification and personalization-oriented knowledge-sharing mechanisms. The mechanisms in all the four quadrants can also be used in a complementary manner to one another.

1 Introduction

Proponents of the resource-based theory of the firm have argued that knowledge is a primary source of competitive advantage for firms (e.g. Galunic & Rodan, 1998), especially for those firms whose critical resource and primary source of value is knowledge. It is important for such firms, not only to have these knowledge resources, but also to ensure they can effectively combine and utilize the knowledge resources that are distributed amongst the employees and groups in the firm (Lowendahl, Revang, & Fosstenlokken, 2001). Professional service and technical organizations, such as research government contractors, accounting firms, and software engineering firms, are typical examples of organizations that regard knowledge as an essential resource (Empson, 2001). These professional service and technical organizations also tend to be project-based, as projects are often their major business endeavor and the normal mechanism for executing new business opportunities (Hobday, 2000). Having a strong focus on projects raises questions about how a project-based organization learns and builds up its knowledge capabilities, and resources. The temporary nature of projects implies that new human encounters and relationships take place whenever a new project is started; this increases the barriers to learning from the previous experience of others (Prencipe & Tell, 2001). Each project is customized, thus it tends to differ from another in several, critical aspects. While there is less scope for routinized learning in non-repetitive project work, firms that can successfully share knowledge across individuals and across projects may be able to recycle their experience from one bid or project for others in the same line of business. Common problems may be encountered across different projects, and effective sharing of knowledge across projects can reduce the organizational costs of duplicating efforts to invent the same solutions (Goodman & Darr, 1998).

2   Knowledge-Sharing Mechanisms

In order to further specify a more concrete and empirically tractable manner of examining how organizations learn from their experience, we focus on knowledge-sharing mechanisms. Knowledge-sharing mechanisms are defined as the formal and informal mechanisms for sharing, integrating, interpreting and applying the know-what, know-how, and know-why embedded in individuals and groups that is relevant to the performance of the organization and its members. Such mechanisms are not only restricted to formal processes adopted by the organization, but also include informal practices such as the stories shared among the technical reps in Orr (1990). The knowledge-sharing mechanisms are the means by which individuals access knowledge and information from other actors, through the organizational memory embedded in individuals, groups, and artifacts of the organization.

Most of the prior work on organizational learning and knowledge-sharing mechanisms has been ad-hoc in nature, focused on describing specific learning mechanisms that have been found in various organizations. It is important to define and operationalize relevant dimensions of different types of knowledge-sharing mechanisms (e.g. in Prencipe & Tell, 2001), so that we can have a typology of different types of knowledge-sharing mechanisms. Hence, in this paper, we specify an overall framework that provides a typology of the types of knowledge-integrating mechanisms used by project-based organizations. We build an overall picture using two important dimensions of knowledge-sharing mechanisms and identify the key relevant mechanisms illustrating each dimension that project-based organizations can adopt to effectively leverage the experience and expertise of individuals and groups. Then, we present the findings of empirical studies conducted in two project-based organizations to identify the types of knowledge-sharing mechanisms they use, and contrast between the two cases to examine insights about how the attributes of the organization affect the types of knowledge-integrating mechanisms used.

2.1 Codification vs. Personalization

Organizations can facilitate the sharing of knowledge between individuals and groups by using the codification or personalization strategy (Hansen, Nohria, & Tierney, 1999), the first dimension of our typology. If knowledge is shared through a codification mechanism, knowledge is carefully codified and stored in databases and documents, where it can be accessed and used easily by employees in the company. Codification can be a good mechanism to store large amounts of knowledge, serving as a means of creating an organizational memory for all employees (Goodman & Darr, 1998). On the other hand, personalization is a knowledge sharing mechanism concerned with the use of people as a method for transferring knowledge. Knowledge shared through a personalization strategy will be closely tied to the person who developed it and will be shared mainly through direct person-to-person contacts. Individuals are effective carriers of knowledge because they are able to restructure knowledge so that it applies to new context (Allen, 1977). Personalization also allows for discussions and sharing interpretations that may lead to the development of new knowledge (Prencipe & Tell, 2001).

2.2 Integration vs. Institutionalization

Another key dimension in our typology of knowledge sharing mechanism is whether the mechanisms facilitate knowledge sharing through integration processes at the individual and group levels, or whether the mechanisms facilitate knowledge sharing through processes institutionalized in various organizational routines, artifacts, or organizational structure (Crossan, Lane, & White, 1999). Integration is defined as the process of developing shared understanding among individuals and of taking coordinated and collective action through mutual adjustment. Knowledge sharing mechanisms supporting the integration process of individual knowledge tends to be more ad hoc and informal. An example is the referral of experts or other colleagues who have been involved in prior projects and proposals, so that people facing a problem can locate an expert who may be able to shed some light on how the same problem was solved in a previous project. On the other hand, institutionalization is defined as the process of embedding learning that has occurred by individuals and groups into the organization. Institutionalized knowledge sharing mechanisms refer to the systems, structure, procedure and strategy that are put in place to ensure that certain actions occur so that knowledge sharing can be effected through these mechanisms. The emphasis in institutionalizing knowledge-sharing mechanisms is to ensure repeatability of the learning and knowledge sharing in the long run. An example is the use of an experts database that provides search capabilities for individuals to locate other experts who have experience or expertise in a particular type of project.

3   Typology of Knowledge Sharing Mechanisms

Table 1 shows how the two dimensions relate with one another to present the overall typology of knowledge-integrating mechanisms.

Table 1. Typology of Knowledge-Integrating Mechanisms for Managing Distributed Knowledge and Expertise in Professional and Technical Services Firm

	Knowledge Sharing Through **Integration** Processes Between Individuals and Groups	Knowledge Sharing Through Processes **Institutionalized** in Routines / Structure
Personalization	*Quadrant 1* **Informal networks and referral system** **Meetings** **Communication**	*Quadrant 2* **Experts Database** **Organization of Support Services** **Deployment**
Codification	*Quadrant 3* **Informal Sharing of Documents**	*Quadrant 4* **Community communication archives** **Repositories** **Standardized Methodologies**

3.1 Quadrant 1

Quadrant 1 describes personalization knowledge sharing mechanisms supporting integration processes between individuals and groups. Within every organization, there is a great deal of knowledge embodied in workers. If an organization made optimal use of the knowledge its employees have, then its performance would benefit enormously. Unfortunately, few organizations enjoy such benefits, because they are not fully aware of the knowledge that they possess. The knowledge is there, but it cannot be used, because too few people (or not the right people) realize that it exists and know how to locate it. To facilitate knowledge sharing through personalization, there are mechanisms that individuals and groups use to affect "who knows what" in the organization. Many organizations depend on their informal network and a system of referrals based on reputations to create an organizational memory of "who knows what" within the organization. Networks of individuals can be a powerful means of storage and retrieval of the organization's experiential knowledge, given that individuals have a general preference for obtaining information from other people, rather than from documents (Allen, 1977).

There can also be mechanisms that individuals and groups use to gain timely access to others' thinking; and reduce the cost of seeking information from another person. Individuals often organize meetings and presentations between groups and within communities. These meetings bring professionals with common interests or in the same practice together so that they can share their experiences and knowledge in free-flowing, creative ways that foster new approaches to problems (Alavi & Leidner, 2001). In addition, broadcast e-mails and communication can facilitate contact between the person seeking knowledge and those who may have access to the knowledge. This is particularly useful for allowing geographically dispersed individuals and groups use to gain timely access to others' thinking.

3.2 *Quadrant 2*

Quadrant 2 describes personalization knowledge sharing mechanisms that are institutionalized in the routines and structure of the organization. While informal networks and a system of referrals may work well in a small firm for learning about who knows what within organizations, it becomes problematic in a large firm. A search for knowledge sources through an informal network is usually limited to immediate coworkers in regular and routine contact with the individual. Individuals are unlikely to encounter new knowledge through their close-knit work networks, because individuals in the same clique tend to possess redundant information (Alavi & Leidner, 2001). Thus, expanding the individual's network to more extended, although weaker connections may help to locate information that individuals would not be aware of from immediate co-workers, especially if the firm is big and there is a potentially large pool of experts to draw on that may have the relevant information. To address this problem, some organizations try to create a formal mapping of internal expertise by publishing corporate directories or experts databases that list the expertise and experience of individuals (Alavi & Leidner, 2001).

In order to enable employees to access the expertise and experience of experts in the organization where needed, another mechanism is to structure the organization such that experts are assigned roles where they can disseminate knowledge based on their own experience and expertise easily to others within the organization. Organizations can also deploy the right individuals into a project, so that they have the right expertise and experience to tap on during the execution of the project. Each project in a project-based organization is often a major business endeavor and the normal mechanism for creating, responding to, and executing new business opportunities (Hobday, 2000). Projects have specific expertise requirements to meet the goals of the project and the needs of clients. In the project environment, appropriate expertise utilization means that the members of projects have expertise that is matched to project requirements. The ability to appropriately deploy the right experts on each project will affect the ability of the organization to integrate the expertise embedded in each individual.

3.3 *Quadrant 3*

Quadrant 3 describes codification knowledge sharing mechanisms supporting integration processes between individuals and groups. This refers to the informal sharing of intellectual capital between individuals and groups. A key way that project-based organizations can make connections between the problems and potential solutions across time, group, departmental, and geographical boundaries (Hargadon & Sutton, 1997), is to facilitate reuse of the intellectual capital that is produced for one engagement for another engagement. In the process of completing projects, individuals and groups convert their experiences and learning into various artifacts. These artifacts include project proposals, project plans, client presentations, client reports, software code, system architectures, system testing cases, strategies, and even lessons learned about what works and what does not for different types of engagements. These different types of intellectual capital codify the experience and learning that the organization has accumulated across different engagements. If an organization can achieve reuse of its intellectual capital, it can build upon prior experience and invest in making improvements to the existing intellectual capital instead of wasting effort on reinventing the wheel. Much of the intellectual capital that are created in the process of completing engagements are stored in the hard disks of individual team members, or they are stored in shared spaces that are accessible only to the team members that are working on the project. Hence, much sharing of such intellectual capital takes place through more informal integration mechanisms where individuals find the right intellectual capital to reuse through personal contacts and their social network. Hence, the mechanisms in quadrant 3 tend to work hand in hand with personalization mechanisms in quadrant 1, where individuals make use of a combination of communicating with one another and making use of various artifacts to effectively share knowledge with one another (Hargadon & Sutton, 1997).

3.4 Quadrant 4

Quadrant 4 describes codification knowledge sharing mechanisms that are institutionalized in the routines and structure of the organization. To support knowledge sharing through codification, information technology (IT) can be used to create the electronic repositories and infrastructure for storing, searching and retrieving the intellectual capital that has been created in the course of different engagements. The rise of networked computers has made it possible to codify, store and share certain kinds of knowledge more easily and cheaply than ever before. With computer-based information technologies playing an increasingly important role in how organizations store knowledge (Olivera, 2000), electronic databases for people to share knowledge and information has become even more widely available.

Another form of knowledge that can be stored and accessed again is the communication between the person seeking knowledge and those who may have access to the knowledge, this communication between individuals can be codified and made accessible to others who may face similar problems, by making use of electronic bulletin boards and forums that archive, and provide search facilities for the history of communication taking place between individuals.

To facilitate the sharing of knowledge, organizations can also institutionalize a common language or a shared interpretive context. In many consulting firms, for example, organizations train their consultants in a common methodology for project management, and define a set of methodology or framework or engagement models for consultants to make use of in different types of engagement. These models including broad methods outlining in detail the activities required, for example, in the execution of re-engineering projects, and more specific tools for tackling a variety of tasks, such as how to design a sales organization, the product-development process or a logistics system in a specific industry. After becoming internalized by each consultant, this set of methodology serves as a common language and approach to thinking of problems that can greatly help the sharing of knowledge and experience across projects.

3.5 From Integration to Institutionalization

As pointed out by Crossan *et al.* (1999), organizations typically adopt a path from integration to institutionalization. Actions that are deemed to be effective will be repeated. Often, by nature of their small size, their open communication and their formation based on common interest and dreams, individual and group learning dominate in young organizations. As organizations mature, however, individuals begin to fall into patterns of interaction by formalizing them. Over time, spontaneous individual and group learning become less prevalent, as the prior learning becomes embedded in the organization and begins to guide the actions and learning of organizational members. Hence, we propose that:

Proposition 1. Organizations that are less mature and smaller in size are more likely to make use predominantly integration knowledge-sharing mechanisms, while organizations that are more mature and bigger in size are more likely to make use of institutionalized knowledge-sharing mechanisms.

3.6 Personalization vs. Codification

Hansen *et al.* (1999) highlighted that effective firms excel by predominantly focusing on using either the personalization or codification mechanism for knowledge sharing, and using the other in a supporting role. They noted that companies do not use both approaches to an equal degree. What determines which mechanisms to focus on depend on the task routineness of the organization. For organizations that face similar problems over and over, their customers benefit from their ability to build a reliable, high-quality information system faster and at a better price than others by using work plans, software code, and solutions that have been fine-tuned and proven successful. Other factors such as the size of the organization and the extent of geographical distribution can also play an important role in determining whether organizations should focus on the use of codification or personalization strategy. Given that individuals have a general preference for obtaining information from other people, rather than from documents (Allen, 1977), the use of personalization strategy tends to be used in most organizations. This is especially since the use of codification strategy requires deliberate investments on the part of organizations to make it work. As the organization grows in size with employees dispersed in different geographical locations, however, relying on the personalization strategy alone can result in insufficient sharing of knowledge amongst employees, as individuals tend to share knowledge with those who have similar experience sets. Hence, we propose that:

Proposition 2. Bigger and more geographically dispersed organizations conducting tasks that are more frequent in nature benefit more from using more codification-oriented knowledge-sharing mechanisms, while smaller, less geographically dispersed organizations conducting tasks that are more unique in nature tend to make use of more personalization-oriented knowledge-sharing mechanisms.

4   Case Studies

To examine how project-based organizations leverage on and integrate the experience and expertise embedded in individuals and groups, we made use of the above framework to examine the types of knowledge-sharing mechanisms adopted in two organizations that differed in terms of size, maturity and nature of projects – Research Inc. and Consulting Inc. We then contrast between the findings of these two case studies to obtain insights about how the attributes of these organizations affect their adoption of these knowledge-sharing mechanisms.

4.1 Case 1: Research Inc.

Research Inc. (a pseudonym) forms projects to do research, consulting, and technical work for other organizations. Peer organizations in the industry include RAND, American Institutes for Research, Educational Testing Service, SAS, Inc., and Westat. The organization is a multi-location firm whose management has formed distributed work teams for some of its projects. The organization creates project teams to bid competitively for work in domains such as elementary education, child health, and Internet-based information services. Research Inc. is an appropriate setting to study our research problem. As a research and professional service firm, its key resource is the expertise of employees. Over 80% of the staff are professionals, and over half of these employees have doctorate degrees. Given the importance of knowledge as a resource in the firm, and the wide usage of teams to supply the complex mix of services required by clients, effective knowledge sharing within project teams is critical for project teams to work together.

I interviewed 36 individuals in three separate sites in Research Inc., and observed 8 meetings, including high-level director meetings, project meetings, staffing meetings, as well as proposal meetings. Based on the interviews and meeting observations, I observed that much learning that is critical to the organization takes place at the management level. These top managers typically supervise multiple projects and many people. Many of them have been with the organization for a long time. They have a rich institutional knowledge of Research Inc., and a good top down view of the capabilities and experience of staff in the organization. With their years of accumulated knowledge, they are the key people driving the strategic direction of the organization, and they are key to bringing in business for the firm. Employees who have less experience at Research Inc benefited more from effective knowledge sharing with one another. Many interviewees observed that Research Inc relies more on integration and personalization mechanisms than on institutionalized and codified mechanisms to share knowledge and capitalize on the experience of their staff. Table 2 shows the different types of knowledge-sharing mechanisms used in Research Inc., based on the typology proposed above.

Table 2. Typology of Knowledge-Sharing Mechanisms Adopted by Research Inc.

	Knowledge Sharing Through **Integration** Processes Between Individuals and Groups	Knowledge Sharing Through Processes **Institutionalized** in Routines / Structure
Personalization	• Brain-storm with other colleagues • Referrals to experts or other colleagues who have been involved in prior projects and proposals • Informal one-on-one office visits for more personal communication • Hallway conversations and informal lunch-time conversations • Monthly meetings to keep colleagues informed about other projects • Project Directors brown bag meetings for sharing experiences • Brown bag presentations to allow others to learn about specific projects • Informal project debriefs • Broadcast e-mails to specific groups to request for certain information	• Deployment • Database of resumes and self-classified expertise categories • Staff Directory • Senior staff as project and program reviewers • Sharing of common researchers across projects that are in similar domains to ensure they have adequate overview of all projects within the same domain area
Codification	• Informal sharing of documents • Writing of manuals and things to take note of on the job and sharing with others	• Database of project abstracts and proposals • Manuals: e.g. Project Directors Manual, Proposal Manual

4.2 Case 2: Consulting Inc.

Our second case study was conducted in Consulting Inc. (a pseudonym), which does technical consulting work for other organizations. Examples of organizations in this industry include Accenture, IBM Global Services, McKinsey, Gartner Group, etc. The organization has more than 50,000 employees distributed in many different countries and in different locations within the US. As a consulting firm, its key resource is the expertise of employees. The organization recognizes the importance of knowledge sharing amongst its consultants and have institutionalized several mechanisms to ensure adequate sharing of knowledge where required.

Given the large size and wide geographical distribution of Consulting Inc, they cannot rely only on integration knowledge-sharing mechanisms to effectively share knowledge amongst consultants. Hence, the organization institutionalized many knowledge-sharing mechanisms. However, Consulting Inc makes use of not only codification mechanisms, such as databases, and archived forums, but they are also aware of the importance of personalized interactions; hence, they institutionalized several mechanisms to support that. For example, they provide a comprehensive expert database, and continually make improvements to this database, so that individuals can easily locate others with the required expertise and experience. Consulting Inc also assigns experts with many years of consulting experience to help and advise other consultants on customer engagements, especially when they encounter problems they cannot solve (Halverson, 2004). Such experts do not simply serve the roles of librarians, of locating and directing users to a set of information, but they actively take a role in generating solutions for consultants on the field, and sometimes even help consultants negotiate through social and political aspects around issues (Halverson, 2004).

Table 3: Typology of Knowledge-Sharing Mechanisms Adopted by Consulting Inc.

	Knowledge Sharing Through **Integration** Processes Between Individuals and Groups	Knowledge Sharing Through Processes **Institutionalized** in Routines / Structure
Personalization	• Referrals to experts or other colleagues who have been involved in prior projects and proposals • Instant Messaging Broadcast Emails • Monthly conference calls within communities to discuss trends and issues and to share experiences • Presentations to allow others to learn about specific projects / topics	• Deployment • Staff Directory • Consultants Support: Senior consultants and experts serve as consultants for more inexperienced consultants on the field • Centers of Excellence: Congregation of domain experts in a particular center, to facilitate drawing of expertise from these centers
Codification	• Informal sharing of documents	• Centralized and local websites and repositories for reusable intellectual capital • Licensing and commercialization of intellectual property • Archived Forums • Formal Language • Common Methodologies

5   Discussion and Conclusion

In this paper, we proposed a typology that identifies two key dimensions of knowledge-sharing mechanisms used by project-based professional service and technical organizations. This typology highlights that researchers should not only focus on knowledge sharing mechanisms that fall in quadrant 1 and quadrant 4 of our typology. Consulting Inc., for example, institutionalizes many knowledge-sharing mechanisms that support personalized interactions between consultants. It is also important to note that not all sharing of documents come about through institutionalized mechanisms such as having a shared database. Sometimes, knowing the right people and using integration mechanisms can also lead individuals to effectively share documents with one another. It should also be highlighted that the mechanisms in all the four quadrants can often be used in a complementary manner to one another. For example, we found that 17% of a sample of individuals we examined approached the authors of documents that they reused for help, even though they found these documents in a database, and most of them did not know the authors of the documents.

Contrasting between the types of mechanisms adopted by Research Inc. and Consulting Inc., we observe that Research Inc., which is smaller in size and less mature, makes use of predominantly integration and personalization knowledge-sharing mechanisms, while Consulting Inc., which is bigger in size and more mature makes use of predominantly institutionalized knowledge-sharing mechanisms. The work conducted by Research Inc. also tends to be more unique than the work conducted by Consulting Inc. In Research Inc., each contract involves a different problem, for which the researchers do not have clear solutions at the outset. Hence, researchers benefit more from seeking advice from colleagues to deepen their understanding of the issues, as they must eventually create a highly customized solution to a unique problem. In contrast, Consulting Inc tends to focus on building upon their experience in similar problems to generate a best practices model or proposed steps for completing the engagement. These observations are consistent with our propositions. Future research can examine in a more systematic manner how the attributes of the organization affect the types of mechanisms used, and the factors that affect the implementation of different knowledge-sharing mechanisms.

References

Alavi, M., & Leidner, D. E. 2001. Review: Knowledge management and knowledge management systems: Conceptual foundations and research issues. *MIS Quarterly*, 25(1): 107-136.

Allen, T. J. 1977. *Managing the flow of technology: Technology transfer and the dissemination of technological information within the R&D organization*. Cambridge, MA: MIT Press.

Crossan, M. M., Lane, H. W., & White, R. E. 1999. An organizational learning framework: From intuition to institution. *Academy of Management Review*, 24(3): 522-537.

Empson, L. 2001. Introduction: Knowledge management in professional service firms. *Human Relations*, 54(7): 811-817.

Galunic, D. C., & Rodan, S. 1998. Resource recombinations in the firm: Knowledge structures and the potential for Schumpeterian innovation. *Strategic Management Journal*, 19(12): 1193-1201.

Goodman, P. S., & Darr, E. D. 1998. Computer-aided systems and communities: Mechanisms for organizational learning in distributed environments. *Mis Quarterly*, 22(4): 417-440.

Halverson, C. A. 2004. *The Value of Persistence: A Study of the Creation, Ordering and Use of Conversation Archives by a Knowledge Worker*. Proceedings of the 37th Annual Hawaii International Conference on System Sciences (HICSS'04), Big Island, Hawaii.

Hansen, M. T., Nohria, N., & Tierney, T. 1999. What's your strategy for managing knowledge? *Harvard Business Review*, 77(3): 196-196.

Hargadon, A., & Sutton, R. I. 1997. Technology brokering and innovation in a product development firm. *Administrative Science Quarterly*, 42(4): 716-749.

Hobday, M. 2000. The project-based organization: An ideal form for managing complex products and systems? *Research Policy*, 29(7): 871-893.

Lowendahl, B. R., Revang, O., & Fosstenlokken, S. M. 2001. Knowledge and value creation in professional service firms: A framework for analysis. *Human Relations*, 54(7): 911-931.

Olivera, F. 2000. Memory systems in organizations: An empirical investigation of mechanisms for knowledge collection, storage and access. *Journal of Management Studies*, 37(6): 811-832.

Orr, J. 1990. Sharing knowledge, celebrating identity: War stories and community memory in a service culture. In D. S. Middleton, & D. Edwards (Eds.), *Collective remembering: Memory in society*. Beverly Hills, CA: Sage Publications.

Prencipe, A., & Tell, F. 2001. Inter-project learning: processes and outcomes of knowledge codification in project-based firms. *Research Policy*, 30(9): 1373-1394.

THE SOURCES OF A FIRM'S COMPETITIVE ADVANTAGE ACCORDING TO THE KNOWLEDGE-BASED SCHOOL: THE CASE OF SLOVENIAN FIRMS

TOMAŽ ČATER

Faculty of Economics, University of Ljubljana, Kardeljeva ploščad 17, Ljubljana 1000, Slovenia

A basic characteristic of the knowledge-based school is that it follows the "inside out" approach of explaining the sources of a firm's competitive advantage. There are at least two important classifications of knowledge in the literature. The first one divides knowledge into its explicit and tacit component, while the second one discusses human and structural capital. Besides knowledge, its adequate management is also necessary to ensure greater competitiveness and performance. Empirical research based on a sample of 225 Slovenian firms shows that the firms see the most relevant sources of their competitive advantage in structural capital, tacit knowledge and the imperfect imitability of knowledge. The more relevant knowledge a firm possesses and the better its management is, the better the firm's performance and competitiveness, which means our empirical support of the knowledge-based school is quite clear. Among the studied firms, knowledge-related sources of competitive advantage, performing the knowledge management tasks and the imperfect imitability of knowledge, seem to be the most relevant factors of a firm's competitiveness and performance.

1   Introduction

The scientific literature usually discusses four basic schools concerning the sources of competitive advantage, i.e. the industrial organization, the resource-based, the capability-based, and the knowledge-based school. The purpose of this paper is to (1) analyze the sources of competitive advantage as seen by the knowledge-based school, (2) examine the relationship between these sources and a firm's competitiveness and performance and, based thereon, (3) offer a judgment on the relevance of the knowledge-based school. After briefly reviewing the relevant theory on the knowledge-related sources of competitive advantage, the paper mainly involves a presentation of the empirical findings of a study of 225 Slovenian firms. By comparing the empirical evidence with theoretical findings, we believe some new insights can be offered to scholars and researchers in the area of competitiveness, especially in the (post)transitional business environment.

2   Knowledge-based School: A Theoretical Review

2.1 The Origins of Competitive Advantage as Seen by the Knowledge-based School

Knowledge is said to be a good source of competitive advantage because it is subject to the effects of the economies of scale and scope. This means that a firm, once it possesses the relevant knowledge, can use this knowledge at many fronts with negligible marginal costs (Grant 1997). One of the first modern notes about knowledge as a source of competitive advantage go back to 1890, when Alfred Marshall in his "Principles of Economics" compared knowledge with the most powerful machine of the business (Truch 2001). In spite of this, the knowledge-based school became an equally important approach for explaining a firm's competitive advantage as late as in the 1990s when several papers on the knowledge-based theory of the firm (Grant 1997) and knowledge as an important factor of firm performance (Martin 2000) and competitiveness (Riesenberger 1998) were published. Although the knowledge-based school derives from the resource-based school there is an important distinction between them. Namely, while the resource-based school primarily treats the sources of competitive advantage on the strategic business unit level, the knowledge-based school, especially within the discussion on knowledge management, treats them on the corporate level (Wiig 1997; Pučko 2002).

If a firm wants to base its competitive advantage on its knowledge several conditions must be met. Since we have already discussed these conditions elsewhere (see, for example, Čater 2001a) we will not discuss them in details again. Let us just mention that knowledge that has a potential to be a source of competitive advantage has to be valuable, heterogeneous, rare, immobile, unsubstitutable and may not be easily imitated (Teece 1998; Ndlela and Du Toit 2001).

2.2 Classification of Knowledge-related Sources of Competitive Advantage

From the firm's point of view not all kinds of knowledge are equally useful. Especially important is that part of knowledge that can be labeled commercial knowledge. The nature of commercial knowledge was perhaps best described by Demarest (1997), who proposed that the goal of commercial knowledge is not to find the truth, but to ensure effective performance. It does not answer the question "what is right" but rather "what works" or even "what works better" where better is defined in competitive and financial contexts.

With regard to its contribution to the creation of competitive advantage, a distinction between explicit knowledge and tacit knowledge (as introduced by Polanyi 1966) should also be mentioned. Explicit knowledge is objectively "codified" knowledge, which is transmittable in formal, systematic language (Riesenberger 1998). It can be found in manuals, textbooks, computer programs, patent documents *etc.*, which means that it can be learned by observing and studying (Edvinsson and Sullivan 1996). Tacit knowledge, on the other hand, is personal, subjective and context-specific, which means that it is hard to communicate (Inkpen 1996; Narasimha 2000) and can usually be acquired only in the direct working experience (Inkpen 1996). If we now ask ourselves, which type of knowledge is more important in terms of creation of competitive superiority of a firm, the answer is quite obvious. Explicit knowledge usually will not play a vital role in competitive battle between firms. Even if it is protected as the intellectual property, such protection is usually limited in time and in many countries also hard to enforce (Pučko

1998). On the other hand, a firm will probably be able to base its competitive advantage on the relevant tacit knowledge (McAulay *et al.* 1997; Leonard and Sensiper 1998).

Another important knowledge-related classification divides a firm's intellectual capital into its human and structural component (Edvinsson and Malone 1997). Human capital is based on the employees' knowledge, their innovativeness and ingenuity, their skills, as well as on their values and culture. This category of intellectual capital cannot be the property of a firm, because employees take their knowledge, skills and experience with them when they leave the firm. Human capital can therefore only be rented, which means that it is highly risky. On the other hand, structural capital is everything left at the office when employees go home. It is the property of a firm and can thereby be traded (Edvinsson and Sullivan 1996). For this reason, a firm's true competitive advantage can mostly be built on its structural capital (Lank 1997).

2.3 Knowledge Management Tasks

The growing importance of intellectual capital naturally calls for its systematic management. If knowledge management is to give proper results, i.e. help create a firm's competitive advantage, its basic goal should be to transform as much of a firm's human capital as possible into its structural capital (Edvinsson and Sullivan 1996; Lank 1997). In order to reach this goal the basic knowledge management tasks should be adequately carried out at strategic, tactical as well as operational level (Macintosh 1999). At the strategic level knowledge management should (a) establish a "knowledge-oriented" mentality in a firm (Lank 1997), (b) make sure that a firm is able to analyze and plan its business in terms of the knowledge it currently has and the knowledge it needs for the future business process (Pučko 1998), and (c) ensure suitable business environment for an efficient process of creating new knowledge in a firm (Rastogi 2000). At the tactical level knowledge management should make sure (a) that existing knowledge is properly identified (Rastogi 2000), (b) that new knowledge for the future use is acquired and properly archived in organizational memories (Macintosh 1999), and (c) that new systems that enable effective and efficient allocation of the knowledge within a firm are created (Argote and Ingram 2000). Finally, at the operational level knowledge management should see that knowledge is used in everyday practice by those who need access to the right knowledge, at the right time, at the right location (Čater 2001b).

2.4 Past Empirical Research on the Knowledge-based School

Despite the fact that it is relatively new the knowledge-based school has considerable empirical support in the related literature. Several studies can be found that confirm direct influence of employees' knowledge on competitive advantage, sales growth, market share, profitability and value added per employee (Hall 1991). Similar conclusions were also reached by Michalisin (1996) who concentrated on the influence of the employees' know-how on firm performance. The relationship between the experience (as a special type of knowledge) and firm performance was studied by Piercy *et al.* (1998) who confirmed the positive influence of the experience on return on investment, market share and sales growth. Pučko's (2002) research revealed that among several types of knowledge the most relevant source of superiority is team knowledge and technological know-how.

Beside the studies that concentrate on the influence of knowledge on a firm's competitiveness and performance also the studies that deal with knowledge management can be found in the literature. These studies can be divided into three categories. The emphasis of the first group of authors is focused on the importance of knowledge management for process and technology improvements (Demarest 1997; Hichs 2000; Raisinghani 2000). The next group of published papers surpasses the thesis that knowledge management is needed to improve a firm's processes and technology and connects knowledge management directly with the improved financial performance of a firm, especially the improved profitability (Hitt *et al.* 2000), productivity (Dyer and Nobeoka 2000) and cash flows (Demarest 1997). Finally, in the third group there are authors who believe that the benefits of successful knowledge management systems are not only in helping improve a firm's financial performance but also in creating a firm's competitive advantage (Sarvary 1999; Ndlela and Du Toit 2001) that cannot be imitated (Lubit 2001).

3   Methodological Background

Based on the aim of the paper two research hypotheses dealing with the knowledge-based school on the sources of competitive advantage were developed as follows:

- H1: A firm's competitive advantage positively depends on the sources of competitive advantage discussed by the knowledge-based school.
- H2: Firm performance positively depends on the sources of competitive advantage discussed by the knowledge-based school.

Empirical research in this paper forms part of a broader study on the strategic behavior and competitive advantages of Slovenian firms. Data was collected by sending questionnaires to the Chief Executive Officers or members of the top management of randomly selected firms by post. The research encompassed the period from May 2002 till October 2002. During those six months, questionnaires from 225 Slovenian firms had been satisfactorily completed and returned to the author, meaning the response rate was 44.3%. The respondents were mostly Chief Executive Officers (36.4%), assistant managers (27.6%) or members of the top management (25.3%). In the remaining 10.7%, the respondents were the heads of different (mostly advisory) departments such as controlling, accounting *etc.* Because of the broader goals[1] of the research we used

---

[1] The goals of the research were much wider than the goals presented in this paper. Among other things, we also wanted to examine the differences in the sources and forms of competitive advantage between large, medium-sized and small firms. In order to have a sufficient number of large firms in the sample, stratified sampling was used.

stratified sampling in selecting firms in the sample. The structure of firms in the sample can be shown according to several criteria:

- Sector: manufacturing (33.3%), service (34.2%), trading (32.4%);
- Size[2]: large (33.3%), medium-sized (33.3%), small (33.3%);
- Year of foundation: founded before 1990 (50.7%), founded in 1990 or later (49.3%).

Since the structure of firms in the sample, especially in view of size distribution, was quite different from the actual structure[3] of Slovenian firms, it cannot be said that the sample is completely representative. The reason for this primarily lies in the use of stratified sampling which, as already explained, was influenced by the research's broader goals.

Most questions in the questionnaire required an answer in the form of (dis)agreement with the offered statements. Respondents were asked to choose between five answers (a five-point Likert scale was used), where 1 means they completely disagree with the statement, whereas 5 means they completely agree with it. In this way we collected data for two groups of variables, i.e. the sources of competitive advantage as discussed by the knowledge-based school and the forms[4] of competitive advantage. Data for the third group of variables, i.e. a firm's performance, were partly collected through the questionnaire (estimations of the nonfinancial performance indicators were obtained in this way) and partly from the Gospodarski vestnik[5] (2002) database (the data needed to calculate the financial performance indicators were collected using this). As for the financial performance indicators, firms were asked to provide the data needed to calculate: (1) return on equity; (2) return on assets; (3) return on sales; (4) revenues–to–expenses ratio; (5) sales–to–operating–expenses ratio; and (6) value added per employee. On the other hand, they were also asked to provide data on six nonfinancial performance indicators, namely: (1) percentage of loyal customers; (2) percentage of loyal suppliers; (3) turnover (of staff); (4) share of expenses on training and education; (5) share of expenses on research and development; and (6) percentage of reclaimed deliveries. The data for all performance indicators were collected for the period between 2000 and 2002.

---

[2] The size of firms in Slovenia (also in this research) is statutorily defined (ULRS 2001).

[3] The actual structure of Slovenian firms shows that at the end of 2001 17.4% of firms were in the manufacturing sector, 45.4% were in the service sector, while 37.2% were in the trading sector. From the aspect of size, there were 95.0% of small firms, 4.1% of medium-sized firms, and 0.9% of large firms (Statistical Office of the Republic of Slovenia 2002).

[4] Since any discussion about the forms of competitive advantage is more reasonable at the strategic business unit (SBU) level than the corporate level, respondents were asked to take this fact into account. Where a firm was diversified, respondents were asked to provide answers for the most important SBU. On the other hand, if a firm as a whole was a single SBU respondents were asked to provide answers for the firm as a whole.

[5] Gospodarski vestnik is a leading Slovenian business newspaper publisher.

We then used these figures to calculate a three-year unweighted mean[6] for each indicator. These means were then used in all statistical analyses instead of individual annual indicators.

In order to test the research hypotheses we need to examine how the number of points for variables representing how firms follow the "teachings" of the knowledge-based school influences a firm's competitive position and performance. For this purpose, we first had to carefully study the relevant literature and, based thereon, form a list of variables that measure as accurately as possible how the lessons within the knowledge-based school are followed by Slovenian firms. Based on these basic variables, the compounded variables (constructs) were then calculated. The formation of these constructs was carried out by calculating unweighted[7] means from the basic variables. The total estimation of the knowledge-based school was for example calculated as a mean from individual types of knowledge, the characteristics of knowledge and the regularity of performing knowledge management tasks (see Table 1).

4   Empirical Findings and Discussion

In the research we first wanted to find out how the firms estimate the importance of the sources of competitive advantage within the knowledge-based school. The results (see Table 1) show that firms on average ascribed the most points to the variables representing the structural capital, the tacit knowledge, the human capital and the imperfect imitability of knowledge. Slightly less important are the explicit knowledge and the regularity of performing knowledge management tasks, while all other variables, i.e. the characteristics of knowledge other than imitability, received considerably lower estimates of importance. Among several knowledge management tasks motivating employees (although according to the literature this is an important knowledge management task) was ascribed the most points. Relatively satisfactory estimates of importance can also be found for acquiring new knowledge and stimulating the creation of knowledge within a firm, while all other knowledge management tasks received considerably lower estimates of importance.

Table 1. The relevance of knowledge, its characteristics and knowledge management

Knowledge-related sources	Mean	St. dev.	Knowledge-related sources	Mean	St. dev.
a) Human capital	3.56	1.16	g) Rareness of knowledge	2.82	1.12
b) Structural capital	3.83	1.07	h) Durability of knowledge	2.19	0.82
c) Explicit knowledge	3.31	1.05	i) Unsubstitutability of knowledge	2.84	1.11
d) Tacit knowledge	3.67	1.05	j) Immobility of knowledge	2.84	1.05
e) Value of knowledge	2.16	0.87	k) Imperf. imitability of knowledge	3.47	1.10
f) Heterogeneity of knowledge	2.16	0.85	l) Knowledge management tasks	3.04	0.78

[6] The measurement of firm performance based on three-year means was necessary to avoid the influence of unique and random events. Also, the measurement of performance over several years follows the logic of competitive advantage as a long-term phenomenon.

[7] Unweighted means were calculated because we were unable to determine different weights for every variable in an objective way.

4.1 Knowledge-related Sources and the Forms of Competitive Advantage

In the first research hypothesis we examine the reasonableness of the knowledge-based school on the sources of competitive advantage. One possible approach here is to calculate the influence of the total estimation of this school as well as individual sources of competitive advantage within it (independent variables) on a firm's competitive advantage (dependent variable). As both groups of variables (independent and dependent) are metric a univariate (linear) regression analysis can be used. The results (see Table 2) show that the strength of a firm's competitive advantage is positively dependent on the total estimation of the knowledge-based school as well as on the estimations of all individual sources of competitive advantage within this school. By the total estimation of the knowledge-based school we can explain a considerable share (39.9%) of variance of the strength of a firm's competitive advantage. Of all studied sources of competitive advantage, the greatest share of variance of the strength of a firm's competitive advantage can be explained by the performance of knowledge management tasks (57.2%) and the imperfect imitability of knowledge (54.8%). The results regarding both basic forms of competitive advantage, i.e. lower price and differentiation, are very similar, which means that *hypothesis 1* can be *confirmed*.

Table 2. Examination of the influence of the knowledge-based sources of competitive advantage on the forms of competitive advantage using the regression analysis (determination coefficients)

Depend. var. (Y) = Form of competitive advantage	Independ. var. (X) = Knowledge-based sources of competitive advantage							
	Knowl. school	Human capital	Structural capital	Explicit knowl.	Tacit knowl.	Charact. of knowl.	Imperf. imitabil.	Knowl. managem.
Total	**$0.399^{(+)}$	**$0.250^{(+)}$	**$0.391^{(+)}$	**$0.204^{(+)}$	**$0.314^{(+)}$	**$0.480^{(+)}$	**$0.548^{(+)}$	**$0.572^{(+)}$
Lower price	**$0.267^{(+)}$	**$0.171^{(+)}$	**$0.267^{(+)}$	**$0.137^{(+)}$	**$0.183^{(+)}$	**$0.381^{(+)}$	**$0.443^{(+)}$	**$0.406^{(+)}$
Differentiation	**$0.419^{(+)}$	**$0.261^{(+)}$	**$0.409^{(+)}$	**$0.215^{(+)}$	**$0.348^{(+)}$	**$0.470^{(+)}$	**$0.532^{(+)}$	**$0.587^{(+)}$

Note: ** Statistical significance at the < 0.01 level

In the research we also examined the relative influence of the studied sources of knowledge-based advantage on a firm's competitive position. Again both groups of variables are metric, which means the partial correlation analysis can be used. This analysis differs from the bivariate correlation analysis in that it excludes the disturbing influence of all other variables when calculating the relationship between two variables.

Table 3. Examination of the influence of the knowledge-based sources on the forms of competitive advantage using the partial correlation analysis (coefficients of partial correlation and their ranks)

Depend. var. (Y) = Form of competitive advantage	Independ. var. (X) = Knowledge-based sources of competitive advantage						
	Human capital	Structural capital	Explicit knowl.	Tacit knowl.	Character. of knowl.	Imperfect imitability	Knowl. managem.
Total	0.097[3]	−0.022[5]	−0.012[6]	0.048[4]	0.005[7]	*0.152[2]	**0.258[1]
Lower price	0.063[3]	0.008[7]	−0.030[5]	0.047[4]	−0.012[6]	**0.205[1]	0.132[2]
Differentiation	0.104[2]	−0.037[5]	0.001[7]	0.097[4]	0.015[6]	0.099[3]	**0.296[1]

Note: * Statistical significance at the < 0.05 level; ** Statistical significance at the < 0.01 level

The results (see Table 3) show that the performance of knowledge management tasks has the largest positive influence on the strength of a firm's differentiation (R = 0.296) as well as total (R = 0.258) competitive advantage, while the imperfect imitability of knowledge has the largest positive influence on a firm's price advantage (R = 0.205). For all other studied sources of competitive advantage this influence is no longer statistically significant as also indicated by the low values of the coefficients of partial correlation (approximately between 0 and 0.1).

4.2 Knowledge-related Sources and Firm Performance

The second research hypothesis examines the reasonableness of the knowledge-based school by testing the direct influence of the total estimation of this school and individual sources of competitive advantage within it on a firm's performance. The fact that both groups of variables (independent and dependent) are metric allows us to use the univariate (linear) regression analysis. The results (see Table 4) show that the total estimation of the knowledge-based school as well as all individual sources of competitive advantage within this school have a positive influence on most performance indicators, except on turnover and the percentage of reclaimed deliveries (which was fully expected since smaller turnover and less reclaimed deliveries mean better performance). In spite of all that, relatively small shares of variance of financial (between 15 and 25%) and nonfinancial (between 5 and 15%) performance indicators can be explained by the total estimation of the knowledge-based school. Of all studied sources of competitive advantage, the greatest shares of variance of most performance indicators can be explained by the performance of knowledge management tasks, the imperfect imitability of knowledge and the total characteristics of knowledge. As a firm's performance seems to be positively dependent on the sources of competitive advantage discussed by the knowledge-based school, *hypothesis 2* can be *confirmed*.

Table 4. Examination of the influence of the knowledge-based sources of competitive advantage on firm performance using the regression analysis (determination coefficients)

Depend. var. (Y) = Firm performance	Independ. var. (X) = Knowledge-based sources of competitive advantage							
	Knowl. school	Human capital	Structural capital	Explicit knowl.	Tacit knowl.	Charact. of knowl.	Imperf. imitabil.	Knowl. managem.
Return on equity	**$0.214^{(+)}$	**$0.212^{(+)}$	**$0.214^{(+)}$	**$0.145^{(+)}$	**$0.197^{(+)}$	**$0.249^{(+)}$	**$0.278^{(+)}$	**$0.277^{(+)}$
Return on assets	**$0.251^{(+)}$	**$0.248^{(+)}$	**$0.253^{(+)}$	**$0.134^{(+)}$	**$0.212^{(+)}$	**$0.304^{(+)}$	**$0.313^{(+)}$	**$0.319^{(+)}$
Return on sales	**$0.260^{(+)}$	**$0.220^{(+)}$	**$0.298^{(+)}$	**$0.131^{(+)}$	**$0.206^{(+)}$	**$0.320^{(+)}$	**$0.320^{(+)}$	**$0.347^{(+)}$
Revenue-to-expen.	**$0.193^{(+)}$	**$0.161^{(+)}$	**$0.217^{(+)}$	**$0.088^{(+)}$	**$0.151^{(+)}$	**$0.261^{(+)}$	**$0.253^{(+)}$	**$0.263^{(+)}$
Sales-to-oper.-expen.	**$0.160^{(+)}$	**$0.201^{(+)}$	**$0.200^{(+)}$	**$0.121^{(+)}$	**$0.139^{(+)}$	**$0.226^{(+)}$	**$0.246^{(+)}$	**$0.243^{(+)}$
Value added per emp.	**$0.104^{(+)}$	**$0.145^{(+)}$	**$0.133^{(+)}$	**$0.064^{(+)}$	**$0.132^{(+)}$	**$0.180^{(+)}$	**$0.170^{(+)}$	**$0.203^{(+)}$
% of loyal customers	**$0.083^{(+)}$	**$0.054^{(+)}$	**$0.060^{(+)}$	**$0.040^{(+)}$	**$0.065^{(+)}$	**$0.050^{(+)}$	**$0.053^{(+)}$	**$0.083^{(+)}$
% of loyal suppliers	**$0.023^{(+)}$	*$0.019^{(+)}$	**$0.030^{(+)}$	$0.009^{(+)}$	*$0.019^{(+)}$	$0.014^{(+)}$	$0.008^{(+)}$	*$0.025^{(+)}$
Turnover (of staff)	**$0.117^{(-)}$	**$0.068^{(-)}$	**$0.090^{(-)}$	**$0.045^{(-)}$	**$0.084^{(-)}$	**$0.100^{(-)}$	**$0.109^{(-)}$	**$0.144^{(-)}$
% of expen. on train.	**$0.141^{(+)}$	**$0.119^{(+)}$	**$0.106^{(+)}$	**$0.071^{(+)}$	**$0.081^{(+)}$	**$0.145^{(+)}$	**$0.131^{(+)}$	**$0.167^{(+)}$
% of expen. on R&D	**$0.096^{(+)}$	**$0.079^{(+)}$	**$0.095^{(+)}$	**$0.032^{(+)}$	**$0.062^{(+)}$	**$0.172^{(+)}$	**$0.147^{(+)}$	**$0.149^{(+)}$
% of recl. deliveries	**$0.175^{(-)}$	**$0.075^{(-)}$	**$0.178^{(-)}$	**$0.076^{(-)}$	**$0.131^{(-)}$	**$0.140^{(-)}$	**$0.175^{(-)}$	**$0.184^{(-)}$

Note: * Statistical significance at the < 0.05 level; ** Statistical significance at the < 0.01 level

In the research we also examined the relative influence of the studied knowledge-related sources of competitive advantage on a firm's performance. Since both groups of variables (independent and dependent) are metric, probably the best approach here is by using a partial correlation analysis. The results (see Table 5) show that the performance of knowledge management tasks has the largest positive influence on most performance indicators. The second largest effect on most performance indicators can be detected for the imperfect imitability of knowledge. For all other studied sources of competitive advantage this influence is no longer statistically significant as also indicated by the low values of the coefficients of partial correlation (approximately between 0 and 0.1).

Table 5. Examination of the influence of the knowledge-based sources on firm performance using the partial correlation analysis (coefficients of partial correlation and their ranks)

Depend. var. (Y) = Firm performance	Independ. var. (X) = Knowledge-based sources of competitive advantage						
	Human capital	Structural capital	Explicit knowl.	Tacit knowl.	Character. of knowl.	Imperfect imitability	Knowl. managem.
Return on equity	0.066(5)	0.068(4)	−0.041(7)	0.124(2)	0.043(6)	0.072(3)	**0.196(1)
Return on assets	0.027(6)	−0.026(7)	*0.135(2)	0.103(4)	0.106(3)	0.072(5)	**0.275(1)
Return on sales	−0.023(6)	0.100(5)	0.103(4)	0.000(7)	0.129(2)	0.108(3)	**0.189(1)
Revenue-to-expen.	−0.013(6)	0.073(4)	0.108(3)	0.003(7)	0.131(2)	0.067(5)	*0.166(1)
Sales-to-oper.-expen.	0.051(5)	0.019(6)	0.077(2)	0.009(7)	0.051(4)	0.064(3)	**0.208(1)
Value added per emp.	−0.046(7)	−0.081(6)	0.126(2)	0.112(4)	0.099(5)	0.124(3)	**0.232(1)
% of loyal customers	−0.058(4)	−0.042(5)	0.010(7)	0.077(2)	0.016(6)	0.131(1)	0.072(3)
% of loyal suppliers	*0.137(1)	0.072(4)	−0.025(6)	−0.006(7)	0.075(3)	0.091(2)	0.057(5)
Turnover (of staff)	0.012(6)	0.041(4)	0.026(5)	−0.048(3)	−0.004(7)	*−0.157(1)	−0.076(2)
% of expen. on train.	−0.086(4)	−0.036(5)	−0.027(6)	0.014(7)	0.109(3)	*0.149(2)	*0.150(1)
% of expen. on R&D	−0.030(5)	0.014(7)	0.110(3)	−0.018(6)	*0.147(1)	0.057(4)	*0.139(2)
% of recl. deliveries	−0.070(3)	−0.102(1)	−0.020(6)	−0.007(7)	0.027(4)	−0.070(2)	0.025(5)

Note: * Statistical significance at the < 0.05 level; ** Statistical significance at the < 0.01 level

5   Conclusion

Three important conclusions can be drawn concerning the relevance of the knowledge-based school on the sources of a firm's competitive advantage. (1) Slovenian firms believe that for creating a firm's competitive advantage the structural capital is more relevant than the human capital and the tacit knowledge is more relevant than the explicit knowledge. Among different characteristics of knowledge the most relevant and desirable seems to be its imperfect imitability. (2) Using the regression analysis it can be concluded that the more firms follow the teachings of the knowledge-based school the greater competitive advantage (hypothesis 1 confirmed) and performance (hypothesis 2 confirmed) they achieve. (3) Using the partial correlation analysis it can be concluded that among all individual sources of competitive advantage within the knowledge-based school the regular performance of knowledge management tasks and the imperfect imitability of knowledge have the largest influence on a firm's competitive advantage and performance. Of all other studied sources (with much smaller relative influence) the human capital takes third place, the tacit knowledge fourth place, the structural capital fifth place, the explicit knowledge sixth place and the total characteristics of knowledge seventh place.

Our findings generally confirm the findings of most empirical research on the sources of competitive advantage within the knowledge-based school that has been carried out in both transitional economies and established market economies. In this respect, our research definitely represents further support of the contemporary theory on firm competitiveness, which teaches us that the "internal" sources of competitive advantage (such as knowledge and its proper management) are extremely relevant and important for the creation of competitive advantage and superior performance.

Irrespective of all the findings of this research, its possible weaknesses should also be mentioned. Perhaps the most important one is that real sources of competitive advantage are usually well hidden, making it impossible for a researcher to measure them objectively. For this reason, we had to use managers' relatively subjective assessments of the basic sources and forms of competitive (dis)advantage of their firms. This weakness might be partially avoided by personally interviewing managers and/or by observing each firm over a longer period of time. Another possible weakness of this research is the use of stratified sampling, which was necessary because of the broader goals of the research. As a suggestion for further research, we believe that similar studies should also be carried out on a much more homogeneous sample of firms. In spite of these weaknesses, we still believe the research has the potential to broaden our knowledge in the field of firm competitiveness. Its most important advantage is probably the relatively large sample of firms involved, which has allowed us to draw certain conclusions with minimum risk.

References

Argote, L. and Ingram, P. (2000) "Knowledge transfer: A basis for competitive advantage in firms." *Organizational Behavior & Human Decision Processes*, 82(1): 150–169.

Čater, T. (2001a) "Hipoteze o osnovah konkurenčne prednosti podjetja." *Organizacija*, 34(2): 64–74.

Čater, T. (2001b) "Knowledge management as a means of developing a firm's competitive advantage." *Management*, 6(1–2): 133–153.

Demarest, M. (1997) "Understanding knowledge management." *Long Range Planning*, 30(3): 374–384.

Dyer, J.H. and Nobeoka, K. (2000) "Creating and managing a high-performance knowledge-sharing network: The Toyota case." *Strategic Management Journal*, 21(3): 345–367.

Edvinsson, L. and Malone, M.S. (1997) *Intellectual capital: The proven way to establish your company's real value by measuring its hidden brainpower*. London: Piatkus.

Edvinsson, L. and Sullivan, P. (1996) "Developing a model for managing intellectual capital." *European Management Journal*, 14(4): 356–364.

Gospodarski vestnik (2002) *FIPO baza 2002* (http://www.gvin.com/fipo2002).

Grant, R.M. (1997) "The knowledge-based view of the firm: Implications for management practice." *Long Range Planning*, 30(3): 450–454.

Hall, R. (1991) "The contribution of intangible resources to business success." *Journal of General Management*, 16(4): 41–52.

Hicks, S. (2000) "Are you ready for knowledge management?" *Training & Development*, 54(9): 71–72.

Hitt, M.A., Ireland, D.R. and Lee, H. (2000) "Technological learning, knowledge management, firm growth and performance: An introductory essay." *Journal of Engineering and Technology Management*, 17(3–4): 231–246.

Inkpen, A.C. (1996) "Creating knowledge through collaboration." *California Management Review*, 39(1): 123–140.

Lank, E. (1997) "Leveraging invisible assets." *Long Range Planning*, 30(3): 406–412.

Leonard, D. and Sensiper, S. (1998) "The role of tacit knowledge in group innovation." *California Management Review*, 40(3): 112–132.

Lubit, R. (2001) "Tacit knowledge and knowledge management: The keys to sustainable competitive advantage." *Organizational Dynamics*, 29(3): 164–178.

Macintosh, A. (1999) *Knowledge management* (http://www.aiai.ed.ac.uk/~alm/kamlnks).

Martin, B. (2000) "Knowledge management within the context of management: An evolving relationship." *Singapore Management Review*, 22(2): 17–36.

McAulay, L., Russell, G. and Sims, J. (1997) "Tacit knowledge for competitive advantage." *Management Accounting*, 75(11): 36–37.

Michalisin, M.D. (1996) *Strategic assets and firm performance: An empirical study of the resource-based view's main prescription (doctoral thesis)*. Kent: Kent State University.

Narasimha, S. (2000) "Organizational knowledge, human resource management, and sustained competitive advantage: Toward a framework." *Competitiveness Review*, 10(1): 123–135.

Ndlela, L.T. and Du Toit, A.S. (2001) "Establishing a knowledge management programme for competitive advantage in an enterprise." *International Journal of Information Management*, 21(2): 151–165.

Piercy, N.F., Kaleka, A. and Katsikeas, C.S. (1998) "Sources of competitive advantage in high performing exporting companies." *Journal of World Business*, 33(4): 378–393.

Polanyi, M. (1966) *The tacit dymension*. London: Routledge & Kegan Paul.

Pučko, D. (1998) "Poslovodenje znanja in vplivi na strateško poslovodenje ter analizo." *Organizacija*, 31(10): 557–565.

Pučko, D. (2002) "Analiza konkurenčnih prednosti slovenskih podjetij." In J. Prašnikar (Ed.), *Primerjajmo se z najboljšimi*: 175–195, Ljubljana: Finance.

Raisinghani, M.S. (2000) "Knowledge management: A cognitive perspective on business and education." *American Business Review*, 18(2): 105–112.

Rastogi, P.N. (2000) "Knowledge management and intellectual capital: The new virtuous reality of competitiveness." *Human Systems Management*, 19(1): 39–48.

Riesenberger, J.R. (1998) "Knowledge: The source of sustainable competitive advantage." *Journal of International Marketing*, 6(3): 94–107.

Sarvary, M. (1999) "Knowledge management and competition in the consulting industry." *California Management Review*, 41(2): 95–107.

Statistical Office of the Republic of Slovenia (2002) *Statistical yearbook of the Republic of Slovenia 2002*. Ljubljana: Statistical Office of the Republic of Slovenia.

Teece, D.J. (1998) "Capturing value from knowledge assets: The new economy, markets for know-how, and intangible assets." *California Management Review*, 40(3): 55–79.

Truch, E. (2001) "Knowledge management: Auditing and reporting intellectual capital." *Journal of General Management*, 26(3): 26–40.

ULRS (2001) *Zakon o gospodarskih družbah (ZGD-F)*. Ljubljana: ULRS.

Wiig, K.M. (1997) "Integrating intellectual capital and knowledge management." *Long Range Planning*, 30(3): 399–405.

A FRAMEWORK FOR KNOWLEDGE REUSE SUCCESS

D.C.Y. LIM, A. KANKANHALLI & K.S. RAMAN

School of Computing, National University of Singapore
3 Science Drive 2, Singapore 117543

Organizations are concerned about the reuse of knowledge since the benefits to be derived from knowledge management depend on the effective reuse of knowledge resources. To facilitate effective reuse of organizational knowledge resources, it is necessary to understand the factors behind reuse success. The purpose of this research is therefore to propose a theoretical framework which can be used to understand and explain the success of knowledge reuse within an organization. Our findings in an exploratory case study with an organization in the ornamental fish industry showed that the antecedents identified in the framework influence knowledge reuse success. This suggests that the proposed framework is relevant from the point of view of practitioners as well as researchers.

1 Introduction

Organizations have always valued the experience and know-how of their employees. Only recently however, have organizations come to understand that they require more than a casual approach towards corporate knowledge if they are to succeed in today's and tomorrow's economies. This understanding has led to knowledge being viewed as a significant organizational resource (Alavi and Leidner, 2001) and the growing interest in knowledge management (KM).

KM involves the management of knowledge processes which are often categorised by whether they involve knowledge creation or knowledge reuse. Knowledge creation is typically viewed as somehow more important than knowledge reuse, more difficult to manage, and less amenable to information technology support. However, in reality organizations are also concerned about the reuse of knowledge since the benefits to be derived from KM depend on the effective reuse of knowledge resources. Given that knowledge reuse is a key organizational concern, it is necessary to understand the factors behind reuse success.

In information systems (IS) research, the DeLone and McLean (1992; 2003) model has been widely used to study IS success. Although DeLone and McLean's model has been applied to a variety of information systems, there have been few attempts (exceptions include Jennex and Olfman, 2003) to extend the model to knowledge management systems (KMS) and knowledge reuse in particular. Markus (2001), however, provides a framework to categorise knowledge reuse situations and find success factors for the different reuse situations, but this framework has not been operationalized to investigate reuse success and its antecedents.

The purpose of this research is therefore to propose a framework which can be used to understand and explain the success of knowledge reuse within an organization. The proposed framework is based chiefly on concepts from the DeLone and McLean IS

Success Model (1992; 2003), the Jennex and Olfman KMS Success Model (2003), Markus' framework for reuse (2001), and previous literature on the determinants of knowledge transfer (Ko, Kirsch, and King 2003).

Before presenting the proposed reuse framework, this paper will discuss briefly the Jennex and Olfman KMS success model and Markus' knowledge reuse framework. This is followed by the description of a case study which was used to validate the framework. The paper concludes with a summary of findings and outline of future work on this topic.

2   Literature Review

2.1 Jennex and Olfman's KMS Success Model

Jennex and Olfman developed the KMS Success Model as an application and extension of DeLone and McLean's IS Success Model. The DeLone and McLean Model (2003) suggests system quality, information quality, and service quality as antecedents of IS use intention and user satisfaction. In the Jennex and Olfman model (2003), service quality is incorporated into system quality since service quality for a KMS is considered a part of system quality. In addition, since the model assesses the use of knowledge, the information quality construct from the DeLone and McLean model is reconceptualized as knowledge/information quality. Further, because the use of a KMS is usually voluntary, the intention to use outcome of the DeLone and McLean model is expanded to include a perceived benefit dimension based on Thompson *et al.* (1991) perceived benefit model, which predicts system usage when usage is voluntary. Jennex and Olfman also proposed sub-dimensions within the system quality and knowledge/information quality dimensions resulting in the overall model shown in Figure 1.

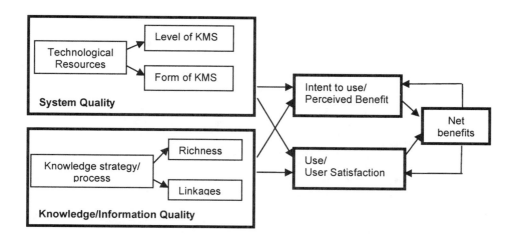

Figure 1. The Jennex and Olfman KMS success model (2003)

2.2 *Markus' Framework of Knowledge Reuse*

Markus (2001) presents a framework of organizational knowledge reuse, with emphasis on the role of KMS. Knowledge reuse follows the processes of knowledge capture, knowledge packaging, and knowledge distribution. This study proposes that reuse consists of four different steps. The first and most essential step is defining the search question. It has been noted that one characteristic that sets novices apart from experts is that experts know what to ask. The second step is the search for experts or expertise. The third is the selection of an appropriate expert, or of expert advice from the results of the previous search. The final step is the application of knowledge in the situation which triggered the need for knowledge.

Typology of Knowledge Reuse Situations

Markus (2001) then outlines a typology of knowledge reuse situations which involve four different types of users i.e., shared work producers, shared work practitioners, expertise seeking novices, and secondary knowledge miners. The basic characteristics differentiating these types of reuse situations are the knowledge reuser (in relation to the knowledge producer) and the purpose of reuse (see Table 1).

Table 1. Types of knowledge reuse situations (from Markus 2001)

Reuse Situation	Description and Purpose
Shared Work Producers	People working together on a team, either homogeneous or cross-functional; producers of knowledge for their own later reuse. They seek to reuse knowledge to: • Keep track of current status and things needing attention • Recall reasons for decisions when decisions need to be revisited or when there is a turnover among team members • Learn how the team can perform better on the next project
Shared Work Practitioners	People doing similar work in different settings; producers of knowledge for each other's use. They seek to reuse knowledge to: • Acquire new knowledge that others have generated • Get advice about how to handle a particularly challenging or unusual situation that is new for the team • Gain access to observations that spur innovations
Expertise Seeking Novices	People with an occasional need for expert knowledge that they do not possess. They seek to reuse knowledge to: • Answer an arcane question or solve an ad-hoc problem • Approximate the performance of experts • Minimise the need for experts
Secondary Knowledge Miners	People who seek to answer new questions or develop new knowledge through analysis of records produced by other people for different purposes. They seek to reuse knowledge to: • Seek answers to new questions or create new knowledge

Because of the differences in reusers, knowledge producers, and reuse purposes, the requirements to make each reuse situation successful tend to be different.

3 Proposed Framework for Knowledge Reuse Success

The Jennex and Olfman KMS Success Model (2003) and Markus reuse framework (2001) indicate that knowledge characteristics and system characteristics are likely to impact knowledge reuse success. Additionally, previous literature on determinants of knowledge transfer (Ko *et al.* 2003) suggests that reuser characteristics and the relationship between knowledge source and reuser also impact reuse success. The framework for knowledge reuse success based on these models and relevant KM literature is shown in Figure 2.

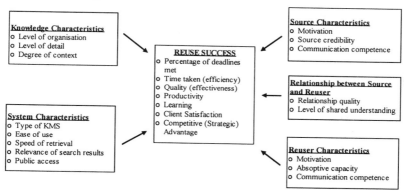

Figure 2. The proposed framework for knowledge reuse success

3.1 The Independent Variables

3.1.1 Knowledge characteristics

In identifying the characteristics which impact knowledge reuse success, Markus (2001) made distinctions between the between the level of organization and level of detail of the knowledge stored in the KMS. Level of organization refers to how well the knowledge is indexed. On the other hand, level of detail looks at how much attention is paid to particular items. Both characteristics are likely to influence the way knowledge is reused. Markus also points out that the information on the interrelated conditions can be important for the successful application of the knowledge resource, and therefore the degree of context of the knowledge plays an important role in knowledge reuse.

3.1.2 System characteristics

For a start, the appropriate type of KMS must be chosen to facilitate the purpose of the reuse. For example, a knowledge repository may be suitable for an expertise-seeking novice, who is trying to tackle a problem already solved by someone else in the organization. This can later be supplemented by an electronic bulletin board system (e.g., to support a community-of-practice), where the novice is able to ask questions which can be answered by experts (Davenport and Prusak, 1998). Ease of use is also an important factor in encouraging users to share and retrieve knowledge to help them in the course of their work. The speed at which search results are returned and their relevance is critical as well because the purpose of the KMS is to reduce task time and in so doing increase effectiveness (Stein and Zwass, 1995). Another contributing factor is whether the KMS has different types of access (Markus, 2001).

3.1.3 Source characteristics

The characteristics of a source of knowledge (knowledge producer) that may influence knowledge reuse success are source motivation, credibility, and communication competence (Ko *et al.*, 2003). Motivation can be intrinsic or extrinsic. Employees are intrinsically motivated when their needs and self defined goals are directly satisfied, or satisfaction lies in the content of the activity itself. In contrast, employees are extrinsically motivated when their needs are indirectly satisfied, e.g., through monetary reward (Ko *et al.*, 2003). Source credibility refers to the extent to which a reuser perceives a source to be trustworthy and an expert. When source credibility is perceived to be high, the knowledge presented by the source is perceived to be useful (Ko *et al.*, 2003). Communication competence takes into consideration various kinds of communication which the knowledge producer may engage in, such as written or oral communication. This is important because this affects whether the producer is able to carry across his or her points clearly and in an understandable manner.

3.1.4 Reuser characteristics

Reuser characteristics measure certain aspects of the reuser as an individual that have an impact on reuse success (Ko *et al.*, 2003). One such aspect is the motivation of the reuser, which determines if a reuser is motivated intrinsically or extrinsically. Absorptive capacity also has an impact on reuse success and is defined as the ability of a recipient of knowledge (reuser) to recognize the importance and value of the external information, assimilate it, and apply it. Communication competence, as defined in the section on source characteristics, is also important as reusers may have to seek clarifications or ask questions about the knowledge which they retrieve.

3.1.5 Relationship between source and reuser

This measures both the relationship quality between the source and reuser, as well as the shared understanding between the two. This has an impact on reuse because, for example, certain knowledge can be omitted when the shared understanding between source and reuser is high, but cannot be in the case where the shared understanding is minimal.

3.2 The Dependent Variable – Reuse Success

Reuse success has been measured in various ways. For example, Jennex and Olfman (2003) highlighted several desired outcomes of knowledge reuse through a KMS, i.e., timeliness in completing assignments, doing assignments right the first time, identification and completion of high priority assignments, completeness of solutions, quality of solutions, complexity of the work, and client satisfaction.

Researchers agree that impacts can be measured at many levels (DeLone and McLean 2003). Juxtaposing DeLone and McLean's success factors with Jennex and Olfman's, several likely success factors were identified. First, reusers' ability to meet deadlines may improve when previous knowledge is available to make use of in their work (the knowledge has to be well indexed in order to avoid overload and facilitate retrieval). Second, the time taken to complete a task may decrease and the quality of work may improve when knowledge from previous experience is available. Individual outcomes for the reuser include potential improved productivity from completing work faster and more accurately. Also reusers may learn from others' experience e.g., documented mistakes can warn reusers about pitfalls and give suggestions on how to avoid them. Client satisfaction, where applicable, can also be an indicator of how the reuser's performance has improved. For the organization, a desired outcome of knowledge reuse is the competitive advantage obtained.

3.3 The Different Reuse Situations

Table 2 shows the requirements in each knowledge reuse situation which are likely to bring about a positive impact on reuse success as outlined in our framework. This table also takes into consideration the situation of self-reuse, which has been added to Markus typology to account for the situation where the knowledge producer reuses some knowledge which he or she has produced in the past.

4   Case Study Description

An exploratory case study was conducted in an attempt to do a preliminary validation of the framework proposed in Figure 2. A positivist approach was used for the purpose of this case study. Positivist studies generally aim to test theory, and increase the predictive understanding of phenomena (Dube and Pare, 2003).

4.1 Case Background: ABC Corporation Limited

ABC Corporation Limited is a leading exporter of ornamental fish and pet accessories. They export a large number of species of ornamental fish to over 50 countries worldwide. They also have subsidiaries in neighbouring countries. ABC was selected for our case study for several reasons. First, ABC is considered to be a leader in its industry. It is one of the first in the industry to implement a KMS. Second, ABC is a new user of IT and despite having some staff members with little computer experience, their sharing of knowledge via the use of the KMS is spread over four countries. Finally, whereas typical KMS implementations are in large organizations with pre-existing successful IS applications and users, ABC started with KM as an integral part of their IS strategy.

Table 2. Requirements of characteristics

	Shared Work Producers	Shared Work Practitioners	Expertise Seeking Novices	Secondary Knowledge Miners	Self-Reuse
KNOWLEDGE CHARACTERISTICS					
Level of organization	High, but tends to be low in this situation	High, but tends to be moderate	High	High	High
Level of detail	High. Sketchy (producers assume reusers know)	High	Moderate. Novices may not understand details.	Low. Reuser need to filter the relevant information.	High.
Degree of Context	Contextualised	Decontextualised; but delivered with context inf.	Decontextualised, but support recontext.	Store metadata to facilitate secondary reuse	Highly contextualised
SYSTEM CHARACTERISTICS					
Type of KMS	EKR or Collaborative space	Communities of Practice (CoP) or EKR	EKR and Yellow Pages	EKR (Electronic Knowledge Repository)	Personal KM tools
Ease of use	High	High	High	High	High
Speed of retrieval	High	High	High	High	High
Relevance of results	High	High	High	High	High
Public access	No public access provided	Restricted to experts and packaged expertise	Restricted to experts and packaged expertise	Restricted to experts and packaged expertise	No public access provided
SOURCE (SENDER) CHARACTERISTICS					
Motivation for producing knowledge	Intrinsic. e.g. Share knowledge within a working team.	Intrinsic. e.g. Share knowledge within a community	Intrinsic. e.g. Help novices to answer questions	Intrinsic. e.g. Usually not produced for knowledge miners	Intrinsic. e.g. For self reuse at a later time.
Source credibility	High	High	High	High	N.A.
Communication competence	High (also for reuser)	High (also for reuser)	High (also for reuser)	High (also for reuser)	N.A. (also for reuser)
REUSER (RECEIVER) CHARACTERISTICS					
Motivation for reuse	Intrinsic. e.g. Keep track of current status	Intrinsic. e.g. Acquire new knowledge from others	Intrinsic. e.g. Answer a question or solve an ad-hoc problem	Intrinsic. e.g. Seek answers to new questions	Intrinsic. e.g. To learn from a past experience
Absorptive Capacity	High	High	High, but unlikely to be because they are novices.	High	N.A.
RELATIONSHIP BETWEEN PRODUCER AND REUSER					
Relationship Quality	High	Low	Low	N.A.	N.A.
Level of Shared Understanding	High	High	Low	Low	N.A.

Two days were spent at ABC where an exploratory study was conducted with the intention of preliminarily validating the proposed framework. During the visits, interviews were arranged with the chief executive and several administrative managers with regards to the reuse of knowledge in their organization and the use of their KMS. This was followed up by e-mail exchanges and telephone conversations with them as well as other staff members. At the time of the study, KM in ABC was still in the process of being implemented in phases. Therefore, their views are based on their experience so far, and their future expectations. Their aim is to make KM organization-wide so that all their staff members, no matter what function they perform, can leverage on the advantages which the KMS provides.

4.2 Knowledge Management in ABC

The chief executive of ABC realised that the business environment had changed with the rise of the Internet. According to him, the only way to maintain competitiveness and increase profits in today's knowledge economy is to ensure that the company knows more about the critical success factors of the industry and has higher productivity than their competitors. To do this, ABC implemented a KMS in conjunction with their IT vendor at the start of 2003. The main purpose of the KMS is to make the company's existing knowledge easily accessible to its staff members both in the headquarters and in their international offices. The system also attempts to ensure that knowledge is retained in the company after an employee has left.

4.3 ABC's KMS

ABC's KMS is a web-based system that contains a central knowledge repository which is systematically organised according to categories. Users are able to search the repository for required knowledge and post questions to experts from any part of the world using a variety of devices. This is because the KMS supports not only desktop and laptop computers, but also handheld devices such as Personal Digital Assistants (PDAs) and mobile phones. In addition, the KMS includes tools for knowledge encryption, compression, version control, and approval control, which attempts to ensure that ABC's knowledge remains accurate and secure.

4.4 Types of Reusers in ABC

Of the five reuse situations mentioned in Table 2, ABC's KMS users fall into four categories i.e., shared work producers, shared work practitioners, expertise seeking novices and self-reusers. While secondary knowledge mining is not being done at the moment, it is ABC's intention to do it in the future so that patterns such as sales trends can be identified and used in forecasting and decision making. Further, while self reuse is obviously present in any organization, it was suggested that self reusers at ABC typically do not utilize the organization's KMS when they are reusing their own knowledge. Instead, they are more likely to use personal tools such as directories in their local hard disk to store their knowledge. Therefore, since the type of personal tools used differs with every user, the impact of such tools on reuse was not assessed. As a result, the situation of self-reuse is not covered in this case study. Examples of knowledge sources and reusers in each of the three reuse situations relevant to ABC are provided in Table 3.

Table 3. Knowledge sources and reusers in ABC

Type of reuse situation	Knowledge Source	Knowledge Reusers
Shared work producers	Members of cross functional teams formed for specific tasks or projects.	
Shared work practitioners	Members of staff who do the same kind of work, perhaps in different countries. For example, a farmer in one country can share his knowledge on a new fish virus he encountered with his counterparts in another country.	
Expertise seeking novices	Experts in various fields	New employees learning new skills and seeking expertise from more experienced staff members

Employees performing other functions who require certain ad-hoc expertise to assist them in their work |

4.5 Relevance of the Proposed Framework in ABC

While ABC has not yet developed a framework to measure reuse success of their own KMS, our interviews with the staff members of ABC suggest that they are in agreement with those variables identified in our framework which are relevant to their company. In particular, they highlighted the following attributes that they considered crucial to the success of knowledge reuse in their organization:

Level of organization
Knowledge in ABC's KMS is well organised in directories. This makes searching for knowledge easy when required. In addition, the nature of organization makes it easier to demarcate the areas for the different supervisors to take care of. The level of organization is also positively related to the ease of use and speed of knowledge retrieval.

Degree of context
Due to nature of ABC's business, certain types of knowledge such as that describing a cure for a fish disease can be highly context-specific. In such cases, if the necessary context information is not present, reuse may not be possible.

Ease of use and speed of retrieval
It is important that the KMS is easy to use because ABC intends to implement KM organization wide. Given that some staff members have little exposure to computers, ease of use can assist to get them started on using the KMS. Speed of retrieval also should be faster than if the user has to flip through physical files to get the desired knowledge, otherwise it will be difficult for the reuser to be able to see the advantages of the system.

Communication competence and credibility of the source

These are two attributes which ABC attempts to control by having an approval system in place. All knowledge submitted to the company's KMS will be published only after it has been approved by a supervisor, who is considered to be an expert in the subject matter he is in charge of. As a result, source credibility is high, and this procedure also helps to ensure that the knowledge is well communicated, is understandable by all levels of staff members, and is accurate.

4.6 Discussion

The findings in the ABC case study reveal that there are some areas which are unique to knowledge reuse in their organization. In particular, the nature of the ornamental fish industry dictates that certain types of knowledge are very context-specific and the level of context is especially important to reusers in this industry. In addition, many interviewees suggested that while source credibility was important in most reuse situations, it did not need to be measured for shared work producers as knowledge exchange takes place only between members in a team. In such teams, members are usually selected because they are experts in their own field, indicating high source credibility.

It is also worth noting that not all five reuse situations outlined in Table 2 were relevant in the case of ABC. This is not uncommon, because the type of reusers present in an organization depends on the nature of the organization's business activities, the size of its operations and how knowledge intensive it is. Finally, our findings showed that ABC is generally in agreement with the framework which we proposed and also with most of the variables, and their attributes which have been identified. Many interviews revealed that users feel that their improved performance ultimately helps them to contribute to the organization's competitive strategic advantage over its competitors. They considered this to be a very important aspect in determining reuse success.

5   Conclusion

This paper has proposed a framework to understand and explain knowledge reuse success. Our findings in an exploratory study with ABC Corporation Limited showed that they are in agreement with the variables and their attributes which have been identified. This research is still a work-in-progress. At the next stage, a set of hypotheses will be developed, refined, and validated quantitatively. For this purpose, a survey instrument will be developed using the method suggested by Churchill (1979) and the construct validation procedure put forth by Moore and Benbasat (1991).

References

Alavi, M. and Leidner, D.E. (2001) "Review: Knowledge management and knowledge management systems: Conceptual foundations and research issues." *MIS Quarterly*, 25(1): 107-136.

Churchill, G.A. (1979) "A paradigm for developing better measures of marketing constructs." *Journal of Marketing Research*, 16(1): 64-73.

Davenport, T.H. and Prusak, L. "Working Knowledge." Harvard Business School Press, 1998.

DeLone, W.H. and McLean, E.R. (1992) "Information systems success: The quest for the dependent variable." *Information Systems Research*, 3(1): 60-95.

DeLone, W.H. and McLean, E.R. (2003) "The DeLone and McLean model of information systems success: A ten-year update." *Journal of Management Information Systems*, 19(4): 9-30.

Dube, L. and Pare, P. (2003) "Rigor in information systems positivist case research: Current practices." *MIS Quarterly*, 27(4): 597-635.

Jennex, M.E. and Olfman, L. (2003) "A knowledge management success model: An extension of DeLone and McLean's IS success model." *Proceedings of the Ninth American Conference on Information Systems*.

Ko, D., Kirsch, L. and King, W.R. (2003) "Determinants of inter-firm knowledge transfer in enterprise system implementations: Transferring knowledge from consultants to clients." *The Academy of Management Annual Meeting*, Seattle, WA.

Markus, M.L. (2001) "Toward a theory of knowledge reuse: Types of knowledge reuse situations and factors in reuse success." *Journal of Management Information Systems*, 18(1): 57-93.

Moore, G.C. and Benbasat I. (1991) "Development of an instrument to measure the perceptions of adopting an information technology innovation." *Information Systems Research,* 2(3): 192-222.

Stein, E.W. and Zwass, V. (1995) "Actualizing organizational memory with information systems." *Information Systems Research*, 6(2): 85-117.

Thompson, R.L., Higgins, C.A., and Howell, J.M., "Personal Computing: Toward a Conceptual Model of Utilization." *MIS Quarterly*, 1991, pp. 125-143.

THE DEVELOPMENT OF KM COMPETENCIES IN LIS PROGRAMS: AN ANALYSIS

SAJJAD UR REHMAN

Library and Information Science, Kuwait University
PO Box 5969, Safat 13060, Kuwait

ABDUS SATTAR CHAUDHRY

School of Communication and Information, Nanyang Technological University
31 Nanyang Link, Singapore 637718, Singapore

Views of selected head of LIS programs were sought on six KM competencies considered to be most pertinent to LIS professionals to play an effective KM role. They held the view that existing LIS programs had certain ingredients that could be transformed into KM competencies. However, there was a need to introduce new coursework in order to develop these competencies. Distinction between IM and KM applications was still blurred for many LIS programs and practitioners. LIS programs are keener to develop infrastructures and technologies that are more germane to codified knowledge. Competencies related to knowledge organization are also emphasized.

1   Introduction

Knowledge management (KM) is fast maturing as a discipline and finding its place on the lists of academic programs in academia. KM courses are commonplace in schools of business, information systems, computer science, library and information science (LIS). A body of literature has emerged that explicitly addresses knowledge management from the perspective of library and information professionals (Broadbent, 1997; Nicholson, 1997; and Loughridge, 1999; Wilson, 2002). Library and information professionals have an important role to play in knowledge management, if they are equipped with the right competencies. Yunhua (1999) makes a clear case for library development from the perspective of KM. Since early 1990s, LIS has taken a lead role in managing the initiatives of information management (IM). A great deal of confusion has prevailed in the LIS community about the relationship of IM to KM (Breen *et al.*, 2002; Davenport & Cronin, 2000; Loughridge, 1999; Oxbrow & Abell, 2002; Southon & Todd, 2001a). Broadbent (1998) clarified the notion of KM that it enhances the use of organizational knowledge through sound practices of information management and organizational learning. KM is at least partially reincarnation or resurrection of familiar library and information management processes and procedures (Koenig, 1996; Broadbent, 1998). Danvenport and Cronin (2000) asserted that librarians were confused about the transition from IM to KM and they mostly took it as a semantic shift. Southon and Todd (2001a) also noted that the concept of KM was reasonably familiar to most participants. In a subsequent paper, Southon and Todd (2001b) identified what understandings were required if these professionals desired to have an effective KM role. Loughridge (1999) holds the view that KM differs significantly from the theory and practice of librarianship, information management, and information resource management. Koenig (2002) noted that the areas of IT applications, corporate culture, business background, and knowledge organization were most significant for LIS professionals Butler (1998) pointed out that many KM initiatives were seemingly concentrated in the familiar territories of LIS, but had not been initiated by the library professionals. Broadbent (1997) maintained that librarians were generally driven by a desire to provide access to information sources, and they matched this desire with values that assumed information sharing as a good thing, which are critical for the practice of knowledge management

Davenport, Javenpaa and Beers (1996 and 1999) explained that knowledge work was about the acquisition, creation, packaging or application or reuse of knowledge. Butler (1998) pointed out that many KM initiatives seemingly concentrated on familiar territories of LIS but had not been initiated by the library professionals. Abram (1999) argued that only the knowledge environment can be managed and here librarians could play a vital role as a key catalyst in the knowledge continuum, a role of "transformational librarianship." Abell & Oxbrow (2001) linked knowledge management competencies to information management skills. Marouf (2004) analyzed the contribution of libraries to KM initiatives in six leading companies. She reported that the largest company was involved in taxonomy building, use of intranet for networking staff from 76 countries, creation of hundreds of portals, development of best practice database, design of new search tools, and emphasis on virtual library. Other companies reported having a greater emphasis on literacy programs, extensive search services, variety of activities for information architecture, creation and maintenance of knowledge repositories, design of research portal, and development of directories.

2   Research Focus

A number of LIS schools have added many KM components to their curricula and degree programs. They also have been trying to attract potential KM practitioners for education in pertinent KM competencies. A review of KM applications suggests that there is a desirable set of competencies that has to be targeted for KM education programs. These include: Leadership competencies for championing KM initiatives in organizations; Communication and public relations competencies; management of dynamic content; using enabling technologies for leveraging knowledge; managing intellectual assets and human capital; facilitating knowledge sharing by creating knowledge friendly environment. The question is whether LIS schools can impart the needed competencies to their graduates who can then perform effective roles in organizations. Since a number of these schools have already initiated degree programs or tracks of specialization in their graduate education programs, it is desirable to see what KM competencies are being targeted in these schools. Assuming that KM offers a major challenge as well as a tremendous opportunity for LIS programs, we find it imperative to conduct a study about the perspectives of heads of LIS programs about the KM competencies these schools can teach in their programs.

3   Procedures

Invitation for participation was sent to LIS deans and directors in North America, UK, and certain countries of the Pacific region. Since the study would interest only those heads of schools that are either currently having KM programs or they are seriously contemplating about taking such an initiative, the study was based on voluntary participation. The study was qualitative in nature and only those who had an apparent interest or commitment were expected to volunteer. Five heads expressed their desire to participate, yet they had constraints inhibiting their participation. Twelve heads, all located in universities, participated in the study. Common denominator among participants is their active interest in KM education programs within the fold of LIS programs. Participants were from the North American continent, Europe and Asia-Pacific regions. The academic heads of these units were asked to explain how the LIS programs in their universities could make a contribution in developing competencies in six KM areas. Their responses have been analyzed in the following section.

4   Analysis

The participants were asked what possible contribution the LIS programs might have in developing professionals in established areas of KM. The heads of these academic departments were provided six areas that are assumed to have critical mass content for KM application. Each of the six areas was provided an operational definition so that the responses were consistent.

4.1 Preparation for Leadership Roles

The leadership role had been defined as promoting knowledge and learning, championing KM initiatives, designing and developing knowledge infrastructure, facilitating, creation, use and sharing of knowledge, and deploying enterprise knowledge strategies. Important points made by the heads of these academic units are summarized in Table 1.

4.1.1 Discussion

There exists diversity of views about the preparation of LIS professionals. Since most of these programs lack commonality, no uniform approach can be projected. It would be appropriate to have a combination that might correspond to the needs of a specific situation. A number of participants were prompt to point out that LIS schools have been attempting all along to prepare their professionals for retrieving, capturing, and exploiting information. The clients take that information and create, use and share knowledge.

Table 1: Leadership

Participant	Significant Points
Participant 1	LIS programs have always been about designing and developing an infrastructure to organize, retrieve, and provide information. We have just called it organizing, retrieving and providing information. Our clients take that information and create, use, and share knowledge.
Participant 2	LIS students are trained to align the information organization with, and be supportive of, the strategic directions of the parent organization or of key client groups through partnerships with stakeholders and suppliers. They are also taught to identify, capture, organize, filter, analyze, and interpret information – one step from using skills to make information actionable. Through their expertise in technology and their sensitivity to information sharing, LIS students are well positioned to creatively develop KM initiatives in a number of areas.
Participant 3	One of the areas where LIS can certainly contribute is in the designing and developing knowledge infrastructure. Another is the use and sharing of knowledge. Yet another is the impact of these areas on developing enterprise knowledge strategies. It is essential that LIS education for KM includes considerations of organizational theory and behavior. This doesn't mean that LISD academics need to develop yet another body of knowledge but they work with other academics who have expertise and research profile in organizational theory and behavior. Under the rubric of leadership, information/knowledge policy development has to be included in the enterprise which is core to LIS theory and practice.
Participant 4	Vast literature on leadership argues that leadership can be learned, inherited, or both. Library schools develop competencies and educate. A lot of the needed leadership component can be taught, competence can be encouraged through learning patters like group work, presentations and tutorial work, but the professional also needs the personal confidence to go forward and play these roles. This comes through professional learning and understanding of what the role is ad how it might be achieved given the background learning achieved though professional education.
Participant 5	Organizational knowledge
Participant 6	We do a great deal with some of these relate to certain, use and sharing, especially, and some on certain contexts with enterprise strategies. However, this probably is not done in the context of KM per se.
Participant 7	The question assumes much about the competence of the institution and its curricula. There could be possibilities in the areas of infrastructure and facilitation.
Participant 8	Developing courses to explain KM to students.
Participant 9	It should be an integral part of the KM course. Many LIS programs have developed KM courses, specializations, and degrees.
Participant 10	LIS programs can offer courses in management and leadership. Once course in information leadership in the school is one example.
Participant 11	LIS professionals are qualified to take leadership in the area of KM – they are the natural people to do so. Without a background or some knowledge about it, though, many librarians will not see themselves in this role.
Participant 12	The question presupposes a commonality, or potential commonality, amongst LIS programs – not to mention what constitutes KM. When we offer 4 0r 5 programs leading to different award titles such as library and information studies, information analysis, electronic information management, knowledge management, and information management. These share many common courses. The extent to which they would contribute towards these learning outcomes would depend on the mix of courses within a particular program.

This way, according to them, they have been spearheading infrastructure development. However, this all is not done in the context of KM per se. It is more oriented to IM applications where the focus is on readily available and exploitable body of information. It is a real question whether they have a clear comprehension of the issues and challenges that are inherent in producing KM leaders for different organizations.

4.2 Preparation for Communication and Public Relations

The next most vital competency for effective contribution to KM roles was related to communication and public relations. It entailed managing relations with external information providers, customers, and influential people within organization. LIS professionals have all along been in the service business, which largely depends on effectiveness of communication and public relations. Yet, KM roles require interaction with untraditional partners and also deals with the capacity of interacting with stakeholders and those having a strategic edge. Significant points of the responses of the 12 participants are displayed in Table 2.

Table 2: Communication and Public Relations

Participant	Significant Points
Participant 1	LIS schools have been teaching it for the last 50 years, if not for a longer period, as an integral part of management.
Participant 2	LIS programs stress the importance of marketing and branding themselves and their services. They understand the importance of client-relations and are trained to develop customized services to their clients. Students are immersed in the politics of organizational behavior in the management course.
Participant 3	Areas pertinent to LIS here are advocacy + design and evaluation of information campaigns + information design. Ideally LIS academics should collaborate with their colleagues who are experts in communication and public relations/advertising/public communication.
Participant 4	Combination of educating the professional, developing competence through certain techniques, and then personal initiative of the individual.
Participant 5	Reference services are relevant to public relations.
Participant 6	Communication and public relations have always been a strong part of the LIS traditions, all part of the traditional LIS curriculum. However, it is done in the public service context rather the private sector.
Participant 7	Traditionally these have been among the weak points of LIS profession. It also comes down to personalities and abilities of the individual on the ground.
Participant 8	Public relations and marketing
Participant 9	It is an integral part of any KM course. Also part of any 'type of library' course, and in particular on the management of special libraries
Participant 10	A course on 'marketing of information services' is offered carefully.
Participant 11	LIS professionals are always not equipped with PR skills. However, they are team players and usually know how to collaborate, so they could elicit help of PR and communication people within the organization.
Participant 12	Comments in Table 2 also apply here.

4.2.2 Discussion

Evidently, communication and PR components are there in LIS curriculum and there has always been an emphasis on effective customer relations. Concurrently, we also note that these professionals are not generally perceived to be as effective in these areas. While it is understandable that these competencies might be cultivated among LIS professionals in their traditional domains of practice and interaction, yet their existence in the KM context might pose new challenges. It is incumbent upon those responsible for their education and training to prove beyond doubt that traditional customer skills would be appropriately enhanced so as to suit the KM context that might be distinctly challenging.

4.3 *Management of Dynamic Content*

The next area on this list of needed KM competencies for LIS professionals was related to management of dynamic content. Such content was found to be in the form of knowledge repositories, best practices, etc. It involved organization of enterprise knowledge using infrastructure services such as Intranets, portals, and Web sites. LIS professionals have long been developing and applying database skills. These competencies have mostly been applied while dealing with knowledge that is coded, defined, public, and explicit. It is worth examining how the LIS education is attempting to cater for the dynamic content of enterprises. Responses are shown in Table 3.

Table 3: Management of Dynamic Content

Participant	Significant Points
Participant 1	Librarians were among the very first groups to adopt new technologies as they were developed whether for administration of functions such as circulation and OPACs, or retrieval of information, Intranets, portals, ad websites are all a part of the duties of the information professional.
Participant 2	LIS students are required to master the management of an array of information technologies. Their role as effective content managers is now stressed highly in LIS programs.
Participant 3	These areas are all spot on for LIS academics provided that they understand the difference between IM and KM as well their limits of expertise in IT.
Participant 4	Absolutely Yes
Participant 5	Content management
Participant 6	We do much of this, but in a different context. The question is how does enterprise knowledge differs from any other type of knowledge? Machlup's categories of knowledge are all represented in what we do, but the purpose of knowledge is not a part of the approach. Is instrumental knowledge different in the context of purpose?
Participant 7	These are all the areas where LIS professionals can make a serious contribution.
Participant 8	Best practices would be most useful.
Participant 9	Core knowledge for any information professional with an interest in special libraries, IT, or digital libraries.
Participant 10	We have several courses in Web development and some attention is given to these issues in these courses.
Participant 11	All LIS programs should now be teaching Web design and development skills as well database design and development. These content organization skills are essential for the KM professional.
Participant 12	Response in Table 1 also applies here.

4.3.1 Discussion

Responses indicate that here is a noted emphasis on Web design, portals, Intranets, database, and digital library technologies. But, as one dean remarked, there is always a problem of differentiating between IM and KM technologies. Dynamic content management would involve a different set of strategies that are to be employed on the top of the traditional use of these skills. When we talk about knowledge repositories and best practice accounts for an enterprise, we are referring to the use of many social engineering approaches, implying the use of technology with some ingenuity, creativity, and wisdom. It is yet to be seen if these sets of competencies are being imparted in LIS coursework and cultures, which simply fall much beyond the traditional realm of IM applications.

4.4 Enabling Technologies

The fourth set of competencies was related to exploitation of enabling technologies for leveraging knowledge. These would require use of text mining, summarization, push and pull technologies, taxonomies, ontologies, semantic Webs, Web directories, knowledge maps, etc. These skills, antecedent technologies, and software utilities have been employed for quite some time. However, in KM context it is their use for leveraging enterprise knowledge. Responses of the participants are presented in Table 4.

Table 4: Enabling Technologies

Participant	Significant Points
Participant 1	Our students can find courses that will prepare them for positions that require the use of these technologies.
Participant 2	All the applications and tools are covered. More needs to be done with text mining and summarization.
Participant 3	Spot on for LIS academics provided that they understand the difference between IM and KM.
Participant 4	Absolutely yes.
Participant 5	Cataloging and classification will be helpful in these areas.
Participant 6	We do it in the context that is different from KM.
Participant 7	These too are areas of considerable possibility for the LIS profession.
Participant 8	Competitive data mining
Participant 9	These should be part of a KM specialization course, somewhat more advanced. Might appear in organization of information course.
Participant 10	Our information organization and representation courses deal with ontologies and directories to a certain extent.
Participant 11	Codification is a major issue in any active KM program. LIS graduates should be able to make substantial contributions in this area in developing taxonomies and ontologies.
Participant 12	Comment in Table 1 also applies here.

4.4.1 Discussion

This is the segment in which LIS can genuinely put in the claim that it can offer a great deal. Librarians have been in the business of organizing recorded knowledge and have developed standards, tools, and schemes that have been universally adopted. Three participants made it clear that employment of these techniques and technologies was still without true appreciation of the demands KM placed on their use. This response is again consistent with the findings of other questions. LIS need to capitalize on these competencies where enterprises would be obliged to turn to analytical and organizational skills of LIS graduates. However, they need to make the KM context and demands amply clear so that these could be befittingly applied in knowledge analysis, codification, and representation.

4.5 *Managing Intellectual Assets*

The next element on this list of competencies for LIS students was related to managing intellectual assets and human capital for e-commerce and e-business applications. Table 5 lists responses of 12 participants.

Table 5: Managing Intellectual Assets

Participant	Significant Points
Participant 1	We are less interested in the management of human capital for e-commerce and e-business, but our graduates are certainly able to support those persons who must manage intellectual assets and human capital for e-commerce.
Participant 2	Many LIS students benefit from cognate courses in business school, if they wish to go in profit sector. Anyone interested in KM as a career path would be required to take courses in e-commerce outside LIS schools.
Participant 3	These areas are germane to LIS but at times additional expertise in law and HR might be necessary.
Participant 4	Absolutely yes
Participant 5	Not covered in LIS
Participant 6	Management of intellectual assets and human capital are important for any organizational effort, but we do little with the e-commerce and e-business applications.
Participant 7	No obvious role for LIS here.
Participant 8	E-applications of all types
Participant 9	It should be part of a more focused program; perhaps oriented toward special libraries or, if offered, an e-commerce course.
Participant 10	We have a course on resource management at the undergraduate level, but not currently at the graduate level.
Participant 11	LIS should facilitate these knowledge activities.
Participant 12	Comment in Table1 applies.

4.5.1 Discussion

It is quite clear from these responses that LIS programs have not considered offering e-commerce or e-business courses. Since these competencies can be developed in other programs as a more appropriate venue; there was no reason that LIS should become active in this area. LIS programs have been active in educating their graduates in corporate information systems and services, business information, competitive intelligence, and special librarianship; these competencies could also be relevant if the graduates of these schools wish to find any career opportunities in this area. When we look at these courses, these look more like a bona fide and genuine packaging for information and knowledge professionals in this area.

4.6 Facilitating Knowledge Sharing

The last competency listed on the instrument was about facilitating knowledge sharing. Strategies spelled out for this purpose were related to creating knowledge friendly environment, deploying appropriate knowledge strategies, and encouraging communities of practice. These are established KM strategies for managing capital assets of an organization. It was considered worth exploration whether LIS professionals were also being made conversant with the application of these strategies. Responses of twelve participants are shown in Table 6.

Table 6: Facilitating Knowledge Sharing

Participant	Significant Points
Participant 1	A definite part of most courses is offered. They learn it throughout the program. Every LIS program must be teaching appropriate knowledge strategies. A strong program of LIS program is developing communities of practice.
Participant 2	All these activities stressed in LIS programs. These need to be taught in a specific KM context, as is done for special library courses.
Participant 3	These areas are also germane to LIS theory and practice as long as there is a strong focus on knowledge as well as information.
Participant 4	Absolutely yes
Participant 5	Limited to user assistance
Participant 6	As these are pretty central to the mission of libraries and the information agencies we serve.
Participant 7	LIS people are good at creating the right environment in their own domain. As for their influence on strategy, including the formation of COPs, this would be a much wider institutional and strategic issue. It also depends on leadership within LIS.
Participant 8	Knowledge friendly/customer oriented/customer friendly would be most useful.
Participant 9	Likely to be in the KM course but not often explicitly covered in traditional LIS course.
Participant 10	We offer a course on communities of practice. The focus of the course is more on knowledge communities and not to facilitate such a community.
Participant 11	The current wave of KM theory and applications value conversation, storytelling and communities of practice, which is the human element of knowledge sharing and information sharing on which knowledge can be created. LIS should facilitate these knowledge activities.
Participant 12	Comment in Table 1 applies.

4.6.1 Discussion

Many of the participants appeared to be defending their stance by asserting that library schools had been cultivating these values and skills all along. One respondent rightly pointed out that LIS people are good in creating environment in their own domain. It was not perceived to be a strategic and institutional issue. When KM literature makes a mention of these initiatives and skills, it has little to do with the traditional services that the profession of LIS has been dealing with. Activities like storytelling have been there in libraries, but the way these are being exploited in creating communities of commerce, traditional library approaches and practices would have little to do with this sort of story telling and communities of practice.

5   Conclusion

The views of heads of LIS programs reflect that the competencies required for KM are already targeted in their programs. A closer analysis of responses, however, suggests that these responses have not taken into account the need for in-depth coverage and the nature of support needed. LIS graduates seem to be closer to KM in terms of possession of relevant competencies as compared with their other counterparts, but LIS sector had traditionally focused on external information sources, emphasized on access to information, and user assistance. The need in the new environment is to make full use of internal knowledge resources, get involved in the knowledge creation process, and have a better focus on effective utilization of knowledge rather than just access. Difference in information and knowledge suggests emphasis on context that comes from the organizational perspectives and use of tacit knowledge in addition to explicit information. These would require a fresh initiative for cultivating appropriate education strategies. It is important that LIS programs look at the need for developing competencies for knowledge management from a more open mind, using out of the box approach. While their current curriculum might include some relevant topics, these topics need to be covered from a different perspective. For example, collection development needs to be expanded to include content management; cataloguing and classification need to be expanded to focus more on taxonomies, ontology, and metadata; and reference and information services need to be covered more from knowledge sharing perspectives. Likewise, the leadership qualities and team building skills needed for promoting and championing knowledge management may not be properly supported by the existing management courses in LIS programs.

References

Abell, Angella; Oxbrow, Nigel (2001) Competing with knowledge: The information Professional in the Knowledge management age. London, England: Library Association Publishing.

Abram, Stephen (1999) "Post information age positioning for special librarians: Is knowledge Management the answer?" In: Matarazzo, James; Connolly, Suzanne; eds. Knowledge and special libraries. Boston, MA: Butterworth-Heinemann, p.185-193.

Broadbent, Marianne (1997) "The emerging phenomenon of knowledge management." The Australian Library journal, 46(1), 6-23.

Broadbent, M. (1998). "The phenomenon of knowledge management: what does it mean to the information profession?" Information Outlook, 2(5), 23-26+.

Butler, Yvonne (1998) "Six months in a leaky boat: issues for Australian and NZ law librarians." The law Librarian, 29(4), 229-233.

Butler, Yvonne (2000) "Knowledge Management – If Only You Knew What You Knew." Australian Library Journal, 49(1), 31-43.

Davenport, E.; Cano, V. (1996). Private sector information work, World-Wide (1996/1997). an annual survey. London: Bowker Saur, 159-258.

Davenport, E., Cronin, B. (2000) "Knowledge management: semantic drift or conceptual shift?" Journal of Education for Library and Information Science, 41(4), 294-306.

Davenport, Thomas; De Long, David; Beers, Michael (1999) "Successful Knowledge management projects." In: Cortada, James; Woods, John. The knowledge Management year book 1999-2000. Boston, MA : Butterworth-Heinemann, 89-107.

Koenig, M. (1996) "Intellectual capital and knowledge management." IFLA Journal, 22(4), 299-301.

Koenig, M. (1999). "Education for knowledge management." Information Services and Use, 19, 17-31.

Koenig, M. and Srikantaiah, T. K. (2002) "The business world discovers the assets of librarianship." Information Outlook, 6(4), 14-15.

Loughridge, Brendon (1999) "Knowledge management, librarians and information managers: fad or future." New Library World, 100(6), 245-253.

Marouf, L. (2004) "Role and contribution of corporate information centers toward KM initiatives: an analysis of managers' perceptions." Journal of Information and Knowledge Management, 3(1), 1-17.

Oxbrow, N. and Abell, A. (2002) "Is there life after knowledge management?" Information Outlook, 6(4) 20-2, 25-6, 29.

Southon.G. and Todd, R. (2001a) "Library and information professionals and knowledge management: conceptions, challenges and conflict." The Australian Library Journal, 50(3), 259-281.

Southon. G. and Todd, R. (2001b) "Educating for a knowledge management future: perceptions of library and information professionals." The Australian Library Journal, 50(4), 313-326.

TEPL LIMITED (1999) Skills for knowledge management: Building a knowledge economy. London, England: TEPL Ltd.

Wang, Yunhua (1999) "Knowledge economy and the development of the library." Library Work & Research, 6, 17-19.

Wilson, D. (2002) "The nonsense of 'knowledge management." Information Research , 8(1).

STRATEGIC APPROACHES TO KM:
AN EMPIRICAL STUDY CONDUCTED IN THE US
GOVERNMENT AND NONPROFIT SECTORS

VINCENT RIBIÈRE

School of Management, New York Institute of Technology
New York, NY, USA
vince@vincentribiere.com

JUAN A. ROMÁN

National Aeronautics and Space Administration
Goddard Space Flight Center
Greenbelt, MD, USA
Juan.Roman@nasa.gov

(Authors listed in alphabetical order since contributions to this work were equal)

The adoption of Knowledge Management (KM) programs and systems in the US government and nonprofit sectors is rapidly growing. The purpose of this study was to assess how knowledge workers obtain, share, and/or use the knowledge that they need to perform their work (knowledge flow). We found a certain agreement on a typology defining two main strategies for knowledge flows: codification versus personalization. A total of 341 knowledge workers from the U.S. government and nonprofit sectors were surveyed in order to assess what KM strategy they employed (at the organizational level as well as their work unit level) for managing knowledge. KM practices, tools and technologies used were assessed and ranked. This paper presents the results of this empirical study.

1   Introduction

1.1 KM in the Government and Nonprofit Sectors

The adoption of KM programs and systems in the US government and nonprofit sectors is rapidly growing. Moreover, in the current environment there is a critical need for the Federal government to effectively integrate Knowledge Management Systems (KMS) efforts with the aim of transcending boundaries and to disseminate essential knowledge throughout many departments, agencies, local governments, and many other entities including nonprofit institutions. As in the private sector, KM is transforming the way government operates its business transactions, the relationship among government organization and citizens, and the value placed on human capital. The US Navy, the General Service Administration (GSA), the Government Accounting Office (GAO), the Federal Aviation Administration (FAA), and many other organizations have recognized the need for formal KM in their organization and are also reaping the benefits of their efforts (Eisenhart 2001). Furthermore, many nonprofit institutions such as the American Association of Retired People (AARP) and several colleges and universities (such as Jackson State University, Mississippi, and Cuyahoga Community College, Ohio) are applying KM to the business of running the university (Graham 2001; Eugene 2001). Although the key reasons for undertaking KM initiatives may differ, the practice of KM in the public, nonprofit, and private sectors are very similar when observed at the highest level. The need to leverage on existing and future knowledge is clear. However, the knowledge that civil servants hold is, for the most part, meant to be shared with colleagues and ultimately with the public. This knowledge becomes truly useful only when it is dispersed to citizens and agencies at the federal, state, and local levels, as well as government partners in the private sector (Chiem 2001).

1.2 Research Objectives

In this paper we report research results that are considered essential for both KM practitioners and researchers alike. Two main research questions drove this study:

- What KM strategy (codification vs. personalization) is primarily deployed in the US government and in nonprofit organizations at the work unit and organizational levels?
- What are the KM practices, technologies, and tools that are most frequently used in the US government and in nonprofit organizations at the work unit and organizational levels?

The following sections present in more detail the different factors and variables that compose these research questions.

1.3 Codification and Personalization Strategies

The generation, acquisition, and sharing of knowledge are primary mechanisms in a knowledge-base enterprise. However, when considering the flow of knowledge throughout an enterprise, there are two main strategies or approaches that emerge in the literature. Various authors identify them differently; however, their purpose and essence are the same. For this research, we employed the knowledge flow taxonomy developed by Hansen *et al.* (Hansen, Nohria, and Tierney 1999). The "Codification" approach is generally defined as the formalization of tacit knowledge that is typically difficult to express or explain by developing processes that acquire it or by developing mechanisms that allow this knowledge to become explicit and then become documented. The Codification strategy is based on a people-to-document approach and uses information systems to carefully codify knowledge and store it in a location that can be accessed and reused by everyone in the enterprise. On the other hand, the "Personalization" approach is the sharing of tacit knowledge by direct contact from person-to-person therefore allowing the flow of knowledge that probably could not be codified. It is focused on dialog among individuals, teams, and groups of employees in formal and informal settings. The Personalization approach can help them achieve deeper insight by engaging in an open dialog. The knowledge is kept close to whoever developed it. Information systems are used to help communicate that knowledge but not to store it. However, the emphasis of one approach over the other, or a balanced approach, depends on the overall strategy of the enterprise and can be influenced by the way the enterprise serves its clients or stakeholders, the economics of its business, and the human capital it possesses.

A model was used to determine the dominant strategic approach (Codification or Personalization) that people predominantly use to facilitate the flow of knowledge throughout the enterprise. It is foundationally based on a tool developed by Ribière in his doctoral dissertation (Ribière 2001). The determination is established on the assessment of the practices, technologies and tools that are predominantly used by employees for the acquisition and dissemination of knowledge throughout the enterprise. However, it was modified for this research based on an extensive literature review (Hoyt 2001; Kemp *et al.* 2001; Shand 1998; Marwick 2001; McKellar and Haimila 2002), and validated using confirmatory factor analysis using path analysis with latent variables (Román-Velázquez 2004).

2   Research

2.1 *Methodology*

A carefully crafted research questionnaire was distributed as hard copy and also made accessible through an interactive web-based environment, using Survey Solutions XP™ software that was located at the George Washington University (GWU) Interactive Multimedia Applications Group server. The introduction and information sheets of the questionnaire explained the intent of the overall survey and the reason and benefits of the study, assured the anonymity of the responders, and gave general instructions. In order to reach the largest number of potential respondents from the government and nonprofit sectors, the questionnaire was distributed through multiple channels. A total of 1,800 e-mail messages and 200 hard copy questionnaires in pre-addressed and stamped envelopes were distributed. Participation in the survey was on a voluntary basis. A total of 346 subjects participated in the research during the data collection period. Only 5 subjects were considered unacceptable for use and were excluded from the analysis. As a result, a sample size of 341 was used as the body of data collected and analyzed. Table 1 and Figure 1 show the questionnaire responses by category and the functional roles and responsibilities of the respondents.

Once the data was collected, it was analyzed using SPSS 10.0 and the SAS System version 8e statistical analysis software packages. The research study employed inferential statistical analysis, using the data collected to make estimates about the much larger government and nonprofit population. The confidence levels and confidence intervals are two key components of the sampling error estimates. Therefore, the accuracy of the sample statistics is expressed in both of these terms. The mathematics of probability proves that for large populations, in this case the government and nonprofit sector, the size is irrelevant unless the sample collected exceeds a few percent of the total population under research (Babbie 1998; Sekaran 1992). For this research, using $N = 341$ as the responses collected and a 95% confidence level, the confidence interval was calculated to be ± 5.31. This implies that for any given statistic in the research, we are 95% confident that it falls within ± 5.3 of the parameter stated.

Table 1. Questionnaire Responses by Category

Category	Respondents	Percent
Federal Departments	104	30.5%
Federal Agencies	137	40.2%
FFRDC	9	2.6%
Federal Administrations	20	5.9%
Federal Commissions	2	0.6%
State Government	6	1.8%
Local Government	0	0%
Universities/Colleges	23	6.7%
Nonprofit Institutions	26	7.6%
Others	14	4.1%
Total	341	100.0%

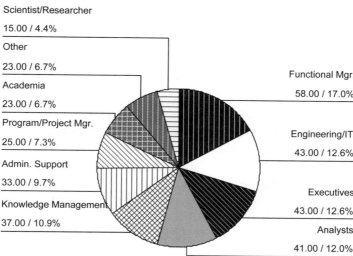

Scientist/Researcher
15.00 / 4.4%

Other
23.00 / 6.7%

Academia
23.00 / 6.7%

Program/Project Mgr.
25.00 / 7.3%

Admin. Support
33.00 / 9.7%

Knowledge Management
37.00 / 10.9%

Functional Mgr.
58.00 / 17.0%

Engineering/IT
43.00 / 12.6%

Executives
43.00 / 12.6%

Analysts
41.00 / 12.0%

Figure 1. Respondents by Functional Roles

The data was collected using a Likert 7-point scale for the dependable variable and a nominal scale for the classification variable. Therefore, it is important to consider three perspectives that were utilized in this study in order to understand the data analysis. First, the absolute rating where 1 is "Very Minimum Extent" and 7 is "Very Great

Extent". Since the midpoint is 4.0, mean scores below 4.0 are considered to be low scores. Second, the change in the rating of an item—that is, how each item mean score differs between the organization level and the work unit level. A test of group difference is performed to calculate the probability that the difference between the two levels occurred by chance. Last is the item ranking – that is, how the rating of each item at the organization level compares with the ratings of similar items in the work unit.

Two types of tests were utilized during the study. The first type was "test of group difference," in order to know whether two sample populations differ with respect to their mean scores on the dependent variable. Examples of this test are independent sample *t* test and one-way analysis of variance (ANOVA). The second type of test was the "test of association" in which a single sample population of respondents was evaluated to find out whether there is a relationship between two or more variables within the population. An example of a test of association utilized in this study involves testing the significance of a correlation coefficient.

Two different types of hypotheses are relevant to the inferential test identified above. The null hypothesis states that there are no differences between the group means or no relationships between the measure variables. The other hypothesis, called a research or alternative hypothesis, is a statement expressing differences or relationships among group means. We considered the research hypothesis to be acceptable only if the null hypothesis is unacceptable (rejected) because of its associated low probability. A significant level of less than 5% ($p < .05$) was used to test the null hypothesis for rejection.

3 Findings

The research findings revealed that KM is being widely accepted and implemented throughout the government and nonprofit sectors. The vast majority (78%) of the enterprises that implemented KMS efforts had them supporting both organization and work unit levels. Of the 341 responses collected, only 18% reported no KMS efforts in place within the enterprise. Furthermore, respondents were asked to evaluate the extent to which KM is critical to the success of the enterprise. For the government sector, a total of 79% at the organization level and 81% at the work unit level reported scores between a Great Extent and Very Great Extent. A very similar response emerged from the nonprofit sector as well. This indicates that there is a significant awareness and understanding of the critical role that KM plays.

3.1 Technologies, Tools and Processes Used for Knowledge Flow

This section describes the technologies, support tools, and processes that respondents use to generate, organize, and share knowledge throughout the enterprise. A total of 20 items were evaluated with a sample size of N = 339 for the organization level and N = 335 for the work unit level. Their mean scores ranged from 3.09 to 5.87 for the organization and 3.04 to 6.12 for the work unit on a 7-point scale, as shown in Figure 2 and Table 2. Ten items at the organization and nine at the work unit had mean scores above 4.0. Items with means below 4.0 are considered to be low scores and therefore provide less impact to the organization and work unit. A close inspection of the results showed that a familiar process, *One-on-One Conversations*, was the most utilized mode for transferring and sharing knowledge at the organization and work unit, with mean scores of 5.87 and 6.12 respectively. This finding demonstrates that direct exchange between two employees remains the most effective means of sharing knowledge and no other technology or tool can surpass it.

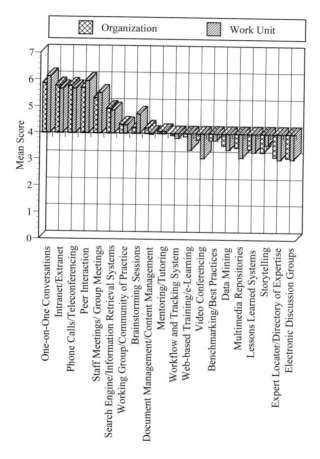

Figure 2. Technologies, Support Tools, and Processes Utilized Throughout the Enterprise

Table 2. Descriptive Statistics for the Technologies, Support Tools, and Processes Utilized Throughout the Enterprise

STRATEGIC APPROACH	TECHNOLOGIES, SUPPORT TOOLS, AND PROCESSES	ORGANIZATION			WORK UNIT		
		RANKING	MEAN	SD	RANKING	MEAN	SD
P	One-on-One Conversations	1	5.87	1.22	1	6.12	1.04
C	Intranet/Extranet	2	5.78	1.37	4	5.67	1.44
P	Phone Calls/ Teleconferencing	3	5.77	1.28	3	5.68	1.49
C	Peer Interaction	4	5.71	1.23	2	5.96	1.13
P	Staff Meetings/ Group Meetings	5	5.33	1.52	5	5.52	1.38
C	Search Engine/Information Retrieval Systems	6	4.93	1.68	6	4.87	1.84
P	Working Group/ Community of Practice	7	4.34	1.81	8	4.32	1.96
C	Brainstorming Sessions	8	4.22	1.79	7	4.73	1.76
P	Document Management/ Content Management	9	4.21	1.83	10	3.97	1.95
C	Mentoring/Tutoring	10	4.08	1.84	9	4.08	2.00
P	Workflow and Tracking System	11	3.93	1.87	11	3.82	1.99
C	Web-based Training/ e-Learning	12	3.89	1.73	15	3.37	1.86
P	Video Conferencing	13	3.76	1.85	18	3.06	1.98
C	Benchmarking/ Best Practices	14	3.75	1.75	12	3.74	1.96
P	Data Mining	15	3.54	1.90	14	3.38	1.99
C	Multimedia Repositories	16	3.47	1.90	17	3.09	1.93
P	Lessons Learned Systems	17	3.42	1.89	16	3.30	1.95
C	Storytelling	18	3.29	1.97	13	3.58	2.04
P	Expert Locator/Directory of Expertise	19	3.12	1.99	20	3.03	2.00
C	Electronic Discussion Groups	20	3.09	1.94	19	3.04	1.94

N = 339 (Organization) and N = 335 (Work Unit), P = Personalization, C = Codification

The data also revealed that *One-on-One Conversations, Peer Interaction, Staff/Group Meetings, Brainstorming Sessions,* and *Storytelling* were tools that had higher mean scores at the work unit. Therefore, these were more frequently utilized at the work unit level than at the organization level. They were mostly used to facilitate the flow of knowledge on a "one-to-one" basis or within a small group environment. However, higher scores at the organization level were found for *Intranet/Extranet, Phone calls/Teleconferencing, Search Engines/Information Retrieval System, Working Group/Communities of Practice, Document Management/Content Management, Workflow and Tracking System, Web-based Training/e-Learning, Video Conferencing, Benchmarking/Best Practices, Data Mining, Multimedia Repositories, Lessons Learned Systems,* and *Expert Locator/Directory of Expertise.* These technologies, processes, and tools allowed the broadcasting or sharing of knowledge from "one-to-many" or "many-to-many." These results demonstrate that the types of technologies, tools, and processes that CKO's, KM Architects, KM Managers, etc., should select for implementation need to be based on the knowledge distribution process that is desired, i.e. "one-to-one" or "many-to-many," for the particular enterprise level where it will be deployed.

Is is worth noting that *Mentoring/Tutoring* had the same mean score ($M = 4.08$) for the organization and work unit levels. This indicates that it has the same effectiveness throughout the enterprise. Formal and informal *Mentoring/Tutoring* are used extensively in many enterprises to enable and foster the sharing and transfer of knowledge in different hierarchical levels—from new hires in a work unit to a senior executive mentoring a new executive.

3.2 Codification and Personalization Strategic Approach

The data collected was used to calculate the respective scores for the *Codification* and *Personalization* processes of transferring and sharing knowledge. Figure 3 and 4 show the factor score distribution with their respective mean and standard deviation for the organization and work unit levels.

Each factor shows similar statistical distributions with only minor variations between the two enterprise levels. A more in-depth analysis of the data revealed that *Codification* was the dominant approach employed by 60% (N = 205) and 58% (N = 194) of the respondents at the organization and work unit levels, respectively. In contrast, *Personalization* was the dominant approach utilized by 32% (N = 107) of the respondents at the organization, with a slight increase to 35% (N = 117) at the work unit level. Only a small number of respondents, 8% (N = 27) and 7% (N = 24) at the organization and work unit levels respectively, utilized both approaches with the same emphasis, as shown in Figure 5. The responses were also divided into government and nonprofit sectors and analyzed independently. A graphical summary of both sectors is shown in Figure 6.

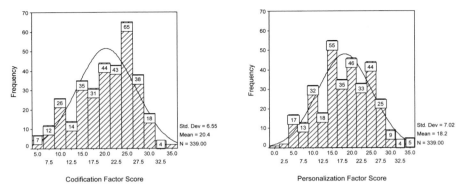

Figure 3. Codification and Personalization Factor Score Distributions at the Organization Level

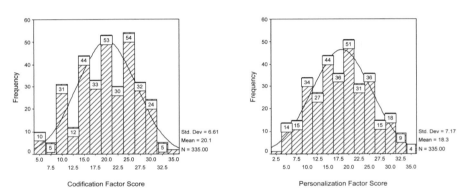

Figure 4. Codification and Personalization Score Distributions at the Work Unit Level

Figure 5. Codification and Personalization Factors as a Dominant Approach for the Knowledge Flow throughout the Enterprise

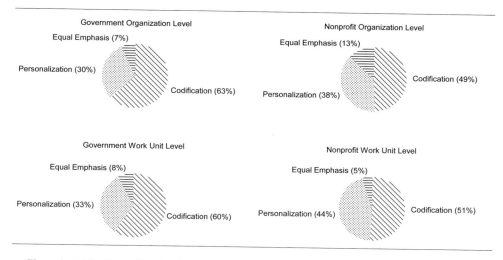

Figure 6. Codification and Personalization Factors as Dominant Approach for the Knowledge Flow in the Government and Nonprofit Sectors

This analysis shows that the nonprofit sector was considerably different from the government sector. Nonprofit institutions had a higher number of respondents employing a *Personalization* approach to transfer and share their knowledge within the enterprise. Also, at the organization level, there was almost double the number of respondents that employ an equal emphasis on *Codification* and *Personalization* compared to the government sector. Furthermore, the work unit level in the nonprofit sector had an almost balanced utilization of the two approaches.

4   Conclusion

It is important to remember that the codification and personalization KM strategies are not incompatible. Organizations must use both strategies simultaneously but might need to put more emphasis on one of these strategies than on the other. Hansen *et al.* (1999) suggested a 20/80 split between these two strategies. However, our empirical study demonstrated that in practice there is not such a clear distinction between the emphasis associated to each. Organizations interested in launching a KM initiative or organizations working on taking their KM initiative to the next level need to asses what strategy will best fit their needs and which will be the most likely to succeed based on their organizational culture (Román, Ribière, and Stankosky 2004). Focusing on the right knowledge flow strategy is one of the keys to a successful KM journey.

References

Babbie, E. 1998. *The Practice of Social Research*. 8th ed. Wadsworth Publishing Company.
Chiem, P. X. 2001. In the public interest. *Knowledge Management Magazine*, August.
Eisenhart, M. 2001. Washington's need to know. *Knowledge Management Magazine*, January.

Eugene, A. C. 2001. KM in education (Readers offer responses and suggestions). *Knowledge Management Magazine*, August.

Graham, R. 2001. Benchmarking Jackson State. *Knowledge Management Magazine*.

Hansen, M. T., N. Nohria, and T. Tierney. 1999. What's your strategy for managing knowledge? *Harvard Business Review*:106-116.

Hoyt, B. J. 2001. *KM Technology & Tools Listing*, Hoyt Consulting. http://www.kmnews.com. November 21 2001 [cited November 6 2001].

Kemp, J., M. Pudlatz, P. Perez, and A. M. Ortega. 2001. KM Technologies and Tools: European KM Forum.

Marwick, A. D. 2001. Knowledge Management Technology. *IBM Systems Journal* 40(4):814-830.

McKellar, H., and S. H., eds. 2002. *KMWorld Buyers' Guide*. Fall 2002 Edition, *Buyers' Guide*: KM World & Information Today.

Ribière, V. M. 2001. Assessing knowledge management initiative success as a function of organizational culture. PhD diss., Engineering Management and Systems Engineering, George Washington University, Washington D.C.

Román-Velázquez, J. A. 2004. An empirical study of knowledge management in the government and nonprofit sectors: Organizational culture composition and its relationship with knowledge management success and the approach for knowledge flow. D.Sc. diss., Engineering Management and Systems Engineering, George Washington University, Washington, D.C.

Román, J. A., V. Ribière, and M. A. Stankosky. 2004. Organizational culture types and their relationship with knowledge flow and knowledge management success: An empirical study in the US government and nonprofit sectors. *Journal of Information & Knowledge Management (JIKM)* 3(2).

Sekaran, U. 1992. *Research Methods for Business,* 2nd ed. John Wiley & Sons, Inc.

Shand, D. 1998. Harnessing knowledge management technologies in R&D. *Knowledge Management Review* 3:20-26.

PART VI

Knowledge Creation

PATENT INTELLIGENCE AND ITS IMPLICATIONS FOR PATENT PRODUCTIVITY *

NILANJANA BHADURI NEE CHAKRABORTY & MARY MATHEW

*Department of Management Studies, Indian Institute of Science,
Bangalore, Karnataka 560012, India*

The prevailing hypercompetitive environment has made it essential for organizations to gather competitive intelligence from environmental scanning. The knowledge gained leads to organizational learning, which stimulates increased patent productivity. This paper highlights five practices that aid in developing patenting intelligence and empirically verifies to what extent this organizational learning leads to knowledge gains and financial gains realized from consequent higher patent productivity. The model is validated based on the perceptions of professionals with patenting experience from two of the most aggressively patenting sectors in today's economy, viz., IT and pharmaceutical sectors (n=119). The key finding of our study suggests that although organizational learning from environmental scanning exists, the application of this knowledge for increasing patent productivity lacks due appreciation. This missing link in strategic analysis and strategy implementation has serious implications for managers which are briefly discussed in this paper.

1   Introduction

Modern organizations exist in a hypercompetitive environment amidst uncertainties stemming in the form of shortened product life cycles, shifting markets, technology proliferation, multiplying competitors and other similar pressures. To maintain technological leadership patenting behavior is seen as critical in this competitive environment. Maintaining a steady generation of commercially viable patents necessitates the existence of a continuous patent related organizational learning mechanism in the system. The organizational learning processes have underlined the importance of 'knowledge', accumulated over a time-line.

The old industrial era has been supplanted by a new knowledge-based economy where ideas and innovation have become the principal wellsprings of economic growth and competitive business advantage (Rivette & Kline, 2000). In an age where ideas that have a proof of concept command enormous value, it is hardly surprising to note that rights to ownership of these ideas - patents, have become priorities in the organizational agenda for performance enhancement. Apart from protecting the core technologies and business methods, patents execute multiple strategic roles in an organization. They include boosting R&D and branding effectiveness, anticipating market and technology shifts, tapping new revenues from licensing and cross-licensing deals, attracting venture capital and new investments by enhancing corporate value as well as exploiting new technology and market opportunities through alliances based on their bargaining power (Pakes, 1985; Narin *et al.*, 1987; Ashton & Sen, 1988; Mogee, 1991; Sullivan & Daniele,

---

* This work is supported by Indian Institute of Science, Bangalore.

1996; Rivette & Kline, 2000). Thus through proper configuration and deployment of patents, organizations can successfully establish proprietary market advantage, improve financial performance and enhance their competitiveness. This insight necessitates the development of a quality patent portfolio as a foundation for realizing better organizational performance. Hence organizations have been concentrating on increasing their patent productivity. Patent productivity refers to the generation of more and more patents. Commercial externalization of the value of the patents incubated within the organization is the further goal. Enhancing this patent productivity with a commercial edge depends upon a host of practices that facilitate organizational learning. Organizational learning requires intelligence gained from both internal and external organizational environmental scanning.

Lorange and his coworkers have explained the indispensability of external environmental scanning in determining organizational performance on grounds that hypercompetition has eroded the buffer between organizations and environment (Lorange *et al.*, 1986). The open systems model clearly states that the organization is affected by and in turn affects its external environment (Cummings and Worley, 1997). Organizations must therefore constantly monitor their environmental "signals" (Liu, 1998) and innovate accordingly. The key to success of innovation lies in the organization's ability to think in terms of the future (Tushman and Nadler, 1986). Consequently, prior knowledge about the "signals" in the external environment would equip organizations with competitive intelligence learning. This in turn will increase patent productivity.

This paper concentrates on how the organizational learning acquired through environmental scanning practices lead to higher patent productivity. We empirically test the validity of this model in the context of two aggressively patenting Indian industrial sectors.

2   Literature Review

Previous studies have illustrated the role of organizational learning towards improved organizational performance and competitive advantage (Stata, 1989; Edmondson and Moingeon, 1996; Grant, 1996). The importance of environmental scanning has also been considerably researched upon in the context of innovation studies (Briggs, 1992; Fiol, 1996; Ozsomer *et al.*, 1997; Keogh, 1999). Environmental scanning has been defined as the acquisition and use of information about events, trends and relationships in a firm's external environment, the knowledge of which would assist management in planning future courses of actions (Aguilar, 1967; Choo and Auster, 1993; Choo, 1998).

The management literature on patents emphasizes upon the strategic role of patents as technology and corporate indicators (Narin *et al.*, 1987; Ashton & Sen, 1988; Mogee, 1991, Berkowitz, 1993, Cantrell, 1997). These studies state that through patent analysis a repository of information can be gleaned with respect to technology status, infringement threats, organizational business intentions, potential markets, corporate R&D spending, future financial performance and like aspects of business, market, technology and legal intelligence. There is also adequate literature establishing that patent filings by organizations lead to better organizational performance (Scherer, 1965; Comanor and Scherer, 1969; Griliches *et al.*, 1991; Ernst, 2001).

In our study we attempt to addresses the application of intelligence extracted from patents for increasing patent productivity in organizations. To the best of our knowledge no previous study has been undertaken in this regard.

3   Methodology

The aim of the study reported here is to understand environmental scanning practices in the context of patent productivity.

3.1 Conceptual Model

Practices that enhance organizational learning to ensure a commercial edge of patents include extraction of market intelligence (SI), prior art analysis (PA), technology assessment (TA), rival analysis (RA) and competitive monitoring (CM).

Extraction of market intelligence can help in identification of potential markets along with the strategic players and their market intentions. Leveraging upon this knowledge, organizations can choose those markets which ideally suit their technology and thus develop the ideal international patent families.

Prior art analysis includes literature searching as well as patent searching. The knowledge gained in this process helps in improving the technological soundness of the inventors and often provides ideas for development of patentable technologies, which leads to increase in patent productivity.

Technology assessment is conducted with respect to both patented and non-patented technologies so that inventors are able to identify patentable ideas. Moreover organizations gain awareness of stage of technology life cycle and can forecast directions of technology development. This knowledge is especially useful in designing patent portfolio for dominating the future market.

Rival analysis relates to closely studying the business strategies of the competitors. Their patents are especially useful in this regard. Blocking the technology development of their competitors through appropriate patents is definitely one of the best ways organizations can outperform their rivals. Moreover, patents need to be designed cautiously in order to avoid infringement threats. This process also provides vital information about the key inventors responsible for patenting in competitor organizations. The recruitment cell is responsible for using this information to attract them over and use their creativity to increase patent productivity.

Competitive monitoring refers to a systematic survey of patents along with other indicators of technological progress and business intentions of organizations in the interested technological spheres. The business, technological and legal intelligence gained aids the designing of patents in diversified areas of interest, thereby leading to higher patent productivity.

We refer to these practices collectively as competitive intelligence (CI) practices as they are essentially concerned with intelligence gathering that makes the organization more competitive. The role of these CI practices in enhancing patent productivity is described in Figure 1.

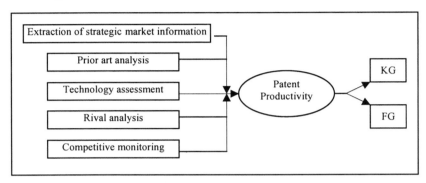

Figure 1. Conceptual Model.

Figure 1 describes the conceptual model of our study. These CI practices lead to organizational learning, which stimulates patenting productivity. An increase in the patenting productivity is discernable through the increase in knowledge gain (KG) and financial gain (FG) realized by the organization. Patenting is an expensive activity and it is logical to file patents provided they reap adequate financial returns. Therefore, FG emerges as an immediate gain realized through higher patent productivity. However, some patents, especially the ones designed for a future market, do not accrue immediate financial gains. These patents are primarily acquired with an objective of using them as bargaining tools to gain entry into new markets. Under such circumstances patents may not lead to immediate financial gains. Therefore, we include KG as delayed revenue gains realized through higher patent productivity. Thus KG and FG reflect increases in patenting productivity.

3.2 Variables and Items

A questionnaire was designed by us to measure the conceptual model. There are five independent variables in our study: SI, PA, TA, RA and CM. These CI variables aim at measuring the output variables of KG and FG which are surrogate measures of the dependent variable, viz., patent productivity.

In order to actually realize the impact of the CI variables on the dependent variables KG and FG a longitudinal research is advisable. This is substantiated by the empirically proven fact that there is a time lag of 2-3 years between patent applications and subsequent changes in organizational performance (Ernst, 2001). However, considering practical research constraints, we opt for a one-time only survey design (Emory, 1976).

Accordingly, the questionnaire is designed for being filled with the perspective of an ideal situation where the CI practices are ideally implemented so that the patenting productivity is optimally realized.

Table 1 lists the 15 items for measuring the CI variables. Each item measures to what extent the ideal implementation of the practice would contribute towards KG and FG. The items are measured on Likert type 5-point scale, the anchors being: 1-very low contribution, 2- low contribution, 3-moderate contribution, 4-high contribution and 5-very high contribution. The reliability analysis of the items reported a Cronbach alpha of 0.97.

Table 1. List of independent (CI) variables and their corresponding items.

CI variables	Item No.	Item
Variable 1: Extraction of strategic market information (SI)	1	Extraction of strategic market information from worldwide patent filings.
	2	Studying the trend of patent filings in the market prior to patent filing.
	3	Monitoring the entry and exit pattern of firms into markets on basis of their patenting activities.
Variable 2: Prior art analysis (PA)	4	Provision of desktop search facilities (access to Delphion, Derwent and like databases) w.r.t. prior patents granted.
	5	Periodic review of organization's own patent portfolio.
	6	Studying previous patent applications filed by the organization.
	7	Conducting patent citation analysis for tracing radical innovations.
Variable 3: Technology assessment (TA)	8	Periodic review of worldwide patents for understanding technology domains.
	9	Periodic review of organization's own technology database.
	10	Assessing the technology status on basis of frequency of patent filings in that field.
Variable 4: Rival analysis (RA)	11	Periodic review of patents of competitors.
	12	Assessing competitor inventors on basis of their patent filings.
	13	Conducting thorough patent analysis of competitors' patents before practicing own innovation.
Variable 5: Competitive monitoring (CM)	14	Having a watchdog mechanism within organization constantly looking out for other technologies that are infringing upon your patents.
	15	Active patenting of incremental innovation to seal off more fundamental patents of competitors.

For measuring the dependent variables KG and FG, we use 4 and 7 items, respectively (Table 2). Each of these items measure the benefits realized in an ideal situation where patent intelligence is proactive in raising patent productivity. A 5-point Likert scale is employed for measuring the benefits. The anchors are: 1-very low, 2-low, 3-moderate, 4-high and 5-very high. The Cronbach alpha of the items measuring KG is 0.70, while the value for the items under FG is 0.83.

Table 2. List of dependent variables and their corresponding items.

Dependent variable	Item No.	Item
Var.1: Knowledge gained by organization (KG)	1	New ideas gained
	2	New products planned
	3	New business opportunities identified
	4	New knowledge gained by organization
Var.2: Financial gains of organization (FG)	1	Licensing income earned
	2	Total profit realized
	3	Venture capital inflow
	4	Stabilization of relationship with suppliers
	5	Customer loyalty increase
	6	Increase in total sales
	7	Brand image upliftment

3.3 Sample

Our sample comprises of randomly selected professionals with patenting experience from the IT and pharmaceutical sectors. We select these two sectors as they represent the most progressive sectors where patenting is being actively pursued worldwide. While IT symbolizes one of the new and most innovative sectors that favor prolific patenting, the pharmaceutical industry represents a veteran innovative sector that has been actively involved in patenting for a considerable period. Owing to the innovative thrust prevailing in both these sectors, patenting is well appreciated. Our sample comprises of 69 respondents from the IT sector and 50 from the pharmaceutical sector, thereby making the total sample size of 119. They represent organizations located in New Delhi, Kolkata, Bangalore and Hyderabad in India.

3.4 Analysis

We performed the analysis with an objective of exploring the contribution of the 5 independent variables of SI, PA, TA, RA and CM towards KG and FG. For arriving at the scores of KG, FG and all the CI variables, we consider a weighted mean of their corresponding items. The weights are the values of the respective first principal components of the measuring items. Table 3 reports the mean and standard deviation (S.D.) of the independent CI variables. Here the composite sample is taken into consideration. The results of the t-tests conducted in order to check whether the CI variables contribute equally towards KG and FG are also reported in the Table 3. For exploring the possibility of any sector-specific differentiation in the scores obtained, we report the sector-wise mean, S.D. and t-test results for the CI variables in Table 4. The sector-wise scores for the actual KG and FG scores are reported in Table 5. Finally we perform simple linear regression analysis using enter method for each of the 2 sectors for understanding the relation between the patent intelligence gathering practices and increase in patent productivity. The regression results are reported in Table 6.

3.5 Results

Table 3 describes the mean, S.D. and t-test results for the CI variables for both the sectors. From the mean scores, it is seen that PA reports the highest contribution to KG while CM reports the highest in the context of FG realized. Both these scores are above the 4 mark out of the 5 point scale. All the CI variables rank higher than the moderate level in their contribution to KG and FG. Except for CM, all the variables contribute significantly higher towards KG than towards FG. In case of CM, FG is seen to be significantly higher than the KG score.

Table 3. Mean, S.D. and t-test results for the CI variables (n=119).

Ideal CI Practice	Contribution towards KG Mean (S.D.)	Contribution towards FG Mean (S.D.)	t-test (p-value)
SI	3.86 (0.86)	3.58 (0.94)	4.38 (.00)**
PA	4.02 (0.77)	3.72 (0.88)	5.87 (.00)**
TA	3.96 (0.68)	3.68 (0.80)	4.28 (.00)**
RA	3.82 (0.63)	3.68 (0.69)	3.04 (.00)**
CM	3.72 (1.04)	4.07 (0.89)	-4.14 (.00)**

$* p \leq 0.05$,　$** p \leq 0.01$

The sector-wise differences in the appreciation of the contributions of the CI variables towards KG and FG are reported in Table 4. The pharmaceutical sector's scores are seen to be significantly higher than that of the IT sector, both in case of KG and FG realized through the ideal implementation of CI practices. With respect to contributions towards KG, it is seen from the mean scores that its highest contributor, both in the IT and pharmaceutical sectors, is PA. However in case of the IT sector, considering their mean scores, TA contributes as much as PA towards KG. The contribution towards FG is highest from CM across both the sectors.

The results of Table 5 highlight that although the pharmaceutical sectors' mean value of the KG and FG realized through patent productivity is higher than that of the IT sector, they do not significantly differ with respect to the KG scores. However, the pharmaceutical sector scores significantly higher than IT in their FG realized through enhanced patent productivity.

The sector-specific regression results are described in Table 6. With respect to the IT sector, none of the CI variables seem to contribute significantly to the enhanced patent productivity indicators of KG and FG. In fact, TA is totally excluded from the regression equation estimating the relation between the CI variables and the KG on higher patent productivity. The relationship between the CI variables and higher FG and KG realized through higher patent productivity improves in case of the pharmaceutical sector. Here SI is seen to be contributing significantly both towards KG and FG, thereby emerging as a significant contributor towards increased patent productivity. RA is also reported as a contributor towards KG. Here too in both instances of KG and FG, TA is not seen to execute any role at all towards increasing patent productivity.

Table 4. Mean, S.D. and t-test results for sector-wise differences in perception of CI practices (n=119; 1: IT, n_1=69; 2: Pharmaceutical, n_2=50).

Ideal CI Practice	Contribution to KG			Contribution to FG		
	1 Mean (S.D.)	2 Mean (S.D.)	t_{12} (p-value)	1 Mean (S.D.)	2 Mean (S.D.)	t_{12} (p-value)
SI	3.43 (0.79)	4.46 (0.54)	-8.50 (.00)**	3.13 (0.82)	4.19 (0.72)	-7.50 (.00)**
PA	3.62 (0.74)	4.57 (0.36)	-9.25 (.00)**	3.34 (0.90)	4.24 (0.52)	-6.89 (.00)**
TA	3.62 (0.62)	4.42 (0.45)	-8.19 (.00)**	3.50 (0.87)	3.92 (0.62)	-3.05 (.00)**
RA	3.55 (0.56)	4.19 (0.53)	-6.46 (.00)**	3.41 (0.67)	4.06 (0.51)	-6.04 (.00)**
CM	3.32 (1.10)	4.48 (0.62)	-6.07 (.00)**	3.80 (0.93)	4.43 (0.67)	-4.26 (.00)**

* p$\leq$ 0.05, ** p$\leq$ 0.01

Table 5. Mean, S.D. and t-test results for sector-wise differences in KG and FG scores due to increased patent productivity (n=119; 1: IT, n_1=69; 2: Pharmaceutical, n_2=50).

Dependent variable	1 Mean (S.D.)	2 Mean (S.D.)	t_{12} (p-value)
KG	3.86 (0.70)	4.04 (0.36)	-1.89 (.06)
FG	3.61 (0.63)	4.04 (0.57)	-3.84 (.00)**

* p$\leq$ 0.05, ** p$\leq$ 0.01

Table 6. Linear Regression Results.

1. IT Sector Regression Results:	
KG=2.31+ 0.11*SI + 0.19*PA + 0.28*RA – 0.19*CM (.00) (.42) (.25) (.89) (.12)	R^2=.12 F=2.70, p-value=.03*
FG=2.54+ 0.21*SI + 0.16*PA – 0.25TA + 0.35*RA – 0.12*CM (.00) (.17) (.40) (.12) (.07) (.27)	R^2=.23 F=3.67, p-value=.01*
2. Pharmaceutical Sector Regression Results:	
KG=2.26+ 0.17*SI -0.21*PA + 0.34*RA (.00) (.00) (.22) (.01)	R^2=.34 F=4.61, p-value=.00**
FG=1.97+ 0.44*SI - 0.25*RA + 0.31*CM (.00) (.00) (.29) (.07)	R^2=.34 F=4.45, p-value=.00**

* p$\leq$ 0.05, ** p$\leq$ 0.01

4 Conclusions

Our results highlight that the perception of the pharmaceutical sector is discernibly better than the IT sector for practices in the context of enhancing patent productivity. Therefore the organizational learning practices are higher in the pharmaceutical sector. The lack of patent legislations supporting software patenting in India probably explains the poorer rating by the IT experts. On the other hand, the higher pharmaceutical sector scores are undoubtedly attributed to their better environmental scanning and organizational learning practices. Based on these observations it can be predicted that provided with a pro-organizational learning environment, the IT organizations would be able to increase their patent productivity significantly.

Additionally, our results show that in the general opinion of the respondents across both IT and pharmaceutical sectors, except for the practice of competitive monitoring, all the other competitive intelligence variables contribute significantly higher towards knowledge than financial gains. This indicates that the organizational employees perceive patent-intelligence gathering and organizational learning practices primarily as a knowledge enhancing activity. But there is a lack of appreciation of the conversion mechanism translating this knowledge gain into financial gains.

Yet another striking observation is that the competitive-intelligence gathering practices are not recognized as having significant relation with patent productivity. In fact only two variables, viz., extraction of market intelligence and rival analysis, are seen to have a significant impact upon patent productivity in the context of the pharmaceutical sector. This lack of appreciation for the contribution of prior art analysis, technology assessment and competitive monitoring may adversely affect organizational patent productivity in the long run.

These observations cumulatively have serious implications for managers. Based on the employee perceptions it is clear that the organizational learning practices are prevalent in both the IT and pharmaceutical sectors. But the application of organizational learning for enhancing financial gain is not perceived. Therefore, we can say that although the foundation required for strategic analysis exists, there is a missing link between the strategic analysis and strategy implementation, i.e. at the strategy formulation stage. The organizational learning in the nature of patent intelligence fails to be incorporated in the revenue generating operation assessments. The situation is expected to improve if this knowledge is considered in the day-to-day decisions relating to increasing patent productivity. This requires that the respondents be well educated about the entire patenting process and have the desired perceptions in this regard. Without a holistic understanding of the patenting process and the implications that it bears for the organizational revenues, the employees cannot be expected to perform their best in enhancing patent productivity that have a commercial edge. Therefore organizations need to launch immediate patent education programmes for creating the awareness about using the data from these environmental scanning practices. Similarly, in light of the fact that external environmental conditions have a serious impact upon the actual patenting process and also on the perceptions of the organizational employees, thereby affecting actual patent productivity, organizations need to boost up their corporate political activity in ensuring that a healthy pro-patenting environment exists. Thus both internal and external infrastructure support has to developed by the organizations for getting into the "generative" rather than the "adaptive" mode (Senge, 1990) of organizational learning for stepping up patent productivity.

References

Aguilar, F.J. (1967) *Scanning the Business Environment.* New York: Macmillian Co.

Ashton, B.W. and Sen, R.K. (1988) "Using Patent Information in Technology Business Planning: I." *Research Technology Management*, 31(6): 42-46.

Berkowitz, L. (1993) "Getting the Most from your Patents." *Research Technology Management*, 32(2): 26-32.

Briggs, J. (1992) *Fractals: The Pattern of Chaos.* London: Thames & Hudson.

Cantrell, R. (1997) "Patents Intelligence from Legal and Commercial Perspectives." *World Patent Information*, 19(4): 251-264.

Choo, C.W. and Auster, E. (1993) "Environmental Scanning: Acquisition and Use of Information by Managers." In Williams, M.E. (Ed.), *Annual Review of Information Science and Technology*: Medford, N.J.: Learned Information Inc.

Choo, C.W. (1998) "Information Management for the Intelligent Organization: The Art of Scanning the Environment." *Information Today*, New Jersey: Learned Information Inc.

Comanor, W.S. and Scherer, F.M. (1969) "Patent Statistics as a Measure of Technical Change." *Journal of Political Economy*, 77(3): 392-398.

Cummings, T.G. and Worley, C.G. (1997) *Organizational Development and Change.* Ohio: South-Western College Publishing.

Edmondson, A. and Moingeon, B. (1996) "When to Learn How and When to Learn Why: Appropriate Organizational Learning Processes as Source of Competitive Advantage." In Moingeon, B. and Edmondson, A. (Eds), *Organizational Learning and Competitive Advantage*, London: Sage Publishers.

Emory, W.C. (1976) *Business Research Methods.* Illinois: Richard D. Irwin Inc.

Ernst, H. (2001) "Patent Applications and Subsequent Changes of Performance: Evidence from Time-series Cross-section Analyses on the Firm Level." *Research Policy*, 30: 143-157.

Fiol, C.M. (1996) "Squeezing Harder Doesn't Always Work: Continuing the Search for Consistency in Innovation Research." *Academy of Management Review*, 21(4): 1012-1021.

Grant, R.M. (1996) "Toward a Knowledge-based Theory of the Firm." *Strategic Management Journal*, 17: 109-122.

Griliches, Z., Hall, B.H. and Pakes, A. (1991) "R&D, Patents and Market Value Revisited: Is there a Second (Technological Opportunity) Factor?" *Economies of Innovation and New Technology*, 1: 183-201.

Keogh, W. (1999) "Understanding Processes and Adding Value Within Innovative Small Firms." *Knowledge and Process Management*, 6(2): 114-125.

Liu, S. (1998) "Strategic Scanning and Interpretation Revisiting: Foundations for a Software Agent Support System: Scanning the Business Environment with Software Agents." *Industrial Management + Data Systems*, 98(8): 362-375.

Lorange, P., Morton, M.S.S. and Ghosal, S. (1986) *Strategic Control.* St. Paul: West Publishing Company.

Mogee, M.E. (1991) "Using Patent Data for Technology Analysis and Planning." *Research Technology Management*, 34(4): 43- 49.

Narin, F., Noma, E. and Perry, R. (1987) "Patents as Indicators of Corporate Technological Strength." *Research Policy*, 16: 143-155.

Ozsomer, A., Calantone, R.J. and Di Bonetto, A. (1997) "What Makes Firms More Innovative? A Look At Organizational and Environmental Factors." *Journal of Business and Industrial Marketing*, 12(6): 400-416.

Pakes, A. (1985) "On Patents, R&D, and the Stock Market Rate of Return." *Journal of Political Economy*, 93(2): 390-408.

Rivette, K.G. and Kline, D. (2000) "Discovering New Value in Intellectual Property." *Harvard Business Review*, 78(1): 54-67.

Senge, P. (1990) *The Fifth Discipline*. London: Nicholas Brealey.

Scherer, F.M. (1965) "Corporate Inventive Output, Profits and Growth." *Journal of Political Economy*, 73(3): 290-297.

Stata, R. (1989) "Organizational Learning-The Key to Management Innovation." *Sloan Management Review*, 30(3): 63-74.

Sullivan, P.H. and Daniele, J.J. (1986) "Intellectual Property Portfolios in Business Strategy," In Parr, R.L. and Sullivan, P.H., (Eds.), *Technology Licensing: Corporate Strategies For Maximizing Value*, New York: John Wiley & Sons Inc.

Tushman, M. and Nadler, D. (1986) "Organizing for Innovation." *California Management Review*, 28 (3): 74-93.

INTELLECTUAL PROPERTY RIGHTS AND THE DEBATE ON RENT SEEKING AND ALLOCATION OF KNOWLEDGE RESOURCES

BRUNO DE VUYST

Vesalius College, and Institute for European Studies, Vrije Universiteit Brussel,
Of Counsel, Lawfort, Pleinlaan 2, 1050 Brussels, Belgium

ALEA M. FAIRCHILD

Vesalius College and Faculty of Economics (ESP), Vrije Universiteit Brussel
Pleinlaan 2, 1050 Brussels, Belgium

Intellectual property rights have been extended in scope and, in some cases, in time to such extent that questions may be raised about the allocation of such proprietary knowledge resources. It may be questioned in particular whether excessive rent seeking opportunities in certain intellectual property-protected knowledge resources may lead to misallocations.

1   Introduction

To encourage investment in innovation, governmental organizations grant innovators limited rights to the innovations they create via intellectual property law mechanisms such as patents, copyrights, and trade secrets. By the creation of these intellectual property (IP) rights, innovators are assisted in obtaining financial benefit generated by their innovation-related investments (Dam, 1995; Liebeskind, 1996). IP rights are stated in absolute terms and, via the Trade Related Aspects of Intellectual Property (TRIPS) agreement, in a globalized way.

IP rights could also be seen as representing a loss relative to the free and unrestricted use by all of the knowledge that the innovators have created. However, society elects to suffer this social loss in order to increase innovators' incentives to invest in the creation of new knowledge by way of a private investment model (Krogh *et al.*, 2003).

2   The Evolution of Material Rights

In Roman law, the first possessor of a thing became the owner by right of occupancy ("*Res nullius fit primi occupantis*"). Occupancy was defined as a person taking physical possession of something, which at that moment was the property of no man ("*res nullius*"), with the view of acquiring property in it for him. In certain cases, that intention was required to be established through formal acts instituting "appropriation". Roman law viewed occupancy as a natural process, a normal mode of acquisition by which the earth and its fruits, originally held as a common good, became the legitimate property of individuals. Medieval (David, 1992) and Enlightenment (Locke, 2000) societal views recognized the acquisition of property through occupancy and possession as a form of natural law, acknowledged in common law as appropriation.

Material property rights as formulated by the 1804 *Code Civil* started out, ostensibly at least, as being as total and absolute as current intellectual property rights. Their natural law origins, however, did not bear out such absoluteness, stressing appropriation by way of labour, and inherently recognizing thereby already that there was a social factor to justify ownership by appropriation. Nevertheless, by the end of the 18th and the beginning of the 19th century, ownership rights, perhaps out of a defensive political concern, were posited as absolute. While requiring law and due process to be the limiting factor on ownership rights, one cannot from these ignore the inherently recognized limitations of social justice and justifiable use. Today's zoning laws, environmental regulations or, simply, good neighbourship, place realistic limits to material ownership.

3   In Search of the Underpinnings of Intellectual Property

Neither Hegel's placing of a person's will, appropriating a thing for oneself (Yen, 1990) or a Lockeian view of intellectual property rights appear to have suitably explained attitudes towards, and to have established a base for, intellectual property rights (Radin, 1982; Schnably, 1993). While natural law, and natural rights, were emphasized in continental European doctrine as justifications for intellectual property rights, the theories have difficulty explaining the dichotomy between absolutist views in intellectual property rights and the checks and balances, social and economical, weighing on material property rights (Hettinger, 1989; Gordon, 1993).

Indeed, the most common explanation given today does not emanate from theory, but is based on economic pragmatism: intellectual property rights are stated to be what they are because they are based on, and fundamentally about, incentives to create and invent. The United States Supreme Court, in Marer v. Stein, summed it up:

> "The copyright law, like the patent statutes, makes reward to the owner a secondary consideration". United States v. Paramount Pictures, 334 U.S. 131, 158. However, it is "intended definitely to grant valuable, enforceable rights to authors, publishers, etc., without burdensome requirements: "to afford greater encouragement to the production of literary [or artistic] works of lasting benefit to the world" Washington Pub. Co. v. Pearson, 306 U.S. 30. *The economic philosophy behind the clause empowering Congress to grant patents and copyrights is the conviction that it is the best way to advance public welfare through the talents of authors and inventors in "Science and useful Arts". Sacrificial days devoted to such creative activities deserve rewards commensurate with the services rendered"* (emphasis supplied) [1]

This approach does not satisfy, however, to explain the recent growth of proprietary knowledge and of IP and its corollary, the withering away of the public domain, as well as the absolute nature of IP ownership.

4   IP Extensions

Intellectual property rights have seen perceptible, indeed substantial extensions in the last decade alone. In patent law, there have been extensions into biotechnology, including into plants tissue and animals, into the protection of software through patent rights, and into the protection of "business methods"[2] . Trademark law was extended to include the protection of smells, sounds and colors[3] . In the area of copyright, extensions were rendered to software and to formats[4] . New intellectual property rights saw the light of day: for semiconductors[5] and for data banks[6]. At the same time, European Community rights were created for trademarks[7], designs[8] and a European Community patent is under way as of writing (2003)[9]. A European Directive was adopted on the legal protection of biotechnological inventions[10].

Domain names have recently become property, making the world of property laws and liabilities apply to the virtual world of the Internet[11]. All of these lead to the consideration of what is left, in the world of creation, to pure liberty. In the words of Prof. Jeremy Phillips:

> "Look at every aspect of intellectual property and the evidence is plain: the public domain, like the mighty rainforests of South-America, is being whittled away almost while we watch it" (Philips, 1996).

5   TRIPS: Global and Absolute Proprietary Knowledge

TRIPS, which was negotiated during the WTO's Uruguay Round, introduced IP rules into the multilateral trading system. TRIPS provides for a monolithic global framework for treating IP. Its stress is on absolute powers to the IP owner. Few exceptions are available. One of these is set, for copyright, in its article 13, entitled "Limitations and Exceptions". The article provides:

> "[M]embers shall confine limitations or exceptions to exclusive rights to certain special cases which do not conflict with a normal exploitation of the work and do not unreasonably prejudice the legitimate interests of the right holder."

Article 13 has already been considered and interpreted. A dispute resolution panel of the World Trade Organization held in June 2000 the United States in contravention of its obligations under art. 13 of the TRIPS accord to confine limitations or exceptions to exclusive rights to certain special cases, which do not conflict with a normal exploitation of the work and do not unreasonably prejudice the legitimate interests of the right holder. In the dispute resolution proceeding, initiated by the European Union at the behest of the Irish performing rights organization, the contested exception, enacted in the 1998 Digital Millennium Copyright Act, exempted a broad range of retail and restaurant establishments from liability for public performance of musical works by means of communication of radio and television transmission (Ginsburg, 2001). The exception, in other words, is restrictively interpreted.

Article 13 TRIPS has as its companion articles 17 (trademark law), 26 (designs and models) and 30 (patents). Their provisions, and the interpretation given to these provisions, stress further the exceptional character of IP ownership as absolute and global. All of this does not explain why IP ownership is as absolute as it is, and modern material property ownership is yet again not, as it needs to be socially and ethically justified to maintain itself.

6 Explaining the Basic Differences Between IP and Material Rights

The fact that IP is created as a (temporary) monopoly, and that material property rights are not, or no longer without economic-social considerations held or exercised, may also not offer a totally suitable explanation. The differentiation between material projects rights and IP becomes perceptibly clearer as one looks at the demise of ownership rights. A material ownership right is perpetual unless otherwise stipulated. Hence, in principle and systemically, material ownership, once acquired, does not end except by destruction of the thing, or incorporation into another. Intellectual property ownership, however, is always temporal, i.e. restricted in time and at some point coming to an end, thereafter ownership falls within the public domain. Hence, systemically, the reverse happens than with material ownership: while in material ownership appropriation implies individualizing and defining individual ownership rights, in principle forever, in intellectual ownership the reverse occurs. Through intellectual labor, an individual may appropriate his work individually for a defined period, and become the single owner. His ownership rights end, however, at the end of a stated monopoly period, thereafter the fruits of his labor will be shared with all in common.

Is the intellectual-philosophical basis for material and intellectual property ownership the same for material property and IP? It is clearly not from a systemic viewpoint. IP is not based on taking a thing from the commons and belaboring it, this labor warranting individual ownership. IP is based on the human mind, and its work alone. It leads not to a tangible good but to knowledge to be applied. Indeed, material ownership involves drawing from a common, as Roman Law already indicates, while IP ultimately gives to a common. The former belabors a thing from the common to validate individual ownership, the latter belabors the mind alone.

This difference may be the explanation for the temporal ownership monopoly which is so striking in IP (and, thus, the temporal ownership is not the explanation for the systemic difference). As it is based on human labor itself and alone, and not on drawing from a common good, it may warrant keeping this ownership to the individual, at least for a while. Indeed, this may also explain why the creation of the mind called IP falls, after a period of monopoly right to its owner, into the common.

Does this mean that intellectual property ownership, when a monopoly to the owner, is bereft of any social dimension? Marer vs. Stein, quoted above, provides for an answer: *"to advance public welfare"*... *"Sacrificial days devoted to such creative activities deserve rewards commensurate with the services rendered"*.

A tentative understanding of the different bases of material and intellectual property rights leads to an appreciation of a key consideration of IP. Intellectual property rights are stated to be what they are because they are based on, and fundamentally about, incentives to create and invent. Hence, it appears that the economic incentive perspective is the key driver in the granting of intellectual property protection. But are these incentives really necessary to ensure and sustain knowledge creation and innovation?

7   Incentives to Create Knowledge

Mainstream literature on IP value creation suggests that all inventors are autonomous and rational profit-maximizing agents (Anderson and Konzelmann, 2004). In this view, there is no recognition of the specific nature of productive knowledge, power-relationships in bargaining situations and the socially embedded nature of inventors' behaviour. Nor does this view account for difficulties associated with technological interdependence, interaction and collaboration in competitive markets, nor opportunity costs of using the IP as a strategic instrument(Anderson and Konzelmann, 2004).. Collaboration, for example, requires a set of rewards for individuals to engage in this action, such as reputation, control over IP and learning opportunities (Krogh *et al.*, 2003).

In the 1970's, Professor (and later Justice) Stephen Breyer argued that lead time advantages and the threat of retaliation reduced the cost advantages of copiers, hence obviating if not eliminating the need for copyright protection of books (Breyer, 1970). Advances in technology may not have strengthened Breyer's argument. George Priest argued that economic analysis (in his case of patent law) is *"one of the least productive lines of inquiry in all of economic thought"* because of the lack of adequate empirical bases for the assessment of theoretical models of innovation (Priest, 1986). Still, this view does not undo the fact that the utilitarian / economic incentive perspective is perhaps most useful for any analysis of intellectual property rights. These rights inescapably clash with a libertarian view that "information wants to be free" (Barlow, 1994). Those arguing against such "Common Ground" – the expression is borrowed from the writings of Professor Lawrence Lessig - insist that knowledge creation incentives will be hampered by the diminishing of intellectual property rights. Perhaps the way out is not to concentrate on this clash, but to restate the debate as one within the realm of property rights itself, as one about possible excesses of property rights and excessive rent-seeking by their owners.

8   Needed: A Justification for IP Protection

Brainpower supposedly drives the post-modern economy. Technology change makes it harder to protect ideas. Globalization made IP spread, and one might fear that in a variant of Gresham's Law, nations that do not protect IP will drive down global standards. Still, current IP may not be suitable as a monopolistic global system: plant breeders rights (PBR) and indigenous people's disputes bear out that more attention needs to be paid, as part of an information economy paradigm, to societal and cultural aspects that may limit the unrestrained execution of intellectual property rights (de Soto, 2000). If the case for intellectual property rights is to be maintained, equitable correctives will need to be introduced. So for example, recognition of the intellectual capital of indigenous people may be required to attain the necessary sensitivity to properly translate the hidden wealth, which de Soto sought. This translation – rather than superimposing a Western capitalist system – may put intellectual property rights in a proper frame as regards indigenous people and respect for their culture and society.

In the battle over intellectual property rights, owners, even in the developed world, may not maintain their rights if they go further than what society considers justifiable. For example, when ASCAP sent thousands of letters to Girl Scout groups, demanding royalties for songs presumably sung around the campfire, the public relations disaster that ensued made them refrain from collecting a full profit, which was their due under black letter law. The popular reaction, deeming ASCAP's demanding excessive made ASCAP relent from a full application of black letter law and instead made them charge the Girl Scouts one USD per group per year (Zittrain, 2002).

9 Protecting Knowledge: Measuring Justifiable IP Protection

Indeed, if intellectual property owners do not see reason, it may hinder their more patently reasonable claims for due compensation – protection for innovation, in other words. This is the more so as the value of intellectual property rights creation as an economic good itself is being questioned by an eminent jurist, Judge Richard Posner:

> "granting property rights in intellectual property increases the incentive to create such property, but the downside is that those rights can interfere with the creation of subsequent intellectual property (because of the tracing problem and because the principal input into most intellectual property rights is previously created intellectual property). Property rights can limit the distribution of intellectual property and can draw excessive resources into the creation of intellectual property, and away from other socially valuable activities, by the phenomenon of rent seeking.

> Striking the right balance, which is to say determining the optimal scope of intellectual property rights, requires a comparison of these benefits and costs – and really, it seems to me, nothing more.

> We do not know how much intellectual property is in fact socially useful, and therefore we do not know how extensive a set of intellectual property rights we should create. For all we know, too many resources are being sucked into the creation of new biotechnology, computer software, films, pharmaceuticals, and business methods because the rights of these different forms of intellectual property have been too broadly defined" (Posner, 2002).

The socio-economic measurement which Judge Posner proposes may appear to set a daunting task, but it points to correctives that may maintain a case for intellectual property rights. Indeed, one may have suggested two correctives to maintain the case for intellectual property rights going forward: a first corrective finding intellectual capital, and hence intellectual property rights, in indigenous societies in the developing world, in line with a better understanding of current development economic policy. Second, there appears to be a more general need for measuring the impact of intellectual property rights to determine its optimal scope vis-à-vis societal values.

In the margin of the Doha Ministerial Declaration of November 2001, outcome of the Fourth WTO Ministerial Conference, there were somewhat dim glimmers as regards suitable and ethically sound limitations to intellectual property rights: through an August 2003 agreement pursuant to the Declaration on the TRIPS Agreement and Public Health, TRIPS is 'clarified' and the accessibility of medicines to developing countries is enhanced, as countries are waived, through an 'interim' waiver, obligations under article 31 (f) of TRIPS until the article is amended (WTO, 2003).

Excessive expression of intellectual property rights appears to correlate with excessive rent seeking by owners. For example, it appears not acceptable if Girl Scouts are being harassed for more than a symbolic dollar for their campfire songs. This excessive rent-seeking may in turn correlate – as Posner suggests – to a misallocation of resources. Even within intellectual property rights itself elements of this misallocation might be detected. For example, an explanation is required why subsequent copyright term extensions are not matched by patent term extensions. One explanation might be the power of the media industry lobby. Still, this appears not satisfactory if one considers the size and might of the pharmaceutical industry. Might the expected - rapid, exceedingly more rapid than in the pharmaceutical industry return on investment in rapsters than in cancer drugs - provide for an explanation?

If such exceedingly higher (than in other investments') returns occur for certain kinds of IP, they might be indicative not only of "excessive" allocation of scarce resources but they might also lead to a conclusion by the general public that the maximized rent-seeking for such investment is "excessive", i.e. unwarranted on societal and likely on long-term sustainable economical, grounds.

10 Conclusion

Taken to the full consequence: IP appears based on the human mind alone, as distinct from material property rights which are linked to appropriation of a common through labor. IP's protection structure appears therefore to rigidly protect the owner, at least for a stated period, so as to preserve the incentive to create.

This rigidity, as currently conceived, might become a driver for overinvestment in societally unfruitful IP, and might lead to rent-seeking that is socially unacceptable.

The adoption of the global and monolithic TRIPS intellectual property rights system was perhaps the high water mark of absolute intellectual property ownership. The system is already being challenged by both libertarians and developing countries. What is perhaps required is an understanding that what is being fought over may perhaps be the symptoms rather than the disease.

Indeed, perceived excessive rent-seeking opportunities may point to excessive returns on investment which may point in turn to misallocations of knowledge resources into societally less valuable investments. If the current intellectual property rights system would be found to be, by its nature, distortive – driving to investment in rapsters rather than roads – then mainstream society may need to act, to correct, for equity reasons but also in the interest of economic investment in long-term questionable investments[12]

11 Directions for Future Research

IP, embodying a proprietary knowledge resource, appears to have a distinctively different systemic-philosophical basis from that of material rights ownership. This may reflect in, i.e. be the reason for, a temporal monopoly right for IP owners, and for the transfer of IP to the public domain, the common, thereafter. Clearly, more reflection is required to study these phenomena and their basis.

Addressing the optimal and the good of IP, i.e. the basis for a right to individual ownership and ownership rights, creates obvious problems of evidencing "excessive" knowledge rent seeking, and currently posits the issue of ethically useful ownership and ownership rights without defining it other than in rent-seeking terms, or as unsound *"because we know it to be so"*.

Much empirical work is needed to measure IP, cost/benefits of IP and knowledge rent-seeking, and to assess IP in terms of social justification. If one wishes to advance towards a usefulness assessment, it will be key to frame such empirical work in a firm methodological basis, so as to progress in assessing IP for societal justification from a current situation akin to Justice Byron White's crude assessment methodology of pornography: *"I know it when I see it"*.

Endnotes

[1]   Marer v. Stein, 347 U.S. 201 (1954).

[2]   The European Patent Office (EPO) issued on May 13, 1992 a patent application covering a process/method for producing a genetically engineered mouse that would develop cancer (the so called 'Harvard-onco-mouse'). The Harvard-onco-mouse could be used as a tool to study the effects of anticancer treatments and products [EPO Patent N° 0169672, *Official Journal EPO*, 1992/10, 588]; The Technical Board of Appeal (TBA) of the EPO decided on July 1, 1998 in the *IBM* case that *"a computer program claimed by itself is not excluded from patentability if the program, when running on a computer or loaded into a computer, brings about, or is capable of bringing about, a technical effect which goes beyond the "normal" physical interactions between the program (software)and the computer (hardware) on which it is run"*. [*See*: TBA, July 1 1998, T 1173/97, *Official Journal EPO*, 1999/10, 609. (cons. 13)]; In the *Pension Benefit* case TBA of the EPO had to decide if a method of controlling a pension benefits program by administering at least one subscriber employer account on behalf of each subscriber employer's enrolled employees each of whom is to receive periodic benefits payments claims to methods and systems for performing business methods are excluded or not form patentability (*i.e.* a business method) was patentable. The TBA decided that *"all the features of this claim are steps of processing and producing information having purely administrative, actuarial and/or financial character. Processing and producing such information are typical steps of business and economic methods. Thus the invention as claimed does not go beyond a method of doing business as such and, therefore, is excluded from patentability"* [*See*: TBA, September 8, 2000, T 95/0931, *Official Journal EPO*, 2001/10, 413 (cons. 3)].

[3]   On February 11, 1999 the Second Board of Appeal Office of the Harmonization for the Internal Market (OHIM), the EC Trade Mark Office, decided in the *Vennootschap Onder Firma Senta Aromatic Marketing* case that an application to register as an olfactory Community Trade Mark (CTM) '*the smell of freshly cut grass*' for tennis balls was an adequate representation of the mark that the applicant was intending to apply these goods. The Board decided that: *"The smell of freshly cut grass is a distinct smell which everyone immediately recognizes from experience. For many, the scent or fragrance of freshly cut grass reminds them of spring or summer, manicured lawns or playing fields, or other such pleasant experiences"* [*See*: Second Board of Appeal, February 11, 1999, R 156/1998-2, *Official Journal OHIM*, 1999, 1239 (cons. 14)]; In *Orange*, the UK company *Orange Personal Communications Services Ltd.* applied on March 1, 1996 for the entry of the

colour mark "orange" in the trade mark register for a large number of goods in class 9 and services in class 38. In the application form, the applicant had ticked, under the heading "Type of mark", the box "other" and had specified as the other type of mark "Colour mark". For a description of the trade mark, it had referred to an attached sheet on which it stated that the mark consisted of the colour "orange". The applicant had not enclosed a reproduction of the specific colour shade or indicated a code number. Following a request by the examiner, the applicant filed subsequently a graphical representation of the colour on a separate sheet of paper. The Third Board of Appeal of the OHIM confirmed that a single colour is in theory registrable as a CTM, although it must be distinctive (*i.e.* capable of indicating the origin of the goods or services for which registration is sought). [*See*: Third Board of Appeal, February, 12, 1998, R 7/19997-3, *Official Journal OHIM*, 1998, 641]; In 1994 the Dutch company *Shield Mark B.V.* applied for a Benelux Trade Mark consisting sounds (Beethoven's *Für Elise*) in class 9 and 16. The trade mark was described as follows: "THE TRADE MARK CONSISTS OF THE NINE FIRST TONES OF FÜR ELISE" [translation from Dutch]. The trade mark was accorded by the Benelux Trade Mark Office (BTO) [*See*: *Official Journal BTO*, 02/1995, Reg. N°: 551849].

4   See Council Directive 91/250/EEC of 14 May 1991 on the legal protection of computer programs, *Official Journal*, L/122, 17 May 1991, 42, amended by Council Directive 93/98/EEC of 29 October 1993, *Official Journal*, L/290, 24 November 1993.

5   Council Directive 87/54/EEC of 16 December 1986 on the legal protection of topographies of semiconductor products, *Official Journal*, L/024, 27 January, 1987, 36-40.

6   Directive 96/9/EC of the European Parliament and of the Council of 11 March 1996 on the legal protection of databases, *Official Journal*, L/077, 27 March 1996, 20-28.

7   Council Regulation 40/94/EC of 20 December 1993 on the Community trade mark *Official Journal*, L/011, 14 January 1994, 1-3, amended by Council Regulation 3288/94/EC of 22 December 1994, *Official Journal*, L/349, 31 December1994, 83; and First Council Directive 89/104/EEC of 21 December 1988 to approximate the laws of the Member States relating to trade marks, *Official Journal*, L/040, 11 February 1989, p.1, amended by Council Decision 92/10/EEC of 19 December 1991, *Official Journal*, L/006, 1 January 1992, 35.

8   Council Regulation 6/2002/EC of 12 December 2001 on Community designs, *Official Journal*, L/003 , January 5, 2002, 1-24; and Directive 98/71/EC of the European Parliament and of the Council of 13 October 1998 on the legal protection of designs, *Official Journal*, L/289, 28 October 1998, 28-35.

9   Proposal for a Council Regulation on the Community patent (COM/2000/0412 final), *Official Journal*, C/337 E, 28 November 2000, 278.

10   Directive 98/44/EC of the European Parliament and of the Council of 6 July 1998 on the legal protection of biotechnological inventions, *Official Journal*, L/213, 30 July 1998, 13-21.

11   As decided in Kremen v. Cohen, 03 C.D.O.S. 6565 (9th U.S. Circuit Court of Appeals, July 25, 2003).

12   See for examples of this debate in the legal field: Anawalt, H. C. (2002). "Internet distribution of intellectual property protected works in the United States, in Japan, and in the future", 18 *Santa Clara Computer and High Technology Law Journal*, 207; Newton, J. (2001). "Global solutions to prevent copyright infringement of music over the Internet: the need to supplement the WIPO Internet Treaties with self-imposed mandates", 12 *Indiana International and Comparative Law Review*, 125; Rajzer, A. (2000). "Misunderstanding the Internet: how courts are overprotecting trademarks used in metatags", *The Law Review of Michigan State University, Detroit College of Law*, 427.

References

Anderson, B. and Konzelmann, S. (2004). "Releasing the Productive Potential of Intellectual Property: Governance and Value Creation Processes", Proceedings of the AHRB Copyright Research Network Conference, June 29-30, 2004.

Barlow, J.P. (1994). "The Economy of Ideas", 2.03 *Wired* 84.

Breyer, S. (1970). "The Uneasy Case for Copyright: A study in Copyright of Books, Photocopies and Computer Programs", 84 *Harv. L. Rev.* 281; see the reply by Tyerman, L. (1971). "The Economic Case for Copyright Protection for Published Books: A Reply to Professor Breyer", 18 *UCLA L. Rev.* 1100; and Breyer, S. (1972). "Copyright: A Rejoinder", 20 *UCLA L. Rev.* 75.

Dam, K. W. (1995). "Some Economic-Considerations in the Intellectual Property Protection of Software". *Journal of Legal Studies*, 24(2): 321-377.

David, P.A. (1992). "The Evolution of Intellectual Property Institutions and the Panda's Thumb", Meetings of the International Economic Association in Moscow, 24-28 August 1992.

de Soto, H. (2000). *The Mystery of Capital; Why Capitalism Triumphs in the West and Fails Everywhere Else*, Basic Books, New York, NY.

Ginsburg, J.C. (2001). "Toward Supranational Copyright Law? The WTO Panel Decision and the "Three – Step Test" for Copyright Exceptions", January 2001, RIDA, 2001, N° 187, 3.

Gordon, W. J. (1993). "A Property Right in Self-Expression: Equality and Individualism in the Natural Law of Intellectual Property", 102 *Yale L. J.* 1533.

Hettinger, E.C. (1989). "Justifying Intellectual Property", 18 *Phil. & Publ. Aff.* 31.

Krogh, Georg von, Haefliger, Stefan & Spaeth, Sebastian (2003). "Collective Action and Communal Resources in Open Source Software Development: The Case of Freenet". PDF available at http://opensource.mit.edu/papers/vonkroghhaefligerspaeth.pdf.

Liebeskind, J. P. (1996). "Knowledge, strategy, and the theory of the firm". *Strategic Management Journal*, 17: 93-107.

Locke, J. (2000). *Two Treatises on Government*. Birmingham: Palladium Pass (Original work published 1720).

Madava, T. "Terminator technology threatening African farmers' rights", http://www.afrol.com/News2001/afr023_terminator_techn.htm, consulted on December 18, 2002.

Philips, J. (1996). "The Diminishing Domain", *European Intellectual Property Review*, at 429.

Posner, R.A. (Spring 2002) "The law & economics of intellectual property", *Daedalus*, 5, at 12.

Priest, G. (1986). "What Economists Can Tell Lawyers About Intellectual Property", 8 *Res. Law & Econ.* 19.

Radin, M.J. (1982). "Property and Personhood", 34 *Stan. L. Rev.* 957

Schnably, J. (1993). "Property and Pragmatism: A Critique of Radin's Theory of Property and Personhood", 45 *Stan L. Rev.* 347.

WTO (2003), WTO News, Press Release 350, 30 August 2003, "Decision removes final patent obstacle to cheap drug imports"; E. Becker, "In Reversal, U.S. Nears Deal on Drugs for Poor Countries", *The New York Times*, August 28, 2003.

Yen, A. (1990). "Restoring the Natural Law: Copyright as Labor and Possession", 51 *Ohio St. L. J.* 517.

Zittrain, J. (2002). "Calling off the copyright war", *The Boston Globe*, November 24, 2002.

PART VII

Knowledge Discovery

KNOWLEDGE SHARING OVER P2P KNOWLEDGE NETWORKS: A PEER ONTOLOGY AND SEMANTIC OVERLAY DRIVEN APPROACH

SYED SIBTE RAZA ABIDI[†] & XIAOLIN PANG

Faculty of Computer Science, Dalhousie University
Halifax, Nova Scotia, B3H 1W5, Canada

Effective knowledge sharing between communities of knowledge workers impacts the productivity, innovation and competitiveness of organizations. The emergence of Peer-to-peer (P2P) technology has provided some solutions to knowledge sharing amongst peers. In this paper we present a sophisticated *Agent-based Semantic Knowledge network*—ASKnet—that features a unique combination of mobile agents, semantic web and semantic overlay networks to realize an effective knowledge sharing environment. ASKnet enables the sharing of personalized knowledge repositories—typically documents thematically organized by a knowledge worker—of individual knowledge workers with the entire community. The premise here is that if we trust the intellectual ability of the knowledge worker then his/her personalized knowledge repository can be regarded as a source of *best-quality*, *relevant* and *validated* knowledge for that domain/organization.

1   Introduction

The prevailing 'knowledge age' or 'knowledge economy' places a premium on the collective knowledge owned and managed by organizations. Knowledge is perceived as a commodity and its flow across the organization—in order to effectuate innovation, competitive advantage, organizational learning and improved productivity—is deemed as an important factor in the sustainability of the so-called knowledge economy (Zack 1999). In fact, Nonaka argues that "in an economy where the only certainty is uncertainty, the one sure source of lasting competitive advantage is knowledge" (Nonaka 1998). For that matter, organizations nowadays are formulating well-defined knowledge management policies that extend beyond the traditional knowledge management activities involving the acquisition and storage of in-house knowledge. The current knowledge management themes focus on the pragmatic effects of knowledge sharing and re-use by knowledge workers (Liebowitz 2000). Our research investigates the formulation of technology-mediated knowledge management solutions for effective knowledge sharing within a community of knowledge workers.

Knowledge sharing entails both knowledge creation and knowledge reuse; in fact these two activities are not orthogonal, as new knowledge builds on the re-use of existing knowledge. Knowledge sharing involves three main activities: (i) location of relevant explicit knowledge; (ii) selection of relevant/significant knowledge; and (iii) application of the knowledge in a particular context.

[†] Work supported by the Canadian NSERC grant # 262072 – 03.

From a knowledge sharing perspective, the notion of a community of practice (Wenger and Snyder 2000), or as we say *community of knowledge workers*, is of significant relevance. In principle, community of practice is an informal group of workers that are bound together by a shared interest, knowledge or enterprise—essentially peers involved in the execution of a common objective. Advances in communication technology has allowed the members of community of practice to be geographically dispersed yet virtually accessible—Internet mediated discussion forums are a case in point. Through collaboration a community of practice not only fosters knowledge sharing and community-wide learning, but it also leads to the 'creation' of new knowledge and 'validation' of existing knowledge/viewpoints/practices/beliefs. Hence, it is fair to state that a community of knowledge workers in itself is a knowledge resource.

In a knowledge sharing parlance, our work focuses on enabling the sharing of private knowledge repositories—i.e. the private collection of specialized documents thematically organized by a knowledge worker—of individual knowledge workers within the entire community. The premise here is that knowledge workers whilst discharging their duties progressively collect and maintain a private knowledge repository that comprises knowledge-rich documents (i.e. research papers, reports, electronic books, notes, guidelines, learning modules, presentations etc) spanning multiple subjects of interest and collected from respectable sources. If we trust the intellectual ability of the knowledge worker then his/her private knowledge repository can be regarded as a source of *high-quality*, *specialized* and *validated* knowledge. Given the escalation in the volume of dispensable knowledge and the proliferation of knowledge dissemination web-sites there is always a question mark on the quality and validity of the available knowledge content. Furthermore there are noted problems of identification, selection and evaluation of the available knowledge (typically over the WWW). In this scenario, we argue that leveraging the private knowledge repository of a 'trusted' knowledge worker's (provided the said knowledge worker allows access to it) can alleviate the problem of knowledge identification, selection and validation; in fact it could serve as the initial point of search for high-quality knowledge. We foresee that an interconnected and ubiquitous collection of private knowledge repositories of a community of knowledge workers can be regarded as *validated* domain knowledge—akin to the intellectual capital of an organization (Liebowitz 2000). We believe that a network of private knowledge repositories can not only serve as a meta-knowledge resource but also act as a vital collaborative learning and innovation medium for the entire community of knowledge workers.

In this paper we focus on the networking aspect of knowledge sharing within a community of knowledge workers. We present a knowledge sharing framework that interconnects the private knowledge repositories of participating knowledge workers using peer-to-peer (P2P) communication technology. P2P technology is being used for sharing digital resources and services between participating peers—i.e. computers, wireless devices and PDAs. However, the existing P2P based knowledge sharing initiatives exhibit certain limitations, such as (a) coarse granularity of knowledge sharing (i.e. only file-sharing) is provided without considering the content of the file; (b) Peer's neighbors are pre-defined and cannot be changed dynamically according to the relativity of shared knowledge on different nodes; (c) no support for semantic interoperability between the peer's indexing of documents; and (d) inability to scale-up a to larger set of documents. In our P2P knowledge sharing solution we:

- Incorporate notions of semantic web with the P2P knowledge network in an attempt to overcome the heterogeneity present in the different private knowledge resources available within the knowledge network. The use of two ontologies—a domain ontology defining the domain and a peer ontology defining the characteristics of peers—allows the conceptualization of both knowledge content and peers. It may be noted that current knowledge sharing over P2P networks do not adequately account for semantic relationships amongst resources. In our case, we use the semantic web technology to overcome this limitation and in turn provide content-based knowledge search and a mechanism for establishing agreements between knowledge searching mobile agents.
- Integrate mobile agent technology within the P2P based knowledge network to facilitate the automatic search for relevant knowledge across the knowledge network. Our mobile agents are designed to perform various knowledge search and collection tasks on behalf of users (Wang *et al.* 2001).
- Formulate a *Semantic Addressable Overlay* network to support the automatic identification of relevant peers (across the P2P knowledge network) based on their profiles and on the content of their knowledge repositories.

Figure 1 illustrates a P2P knowledge network from a peer's point of view.

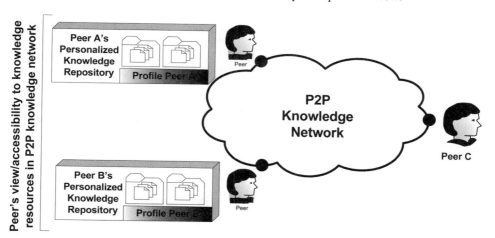

Figure 1. A P2P based knowledge network

2   Background

P2P technology is rapidly emerging as a potential solution for sharing of digital content over the Internet. P2P systems can be classified into two distinct categories according to their architectures. Category 1 is the "pure" P2P architecture (as shown in Figure 1), which consists of peers that have equal responsibility and capability, and may join or leave the network at any time, thus eliminating the need for a centralized server. Peers dynamically discover other peers on the network and interact with each other by sending and receiving messages. Category 2 is the "server-mediated" P2P architecture—also termed as hybrid systems. In this architecture, the central server is responsible for peer discovery and information search as it maintains a registry of shared information about peers. For instance, if peer A is looking for a file it sends a request to the central server. The central server replies to peer A with a set of peers who possess this requested file. Subsequently, Peer A directly interacts with the candidate peers to retrieve the file. In short, P2P technology realizes a de-centralized computer network architecture between 'willing' computers.

With regards to knowledge sharing, a general framework for ontology-based knowledge sharing in P2P systems, called *Helios*, was proposed by Castano *et al.* (2003a). Most significantly, Helios features a peer ontology (Castono *et al.* 2003b) that characterizes the different types and attributes of peers sharing knowledge. Interactions amongst peers, knowledge search and knowledge acquisition/extension are supported by pre-defined query models and semantic techniques for ontology matching.

Subsequently, by combing a communication infrastructure layer (called Hermes) with Helios's knowledge infrastructure layer an enhanced knowledge sharing framework, called H3, was presented by Castano *et al.* (2003c). H3 proposes to build an overlay network among peers in which each peer maintains a peer ontology describing its knowledge of the network. For query routing, the topology of the overlay network mirrors the semantic neighborhood of the peers given by the semantic relationships among the ontologies they own. This approach allows peers to dynamically join communities of interest and to share their knowledge without regard to physical network neighborhood constraints imposed by P2P networks—in this case two peers are neighbors if they possess similar or equivalent semantic concepts (Castano 2003d; Yang and Garcia-Molina 2003).

Nejdl *et al.* (2002) introduced Super-Peer Networks to perform effective content retrieval. In Super-Peer Networks, peers are clustered with respect to their interests, and for each cluster a Super-Peer node is designated, acting as a centralized server for queries in a cluster. Moreover, Super Peers are also connected to each other to create an overlay network.

3   Knowledge Sharing over P2P Networks

To facilitate knowledge sharing amongst a community of knowledge workers we present the design of an *Agent-based Semantic Knowledge network* (or ASKnet) that creates and manages a P2P knowledge network for sharing the private knowledge repositories of a community of knowledge workers. ASKnet is an extension to existing P2P knowledge networks in that it features a novel *Semantic Overlay Network* (or SON) to characterize the semantic relationships between the knowledge available within the P2P knowledge network as shown in Figure 2. Each peer node in ASKnet consists of several components: agent management, query management, knowledge management (comprising ontology management and matching management), discovery management (including peer locating and peer routing management), as shown in Figure 2.

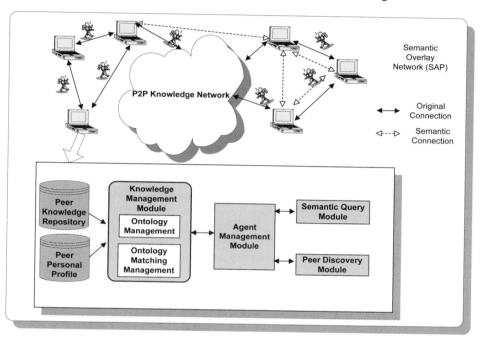

Figure 2. Functional architecture of ASKnet

We discuss ASKnet from two different views—i.e. internal and external view. The internal view refers each peer as an individual and independent unit. In this case, the corresponding knowledge management module is discussed. The external view considers peer's external operations (i.e. the interaction among peers) within the P2P knowledge network. For external view, the function of discovery management, query management, agent management will be discussed.

3.1 Peer Ontology

For knowledge sharing amongst peers we provide a peer ontology that semantically describes each peer and his/her knowledge contents. The peer ontology comprises two components: (1) a *peer personal profile* that characterizes each peer on ASKnet and (2) a *peer knowledge repository profile* that describes the content of each peer's personalized knowledge repository. Figure 3 shows a template for the peer personal profile.

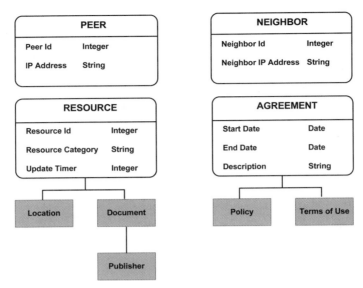

Figure 3. Template of a peer personal profile

The provision of a peer ontology enables peer-to-peer interoperability at different levels of abstraction in terms of both peer matching and subsequent knowledge sharing (Noy and McGuinness 2001). In practice, for each peer we create a peer defining ontology (using a common peer ontology template) that is made available to all other peers as an external view. We argue that by using a peer ontology we achieve the following advantages: (i) ability to share common understanding of the structure of knowledge amongst both peers and software agents; (ii) re-use of domain knowledge; (iii) making domain assumption explicit; (iv) separation of domain knowledge from the operational knowledge; and (v) clear characterization of domain knowledge.

3.2 Peer-Specific Knowledge Management

Within ASKnet the knowledge management activities associated with each peer mainly constitutes ontology management and ontology matching management.

Ontology Management Module performs the definitions and maintenance of the peer ontology. This module presents each peer's profile for an external view; provides its resource for sharing; maintains a list of neighbors; manages access constraints such as access and privacy policy.

Ontology Matching Management Module involves the comparison of a concept within a knowledge query against the peer ontology of other peers in order to match semantically related concepts within another peer's personal profile.

Ontology matching is achieved by a variety of methods that are classified along the lines of instance vs. schema; element vs. structure matching; language vs. constraint; matching cardinality; auxiliary information and so on (Erhard and Bernstein 2001). We note that existing ontology matching methods do not support instance-level matching. In our solution, ontology matching is achieved via both structure level and instance level matching.

3.3 *Semantic Addressable Overlay Network (SON)*

We have developed a *Semantic Addressable Overlay Network* (SON) to support semantically-driven knowledge search across ASKnet. SAP characterizes the peer neighborhood in a semantic way to ensure that peers with similar interest are grouped together according to their personal profiles.

Our approach builds on the notion of Content Addressable Network (CAN) proposed by Ratnasamy *et al.* (2001) that dynamically partitions a virtual d-dimensional Cartesian space into zones and assigns each zone to a peer node. In a CAN the space is used for logically representing the index of shared documents (points). Routing is conducted from one zone to another in the Cartesian space. When a node joins the network, it randomly selects a point in the Cartesian space and migrates to the zone that contains the point, and splits the zone with its current peers.

We have developed and incorporated a SON that models a virtual d-dimensional Cartesian space to logically store the index of each peer's knowledge, where each index is positioned as a point in the space. The indices of peer knowledge are created by a hash function, which is denoted as (key, value) pairs, and each node stores a chunk (called a zone) of the entire hash table. In addition, a node keeps information about a small number of "adjacent" zones in the table. The semantic vector of each peer's ontology is generated as the key. To store a pair (K, V), key K is deterministically mapped onto a point P in the coordinate space. The corresponding (key, value) pair is then stored at the node that owns the zone within which the point P lies. To retrieve an entry corresponding to key K, any node can apply the same deterministic hash function to map K onto point P and then retrieve the corresponding value from the point P. If the point P is not owned by the requesting node or its immediate neighbors, the request is routed from one zone to another until it reaches the node in whose zone P lies.

Functionally speaking, SON mirrors the semantic neighborhood of the peers by providing the semantic relationships among the ontologies they own. SAP creates indices for peer ontology description and distributes them to different peer, which is replicated by several of its neighbors in case of failure by one peer. The main advantage of SON is that it provides the peer neighborhood in a semantic way, which means peers with similar interest are grouped together according to their indices. Furthermore, SAP ensures that isolated peer nodes do not exist and different communities are 'somehow' connected to support atypical queries.

In conventional P2P scenarios, each peer's neighborhood is statically predefined and doesn't change during run time. Whereas, two nodes are treated as neighbors if they possess similar peer knowledge in our approach. And each node's neighbor list can be changed dynamically according to the semantic measuring among peers.

Figure 4a depicts a peer's neighbors in a conventional way. Peer M is a node that request for a certain information and peer M initially has three directly connected peers - Peers A, C and N. However, only peer B and peer D contain information that match peer M's current query. Peer M will forward its request to peer A and peer C to reach peer B and D. Whereas, in our approach, Peer M can send request directly to peer B and D since they have been as its neighbours according to our established semantic overlay network, which is shown in Figure 4b.

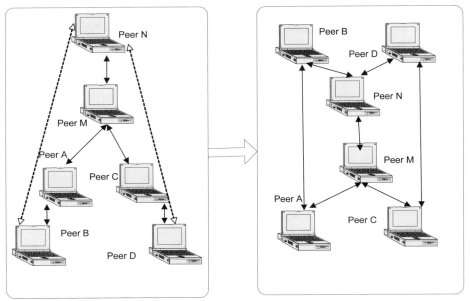

Figure 4a. Conventional Peer's neighbors   Figure 4b. Peer's semantic neighbors

The benefits of SON construction are truly reflected in the functionalities of the agent, peer discovery and query management modules that are discussed below.

3.4 Agent Management Module

The *agent management module* is responsible for the generation and dispatching of mobile agents to retrieve knowledge from their peer's private knowledge repositories. When a peer searches for a knowledge item (say a research paper), a pool of mobile agents on behalf of the asking peer are dispatched to its neighbors—the neighborhood of the asking peer is determined by SON. It may be noted that, in the absence of SON, the agents may need to search over the entire knowledge network. In our approach, the SON keeps an index of each peer's ontology description which helps in focusing the search in a smaller, yet potentially most relevant, region of the knowledge network. Each agent performs semantic matching by comparing with the other peers' ontology to find an accurate match. After the mobile agent finishes the matching task, it takes back the desired results to the asking peer for further action.

3.5 Peer Discovery Module

A P2P network can be evaluated by the quality of peer discovery, which refers to peers that each node of the network selects (Kaplan and Duchon 1998).In semantic-based P2P applications, peer discovery are more desired on the conceptual approximation between one peer with other peers in the network. In conventional P2P networks, peer discovery is conducted in a centralized manner by the use of a central index server or the request of peer discovery is flooded from peer neighbors to neighbors (Kaplan and Duchon 1998). Obviously, these approaches are not scalable and need to be improved.

Our peer discovery approach seeks semantic routing/search (as human do), by using the SON, by implementing a decentralized non-flooding P2P knowledge discovery model: no central index server is provided and peers are grouped with respect to their community of interest based on the SON. Note that SON reflects the similarity approximation between different peers over ASKnet. In practice, when a knowledge-item is needed, the request is initially routed to a group of decentralized peers possessing similar interest as the asking peer, as opposed to broadcasting the request from one peer to another.

3.6 Semantic Query Module

The *semantic query module* is used by a peer to find specific knowledge-items within the P2P knowledge network. The semantic query module is based on the SON as shown in Figure 5. Each peer's ontology is positioned as a point in the semantic space. The distance among points denotes the degree of peer interest similarity. The closer among points are, the higher similar of peers' interest and the vice versa. For instance, the points A and B are close; we say that their interest is similar. Each query can also be positioned in the semantic space. q refers as a query point in this figure. To match peer ontology relevant to a query, the searching can be performed in a small region centered at the query point since the relevance of peer ontology outside the region is a relatively low. Therefore, the search space for the query is effectively limited without affecting the accuracy of results.

In ASKnet the pSearch approach is adopted to perform the query. The search is conducted within a region which has a radius of r centred at a query point. We elucidate the process in the below discussion:

(1) When a node A joins the network, it dispatches a pool of agents to its neighbors to update its peer ontology and its neighbors generate the semantic vector V_n to use it as a key to store the index of A.

(2) When node A looks for a particular resource, a pool of mobile agents are created and dispatched to A's neighbors to send its request. When one of its neighbour,

say node *B*, receives the query, it generates semantic vector v_q of the query and routes the query in the overlay network using v_q as the key.

(3) Upon reaching the destination, the query is flooded to nodes within a radius *r*, determined by the similarity threshold or the number of wanted resources specified by the user.

(4) All nodes that receive the query do a local similarity search and agents respond the best matching resource back to the user. Some kind of matching measure is performed to locate the target concepts.

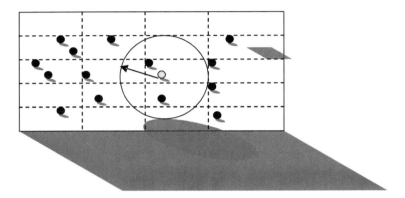

Figure 5. Semantic searching region for a semantic query

4   Concluding Remarks

Knowledge sharing networks are necessary and important in international business, R&D, management and innovation activities. However, organizations and more so knowledge workers are facing problems in identifying, selecting, operationalizing and evaluating validated knowledge resources. The emergence of P2P technology has provided some solutions to knowledge sharing amongst a community of knowledge workers.

For effective knowledge management it is therefore contingent that the knowledge sharing environment deals with the dynamic needs of knowledge workers and adapts the peer configuration accordingly. This brings to relief the need for dynamic knowledge networks that self-configure, based on the semantic content of the knowledge and the profiles of the available knowledge workers, to locate and deliver best quality and validated knowledge.

This concept paper outlines a research program for next-generation knowledge sharing vis-à-vis the incorporation of sophisticated knowledge management methods— i.e. ontologies, semantic web and mobile agents—to design an agent-based semantic knowledge network in a P2P environment. In this concept paper, some limitations on existing P2P application are investigated and the corresponding solutions are proposed: firstly, the semantic web technology as a novel paradigm is combined into P2P network, which overcome the heterogeneity of resources on the network by the use of peer ontology for knowledge conceptualization. Secondly, since mobile agent has the capability of performing operations at remote sites, mobile agent technology is integrated into P2P systems to facilitate semantic search. Thirdly, a semantic overlay network is built which provides efficient peer discovery and query processing.

In closing we will like to point out that our research aims to increase knowledge-workers' effectiveness by allowing them to share their knowledge—vis-à-vis private knowledge repositories of documents—and learn through collaboration in virtual communities.

References

Castano, S., Ferrara, A., Montanelli, S., Zucchelli, D. (2003a) "Helios: A General Framework for Ontology-Based Knowledge Sharing and Evolution in P2P Systems". *Proceeding of the 14th International Workshop on Database and Expert Systems Applications (DEXA '03).*

Castano, S., Ferrara, A., Montanelli, S. (2003b) "H-MATCH: an Algorithm for Dynamically Matching Ontologies in Peer-based Systems." *Proc. of the 1st Int. Workshop on Semantic Web and Databases (SWDB) at VLDB 2003*

Castano, S., Ferrara, A., Montanelli, S. (2003c) "Ontologies and Matching Techniques for Peer-based Knowledge Sharing". *Proc. of the 15th Conference on Advanced Information Systems Engineering (CAISE 2003).*

Castano, S., Ferrara, A., Montanelli, S., Pagani, E., Rossi, G.P. (2003d) "Ontology addressable contents in P2P networks." *Proc. of WWW '03 1st SemPGRID Workshop,* Budapest.

Erhard, R., Bernstein, P.A. (2001) 'A survey of approaches to automatic schema matching". *VLDB Journal,* 10, 334-350

Liebowitz, J. (2000) "Building organizational intelligence: A knowledge management primer". Boca Raton:CRC Press.

Kaplan, B., Duchon, D. (1998) "Combining qualitative and quantitative methods in information systems research: A case study". *Management Information Systems Quarterly,* 12, 571-586.

Nejdl *et al.* (2002) "EDUTELLA: a P2P networking infrastructure based on RDF". *Proc. of the International World Wide Web Conference 2002 (WWW2002),* Honolulu, Hawaii.

Nonaka, I. (1998) 'The Knowledge-Creating Company". *Harvard Business Review on Knowledge Management,* Harvard Business School Publishing, Boston.

Noy, N., McGuinness, D. (2001) "Ontologies Development 101: A Guide to Creating your First Ontology". *Stanford Knowledge Systems Laboratory Technical Report KSL-01-05 and SMI-2001-0880.*

Ratnasamy, S., Francis, P., Handley, M., Karp, R., Shenker, S. (2001) "A scalable content-addressable network". *ACM SIGCOMM '01.*

Wang, Y., Tan, K.L., Ren, J., Pang, X.L. (2001) "An agent-mediated, secure and efficient Internet marketplace", *Proc. of the 4th International Conference on Electronic Commerce Research (ICECR-4),* Dallas.

Wenger, E.C., Snyder, W.M. (2000) "Communities of practice: The organizational frontier". *Harvard Business Review,* 78, 139-145

Yang, B., Garcia-Molina, H. (2003) "Designing a super-peer network'. *Proc. of the International Conference on Data Engineering,* Bangalore, India.

Zack, M.H. (1999) "Developing a Knowledge Strategy". *California Management Review,* 41, 125-146.

ASSESSING THE MICROECONOMIC FACET OF ASSOCIATION RULES VIA AN EFFICIENT WEIGHTING SCHEME

IOANNIS N. KOURIS, CHRISTOS H. MAKRIS & ATHANASIOS K. TSAKALIDIS

University of Patras, School of Computer Engineering and Informatics,
26500 Patras, Hellas (Greece)

and

Computer Technology Institute, P.O. BOX 1192, 26110 Patras, Hellas (Greece)
{jkouris, makri, tsak} @ceid.upatras.gr

Most algorithms and approaches dealing with the task of association rule mining have assumed all itemsets to be of the same nature and importance and used a single support. Very few have tried to address the non-uniformity and non-homogeneity of both the items and also their frequencies. Nevertheless none of the approaches that we are aware of have proposed a concrete way of identifying and assigning the correct measure of importance to every itemset; neither have they taken into consideration the framework within which a data mining activity should be viewed and implemented. In the paper we look into mining for retail organizations and view itemsets and associations rules through the appropriate microeconomic framework. We propose a weighting scheme that assigns the correct supports to all itemsets, automatically finds the most interesting ones and yet proves very efficient.

1   Introduction

Since its first introduction by Agrawal *et al.* (1993) the task of association rule mining has been one of the most popular and well-studied applications in data mining. The goal of this task is to find all frequent itemsets above a user specified threshold (called support) and to generate all association rules above another threshold (called confidence) using these frequent itemsets as input. More formally let I={i1,i2,...,Im} be a set of literals called items. Let D be a set of transactions, where each transaction T is a variable length set of items such that $T \subseteq I$. An association rule is an implication of the form $X \Rightarrow Y$, where $X, Y \subset I$, and $X \cap Y = \emptyset$. The rule $X \Rightarrow Y$ holds in the transaction set D with confidence c if c% of transactions in D that contain X also contain Y. The rule $X \Rightarrow Y$ has support s in the transaction set D if s% of transactions in D contain $X \cup Y$.

The prototypical application of this task has been the market basket analysis, but the specific model is not limited to it since it can be applied to many other domains (e.g. text documents, census data, telecommunication data, medical images etc.). All subsequent works (e.g. Brin *et al.* 1997; Park *et al.* 1995; Savasere *et al.* 1995; Toivonen 1996) tried to improve various aspects of the best-known strategy for the task of association rule mining, called Apriori (Agrawal and Srikant 1994). However most works thus far assumed all itemsets to be of the same importance and relied on the model of one single support for all itemsets in the database. In real life applications though this measure proves inefficient, since the frequency of appearances of itemsets in a database as well as the itemsets themselves are far from being uniform. For example there are many cases where non-frequent itemsets are more interesting than the frequent ones, or the nature and characteristics of the items themselves are too diverse to be dealt as a whole, like e.g. loss leaders products, highly profitable products, products that are in the process of market testing etc. Kotler (2000).

Various approaches and algorithms have been proposed to deal with this problem (Lee at al. 1998; Han and Fu 1995; Srikant and Agrawal 1995; Kim 1990) with the best solution in our opinion being the work by Liu *et al.* (1999). The performance of this work was improved by Kouris *et al.* (2003), but the main idea remained the same. Despite its advantages the approach of Liu *et al.* (1999) suffers too from serious drawbacks such as the support values assigned to all the items or the procedure used for assigning these values. What's most important though is that this as well as all other approaches did not suggest which itemsets should be considered as important nor proposed a way of automatically identifying them.

In this paper we propose and examine a weighting scheme that assigns the correct support value to every itemset in the database automatically. The whole procedure follows a self regulatory logic, where the data miner does not have to define something but rather lets the itemsets assume their own support value according to a series of factors such as their appearances in the database as well as the appearances of all other itemsets. The final approach proves more efficient in terms of the generated suggestions. The rest of this paper is organized as follows. In section 2 we give a brief description of the most relevant previous works. In section 3 we give a description of the problem solved and in section 4 we present the solution we propose. In section 5 we present the experimental results of evaluating our approach and we conclude with section 6 where we summarize the main results of this work and give some future directions.

2 Related Works

2.1 Algorithm MSApriori

To encompass the importance of data, Algorithm MSApriori employs minimum item support (MIS), the minimum support of each data item. A very important itemset will enjoy a small MIS value while an unimportant one a large value. That way we try to make sure that important itemsets will be identified irrespectively what their frequency is as compared to the frequencies of other itemsets in the database. The MIS for every 1-itemset i is expressed as MIS (i), and is calculated using the following formula:

$$MIS(i) = \begin{cases} M(i) & M(i) > LS \\ LS & Otherwise \end{cases}$$

Equation 1

$$M(i) = \beta \cdot f(i)$$

Where f(i) is the actual frequency of an item in the dataset, LS is a user defined lowest minimum item support allowed and β is a parameter that controls how the MIS values should be related to their frequencies. Algorithm MSApriori also works level-wise, i.e. by finding the frequent itemsets at every step then using these frequent itemsets to generate the candidate itemsets of the next step, finding the frequent ones and so on. All higher order itemsets now (i.e. k-itemsets, where k>1) take as MIS value the least MIS value among the MIS values of the data items that compose an itemset. Namely, the minimum support for itemset $I_{1,2,...,m}$ is equal to min[MIS(I_1), MIS(I_2),...MIS(I_m)]. So if all items within an itemset occur frequently then a high MIS value will be assigned while if there exists even one 1-itemset that occurs rarely then a low MIS value will be assigned so that the rules corresponding to that itemset will be found. Of course assigning every itemset a different MIS value means that the downward closure property that prunes itemsets in the single support algorithms no longer holds. This problem is nevertheless solved by introducing and using the sorted closure property, where the 1-items are sorted according to their MIS values in ascending order and also all items within every itemset are sorted according to their MIS values.

MSApriori successfully addresses the problem of having mixed rare and frequent important itemsets in a database, but rather leaves a very important prerequisite parameter blank. More specifically it does not answer the question of how should these itemsets be identified and what would be the best MIS value assigned to them. According to Liu *et al.* (1999) a user has two options for assigning MIS values to the data. The first option is by using Equation 1. But if parameter β in the specific equation is set equal to 0 then algorithm MSApriori decays to any algorithm using a single support value. If on the other hand β is set close to 1, every itemset with number of appearances above the user specified lowest minimum support – LS, is considered as significant and is taken into account with all other itemsets practically discarded (since they cannot possibly be large). Consequently, in both cases the specified algorithm works similar to any algorithm using a single support with the only difference in the later case where every itemset with count above the lowest minimum support has its own MIS value. Practically all itemsets are considered of the same importance, with the only thing distinguishing them being their number of appearances. Whether an itemset should receive some extra attention is not taken into account in any way. In essence the rules created by that option are determined based on parameter β rather than on the frequency of every itemset. The other option now for assigning MIS values to all 1-itemsets without using the formulas described above would be simply by guessing them. Of course if one is not satisfied with the final output he would have to run again and again the algorithm, guessing each time new MIS values until he is finally satisfied, thus wasting both time and resources. In any case though there is not proposed some method to discover the rare but important itemsets.

3 Assessing the Microeconomic Facet of Association Rules

3.1 Problem statement

Association rule mining algorithms mine the database with a fixed minimum support value for all itemsets (or with different but also fixed minimum support values for every itemset in the case of algorithm MSApriori). Essentially they work on the assumption that the correct support value is already known. In practice though the correct minimum support value is not known and can only be estimated based on domain knowledge or on previous experience. Also when talking about the "correct" value, this is determined based on the number of discovered frequent itemsets (i.e. too few or too many itemsets as compared to what has been anticipated), or in other words only through completely subjective and rather trivial criteria. Consequently if the support threshold changes, then the mining process has to repeated from the beginning requiring at least the same number of passes over the database as the previous run (if the new threshold is lower than before), and what's most important without being able to use knowledge from previous runs of the same algorithm. Especially in the case when we must assign every itemset a different support value, managing all these itemsets becomes a very daunting task. So we are talking about an iterative process, where the minimum support value needs fine-tuning which can only be achieved through multiple complete runs of an association rule mining algorithm.

Going through the whole database multiple times and searching and counting all possible combinations of items may not be as practical as it seems, especially in real life applications or for data other than that used for classic market basket analysis (e.g. highly correlated data like census data or data with multiple non-binary attributes). As an example the Cover Type dataset from UCI repository[1] with only 120 1-itemsets, but with most of them appearing almost all the time, results in about 15 million large itemsets. Using algorithm Apriori just to find all these large itemsets requires more than 96 CPU hours (Webb 2000). Or in large real life businesses such as Walmart, Amazon, or UPS with databases reaching Terabytes, with hundreds of thousands of distinct itemsets and with several tenths of items in each transaction, then traversing the database even once requires immense resources. So, the whole process of assigning support values to all the itemsets in a database has to be as accurate as possible in order to avoid unnecessary runs of the same algorithm over the data.

What's most important though is the fact that current techniques for determining the support of an itemset take no provision in the business value of itemsets and the associations between them (Cabena *et al.* 1997), and as a consequence the support assigned does not reflect the real value of the itemsets. This has as an effect the homogenization of all itemsets in any dataset, or in other words the sale of a can of expensive caviar is treated in much the same way as the sale of a packet of chewing gums. According to Kleinberg *et al.* (1998), "*a pattern in the data is interesting only to*

---

[1] http://kdd.ics.uci.edu/

the extent in which it can be used in the decision-making process of the enterprise to increase utility". So the utility of extracted patterns (such as association rules and correlations) in the decision-making process of an enterprise can only be addressed within the microeconomic framework of the environment they are operating in. But before even coming up with patterns, the same provision must be made also for the itemsets themselves which are the basic component of patterns (i.e. the business value of the itemsets must also be taken into account when finding frequent itemsets). The way current algorithms treat itemsets as mere statistical probabilities and as Boolean variables is rather a simplification of a complex problem, that needs to be addressed differently.

In our work we take all the afore-mentioned requirements into consideration and address them in a simple (but not naïve) and general framework. Subsequently we propose an alternative for finding the frequent itemsets in a database, whose main feature is an efficient weighting scheme.

3.2 Our weighted approach

As mentioned above our approach works on the same logic as the traditional association rules algorithms, i.e. by finding all frequent itemsets using multiple minimum support values (like algorithm MSApriori) and then by generating the corresponding association rules. The cornerstone of our approach is the weighting scheme it uses since this allows it to take into consideration the dissimilarities among the itemsets as well as the special conditions of the environment we are operating in. In this work we will be concerned only with one application. More specifically we will propose a weighting scheme specially tailored for the case of a retail store and so we will focus entirely on the microeconomic side of the itemsets. Nevertheless the philosophy and the logic of our approach could be used with little modifications in all kinds of businesses and applications.

So when developing our weighting scheme the first task was to identify and select the factors and their corresponding parameters, which are most important and present the greatest influence in determining the significance of an itemset. We concluded in the following three factors:

(1) What are net profits of an itemset compared to the average net profits from all itemsets in a dataset?
(2) What are the total sales of an itemset compared to the average total sales from all itemsets?
(3) What is the number of transactions an itemset appears in compared to the average number of transactions all itemsets appear in.

In the calculation of every factor we used the average rather than the minimum numbers, cause in such databases the values of these factors present very high deviations and we would probably get a contradicting scheme[2]. The first factor is fairly straightforward since the simplest and more accurate measure of importance of an itemset in a retail store is the net profits it presents. Care must be taken with this factor not to use the sale price, since this does not necessarily reflect its true business value (i.e. an expensive product can present very low net profits for a company and the inverse). The second factor actually links the net profits of an itemset with its presence in the database. More specifically a highly profitable itemset is important only if it has also high sales and a not so profitable itemset can be interesting provided it has large sales. Last but not least is the third factor that has to do with the actual presence of an itemset in the database. The fact that an itemset appears many times in a database is indeed important but it is most important viewed from the point of view of the number of transactions it appears in. In other words the more transactions an itemset appears in the more important it should be considered, since statistically it presents more probabilities to be bought again. In order to quantify these three factors, some parameters need to be known. More specifically we need to have values about the following parameters:

(1) In how many transactions does an itemset appear, noted as Ti.

(2) What is the average number of transactions all itemsets appear in, noted as $\overline{T}_{total}$
(3) How many times does an itemset appear in general, noted as Si.

(4) What is the average number of appearances of all itemsets, noted as $\overline{S}_{total}$
(5) What is the net profit per itemset, noted as Ni.

(6) What is the average net profit from all itemsets, noted as $\overline{N}_{total}$.
(7) How many transactions are there in general, noted as Ttotal.

The next step was to combine all these factors along with their parameters in one equation that would give us the weight of every itemset. Our intuition for finding that function was quite simple. Every itemset can have support at maximum: $\max \sup(i) = T_i / T_{total}$. The closest we set the support of an itemset to its maximum support, the more appearances there are needed in order for it to quantify as a frequent itemset and the less important it is considered. Practically if we set the support of an itemset equal to maxsup(i) it is like eliminating it from further consideration cause then it is required that it appears at a percentage of 100% with any other itemset (which is practically very difficult). The lower we set the support from the value of maxsup(i), the less appearances there are needed for an itemset to quantify as frequent and so the more important we consider it. So after having run many experiments with different forms of equations we concluded in the following form that best approaches the behavior described above:

---

[2] If one bears in mind mottos such as that of department store Harrods (http://www.harrods.com) *"from a pin to an elephant"*, it is easy to understand why prefer average values to the minimum ones.

$$wf = \log_A \left(1 + \frac{\overline{T}_{total}}{T_i} + \frac{\overline{S}_{total}}{S_i} + \frac{\overline{N}_{total}}{N_i} \right)$$

Equation 2

$$\text{where} \quad A = \max\left(1 + \frac{\overline{T}_{total}}{T_i} + \frac{\overline{S}_{total}}{S_i} + \frac{\overline{N}_{total}}{N_i} \right)$$

The logarithm in the specific equation was used in order to avoid the effect where an item with a factor twice as small as that of another one being regarded twice as important (e.g. an itemset having twice the net profits of another one being considered twice as important and getting the half weight). The main advantage of the specific equation is that it takes into consideration all three factors, and an item must have all three factors small in order to be considered as very important. It is not enough for an item to appear in many transactions, or to appear many times in total, or to have large net profits in order to get a very low support value. It is the combination of all these three factors that make it most important. Also in Equation 2 one is free to enter a different degree of influence to every factor he decides to. For example if a company is more interested in increasing its market share (i.e. its actual sales) rather than its net profits it could boost the effect of the factor $\overline{S}_{total}/S_i$ by multiplying it with a constant positive value bellow one. Also the specific equation allows the introduction of any new factor a user considers important. After having found the weight of every item, the final step is to assign a support according to the following formula: $sup(i) = wf * \max sup(i)$.

3.2.1 Interest margin

Up to now our approach considers all 1-items as important, and does not eliminate any of them. We noted before that the higher we set the support of an itemset to its maximum support, the less important it is considered, and if we set its support to 100% of its maximum support it is like eliminating it from the next passes. Nevertheless at least for the second pass a very big number of candidate itemsets would have to be counted (in fact all possible candidate 2-itemsets), despite the fact that at the end of this pass only very few will qualify as big. If the number of 1-itemsets is fairly low then not eliminating any itemsets does not create any serious problem. But if the number of 1-itemsets is quite big this leads to a very big amount of candidate 2-itemsets that might finally act as a bottleneck to the whole process[3]. In practice only itemsets that have a low weight value are important, and should be included in the next passes of our approach. So in order to eliminate some not interesting items from further consideration we introduce the interest margin. The interest margin is a measure of importance of the itemsets, a user defined value above which any itemset is not interesting. For example if we set the interest margin to 80%, then any itemset having a value of w_f above 80% is considered

---

[3] According to Park *et al.* (1995) the first candidate sets of itemsets, with most important that of 2-itemsets are key to the performance of a data mining algorithm.

unimportant and is discarded. The choice of the specific value depends upon the application and the user is free to adjust this value to his needs. Also he can adjust different values for the interest margin for different products or for even for whole families of products. The difference of this value which also comes as it greatest advantage from measures like the minimum support, is the fact that it is computed in relation to the weight of every itemset rather than as a global value that ignores the peculiarity of every itemset.

4   Experimental Results

The best way that we could think of for comparing the performance of our approach with all other approaches in terms of quality is to check the final net profits it produces. As noted before the utility of association rules (or any other pattern being extracted) in the decision-making process of an enterprise can only be addressed within the microeconomic framework of the enterprise or the application we are operating in. So in our case there is no clearer yardstick for the correctness and the value of the suggestions made by our approach than the net profits it finally manages to produce.

Consequently we decided to build a web store, accessible through the internet and to let users make some buys. For the specific test we used a number of human subjects divided into four sets. All sets consisted of people in the age of 18 to 25 years old, all studying at the same university and at the same department. All of them were technology savvy quite familiar with the computers and the Internet. We chose to build a fictitious web store selling cell phones and accessories. The products, their names and the prices used in our web store were all real. The reason we chose the specific product was because the people in our test audience had a cell phone and/or have visited a store selling them at a percentage almost 100%.

Consequently the test was implemented as follows. We let the first set of people make some buys from the store so that we could sum up enough data. The specific buys were made without making any products recommendations to the users at all. Then we had the other three sets of people making buys with recommendations made using a different system. More specifically the first set of people got recommendations from algorithm Apriori, the second from algorithm MSApriori and the third from our approach. The users were unaware of the system used, as well as the subject of our experiment so that they would make all buys uninfluenced. They only knew that they would have to make some buys, and that they had a specific amount of money to spend every time as well as in total.

The goal was to check after having summed up a number of sales, which solution would generate the largest net profits. The outcome was that the solution that suggested itemsets to the users by using algorithm MSApriori presented practically the same net profits as algorithm Apriori. Our approach on the other hand managed to increase the net profits by a percentage of almost 10% and so we can conclude that our system indeed provides better suggestions to its users, since our main objective of increasing the net profits was accomplished.

5   Conclusions and Future Work

We have proposed a weighting scheme in order to take into consideration the special characteristics every itemset carries and to address them through the exact environment that such an approach is implemented. The outcome was an approach that indeed produces better recommendations to the users, and manages to increase the net profits as compared to the traditional approaches. Maybe the most important conclusion of our approach is that an expensive or a very frequent itemset does not present higher business value and opportunities than a cheap or an infrequent one. It is the identification and the combination of all parameters that influence the significance of an itemset that make it more or less important than the other itemsets in a database. Also we have managed to address a problem ignored by all approaches thus far, that of assigning the correct support values or generally any other measure of importance to every itemset in a database and not regarding these values as already known.

Despite the fact that our approach was tested in a comparably very small and artificial environment we nevertheless have strong indications that it accomplishes its purposes based on the outcome of our experiment. In the future we would like to test our approach in a real enterprise, with all kinds of products and far more customers that would actually spend their own real money to buy products. However this option appears highly improbable if we take into consideration the reluctance we faced mainly due to legal as well as to competition and confidentiality considerations, in our current attempts to apply our technique in a real enterprise.

Acknowledgments

Work of the first author (Mr. Kouris Ioannis) was supported by the European Social Fund (ESF), Operational Program for Educational and Vocational Training II (EPEAEK II) - IRAKLEITOS Program.

References

Agrawal, R., Imielinski, T. and Swami A. (1993) "Mining Association Rules between Sets of Items in Large Databases." In Proceedings of ACM SIGMOD Conference, pp. 207-216, Washington, D.C., USA.

Agrawal, R. and Srikant, S. (1994) "Fast Algorithms for Mining Generalized Association Rules." In Proceedings of the 20th VLDB Conference, pp. 487-499, Santiago, Chile.

Brin, S., Motwani, R, Ullman, J.D. and Tsur, S. (1997) "Dynamic itemset counting and implication rules for market basket data. In Proceedings of ACM SIGMOD Conference, pp. 255-264, Tucson, Arizona, USA.

Cabena, P., Hadjinian, P., Stadler, R., Verhess, J. and Zanasi, A. (1997). *Discovering data mining: from concept to implementation.* NJ: Prentice Hall.

Han, J. and Fu, Y. (1995) "Discovery of multiple-level association rules from large databases." In Proceedings of 21st VLDB Conference, Zurich, Switzerland, pp. 420-431.

Kim, W. (1990) *Introduction to Object-Oriented Databases.* The MIT Press, Cambridge, Massachusetts.

Kleinberg, J., Papadimitriou, C. and Raghavan, P. (1998) "A microeconomic view of data mining." In Data Mining and Knowledge Discovery Journal, 2(4): 311-324.

Kotler, P. (2000) *Marketing Management.* Tenth Edition, Prentice Hall, Upper Saddle River, New Jersey.

Kouris, I. N., Makris, C.H. and Tsakalidis A. K. (2003) "An Improved Algorithm for Mining Association Rules using multiple support values." In Proceedings of FLAIRS Conference, St. Augustine, Florida, USA.

Lee, W., Stolfo, S. J. and Mok, K. W. (1998) "Mining audit data to built intrusion detection models." In Proceedings of ACM SIGKDD Conference, New York, USA.

Liu, B., Hsu, W. and Ma Y. (1999) "Mining Association Rules with Multiple Minimum Supports." In Proceedings of ACM SIGKDD Conference, pp. 337-341, San Diego, CA, USA.

Park, J.-S., Chen, M.-S. and Yu, P.S. (1995) "An effective hash based algorithm for mining association rules." In Proceedings of the ACM SIGMOD Conference, pp. 175-186, San Jose, CA.

Savasere, A., Omiecinski, E., and Navathe S. (1995) "An efficient algorithm for mining association rules in large databases." In Proceedings of the 21st VLDB Conference, pp. 432-443, Zurich, Switzerland.

Srikant, R. and Agrawal R. (1995) "Mining Generalized Association Rules." In Proceedings 21st VLDB Conference, pp. 407-419, Zurich, Switzerland.

Toivonen, H. (1996) "Sampling large databases for finding association rules." In Proceedings of the 22nd VLDB Conference, pp. 134-145, Mumbay, India.

Webb, G. I. (2000) "Efficient search for association rules." In Proceedings of the 6th ACM SIGKDD, pp. 99-107, Boston, MA, USA.

A STUDY OF THE "MULTI-AGENT BASED USER ACCESS AND CORRELATED PATTERN IN OPTIMAL CONTENT ALLOCATION METHOD FOR FEDERATED VIDEO DIGITAL LIBRARIES"

R. PONNUSAMY

Dept. of Computer Science & Engg. Anna, University, Chennai – 600 025 &
Dept. of Computer Science & Engg,A.A.M.Engg. College, Kovilvenni – 614403 Tamilnadu India.

T.V. GOPAL

Dept. of Computer Science & Engg. , Anna, University
Chennai – 600 025, Tamilnadu,, India.

Digital libraries are emerging technologies for content management. These contents include multimedia and video objects which involve high storage and bandwidth costs. It is necessary to formulate a new method by taking into account all aspects of multimedia and video-on-demand content management. This paper describes a new approach called the "multi-agent based user access pattern oriented optimal content allocation method" for digital libraries and is concerned with various behavioral patterns of digital library systems. The content access pattern not only varies based on regional interest, subject interest, cultural interest etc. but also over time because of the movement of various user communities. A mathematical technique is adopted in finding the intra-correlation between different languages and regions among the number of individuals in any region who access any language at any time based upon the unit bandwidth cost, storage cost and delay time cost for the additional requirement of bandwidth. The suggested model proves to be a more cost-effective method with regard to the design for dynamic content allocation when compared with other mathematical models for content allocation available in literature.

1 Introduction

Digital libraries are modern social virtual institutions for information collection, preservation and dissemination. The design and development of digital library requires that many issues be addressed (Andreson; Fellner; Frew 2002; Mazurek; Chellappa; Jhao 1999) and it must be able to perform intelligent human-oriented tasks in order to make it highly sophisticated and effective. Content storage management is one of the important issues which decide the fast and economical retrieval of information in the federated or distributed digital libraries (Frew 2002; Jhaon 1999). The system design and development necessitates the need for an intelligent solution in order to address the above requirements.

The delivery of large files to individual users such as video on demand or application programs (Frew 2000; Mazurek; Chellappa; Jhao 1999; Leung *et al.* 2002; Cardellini 1999; Cidon *et al.* 2002) in the envisioned federated web enabled video digital library network is one of the important tasks to be envisaged. As the members of the libraries are scattered across the globe contributing to the unpredictable, simultaneous user requests from various regions (Leung *et al.* 2002; Teodoro *et al.*; Bestavros *et al.* 1998; Cardellini *et al.* 1999), various approaches such as replicating the information across mirrored server architecture (Cardellini *et al.* 1999) and increasing the bandwidth capacity (Leung *et al.* 2002) to provide fast and dense server capacity are implemented.

The huge rate of increase in the data necessitates the need for massive scale storage architecture at a faster rate than the growth of processor and disks. In addition, reliance on hardware improvements alone is not sufficient to keep pace with the demand for data storage.

There is another approach to reduce the bandwidth which consists in program caching (Nussbaumer *et al.* 1995). This approach is more reasonable than server replication. In this method, a number of caches are distributed throughout the network to cater to the multiple requests from its caches rather than going for individual requests. The expected competition among multi-media providers may benefit those that can provide these services at the expected quality level of service at the lowest price. For example the VOD servers, the VOD providers pay for the storage of video copies in the servers and also for using communication links for transferring information on the network to the content consumers. The video providers have to manage the storage of video copies within the servers such that the overall cost is minimized. The question is how many copies should be allocated to each video and at which server? As a consequence the researchers are motivated to focus on optimizing not only the delivery network but also electronic content allocation.

Nussbaumer *et al.* (Cidon *et al.* 2002; Mather 2001; Gavalas *et al.* 2002) introduced in 1994 (later improved on by Cidon *et al.* 2002) a hierarchical architecture which takes into account the trade-off between bandwidth and storage requirements and computed the best level of hierarchy for the server location which minimizes the combined cost of communication and storage. Since the requests are unpredictable as in real networks (Internet), the problem can be perceived as the Partially Observable Markov Decision Problem (POMDP) for determining the optimal policy. Chean (2003) had proposed another hierarchical storage system, by classifying video-objects as "so-popular" and "not-so-popular" objects according to the frequency of video object access. Here the frequently accessed "so-popular" objects are moved to secondary levels and less frequently accessed objects are stored at the root level itself.

All the above methods have not taken into account using content access semantics. In this present work, a multi-agent based user access pattern oriented optimal content allocation method for federated digital libraries is proposed which takes into account the content semantics and frequency of content access in particular region, in addition to the storage and bandwidth. Normally no guarantee can be given for frequency of content access. While considering the group of user accesses, the semantics of content access pattern can be learned using the multi-agent system. By taking the apriori information of the particular pattern for the particular period, the content is moved to the particular region. The content access will vary according to the regional, subject, cultural, research interest and so on. The cost effective method for content allocation in a dynamic environment is possible by considering the content semantics of user communities. As the number of requests for an object is unknown, it is assumed to be zero and will be stored in the root server. If it is accessed from the root then the total traffic in the system will increase unpredictably, where the number of requests increase The user access pattern learning aids in identifying the (i+1)th object pattern for allocation in the same locations, if the (i+1)th object belongs to the ith object pattern.

Brazier *et al.* (1998) has designed a dynamic electrical grid load management system for cost effective usage of electrical production. Such a system is able to do user community classification based on the negotiations between utility companies and their customers. This kind of system design needs the user content access pattern learning for adaptation because this access pattern will change dynamically over time. Whereas the electrical power produced has to be used immediately, the electronic content once it is made available can be used at any point of time and has content semantics. This paper considers the semantics of various content types, user communities, access patterns, locations and the relation between the user groups and key contents. Also in order to use the bandwidth effectively, the user must move the content to the frequently accessed area.

2   User Access Pattern Modeling

The user access pattern furnishes information that explains the essential structure of which type of contents is accessed by which regions. For a language region the user access pattern explains how the number of the ith language requests are received from the region j. The digital video-on-demand libraries are designed for various specific purposes such as movie broadcasting, tourism advertising, virtual universities, geo-referenced information system etc., wherein the contents are accessed across different parts of the world. A video digital library offers video movie services (http://www.themovies.com) to users all over the world and also movies of different countries in regional languages. Usually movies of a specific language are accessed frequently by a set of people in a specific region. However, because of transmigration people of a specific group move from one country to another country, they may have to search for the specific movies of their own language (or mother tongue). Besides this, there are people who are very specific in accessing movies of certain specific actors irrespective of their locations. Considering these factors, the static policy for content storage is not applicable and hence storing the video objects of the respective region will not always be optimal, necessitating the need for a dynamic allocation policy.

A video browsing system (Holffelder *et al.*) designed to overcome information overload has the facility to pre-select the shots of the interest and also to kept it in the buffer for effective browsing. This mechanism supports interactive multimedia browsing applications by exploiting information about the expected browsing behavior of the user, which is estimated on the basis of a rationalistic exploration strategy for the retrieval of results. There is need for a content conceptualization.

In the present design of a multi-agent system, an agent tries to fix it in every distributed server and do content conceptualization through content analysis. The content specification gives the details of content language, content style, content region, etc. The agent collects the user profile while accessing the requests. By processing the requests of every user, the agent is able to identify the region from where those requests have come. The multi-agent system formulates a pattern for that type of access and correlates the frequency of access. This system is able to identify the specific type of content which is normally accessed by users in these regional people and groups. Such a system is called the user access pattern learning which takes a very long period and also changes over time. The new movie objects are frequently uploaded into the system which is able to allocate the content in the optimal location instead of replicating the object to all servers.

Table 1. Language Profile

Language Code	Language
L001	Arabic
L002	Bulgarian
L003	Catalan
L004	Chinese
L005	Croatian
L006	Czech
L007	Danish
L008	Duch
L009	English
L010	Estonian

Table 2. Object/Content Profile

Attributes	Values
Movie Name	TITANIC
Movie Id.	M0025
Language	English
Language Id.	L009
Director Name	James Cameron
Hero Name	Leonordo DiCaptio
Heroine Name	Kate Winslet
Story Writer	James Cameron
Size	1 GB

Table 3. User Profile

Attributes	Values
User Name	James Ronold
User id.	U045
Spoken Language	English
Region	London
Region Code	R006
Address	#8, Downing St., London, UK
Gender	Male

Table 4. Language Region Patterns

Language Code	Region Code	No. of Requests / Month
L009	R009	80
L009	R010	15
L009	R011	18
L009	R012	20
L009	R006	30

Table 5. Regional Profile

Region Name	Country Name	Region Code	Region Name	Country Name	Region Code
Delhi	India	R001	NewYork	U.S.A.	R008
Chennai	India	R002	Washington	U.S.A.	R009
Mumbai	India	R003	California	U.S.A.	R010
Kolkotta	India	R004	Florida	U.S.A.	R011
Tokyo	Japan	R005	Texas	U.S.A.	R012
London	England	R006	Sydney	Australia	R013
Paris	France	R007	Moscow	Russia	R010

The user profile is collected at the first time of user request and the content profile is built at the time of up-loading the content. The content access details are collected through the user requests. Language profile and regional profile are collected and updated as and when they are required. All these profiles are shown in Tables 1 to 5.

3   The System Model

As the set of servers are located in a non-hierarchical order, there is a need for a virtual hierarchical tree T = (V, E), (V being the set of nodes and E the set of directed communication links) to represent the communication network. The hierarchical tree approach for content management permits high-level of scalability, with each node representing the server's capability of storing video objects and each server representing the agent program. The system has three types of nodes – head-end, intermediate node and root node. The head-end (switches) connects all the user nodes through a client node; and stores the video objects, depending on the user access. Each head-end has an agent program, called Head-end accessor which is responsible for storing the video objects in the head-end nodes and also performing the user classification and content access pattern learning by analyzing the user requests. It also collects the information (user profile) about the user who is accessing the object. Such types of information are forwarded to the intermediate nodes. New video objects are also up-loaded into the system through any one of these nodes, during the process of loading. It collects the information (object profile) about the object copies of these profiles are then moved to the root node.

The intermediate node stores an agent program and receives a user profile from the head-end and classifies users into different categories. Normally, the system (virtual tree) contains a number of intermediate levels. The very first (line before the head-end) and the intermediate level of nodes does the user classification and also the object profile analysis. After analysing the user content frequency access over the previous period, a pattern is formed to include the probability of user access to particular language objects by combining previous access over the particular period of time in various regions. The entire user requests, object information and object copy are moved to the root server. This model is shown in the following Figure 1. Here '*' indicates the content/object availability in the particular node.

The following model assumptions are made

(1) While satisfying the head-end's requests for object in the network, any one of the nodes on the path from the root to head-end invariably contains the object.
(2) The link capacities are sufficient to provide all types of requests for delivery of the object to all head-ends.
(3) The links are bi-directional in terms of message exchange, but necessarily distributed from root node to the leaf node for providing the objects at the head-ends.

(4) A labeling process identifies each node. The agent is capable of not only identifying each node connected to all its leaf nodes but also the number of links to which the leaf nodes are linked to the root of the tree.

(5) Each head-end represents the regional server located in different regions. (For example above Figure 1, H1 represents region 1 (R1), H2 represents region 2 (R2) and so on.

(6) The root server is initially storing the complete set of objects of all language.

(7) Generally, other relevant assumptions are made for network representations, pertaining to node linking and message receipt.

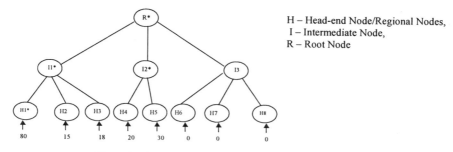

H – Head-end Node/Regional Nodes,
I – Intermediate Node,
R – Root Node

Figure 1. Hierarchical Network Object/Content Location Model

4   The Multi-Agent System Framework

In the Multi-Agent Framework every agent comprises of a single component are able to play various roles according to the place in which agent lives. The intelligent agent emits specialised behaviour for handling different tasks. Such behaviour can be modelled using role (Gottlob *et al.* 1996). Since, the agent is perceived as entity with different roles. In the current design, it is performing tasks such as (1) Head-end Accessor, (2) User Access Pattern Analyser, (3) Content Location Analyser, (4) Agent Replicater, (5) Content Allocator. The basic objective design of this system is capable to adapt any changing conditions that may occur in any part of the system in such a manner that every module is independent of each other as is shown in Figure 2. The various roles played by the agents are

i. Head-End Accessor: This task is equipped with a browser style GUI, which is able to collect the user semantic information about the content request with the user profile (if he has not been profiled earlier) and subsequently the user is classified in a particular category. It stores this information in the local server. This is forwarded to the immediate ancestor. The location of the user is also identified by the system by fetching the IP address of the user access location. Also, it provides a provision to load the video objects in the system.

ii. User Access Pattern Analyser: This is a non-interactive component, which will analyses the different type of users and contents, according to the various attributes and put them in certain category. Based on the frequency of access in particular location the content access frequency is computed based on the type of content is assumed to be accessed in the particular region. This pattern of information is moved to the root node.

    iii. Content Location Analyser: This is also a non-interactive component, which will analyses regional information and compare the best level of hierarchy location for every individual pattern. It also takes into account the parameters of storage and bandwidth, apart from the access pattern of the user. It uses a distributed algorithm as given in the section 6. It also identifies the intra-correlation between languages and regions. If it finds any intra-correlation between two language and regions then it will automatically allocate the content of one language to the other related language regions. This correlation pattern identification method is explained in section 7.

    iv. Agent Replicater: This component performs the agent cloning when any one node is added, and instructs the necessary nodes to do the adjustments if any one of the components is removed.

    v. Content Allocator: For every pattern, this component performs the content allocation according to the information given by content location Analyser.

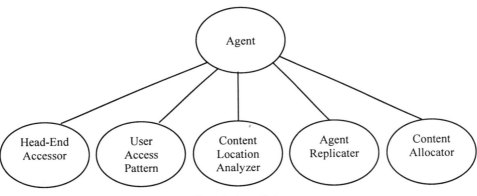

Figure 2. Agent Roles

5   Distributed Algorithm

In this system an agent fixes itself in every server and uses three different algorithms according to the location. The first algorithm is used by the head-end, second one is used by the intermediate nodes and the root server uses the third one. The agent is able to pass the computed information to the parents. In turn each of the parent nodes also passes the required information to its entire children. This agent also passes the depth of information while cloning the new server. These algorithms compute the average request service cost for storing the particular language pattern objects in the concerned nodes.

5.1 Algorithm for Head-End Node

    (1) C_{ci} - Cost of moving particular language (L_j) pattern objects from the root to the Head-end node H_i.

(2) S_{ci} - Storage Cost for the objects at node i, T_i - total number of requests at Head-end H_i for various objects of particular language (L_j) pattern, Set LOCATION = "UP".

(3) $C_i = S_{ci} + C_{ci}$

(4) Compute the average request cost at Head-end Hi (for L_j) using the following equation $C_{avg} = C_i / T_i$

(5) Communicate the average cost, depth, and number of requests to the parent node.

5.2 Algorithm for Intermediate Node

(1) C_{ri} - Cost of moving particular language (L_j) pattern objects from the root to the current node.

(2) C_{si} - Cost of serving the particular language (L_j) objects to the Head-ends.

(3) $C_{ci} = C_{ri} + C_{si}$

(4) S_{ci} - Storage Cost for the particular language (L_j) objects at the ith node, Ti- the total number of requests at Node I_{ij} from its Childs for the particular language (L_j) pattern objects. Set LOCATION = "UP"

(5) $C_i = S_{ci} + C_{ci}$

(6) Compute the average request cost at Node I_{ij} using the following equation $C_{Avg} = C_i/T_i$

(7) If any of the child's average is less than the Caver and not equal to zero then
    i. Pass the LOCATION = "HERE" to those nodes.
    ii. Drop the requests from that node, recompute the value of T_i, C_{si}, C_{Avg}

(8) Communicate the average cost, depth, and number of requests to the Parent nodes.

5.3 Algorithm for Root Node

(1) C_{si} - Cost of serving the particular language (L_j) pattern objects to the Head-ends.

(2) $C_{ci} = C_{si}$

(3) S_{ci} - Storage Cost for the particular language (L_j) pattern objects, T_i- the total number of request at root from its child for the particular language (L_j) pattern objects.

(4) $C_i = S_{ci} + C_{ci}$

(5) Compute the average request cost at root using the following equation $C_{Avg} = C_i/T_i$

(6) If any of the child's average is less than the Cavg and not equal to zero then pass the LOCATION = "HERE" to those nodes.

Notations: C_{ci} – Communication Cost for particular patterned objects at node i, C_{ri} - Cost of moving particular patterned objects from the root to the current node i, C_{si} - Cost of serving particular patterned objects to the Head-ends from the current node i S_{ci} - Storage Cost for particular patterned objects at node i, C_i – Total Cost for particular patterned at node i, C_{Avg} – Average Total Cost/Request for particular patterned objects, T_i – Total number of requests served from node i for particular patterned objects, L_j – j^{th} Language.

The content allocator is moving all the objects of the specific language pattern to all the nodes having LOCATION information "HERE".

6   Empirical modeling

Consider the ith object pattern, it has Ci as the cost element for optimal storage and communication given by.

$$C_i = S_{ci} + C_{ci} \tag{6.1}$$

The ith object may pertain language Li, (i=1,2,3, ... , n) and may spread over different regions R_j (j=1,2,3, ... , n). The first region R_1 takes x_1 number of requests for object 1, x_2 number of requests for object 2, x_3 number of requests for object 3 and so on under this category.

For example, it is known $x_1+x_2+x_3+x_4=163$ pertaining to the current (starting) month; $x_4+x_5+x_6=736$ and $x_7+x_8+x_9+x_{10}=101$ totaling 1000 requests for the required regions for different objects pertains to language L_1. The set of requests $(x_1,x_2,x_3, ... , x_n)$ is random in nature and distributed over specific types of regions needing L_1(Language 1).

The distribution of objects pertaining to Language L_2 to various regions, is assumed to take into account, the semantic aspect reveled by the requirements indicated by $(x_1, x_2,x_3, ... , x_n)$ for the current month. It may spread over different types of regions irrespective of the objects in L_1 in various regions the previous month. If the successive stage of transition from the current period to the immediate successor period follows Markov property, then the corresponding one step transition probability matrix with the transition probability.

$$þ_{jk} = P(x_n = k \mid x_{n-1} = j), n >= 1 \tag{6.2}$$

is given by $P = [þ_{ij}]$, i, j = 1,2, ... , n, such that

$$\sum_{j=1}^{n} þ_{ij} = 1 \text{ for } i=1,2,...,n \tag{6.3}$$

In terms of the conditional probability notation, the probability distribution of the language L_i to the various regions R_j is given by

$$P(L_i) = P(L_iR_1) + P(L_iR_2) + ------------- +P(L_iR_j)+----------+ P(L_iR_n)$$

Where $P(L_iR_j)=P(R_j/L_i)P(L_i)$ for i,j=1,2,3.....n. In other words, the conditional probabilities $P(R_j/L_i)$ are given by $P(L_iR_j)/ P(L_i)$ for i,j=1,2,3, ... , ,n.

Similarly the conditional probabilities of L_i with respect to R_j are given by $P(L_i/R_j)$ =$P(L_iR_j)P(R_j)$, for i,j = 1,2, ... , n. It is necessary to assume that the conditional probabilities are already known for the current month. This prior information of knowing the language L_i, access frequency at the region R_j is explained as a pattern for content allocation of new objects pertaining to language L_j. Form the given requests; the content semantics of a particular specific region for every given language is identified. Instead of storing all the objects in the root node for unknown future requests, we are moving only the particular language objects needed to the required regions. This will enable us to achieve optimal content allocation.

7 Intra-Correlation Pattern

A mathematical technique is adopted in finding the intra-correlation between different languages and regions. Assume that there are n languages L_i (i=1,2,3, ... , n) and there are n regions R_j (j=1,2,3, ... , n). Let x_{ij} denote the number of object content requests accessed by the customers (users) for the language Li in the region R_j at any point of time. (The number of request for L_i accessed by the region R_j need not be the same). This number x_{ij} takes into account the unit bandwidth cost B_{ij}, unit storage cost S_{ij} and delay time cost D_{ij} for additional bandwidth. The movie object is accessed from local/remote server, reckoned to compensate the latency that may be inherent in certain environments. Among these individual costs some of the costs may not be reckoned at all, consistent with the location, any where in the hierarchical graph tree representation. All these costs are added to constitute C_{ij} as unit cost representation for the concerned (i,j)th entry.

$$C_{ij} = B_{ij} + S_{ij} + D_{ij} \qquad (7.1)$$

where Bij and Dij become zero, if and only if Sij >=0, indicating the availability of the object at the local server (Head-end). The set of measurement x_{ij} can be represented in a bi-variate table in a matrix form [Xij], i,j=1,2, ... , n indicating $(L_i, R_j)^{th}$ measurement. From this matrix, we shall have n(n-1) pairs in the Rj region, like (x_{ij}, x_{il}), j ≠ l. There will be n.n(n-1) = N (say) enters for all the n regions. Such a table is called the intra-class correlation table and the correlation is called intra-class correlation.

As there is nothing to distinguish xij (x) from xil (y), we have

$$\bar{x}_j = \bar{y}_j = \frac{1}{n(n-1)} \sum_{i=1}^{n(n-1)} x_{ij} \qquad (7.2)$$

and
$$\sigma^2_{x_j} = \sigma^2_{y_j} = \frac{1}{n(n-1)} \sum_{i=1}^{n(n-1)} \left(x_{ij} - \bar{X}_j\right)^2 \qquad (7.3)$$

$$cov(x_j, x_l) = \frac{1}{n(n-1)} \sum_{\substack{j,l \\ j \neq l}}^{n(n-1)} (x_{ij} - \bar{x}_j)(x_{il} - \bar{x}_j) \qquad (7.4)$$

For instance for j=1,

$$\bar{x}_l = \bar{y}_l = \frac{1}{n(n-1)} \sum_{i=1}^{n(n-1)} x_i \quad \text{etc.} \qquad (7.5)$$

For the entire measurements as L_i and R_j we have

$$\bar{x} = \bar{y} = \frac{1}{n} \sum_{j=1}^{n} x_j \qquad (7.6)$$

$$\sigma_x^2 = \sigma_y^2 = \frac{1}{n} \sum_{j=1}^{n} \left(\bar{x}_j - \bar{x}\right)^2 \qquad (7.7)$$

$$r = \frac{cov(X,Y)}{\sqrt{V(X)V(y)}} = \frac{n^2 \sum_{j=1}^{n}\left(\overline{x_j}-\overline{x}\right)^2 - \sum_i\sum_j\left(x_{ij}-\overline{x}\right)^2}{(n-1)\sum_i\sum_j\left(x_{ij}-\overline{x}\right)^2}$$ (7.8)

$$r = \frac{1}{n-1}\left[\frac{n\sigma_m^2}{\sigma^2}-1\right]$$ (7.9)

It can be shown that

$$r = -\frac{1}{n-1}\le r \le 1$$ (7.10)

An example from the observed data is worked out.

Table 6. Number of requests for five different regions and five different languages

j

REGION/ LANGUAGE	R8 (New York)	R9 (Washington)	R10 (California)	R11 (Florida)	R12 (Texus)
L1	80	15	18	20	30
L2	62	65	62	66	69
L3	70	30	15	20	10
L4	5	3	2	0	9
L5	70	80	90	50	40

i (to the left of the rows L1–L5)

Table. 7 Intra-Correlation between languages and regions

R8		R9		R10		R11		R12	
80	62	15	65	18	62	20	66	30	69
80	70	15	30	18	15	20	20	30	10
80	5	15	3	18	2	20	0	30	9
80	70	15	80	18	90	20	50	30	40
62	70	65	30	62	15	66	20	69	10
62	5	65	3	62	2	66	0	69	9
62	70	65	80	62	90	66	50	69	40
62	80	65	15	62	18	66	20	69	30
70	5	30	3	15	2	20	0	10	9
70	70	30	80	15	90	20	50	10	40
70	80	30	15	15	18	20	20	10	30
70	62	30	65	15	62	20	66	10	69
5	70	3	80	2	90	0	50	9	40
5	80	3	15	2	18	0	20	9	30
5	62	3	65	2	62	0	66	9	69
5	70	3	30	2	15	0	20	9	10
70	80	80	15	90	18	50	20	40	30
70	62	80	65	90	62	50	66	40	69
70	70	80	30	90	15	50	20	40	10
70	5	80	3	90	2	50	0	40	9
1148	1148	772	772	748	748	624	624	632	632
$x_1 = y_1 = 57.4$		$x_2 = y_2 = 38.6$		$x_3 = y_3 = 37.4$		$x_4 = y_4 = 31.2$		$x_5 = y_5 = 31.6$	

7.1 Calculation of Intra Correlation among Languages and Regions

$$\overline{x} = \frac{\overline{x}_1 + \overline{x}_2 + \overline{x}_3 + \overline{x}_4 + \overline{x}_5}{5} = 35.24 = \overline{y} \tag{7.11}$$

$$\sum_{i=1}^{5}\left(\overline{x}_i - \overline{x}\right)^2 = 456.6257 \tag{7.12}$$

$$\sum_{i=1}^{5}\sum_{j=1}^{5}\left(x_{ij} - \overline{x}\right)^2 = 29414.51 \tag{7.13}$$

$$r = \frac{x^2 \sum_{i=1}^{n}\left(\overline{x}_i - \overline{x}\right)^2 - \sum_{i=1}^{n}\sum_{j=1}^{n}\left(x_{ij} - \overline{x}\right)^2}{(n-1)\sum_{i=1}^{n}\sum_{j=1}^{n}\left(x_{ij} - \overline{x}\right)^2} \tag{7.14}$$

$$r = \frac{25 \times 456.6257 - 29414.51}{4 \times 29414.51} \tag{7.15}$$

$$r = -0.153 \quad (7.14)$$

This indicates that the inter correlation among the languages and the region coefficient is negative. Also the regression lies of Y and X is

$$Y = -0.153 \quad \text{where } Y = y - \overline{y} \qquad X = x - \overline{x} \quad Y = y\text{-}57.4 \qquad X = x\text{-}57.4$$

And this regression line lies in the second and fourth quadrants indicates that negative correlation.

7.2 Calculation of correlation among Languages in region R8

$$\overline{x}_1 = \overline{y}_1 = 57.4 \tag{7.16}$$

$$\sigma_{x1}^2 = \sigma_{y1}^2 = 1219.04, f_{x,y} = 320.24 \tag{7.17}$$

$$r = 0.2626. \tag{7.18}$$

There is a low pointer correlation among languages within the region R8. Similar calculations are made for the other languages.

8   Simulation Experiment Results

The system under consideration is simulated using the Java RMIServelets. It is able to pass all the user requests to the parent servers. Also, two RMI clients are developed to get the user request for object and the content uploading. These RMI clients are passing their requests to the RMIservelet server. This RMIserver agent of the video content server will automatically perform the aforesaid (as explained in Section 4) roles.

In current design the RMIserver agent process listens on a particular port. When the server receives an RMI request message, it parses the request and finds the content availability. If it is available then it will supply it from the local server otherwise it will forward the request to the parent server. In order to elicit the effective functionality; the system is designed to accept the RMI messages. This agent is also able to replicate itself, as and when the new server is installed and will automatically replicate to that server and is playing various roles as explained in above design; these roles are played in according to the location (as explained in Section 5).

The system is tested with 20 data sets collected from Internet. Simulation of such system allocates various types of movies of different languages at different regions. Especially the English language pattern is identified in five regions. There are also 4 English language video objects whose data are loaded into the system. It is assumed that the storage cost is 25 Units/object and Communication cost is 1 Unit/link for all objects irrespective of size.

Initially all the head-end's average access cost is computed using the head end algorithm. This is shown in Figure 3. Later all the intermediate average cost is computed and it is compared with the head-end's average cost. This is shown in Figure 4. Here the average cost of H1 is less than the node I1 cost, so this pattern object copy is moved to the node H1. Again the intermediate node I1 recomputes the average cost and it is forwarded to the root. The roots average cost is computed and is compared with intermediate average cost if it is less then a copy will be moved to that node. But, it is testing whether the average value is non-zero. Here it allocates copies of objects in nodes I1 and I2, because the computed average cost of I1, I2 is less than that of R1. The resulting request cost average is shown in Figure 5 and the resulting content allocation is shown in Figure 1.

It is found from the experiment that language L009 (English) requests are occurring from the regions R008 (New York), R09 (Washington), R010 (California), R011 (Florida) and R013 (Texas). That is L009 is receiving 80 requests from region R008, 15 requests from region R009, 18 requests from region R010, 20 requests from R011 and 30 requests from R012. Such a pattern is called language-region pattern. The identification of correlation inherent among all the languages in all the regions reflects over all relationship among them. The correlation of all languages distributed in one specific region revels the inherent relationship between the languages pertaining to that region. Future work can be attempted by making use of bivariate frequency distribution, based upon region/language will estimate the relationship between any two languages in particular regions and the relationship between regions for any specific language can also be distributed. This will enable to allocate related language objects for additional allocation to the regions. New objects (uploaded in to the network) belong to this language and need to be allocated in these regions, because requests for these objects usually occur only from these regions. But, at the same time, it is necessary to compute the best level of hierarchy for these objects for optimal delivery. Likewise it is necessary to identify the occurrence of sub-patterns within the particular language pattern. Thus a particular set of movies may have similar set of attributes, which need to be identified, and its best location can be computed for content allocation.

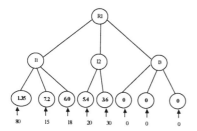

Figure 3. Head-End's algorithm average request cost

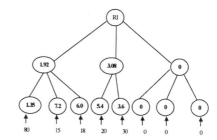

Figure 4. Intermediate Node algorithm's average request cost

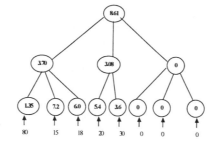

Figure 5. Intermediate Node algorithm's recomputed average request cost and root algorithm's average cost

9   Conclusion

An attempt is made in this paper to design and develop a multi-agent framework for optimal content allocation on federated video digital libraries. This work has revealed that the user access pattern learning contributed to improve the dynamic optimal content allocation which is established by means of simulation, even though the simulations does not take into account the transmission delay time. Such handling of dynamic requests will be the focus on future research for improvement in optimal content allocation by means of sub pattern identification.

References

Andreson, Daniel *et al.* "Scalability Issues for High Performance Digital Libraries on the World Wide Web", Department of Computer Science, University of California, Santa Barbara, CA93106.

Bestavros, Azer *et al.*, "Distributed Packet Rewriting and its application to scalable server architectures", In Proceedings of the 1998 Intl. Conf. On Network protocols (INCP '98), October 1998.

Brazier, Frances *et al.*, "Agents Negotiating for load balancing of electricity use", Proceedings of the 18th International Conference on Distributed Computing Systems, ICDCS'98, IEEE Computer Society Press, 1998.

Cardellini, Valeria *et al.*, "Dynamic load balancing on web-server systems", 28-39, May-June 1999, IEEE Internet Computing.

Chean, S.H. Gray and Fouad A. Tobagi, "Modeling and Dimensioning Hierarchical Storage Systems for Low-Delay Video Services", IEEE Trans. on Computers, Vol 52, No. 7, July 2003.

Chellappa, Rama "Digital Image and Video Libraries", http://www.wtec.org/loyola/diglibs/ob_01.htm

Cidon, Israel *et al.*, "Optimal allocation of electronic content", Elsevier Computer Networks 40 (2002) 205-218.

Fellner, Dieter W., "Research Issues for Digital Libraries", TU Braunschweig, http://graphics.tu-bs.de/DLResearch/Issues/df-DlresIssues010313.pdf

Frew, J. *et al.* "The Alexandria Digital Library Architecture", Int Jour. Digital Libraries (2000) 2: 259-268, Springer-Verlag 2000.

Gavalas, Damianos *et al.*, "Hierarchical network management: a scalable and dynamic mobile agent based approach", Elsevier Computer Networks 38 (2002) 693-711.

Goodwill, James "Developing Java Servelets: The authoritative solution", Techmedia 1999. http://www.themovies.com

Gottlob, Georg and Michael Schrefl *et al.*, "Extending Object Oriented Systems with Roles", ACM Trans. on Info. Systems, Vol. 4, No. 3 pp 268 – 296, July 1996.

Holffelder, Silvia *et al.*, "Designing for semantic access: A Video Browsing system", GMD Report 43, German National Research Center for Information Technology, Germany.

Jhao, J. Leon *et al.*, "Data Management for Multi-User Access to Digital Video Libraries", Tech. Report, School of Business Management, The Hong Kong University of Sc. & Tech, Hong Kong, 1999.

Leung, Y.Y. *et al.*, "Use of Analytical Performance Models for system sizing and Resource Allocation in Interactive Video-on-Demand systems Employing Data Sharing", IEEE Trans. on Knowledge and Data Engineering, Vol 14, No. 3, May/June 2002.

Mather, Paul "Scalable Storage for Digital Libraries", Ph.D. Report, Dept. of Computer Science, Virginia Polytechnic Institute and State University, Blauk Burg, USA, 23 Oct. 2001.

Mazurek, Cezary *et al.*, "Digital Library for Multimedia Content Management", http://www.mon.poznan.pl.

Nelson, Jeff "Programming Mobile Objects with Java", John Willey & Sons, Inc. 1999.

Nussbaumer, J.P. *et al.*, "Networking requirements for interactive video on demand", IEEE Journal on Selected Areas in Communications 13(5) 1995 (Also presented at INFOCOM 94).

Schafa, F. and J.P. Nussbaumer, "On bandwidth and storage tradeoffs in multimedia distribution networks", Fourteenth Annual Joint Conference of the IEEE Computer and Communication Societies (Vol. 3), April 02-06, 1995.

Song, Junehwa *et al.*, "Architecture of a Web Server accelerator", Elsevier Computer Networks 38 (2002) 75 – 97.

Teodoro, G. *et al.*, "Load balancing on stateful clustered web servers". http://www.dcc.ufmg.br/~dorgival/artigos/sbac03.pdf

Weiss, Gerhard "Multi-Agent System : A Modern Approach to Distributed Artificial Intelligence", The MIT Press, 1999.

INTELLIGENT CONTENT DISCOVERY WITHIN E-LEARNING WEB SERVICES

GOTTFRIED VOSSEN &
PETER WESTERKAMP

ERCIS - European Research Center for Information Systems, University of Muenster
Leonardo-Campus 3, Muenster D-48149, Germany

The various e-learning platforms that have been developed in recent years share a variety of functionalities. Recent standardization efforts in e-learning have concentrated on the reuse of learning material, but not on the reuse of these system functionalities. To fill this gap, Web service-based e-learning systems build on the assumption that a typical learning system is a collection of activities or processes that interact with learners and suitably chosen content, and that can be obtained from various sources when it comes to execution. In addition, content typically comes in the form of learning objects that are also accessible via a Web service. This scenario leads to a number of challenges, including the provision and the discovery of services; on the other hand, it has potentials such as the ability to directly integrate e-learning services into business applications or to communicate with a knowledge management system. This paper focuses on the discovery process of content Web services; it first analyzes limitations of traditional discovery mechanisms and then presents an ontology for content services that enables intelligent search and appropriate classification of results.

1 Introduction

The emerging paradigm of Web services (Casati and Dayal 2002) promises to enable partners to exploit vastly arbitrary applications via the Internet. In a nutshell, a Web service is a stand-alone software component that has a unique URI (Uniform Resource Identifier is a unique address), and that operates over the Internet and particularly the Web. Web services come with a specification that is published by its provider, and that is found and used by potential users or subscribers. The latter can compose Web services in order to build comprehensive applications with specific and customized functionality. Nowadays, the benefits of a Service Oriented Architecture (SOA) are well-understood in the area of business-to-business (B2B) applications, and even in business-to-customer (B2C) scenarios (such as e-learning) Web services are of growing importance (Vossen and Westerkamp 2003). In this paper, we discuss the finding or discovery process of e-learning Web services that are offered to present given content and show how this process can be done enhanced through the exploitation of ontologies.

A major application domain that we envision for electronic learning is that of executive education, where learners need to enhance their knowledge or capabilities based on job requirements, or in order to be promoted to a new position. In such cases, learning appears on-demand (as opposed to in-advance) and is often driven by predefined requirements that have been established by a job description, a skill map, or even a certification agency. The content discovery process then becomes a core activity within a learning process and in a learning platform, as learners need to search for appropriate content to consume, authors search for content for reuse in or adaptation to courses or classes, and people from official institutes may want to certify or evaluate content. Similar demands also appear in knowledge management systems.

Since the discovery scenario just described typically needs to refer to a variety of sources, it is near at hand to employ the Web services paradigm for making this work. Indeed, course offerings can be made by some providers, exams can be taken with others, and certification can be granted from parties overseeing an entire learning process. We imagine that any such component is made available as a service. Basically, learners can, for example, search for content suitable to their needs, book it, pay for it, and finally consume it, all by composing appropriate lookup, payment, and presentation services, resp. Several research platforms exist to realize e-Learning Web services, e.g., from Carnegie Mellon's Learning Systems Architecture Lab (Blackmon and Rehak 2003), Bergen University (Chen 2002), University of Muenster (Vossen and Westerkamp 2003), and University of Munich (Bry *et al.* 2003).

From a technical perspective, Web services need to be interoperable, since individual services typically are of limited functionality. Moreover, they have to be independent of the underlying operating system, they should be usable on every Web service engine regardless of the respective programming language, and they should be able to interact with each other. To achieve these goals, Web services are commonly based on generally accepted standards; currently most used are the XML-based specifications SOAP (Simple Object Access Protocol), UDDI (Universal Description, Discovery and Integration), and WSDL (Web Services Description Language, cf. Newcomer 2002). Even for the composition of Web services, XML-based languages are being introduced or even used already (e.g., XLANG, WSFL, BPEL4WS).

Building a decentralized system by composing Web services to achieve functionality similar to that of a traditional, comprehensive e-learning system clearly leads to a variety of novel challenges, among them that of managing the content for the learner. Indeed, in a distributed system organization learning objects cannot simply be imported into a particular learning management system. Instead, content needs to be stored on distributed servers and be called on demand. This paper is to show how content provided as Web service can be discovered in different ways. We describe the limitations of traditional search functionalities and sketch a semantic description to provide more powerful search mechanisms. To simplify matters, we just focus on the content Web services (called content learning service below) and use content from the software engineering field as an example.

Once a Web service-based e-learning platform is in place and ready to roll, the usage of Web services will enable the integration of e-learning functionalities directly to business applications (e.g., as external help for users to understand certain concepts used in an ERP system), since it will become possible to directly interact with applications, processes, and other information sources. Even the direct communication with knowledge management (KM) systems could easily be supported. As already indicated, this could provide benefits for a number of learners particularly in secondary and tertiary education because knowledge stored in KM systems can be used by a learner to get a broader view on a certain topic. Indeed, in a society where on the one hand it becomes more and more common to change jobs several times during a work life, and service provision based on the Web becomes more and more mature on the other, it is more than feasible to bring these two developments together so that one can benefit from the other, and flexibility for the learner is supported as far as current technological developments allow.

The organization of the paper is as follows: Section 2 sketches the notion of a learning object and describes a metadata format used in the field of e-learning; it then illustrates the limitations of existing search mechanisms for e-learning content. To give advanced abilities for the discovery process, Section 3 develops the essence of an ontology for content learning services. Section 4 concludes the paper with a discussion of several problems that deserve further study.

2   Learning Objects and their Discovery

We begin by recalling the notion of a learning object, and we describe a metadata format used in the field of e-learning. After that, we discuss the limitations of existing search mechanisms for e-learning content, when applied to a service-based scenario.

2.1 Learning Objects

Content consumed by learners and created by authors is commonly handled, stored, and exchanged in units of learning objects (LOs). Basically, LOs are units of study, exercise, or practice that can be consumed in a single session, and they represent reusable granules that can be created no matter what kind of delivery medium is used. LOs can be accessed dynamically, e.g., over the Web. Ideally, LOs can be reused by different learning management systems (LMS) and be plugged together to build classes or courses that can serve a particular purpose or goal. Accordingly, LOs need to be context-free in the sense that they have to carry useful description information on the type and context in which they may be used. For example, an LO dealing with the basics of SQL can be used in courses on software engineering, database administration, and data modeling. As have been shown by Vossen and Jaeschke (2003), LOs can conceptually be interpreted as specializations of knowledge objects and thus most concepts presented in this paper can be transferred to knowledge objects accordingly.

As the number of learning objects and of authors grows, metadata on the objects become a critical factor; indeed, metadata are needed for an appropriate description of learning objects so that plug-and-play configuration of classes and courses as well as an efficient search for content is rendered possible. Several standardization efforts have been launched in this direction, including IEEE's Learning Object Metadata (LOM, (IEEE 2002)), and the Sharable Content Object Reference Model (SCORM, (ADL 2001)), which is a collection of specifications adapted from multiple sources to provide a comprehensive suite of e-learning capabilities that enable interoperability, accessibility, and reusability of Web-based learning content. We remark that descriptions of learning content can be formed by an author using one or more of these standardization proposals. This resembles those of electronic services found in e-commerce that are prepared using the UDDI framework.

LOM distinguishes 9 categories of content description explained next. Each category can be structured into subsections to enable a detailed specification of content.

(1) General: general description of a learning resource (e.g., name, language)
(2) Lifecycle: history of development of the learning resource and current version (e.g., version, status, date, author)
(3) Meta-Metadata: description of the metadata used (e.g., metadata-schema)
(4) Technical: technical properties and requirements (e.g., format of data, size)
(5) Educational: pedagogical properties and features (e.g., type of learning object)
(6) Rights: copyright, intellectual property right, condition of use (e.g., price)
(7) Relation: relationship between multiple resources (e.g., name of relationship)
(8) Annotation: remarks on respective e-learning resource (e.g., author)
(9) Classification: positioning of a resource within the classification system (e.g., classification system)

Learning objects can be stored in a relational or an object-relational database and are typically a collection of attributes, some of which are mandatory, and some of which are optional. In a similar way, other information relevant to a learning system (e.g., learner personal data, learner profiles, course maps, LO sequencing or presentation information, general user data, etc.) can be mapped to common database structures.

Web services based e-learning platforms provide not only administrative functionality but also content stored in LOs as services. Technical details of this approach are beyond the scope of this paper and will not be discussed here. Although some of these services already exist, search mechanisms are rather poor, as we will describe next.

2.2 Limitations of Existing Content-Discovery Approaches

In traditional e-learning systems, a learner logs on to the platform to be used and becomes part of a closed community. He can search for content provided inside this learning environment. The quality of the search-results depends on the quality of the implementation of the search mechanism. A retrieval of learning objects outside the system is typically not supported. Thus, the learner's scope is limited to the content offered by the authors that are part of his community - access to content that is not stored inside the learning platform is, however, not possible. Apart from the closed systems, several stand-alone repositories provide access to content via the Web. These repositories can be used by learners to get more information on the topic they are working on. However, almost all traditional learning platforms do not provide an interface for letting a learner import discovered content. Even though these repositories give access to a larger number of content sources, the quantity is still limited to the content referenced by the repository. Most of these repositories are only accessible via a Web interface and do not provide a mechanism to integrate their search functionality into an existing platform (except for simple linking, which is not a useful integration for a Web services based e-learning platform).

The use of search-engines such as Google[1] or Altavista[2] fixes the problem of having restricted search abilities, but the quality of the results is bad because these engines are not intended to specifically search for e-learning content. The results will contain a lot of irrelevant hits in the form of Web sites or documents that were not created to be used as e-learning content. In addition, the information about learning objects provided by metadata like LOM will be not handled and indexed in an adequate way, as the index mechanisms of general search engines have a broader range of application. However, as some of these engines provide a Web services interface, they could be used in a Web services based e-learning platform to search for content.

To search for commercial Web services, the UDDI directory[3] is in common use today. As we focus on e-learning content to be provided as a Web service, it might be obvious to use UDDI for the discovery of this kind of Web service, too. UDDI is a global directory service that is made up of several connected servers, which use a replication mechanism to offer the same amount of knowledge on each node. The provider of a Web service registers his service at one of the UDDI nodes by providing meta information about the service, but the service itself, i.e., its implementation, is stored on a server of the provider and not inside the UDDI directory. This meta information includes, for example, the author, the service category, and technical specifications and is stored in data structures inside the UDDI directory. UDDI further defines a query language to ensure that a service can effectively be found in response to a request; a request is answered by delivering information on how to use and call the service at the server of the provider. The communication rules for client and Web service are described in a WSDL file, which is not part of the UDDI directory; instead, it is referenced by the information a client obtains from the UDDI directory upon his request. The WSDL document includes technical information about the service and primarily can not be used to search for certain e-learning content. UDDI itself can be accessed via a Web service interface.

UDDI uses an XML-based language to represent service descriptions. Since this language is not as flexible as it could have been, a well-structured description of functional and non-functional characteristics of the service is not possible (Trastour *et al.* 2001). Instead, it has to be stored as an unstructured string. For an e-learning content service this means that typical metadata (e.g., price and category of the content) has to be stored as a string without any further structuring or annotation. Although a more detailed structuring is possible in documents outside of UDDI referenced by tModels, this infor-

---

[1] http://www.google.com
[2] http://www.altavista.com
[3] http://www.uddi.org

mation cannot by handled inside UDDI (Dumas *et al.* 2001). Apart from its restricted flexibility, UDDI does not provide a type-system in the description of Web services. In particular, this would have been important to describe non-functional characteristics like the price of the content (or the service). In addition, the support of generalizations and specializations would have been important to offer information about a service on different levels of abstraction, which is particularly useful to classify content.

The query-language of UDDI is unable to handle restrictions of certain characteristics of a Web service. For example, a learner would not be able to formulate a condition to search for content learning services that are cheaper than a special price. Problems also appear in the interpretation of descriptions, as they can be ambiguous. UDDI does not support a formal and machine-readable representation of service characteristics. Thus, the semantics of a search condition might not match the semantics of the service characteristics. Due to these ambiguous data, an automatic use of the results of the search in the UDDI directory is difficult. Clearly, some of the content learning services in software engineering would not be found because the identical semantics of different terms would not be recognized. On the other hand, wrong hits would be in the result due to homonyms. Of course, UDDI is not able to present results of related content learning services because of the missing semantics.

Some of the integration and flexibility problems are addressed by specialized repositories that are built to search for learning content and that also provide a Web service interface. For example, LORAX[4] and the LearnServe repository (Westerkamp and Vossen 2003) both provide a Web service access to special data structures that contain LOM metadata. The search mechanism of these repositories can operate on structured data with a well-defined semantics (e.g., price, author). However, some descriptions are still text strings that can be misunderstood because of different interpretations.

The next chapter illustrates how the use of an ontology can support an advanced mechanism to search for content learning services. In the context of knowledge sharing, the term ontology means a specification of a conceptualization. Thus, an ontology is a description of the concepts and relationships that can exist for an agent or a community of agents (Gruber 1993).

3   An Ontology for E-Learning Web Services

The construction of a semantic Web service description can be done in four steps (Klein and König-Ries 2003):

(1) Define model,
(2) find task ontology,
(3) specify domain-specific ontologies,
(4) derive application ontology.

---

4 http://www.thelearningfederation.edu.au/

This incremental approach defines a structured way and enables a reuse of already existing ontologies. Each step gives a more precise description of the Web service by using or creating ontologies. The first step defines a model for the description of Web services in general. For this purpose, the OWL-S (OWL 2003) language (formerly known as DAML-S) was developed. It is a top-level ontology that offers a uniform and well-accepted model. Since this ontology has a broad focus, the second step defines a task ontology for a certain domain. As we are interested in Web services to offer content, the domain of our services is e-learning. Thus, the task ontology specializes the top-level ontology to a specific application and is also called service-category ontology. The third step includes or creates ontologies that carry the descriptions of a Web service in a concrete application domain. For an e-learning content service this step specifies if the Web service contains content about computer science, biology, or musicology etc. The last step creates an application ontology and uses the concepts of the top-level-, task-, and domain ontologies.

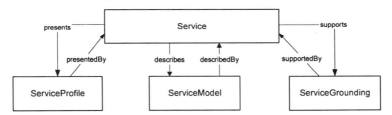

Figure 1. Main parts of OWL-S.

Top-Level-Ontology

As mentioned above, we use OWL-S as top-level ontology language for a description of the general Web service in the field of learning Web services, as indicated in Figure 1. In OWL-S a Web service is an instance of class Service and has the properties presentedBy, supports, and describedBy. Class ServiceProfile offers a description of the service that can be used to discover a service, whereas class ServiceModel contains information about the way a service works. Detailed technical information on how a service can be used is provided by class ServiceGrounding. As we are interested in the discovery process, we just concentrate on the ServiceProfile in this paper. OWL-S does not determine a fixed representation of the service in ServiceProfile, but provides a way to define profiles for specific application domains. This can be done by task ontologies, and we will present one for the learning Web services next.

Task-Ontology

The task ontology for learning Web services just considers those services that are responsible for the provision of learning content and are simplified for a better understanding in this paper. As shown in Figure 2, two items have to be modeled in order to build the ontology: the learning object and the learning service profile as specialization of the OWL-S ServiceProfile class. The modeling of the learning object can be done on the basis of LOM as presented in Section 2. Several RDF approaches exist for modeling LOM[5] (Nielsson *et al.* 2003, Brase and Nejdl 2004). Our model uses a LOM description in OWL that has a class LearningObject to represent the LO that is related to an instance of the class Author via the hasAuthor relation. An author is characterized by attributes hasName and hasEmail which point to the XML Schema datatype string. The author can be found in LOM in the Lifecycle subsection. Properties requires, isRequiredBy and hasPart, isPartOf are used to model contents as well as structure dependencies and can be extracted from the LOM portion named relation. The technical format (corresponding to LOM section Technical) and the category of the content (corresponding to LOM section Classification) are described by properties hasFormat and hasCategory. It is important to mention that the values of these properties are not restricted, in order to enable a categorization of learning objects by referencing classes of (domain-) ontologies of additional descriptions. We will focus only on the usage of hasCategory and will use an existing specification for the area of software engineering.

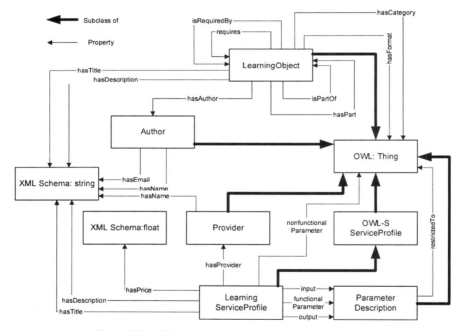

Figure 2. Simplified task-ontology for content learning services.

Apart from class LearningObject, class LearningServiceProfile as a specialization of class ServiceProfile is the central concept in our ontology. Its modeling is similar to the modeling of class Profile in OWL-S and contains information about the provider of the

---

[5] http://www.imsproject.org/rdf/

service in question, the functionality of the service, and information about special non-functional characteristics of the service. Information about the provider is captured by property hasProvider. The provider is described by the property hasName that has type XML Schema datatype string. Functional characteristics of the content learning service are a specialization of functionalParameter, and are modeled by input and output. In addition, our ontology has a non-functional property hasPrice, which is of data type float.

Domain-Ontology

The task ontology enables a characterization of a content learning service by categorization. Properties hasFormat and hasCategory are not restricted. This enables a classification by existing systems. As we want to focus on learning content for software engineering, the system of the Software Engineering Body of Knowledge (SWEBOK)[6] can be used for this purpose. SWEBOK is a well-accepted classification of the field of software engineering created by specialists and contains 10 areas of the software engineering domain and covers about 300 topics. We have modeled a SWEBOK ontology in OWL that uses classes to represent areas and topics that reference properties hasName and hasDescription of the XML Schema datatype string. The hierarchies are modeled by subclasses.

In the last step special information for a certain system can be modeled in an application ontology. After modeling the overall ontology, the representation of a given content learning service is an instance of LearningServiceProfile, which we do not describe in detail in this paper.

The search for a learning service based on a semantic matchmaking will generally provide better results because hits without an exact match will be also recognized. The results can be classified depending on how close a given query matches the content learning services to be delivered. The search query can be interpreted as a restriction on the characteristics of a potential content learning service. Thus, the services provided as a result of a query can be interpreted as set of all services that do not ``contradict" the query. This means that the result set is much bigger compared to an exact match of characteristics of the services. Li and Horrocks (2003) also specify five classes of possible results that are feasible for content learning services. The class of exact results contains all services that have an equivalent description of concepts compared to the query. Class PlugIn is slightly less precise and contains all services that represent generalizations of the query.

Note that traditional repositories without a semantic annotation are generally not able to provide results other than exact matches. Class Subsumption contains all results that are specializations of the query. Although PlugIn and Subsumption are less precise than the exact match, they can still offer useful information. If a service with a certain description is not found, the requestor might want to use a more general one. In the software engineering field this might be the case if the learner searches, say, for content

---

[6] http://www.swebok.org/

about a certain process modeling language. If no adequate service is found he might prefer a more general content learning service. The same is possible if the search for process modeling does not result in exact matches but might offer services about a special process modeling language. In this case the results of class Subsumption are helpful. In general, requestors and providers might formulate their requests and offerings in a more imprecise way than it was initially intended to look at other results in addition to the exact match they are looking for. The two additional classes not mentioned yet are the Intersection and the Disjoint. Both are not very interesting as they do not match a query well. Intersection contains all results that match the query to a certain satisfaction; otherwise, the result ends up in class Disjoint.

4 Conclusions

The usage of OWL-S and OWL enables a flexible approach to describe Web services that deliver e-learning content to learners and provides advanced possibilities for the discovery process. Specifically, this approach is more flexible than approaches without the incorporation of ontologies, since domain- and application-specific knowledge can now be exploited in a discovery process. However, in contrast to existing repositories that are able to extract the metadata from existing documents (such as an imsmanifest.xml file of SCORM) automatically to some extend, the process of describing content in ontologies is much more complex. This is not only the case because Web services deliver the content, but is also a problem for RDF descriptions of content that are offered as traditional learning objects. Of course, the approach depends on the existence or the creation and distribution of well-accepted ontologies for the various levels of a description. This already applies to the top-level-ontology, although several workarounds have been proposed for OWL-S (DAML-S, resp.). For the other levels we have pointed out how already existing and established classification systems can be used to provide formal descriptions. These classification systems have to be formulated as ontologies and communities have to agree on them. The entire process of developing the ontologies has to be supported by tools in order to be efficient and error-free.

Every semantic search engine can be used to search for LOs and content learning services that are annotated in a semantic way as described. As the development of these search engines is still in an early stage, the usage of the additional description is limited to existing repositories. This could be UDDI, which can be enhanced to provide a more powerful way to search for content learning services, but it seems to be more reasonable to use the annotations in a repository like the one provided by LearnServe, as the entire platform focuses on e-learning Web services.

Acknowledgments

The authors would like to thank Jan Werner Schemm for his work on the topic of this paper.

References

Advanced Distributed Learning Initiative (2001): "Advanced Distributed Learning Sharable Content Object Reference Model, The SCORM Overview", Version 1.2.

Blackmon, W.H., Rehak, D. R. (2003): "Customized Learning: A Web Services Approach." In Proc. Ed-Media 2003, June 2003.

Brase, J., Nejdl, W. (2004): "Ontologies and Metadata for eLearning". Handbook on Ontologies 2004: 555-574.

Casati, F., U. Dayal, eds. (2002): "Special Issue on Web Services." IEEE Bulletin of the Technical Committee on Data Engineering, 25(4), December 2002.

Bry, F., N. Eisinger, G. Schneemeyer (2003): "Web Services for Teaching: A Case Study." In Proc. First International Conference on Web Services (ICWS'03), Las Vegas, USA, June 2003.

Chen, W. (2002): "Web Services - What Do They Mean to Web based Education." In Proc. Int. Conf. on Computers in Education, Auckland, Newzealand, December 2002, pp.707-708.

Dumas, M., J. O'Sullivan, M. Heravizadeh, A. ter Hofstede and D. Edmond (2001): "Towards a Semantic Framework for Service Description." In Proc. of the IFIP Conference on Database Semantics, pages 277-291, Hong Kong, China, April 2001. Kluwer Academic Publishers.

Gruber, T. R. (1993): "A Translation Approach to Portable Ontology Specifications." Knowledge Acquisition, 5(2), 1993: pp. 199-220.

IEEE Standards Department (2002): "Draft Standard for Learning Object Metadata." IEEE Publication P1484.12.1/D6.4, March 2002.

Klein, M.; B. König-Ries (2003): "A Process and a Tool for Creating Service Descriptions Based on DAML-S." In Proc. of the 4th VLDB Workshop on Technologies for E-Services, TES 2003: 143-154.

Li, L., Horrocks, I. (2003): "A software framework for matchmaking based on semantic web technology." In Proc. of the Twelfth International World Wide Web Conference (WWW 2003), ACM 2003: 331-339.

Newcomer, E. (2002): "Understanding Web Services: XML, WSDL, SOAP, and UDDI." Addison-Wesley.

Nilsson, M., Palmér, M., Brase, J. (2003): "The LOM RDF binding - principles and implementation." In Proc. of the 3rd annual ARIADNE conference, Katholieke Universiteit Leuven, Belgium, November 2003.

OWL Service Coalition (2003): "OWL-S: Semantic Markup for Web Services." http://www.daml.org/services/owl-s/1.0/owl-s.pdf

Trastour, D., C. Bartolini, J. Gonzalez-Castillo (2001): "A Semantic Web Approach to Service Description for Matchmaking of Services." In Proc. International semantic web Working Symposium (SWWS) 2001: 447-461.

Vossen, G., P. Jaeschke (2003): "Learning Objects as a Uniform Foundation for E-Learning Platforms." In Proc. 7th International Conference on Database Engineering and Applications (IDEAS), Hong Kong, China, IEEE Computer Society Press: 278-287.

Vossen, G., P. Westerkamp (2003): "E-learning as a Web service (extended abstract)." In Proc. 7th International Conference on Database Engineering and Applications (IDEAS), Hong Kong, China, IEEE Computer Society Press: 242-249.

Westerkamp, P., G. Vossen (2003): "UDDI for E-Learning: A Repository for Distributed Learning Objects." In Proc. 2nd International Conference on Information and Knowledge Sharing (IKS2003), Scottsdale, AZ, USA, November 2003: 101-106.

PART VIII

Abstracts of
Poster Presentations

COLLABORATIVE KNOWLEDGE MANAGEMENT PORTALS FOR LEARNING ORGANIZATIONS

RUSLI ABDULLAH &
MOHD. HASAN SELAMAT

*Information System Department, Faculty of
Computer Science and Information System,
Universiti Putra Malaysia, 43400 UPM
Serdang, Selangor, Malaysia*

SHAMSUL SAHIBUDIN &
ROSE ALINDA ALIAS

*Faculty of Computer Science and
Information System,
Universiti Teknologi Malaysia, 81310 UTM
Skudai, Johor, Malaysia*

A knowledge management system is a concept which can be used for creating knowledge repositories, improving knowledge access and sharing as well as communicating through collaboration, enhancing the knowledge environment and managing knowledge as an asset for an institution or organization. In this paper, we will analyze the concept, system and architecture framework of KMS for Learning Organization (LO) and discuss various issues that are involved in this field that will help organizations to increase productivity and quality as well as to gain return on investment (ROI). Issues that are highlighted in this paper also involve the acquiring and disseminating knowledge. The issues are about how to determine the best way of approaching and acquiring knowledge effectively including motivating people to share knowledge and access through the system, how to determine the good metrics for evaluating efficiency, how to determine the best way to perform a knowledge audit, how to determine how people create, communicate and use knowledge, and how to determine more inclusive, integrated KMS software packages with others.

References

Alavi, M. and Leidner, D., (1999), "Knowledge Management Systems: Issues, Challenges, and Benefits" *Communication of AIS*, Vol. 1, Article 14.

Anumba, C.J. Ugwu, O.O. Newnham, L., and Thorpe, A., (2001), "A multi-agent system for distributed collaborative design", *Journal of Logistics Information Management"*,, MCB University Press. Volume 14. Number 5/6, pp. 355-366

Arthur Andersen and The APQC (1996), "The KM Assessment Tools: External Benchmarking Version", *Winter.*

Bostrom, R.P., Watson, R.T., and Kinney, S. (1992),"Computerized Collaborative Work Support at the University of Georgia," *Computer Augmented Teamwork: A Guided Tour*, Van Nostrand Reinhold, pp. 251-267

Chih-Ping W. Jen-Hwa H., and Hung-Huang C., (2002). "Design and evaluation of a knowledge management system". *Software Journal.* 19(3), 56-59.

Davenport, T.H. and Prusak, L. (1998), *Working Knowledge: How Organizations Manage What They Know* Boston, MA: Harvard Business School Press.

Fennessy, G., (2002), "Understanding and selecting knowledge management systems for a health information provider", *Proceeding of 35th Hawaii International Conference on System Sciences, IEEE.*

Lotus Company, (www.lotus.com) at 2002.

McKinsey (1998), "Best Practice and Beyond: Knowledge Strategies" *The McKinsey Quarterly*, Num. 1, pp. 19-25

Meso, P. and Smith, R. (2000), "A Resources-based View of organizational knowledge Management Systems", *Journal of Knowledge Management*, Vol. 4, No. 3, pp. 224-234.

Nonaka, I., and Takeouchi, H. (1995), The knowledge-creating company. NY: *Oxford University Press.*

O'Leary, D.E., (1998). "Enterprise Knowledge Management", *IEEE Computer*, 54 - 61.

Polanyi, M. (1966), The tacit dimension. *MA: Gloucester.*

Van der Spek, R. and Spijkervet A. (1997), "Knowledge Management: Dealing Intelligently with Knowledge", *Knowledge Management And Its Integrative Elements*, eds (Liebowitz, J. & Wilcox, L.). New York: CRC Press.

Wiig, K. M. (1997). "Roles of knowledge-based systems in support of knowledge management". In J. Liebowitz & L. C. Wilcox. *Knowledge management and its integrative element*, (pp. 69-87). New York: CRC Press.

A STUDY OF THE ALIGNMENT OF KNOWLEDGE AND BUSINESS STRATEGIES AND THEIR EFFECT ON THE PERFORMANCE OF THE KINGDOM OF BAHRAIN'S BANKING AND FINANCIAL INSTITUTIONS

JAFLAH ALAMMARY,
CHUN CHE FUNG &
PAULA GOULDING

*School of Information Technology, Murdoch University,
South Street, Murdoch, W.A. 6150, Australia*

Today, knowledge management (KM) is considered as an enabler to achieve the strategic business objectives of an organisation. It is realized that KM must evolve from business strategy and contribute to the achievement of business results. This study proposes a conceptual framework focusing on the importance of aligning the knowledge strategy to the overall business strategies. The study will be primarily based on the identification and analysis of the effects of this alignment with respect to the organizational performance of the Kingdom of Bahrain Banking and Financial Institutions (KBBFI). The study will focus on KBBFI because they are facing major challenges from competitors, a new business environment, changes in technologies and the increasing demands of customer services and products. This paper argues that the alignment between knowledge strategy and business strategies can enhance the success of the KM initiatives in the KBBFI. This will in turn help the institutes in distinguishing their financial services and products from those in other parts of the world and enable them to expand and sustain a leading competitive advantage.

References

Choi, Young S. (2003) "Reality of knowledge management successes", *Journal of academy of business and economics*, Vol. II, Issue 1, pp. 184-188.

Davenport, T. H., (1999). "Knowledge management and the broader firm: Strategy, advantage, and performance", in *J. Liebowitz (Ed.), Knowledge Management Handbook:*2.1-2.11, CRC Press.

Martin, Bill (2000) "Knowledge management within the context of management: An evolving relationship", *Singapore Management Review*, Singapore, Vol. 22, Issue 2, pp. 17 – 26.

Okkonen, J.; Pirttimaki, V.; Lonnqvist, M. & Hannula, A. (2002) "Triangle of performance measurement, business intelligence and knowledge management", *2nd Annual Conference on Innovative Research in Management*, May 9 - 11, Stockholm, Sweden.

Smith, H & McKeen, J. (2003) "Developing and aligning a KM strategy", *Queen's Center for Knowledge-Based Enterprises*, May, Ontario, Canada.

Sunassee, Nakkiran; Sewry, David (2002) "A theoretical framework for knowledge management implementation", *Proceeding of SAICSIT*, Port Elizabeth, S. Africa, Sept. 16-18, pp. 235-245

Zack, Michael H (1999). "Developing a Knowledge Strategy", *California Management Review*, Vol. 41, No. 3, Spring, pp.125-145.

Zack, Michael H, (2002). "A strategic Pretext for Knowledge Management", *Proceeding of The Third European Conference on Organisational Knowledge, Learning and Capabilities*, Athens, Greece, April 5.

MODELING AIR TRAFFIC LANDING SEQUENCES AND CONTROL: A SIMULATION

QURBAN ALI

United Arab Emirates University, Al Ain, P.O Box 175551 UAE

ATIF RAFEEQ

Karachi Institute of Information Technology, Karachi Pakistan

Due to a high increase in air traffic around the globe, the tasks for the air traffic controllers have increased multi-fold. Air traffic control continues to grow in complexity. Hence, the system for its representation needs to be flexible and dynamic to accommodate the present-day requirements of air traffic controllers. This paper is aimed at developing an air traffic control simulation, which assigns the sequence of landing to the airplanes when there are a number of airplanes approaching the airfield. The proposed solution is aimed to automate and optimize the prioritization of additional landing requests once they are transferred to the knowledge base. Two alternatives are proposed in this work: one is based on rule-based expert system, and another is based on artificial neural networks. We show that an artificial neural network based model suits a larger knowledge base situation where additional (and more than scheduled) landing requests are being handled by air traffic controllers, and thus helps optimize the prioritization of overall landing requests in any given time. During the optimization process, we combine various parameters including emergencies, aircraft type, mission critical level of the aircraft, type of the aircraft before an optimized sequence of landing is generated for upfront information to the air traffic controller.

THE STATE OF IMPLEMENTATION OF KNOWLEDGE MANAGEMENT IN SINGAPORE

SATTAR BAWANY

International Professional Managers Association (UK)
IPMA Asia Pacific Academic Advisor - 259 Tampines Central, Singapore 915209

What is the status and role of knowledge management in small- and medium-sized enterprises and global/multi-national companies in Singapore? What are the factors that contribute to the successful implementation of knowledge management? What is the overall perception about knowledge management? What are the significant differences between perceived important factors and actual knowledge management implementation factors? In today's hyper competitive global and market-driven economy, effective knowledge management is becoming a fundamental requirement for baseline corporate success. The underlying rationale for this study is that the majority of Knowledge Management (KM) research to date concentrates on technology as a solution to KM issues. Conversely this study focuses on investigating and developing the softer, human issues within KM. This paper explores the critical success factors in knowledge management implementation within organisations in Singapore. The results presented in this paper are based on survey conducted by the author in collaboration with a leading professional organisation in Singapore. The critical success factors identified and classified broadly includes leadership and policy, performance measurement, knowledge sharing and acquisition, benchmarking and training, and teamworking and empowerment.

References

Choi, Y.S. (2000). An empirical study of factors affecting successful implementation of knowledge management. Unpublished academic dissertation, University of Nebraska.

Drucker, P. (1999). Management challenges for the 21st century. Harper Business, New York.

Mintzberg, H. (1993) Structure in Fives: Designing Effective Organizations, Prentice Hall, Englewood Cliffs, NJ

Nonaka, I., & Takeuchi, H. (1995). The knowledge creating company: How Japanese companies create the dynamics of innovation. New York: Oxford University Press.

Ruggles, R. (1998). The State of the notion: Knowledge management in practice. California Management Review, 40(3), pp. 80 – 90.

ORGANIZATIONAL EFFECTS ON KNOWLEDGE SHARING

KRISDA BISALYAPUTRA

Industrial Engineering Department, Chulalongkorn University, Bangkok, 10240, Thailand

CHUVEJ CHANSA-NGAVEJ

School of Management, Shinawatra University Bangkok, 10900, Thailand

TONY GARRETT

Department of Marketing, School of commerce, Otago University Dunedin, New Zealand

Organizations attempt to establish effective and successful knowledge transfer. The objective of this study is to investigate the relationship between organizational cultures and knowledge sharing. The paper proposes a framework for analyzing the effects of organizational culture in four contexts of knowledge transfer. Organizational culture is assessed based on Schein's organizational culture framework; and knowledge sharing is examined using four groups of factors, including knowledge context, recipient context, interaction context, and transfer activity context.

An appropriate organizational culture significantly strengthens knowledge transfer success. The results of this study can be applied by management in organizations to create the organizational culture which will support knowledge transfer that will stimulate and sustain success in organizations.

References

Brown, A. Organizational Culture: The key to effective leadership and organizational development. *Leadership & organization development Journal.* Vol. 13 No. 2 1992: p.3-6.

Darr, E. D., and Kurtzberg, T. R. An investigation of partner similarity dimensions on knowledge transfer. *Organizational Behavior and Human Decision Processes.* Vol. 82,2000: pp. 28–44.

Davenport, T. H. and Prosak, L. *Working knowledge: How organizations manage what they know.* Boston, Massachusetts: Harvard business school press, 1998.

Schein, E. H. Culture: The missing concept in organization studies. *Administrative science quarterly.* Vol. 41. No.2 June 1996: pp. 229-240.

Schein, E. H. Three Cultures of Management: The key to organizational learning. *Slone Management Review.* Vol. 38 Fall 1996: pp. 9-20.

LEARNING IN PROJECT-BASED ORGANIZATIONS

WAI FONG BOH

Nanyang Business School, Nanyang Technological University Nanyang Avenue, Singapore 369798

This paper examines the question of how a project-based organization manages its knowledge resources and builds up its capabilities. This paper describes a research program consisting of three studies that were conducted to address this research question. Study 1 examined whether different types of experience at the individual, group and organizational levels affect the productivity of an organization doing large-scale software development (Boh *et al.* 2003). I found that project-based organizations face significant challenges in learning and sharing knowledge across projects. Studies 2 and 3 examined the mechanisms organizations use to share knowledge across projects. Study 2 examined how an organization deployed its expertise across projects by sharing personnel amongst several projects (Boh *et al.* 2002). Study 3 examined an organization that uses a repository for sharing project documents such as client presentations, project proposals, project report and templates (Boh 2003). The three studies, together, highlight that project-based organizations face many difficulties in ensuring adequate learning and knowledge sharing across projects. Effective use of knowledge-sharing mechanisms can help organizations to overcome the difficulties and ensure effective knowledge sharing across projects, and result in positive outcomes such as improved project financial performance, and time-savings.

References

Boh, W.F. (2003), "Knowledge Sharing Mechanisms in Project-Based Knowledge Work: Codification Versus Personalization," in *International Conference on Information Systems.* Seattle, WA.

Boh, W.F., Y. Ren, and S. Kiesler (2002), "Managing Expertise in a Distributed Environment," in *International Conference of Information Systems.* Barcelona, Spain.

Boh, W.F., S.A. Slaughter, and J.A. Espinosa (2003), "Individual, Group and Organizational Learning in Software Development: A Learning Curve Analysis," in *Academy of Management Meeting.* Seattle, WA.

APPLYING SOCIAL NETWORK ANALYSIS TO KNOWLEDGE MANAGEMENT

PETER BUSCH & DEBBIE RICHARDS

Department of Computing, Macquarie University North Ryde, NSW, 2109, Australia

Tacit knowledge is either learnt through repeated experience on the job or by being transferred through example or verbally from one individual to the next in informal and often unplanned meetings (Raghuram 1996). Not only is tacit knowledge typically transferred in this manner within an organization, but in order for the knowledge to be passed, the groups are on average required to be very small (von Krogh, Ichijo and Nonaka 2000). This teamwork then permits knowledge to be transmitted back into the organization, through various but characteristically social means. An excellent means of gauging the flows of knowledge between groups of people, is that of Social Network Analysis (SNA) (Scott 1991). Thus, we have adopted the use of SNA as a means of determining how well people in the organization are transferring their tacit knowledge. We have examined three organizations with regard to how their tacit knowledge is being transferred. The outcomes from the research suggest that factors such as organizational size, level of usage of IT and type of meetings employees have with one another will affect how likely tacit knowledge can be transferred within the company.

References

Raghuram, S., (1996) "Knowledge creation in the telework context" International *Journal of Technology Management* 11(7/8):859-870

Scott, J., (1991) Social *Network Analysis: A handbook* Sage Publications London U.K.

Von Krogh, Georg; Ichijo, Kazuo; Nonaka, Ikujiro: (2000) *Enabling Knowledge Creation - How to Unlock the Mystery of Tacit Knowledge and Release the Power of Innovation*, Oxford University Press, Inc., New York.

TACIT KNOWLEDGE DIFFUSION VIA TECHNOLOGY AND HUMAN NETWORKS

PETER BUSCH & DEBBIE RICHARDS

Department of Computing, Macquarie University North Ryde, NSW, 2109, Australia

The management of knowledge has become a critical concern for many organizations. To assist, numerous vendors offer an array of technologies. But, as the conference theme asks, "what have we learnt so far?" with respect to the role, interplay and appropriate balance of "People, Knowledge and Technology". Our work is specifically focused on tacit knowledge, which is that component either gained through self-experience or through working with people who possess "know-how" (Roberts 2001). Research indicates the only way for soft knowledge to be effectively transferred is through the socialization process (Roberts 2001). Furthermore the dissemination of tacit knowledge can be a problem where organizations rely too heavily on information technology (Koski 2001; Walsham 2001). For an organization to benefit from its tacit knowledge resources it must undertake to examine the richness of the different forms of communication mediums it makes use of (Schulz and Jobe 2001; Koskinen 2000). Based on the literature and three case studies, the optimal organization for tacit knowledge transfer contains highly interconnected social human networks and is minimally reliant on the use of technology for communication. Our findings bring into question whether the modern organization is the most appropriate environment for tacit knowledge diffusion.

References

Koski, J., (2001) "Reflections on information glut and other issues in knowledge productivity" *Futures* (London, England) 33(6) August :483-495

Koskinen, K., (2000) "Tacit knowledge as a promoter of project success" *European journal of purchasing & supply management* Vol 6 :41-47

Roberts, J., (2001) "The drive to codify: Implications for the knowledge – based economy" *Prometheus* 19(2) :99-116

Schulz, M., Jobe, L., (2001) "Codification and tacitness as knowledge management strategies: An empirical exploration" *Journal of high technology management research* Vol. 12 :139-165

Walsham, G., (2001) "Knowledge management: The benefits and limitations of computer systems" *European Management Journal* 19(6) December :599-608.

HOW DOES KNOWLEDGE MANAGEMENT INFLUENCE THE INNOVATION MANAGEMENT PROCESS?

DANIEL K.S. CHANG

Prime College, School of Business and Information Technology
Subang Jaya, Selangor D.E. 47600, Malaysia

Innovation is the latest buzzword in the corporate boardroom and in today's news headlines. However, confusion still exists on what innovation is, and where the original source of innovative knowledge lies. This paper sets out to focus on the correlation between Knowledge Management and its influences on the Innovation Management Process. It discusses the basic definitions, applications and perspectives of these two evolving disciplines. It intends to demystify the innovation management model and knowledge management processes in order to draw an integrative framework in managing knowledge for the innovation process. It intends to understand knowledge as the force that influences the nurture, development, implementation and exploitation of the innovation activities cluster.

References

Abraham B. Shani, James A.Sena & Olin, T., (2003) *Knowledge Management and New Product Development: A study of Two Companies,* European Journal of Innovation Management, Vol 6. no.3, November, MCB UP Ltd, pp.137-149

Afuah, A. (2003) *Innovation Management: Strategies, Implementation and Profits,* 2 edn. Oxford University Press, New York.

Aranda, D.A. & Molina-Fernandez, L.M. (2002) *Determinants of Innovation Through a Knowledge-based Theory Lens,* Journal of Industrial and Data Systems. Vol.105/5, MCB UP Ltd. pp.289-296

Bean,R. & Radford, R. (2002) *The Business of Innovation: Managing The Corporate Imagination for Maximum Results,* 1edn. AMACOM, New York pp. 2-7

Bukowitz, W.R. & Williams, R.L.(1999) *The Knowledge Management Fieldbook,* 1edn. Pearson Education, London. pp.2-3.

Carneiro, A. (2000). *How does Knowledge Management Influence Innovation and Competitiveness,* Journal of Knowledge Management. Vol.4 No.2. MCB University Press Vol 4 No.2, pp. 87-98

Darroch, J. & McNaughton, R. (2002), *Examining the Link between Knowledge management Practices and Types of Innovation,* Journal of Intellectual Capital, Vol.3 No.3 MCB UP Ltd, pp.210-222

Davenport,T.H.(1998) and Prusak, L. (1998), *Working Knowledge: Managing What Your Organization Knows,* Harvard Business School Press, Boston, MA.

Davenport,T.H (1999) *Knowledge Management Round Two; Making The Most of Information Rich Environment*, CIO Magazine, November Issues 1999

Drucker,P (1985)*The Discipline of Innovation, The Innovative Enterprise 2002*, Harvard Business School Press, Boston MA, August Issues, pp.95-102

Hiltzik, M.A.(1999) *Dealers of Lightning; Xerox PARC and the Dawn of the Computer Age*, HarperCollins Publishers Inc. New York, pp.389-398

Hong, J.C. & Kuo C.L. (1999) *Knowledge Management in the Learning Organisation*, Journal of the Leadership & Organisation Development, Vol.20 No.4, MCB University Press, pp.207-215

Van Beveren, J. (2002) *A Model of Knowledge Acquisition that Refocuses Knowledge Management*, Journal of Knowledge Management, Vol.6. No.1, MCB UP Ltd., pp.18-22

Yang, J. & Yu, L.(2002) *Electronic New Product Development – A Conceptual Framework*, Journal of Industrial Management and Data Systems, Vol.102/4, MCB UP Ltd. pp.218-225

A MEASUREMENT MODEL FOR ASSESSING THE KNOWLEDGE-BASED ECONOMY

CHIH-KAI CHEN

*Department of International Business,
National Taiwan University
8F, No.50, Lane 144, Section 4, Kee-Lung
Road, Taipei 106, Taiwan, R.O.C.:*

Through theoretical and empirical study, this study focuses primarily on the construct model of Knowledge-Based Economy (KBE) assessment. The analytical results have indicated that the KBE construct model consists of five parts: 1. Economic Incentive and Institutional regime: gross capital formation as % GDP and trade, business environment and local institutional regime. 2. Innovation system: innovation input, foreign direct investment, and innovation entrepreneurship. 3. Education and human resources: educational investment, human structure, extent of mathematics and science, extent of open competitiveness. 4. Information infrastructure: information structure, investment in telecom, rating of computer processing power as % of total worldwide MIPS. 5. Performance indicators: human resources development, employment and productivity. Finally, this study concludes that, in order to construct the model of KBE, one needs to look into the essentiality of the innovation system, education and human resources, information infrastructure factors, all together.

References

APEC (2000), Towards Knowledge Based Economy in APEC.

Bagozzi, R. P., & Yi, Y. (1998). On the evaluation of structural equation models. Academic of Marketing Science, 16 74-94.

Campbell. D. & Fiske. D. W. (1959), Convergent and discriminant validity by the multitrait-multimethod matrix. Psychological Bulletin. 56, 81-105.

Hair J. F. Jr., Anderson, R. E., Tatham, R. L., & Black, W. C. (1998). Multivariate data analysis (5th ed.). Englewood Cliffs, Nj: Pretice-Hall.

IMD, The World Competitiveness Year Book, 2001.

Joreskog, K. G., & Sorbom, D. (1993). LISREL 8: Structural equation modeling with the SIMPLIS command language. Chicago: Scientific Software International.

OECD (1999), OECD Science, Technology and Industry Scoreboard 1999: Benchmarking Knowledge-Based Economies, Paris.

Pisano, G.P. (1991), "The governance of innovation: Vertical integration and collaborative arrangements in the biotechnology industry," Research Policy, 20, pp. 237-249.

Solow, Robert M. (2000), Growth Theory: An Exposition, Oxford University Press.

Teece, D. J. (1999), Managing Intellectual Capital – Organizinational, Strategic, and Policy Dimensions

Teece, D. J (2000), "Managing Intellectual Capital - Organizational, Strategic, and Policy Dimensions," OXFORD University Press.

Thurow, Lester C. (2000), Building Wealth: the New Rules for Individuals, Companies, and Nations in a Knowledge Based Economy.

TRAVERSING THE FUTURE OF KNOWLEDGE MANAGEMENT (KM): AN EMERGING THEME IN HIGHER EDUCATION RESEARCH?

CHIAM CHING LEEN,
JOHN HEDBERG &
PETER FREEBODY

Centre for Research in Pedagogy and Practice, National Institute of Education, Nanyang Technological University, 1 Nanyang Walk, Singapore 637616

Higher education research needs to respond to the changing environment and anticipate key themes that could be of major concern in the future (Teichler, 2003). This paper presents a brief review of the importance of identifying key themes for higher education research and explores the potential of KM to become a significant theme in higher education research in Singapore. It takes readers on a quick tour of the origins of KM and provides empirical evidence that supports the significance of KM in Singapore's higher education research enterprise. The paper aims to stimulate and provoke educational researchers to add to the debate on the future of KM in higher education research in Singapore.

References

Al-Hawamdeh, S. (2003). *Knowledge management: Cultivating knowledge professionals*. Oxford: Chandos Publishing.

Chabrow, E. (2003). *Homeland security will drive federal spending on knowledge management: Government spending on software and services will top $1 billion in five years*. Retrieved March 25, 2004, from http://www.informationweek.com/story/show Article.jhtml?articleID=12803698

David, P. A. (1997). The knowledge factory: A survey of universities. *The Economist*(October 4, 1997).

Fullan, M. (1993). *Change forces: Probing the depths of educational reforms*. London: The Falmer Press.

Guiney, S. Z., & Petrides, L. A. (2002). Knowledge management for school leaders: An ecological framework for thinking schools. *Teachers College Records, 104*(8), 1702-1717.

Hall, B. (2004). Are you ready for the future? *Training, 41*(1), 14.

Inglis, A. (2003). *Will knowledge management technologies be behind the next generation of e-learning systems?* Paper presented at the 16th ODLAA Biennial Forum Conference Proceedings 'Sustaining Quality Learning Environments', Australia.

Kidwell, J. J., Linde, K. M. V., & Johnson, S. L. (2000). Applying corporate knowledge management in higher education. *Educause Quarterly, 4*, 28-33.

Koenig, M., & Ponzi, L. J. (2002). Knowledge management: Another management fad? *Information Research, 8*(1), Paper 145. Retrieved December 13, 2002, from http://informationr.net/ir/2008-2001/paper145.html

Sallis, E., & Jones, G. (2002). *Knowledge management in education: Enhancing learning & education*. London, UK: Kogan Page.

Straits Knowledge. (2002). *Knowledge management in Singapore organizations*. Singapore: Straits Knowledge.

Straits Knowledge. (2003). *Knowledge-based strategy in Singapore Organizations*. Singapore: Straits Knowledge.

Swartz, N. (2003). The 'wonder years' of knowledge management. *Information Management Journal, 37*(3), 53-57. Retrieved July 28, 2003, from ProQuest Education Complete database.

Tan, E. (2004, February 22). *Moving up the experience curve: KM in Singapore*. Retrieved February 22, 2004, from http://knowledge.typepad.com/ikms_newsletter/2004/02/moving_up_the_e.html

Teichler, U. (1996). Comparative higher education: Potentials and limits. *Higher Education, 32*(431-465).

Teichler, U. (2003). The future of higher education and the future of higher education research. *Tertiary Education and Management, 9*, 171-185.

The Task Force of Higher Education and Society. (2000). *Higher Education in Developing Countries: Peril and promises.* Washington, US: The International Bank for Reconstruction and Development (The World Bank).

Tuomi, I. (2002). The future of Knowledge Management. *Lifelong Learning in Europe (LLinE), VII*(2), 69-79.

PROMOTING PROFESSIONAL COLLABORATION BETWEEN MEDICAL PRACTITIONERS: LEVERAGING AN ONLINE DISCUSSION FORUM

JANET CURRAN & SYED SIBTE RAZA ABIDI

Faculty of Computer Science, Dalhousie University, Halifax, Canada

PAULA FORGERON

IWK Health Centre, Halifax, Canada

Effective management of pediatric pain requires pro-active and effective collaboration between health practitioners from a variety of health disciplines. This paper investigates the merits of a collaborative learning environment to address the knowledge gaps experienced by a community of pediatric pain practitioners. We present a knowledge management solution that leverages on an online discussion forum as a collaborative learning environment rooted in team members sharing experiences, offering support to solve problems, guiding members to information/knowledge resources, informing peers about clinical practice guidelines and to simply seek advice on matters pertaining to pediatric pain management. Team interactions, via the discussion forum, were captured and represented as a social network to provide useful insights into the dynamics of team collaboration and to identify the patterns of knowledge flow amongst team members. Practitioner's experiences with the use of the online forum were explored using an online questionnaire and small focus group.

References

Eraut, M. Non-formal learning and tacit knowledge in professional work. *British Journal of Educational Psychology*, 70,113-136, 2000.

Handzic, M. Managing knowledge through experimentation and socialization. *Proceedings of the Third International Conference on Practical Aspects of Knowledge Management (PAKM2000)*, Basel, Switzerland, 1-6, October 2000

Pear, J., Crone-Todd, D. A social constructivist approach to computer mediated instruction. *Computers and Education,*38:221-231, 2002.

Safran, C., Jones, P., Rind, D., Bush, B., Cytryn, K., Patel, V. Electronic communication and collaboration in a health care practice. *Artificial Intelligence in Medicine.* 12: 137-152, 1998.

Yu-N, C., Abidi, S. S. R., The Role of Information Technology in the Explication and Crystallization of Tacit Healthcare Knowledge. *Health Informatics Journal*, 7 (3/4), 158-167, 2001.

MANAGING KNOWLEDGE IN GENERAL PRACTICE SURVEYING FIRMS: A COMPARATIVE STUDY BETWEEN SME AND LARGE FIRMS

PATRICK S.W. FONG

Department of Building & Real Estate, Hong Kong Polytechnic University Hung Hom, Kowloon, Hong Kong

Y. CAO

*KPMG Huazhen, 50th Floor, Plaza 66
1266 Nanjing West Road, Shanghai 200040,
China*

It is widely held that knowledge is the most critical asset for a company and a source of lasting competitive advantage. It follows that managing knowledge is becoming a crucial skill and is critical to business success, if not to business survival. General practice (GP) surveying firms, which are knowledge-intensive in nature, are facing intense local and global competition in the changing commercial environment. Thus, the aim of this study is to investigate the level of awareness of the concept of knowledge management (KM) among GP surveying firms in the UK and Hong Kong, and to create an understanding of how those firms manage their knowledge. Questionnaires were sent to 217 GP surveying firms with a response rate of 18.9%.

Qualitative and quantitative analyses of the survey showed that the management of professionals and the use of information technology were integrated into the processes of knowledge storage, sharing, distribution, transfer and evaluation in these GP firms. While managers confirmed the value of knowledge management, there was still a lack of understanding of the KM concept and its potential benefits. They perceived the most important goal of KM to be increasing customer satisfaction, and the biggest obstacle to be lack of time. Knowledge sharing was perceived to be difficult due to fierce internal competition as well as a lack of

incentives and rewards. Respondents preferred experience-based face-to-face methods of knowledge acquisition. Most IT tools in use were basic and related to knowledge storage and daily communication, whereas systems enabling virtual meetings and knowledge creation had not been implemented. In addition, the size and location of the firm also plays a part: statistical testing revealed that large and global firms had higher awareness of KM and took the lead in implementing KM strategies. Suggested managerial implications include the promotion of knowledge management awareness, the creation of corporate and interpersonal trust, and the formulation of practical attitudes towards technology-based KM systems.

References

Alvesson, M. (2000). Social identity and the problem of loyalty in knowledge-intensive companies. *Journal of Management Studies*, 37(8), 1101-1123.

Bannister, A. and Raymond, S. (1984). *Surveying*. Bath: English Language Book Society/Pitman.

D'Arcy, E., Keogh, G. and Roulac, S.E. (1999). Business culture and the development of real estate service provision in the United Kingdom and the United States since 1945. *Paper presented at the 46th North American Meetings of the Regional Science Association International*, Montreal, Canada, November.

Dawson, R. (2000). *Developing Knowledge-based Client Relationships: The Future of Professional Services*. Boston: Butterworth-Heinemann.

Gray, J.T., Hinings, C.R., Malhotra, N., Pinnington, A., and Morris, T. (2001). Internalization and change in professional service firms. *Paper presented to the ANZAM Conference*, Massey University, New Zealand, December, 09-21.

Hinds, P.J. and Pfeffer, J. (2003). Why organizations don't "know what they know": Cognitive and motivational factors affecting the transfer of expertise. In Ackerman, M., Pipek, V. and Wulf, V. (Eds.), *Sharing Expertise: Beyond*

Knowledge Management, Cambridge, MA: MIT Press, 3-26.

Hitt, M.A., Bierman, L., Shimizu, K., and Kochhar, R. (2001). Direct and moderating effects of human capital on strategy and performance in professional service firms: A resource-based perspective. *Academy of Management Journal*, 44(1), 13-28.

HKIS (2001). Directory and annual report 2000/2001. Hong Kong: Hong Kong Institute of Surveyors.

IDC/KMM (2001). The state of KM. *Knowledge Management Magazine*, May. Visited website: www.destinationKM.com, on 24 January 2003.

Matzdorf, F. and Price, I. (2000). Barriers to organizational learning in the chartered surveying profession. *Property Management*, 18(2), 92-113.

Meyer, M. (1972). Size and structure of organizations: A causal analysis. *American Sociological Review*, 37, 434-440.

Newell, S., Swan, J., Galliers, R. and Scarbrough, H. (1999). The intranet as a knowledge management tool? Creating new electronic fences. In: Khosrowpour, M. (Ed.), *Managing Information Technology Resources in the Next Millennium*, Proceedings of the 1999 IRMA International Conference, May 17-19, Hershey, USA, 612-619.

RICS (2001). Royal Institution of Chartered Surveyors directory 2001: Geographical directory. Exeter, UK: Polestar Weatons.

Ruggles, R. (1998). The state of the notion: Knowledge management in practice. *California Management Review*, 40(3), 80-89.

Watkins, J., Drury, L. and Preddy, D. (1992). *From Evolution to Revolution: The Pressure on Professional Life in the 1990s*. Bristol, UK: University of Bristol.

AN EMPIRICAL EVALUATION OF A CORPORATE E-LEARNING PORTAL

MELIHA HANDZIC & JOON-HO HUR

School of Computer Science and Engineering, The University of New South Wales Sydney, NSW 2052, Australia

This paper examines the perceptions and attitudes of employee-trainees from a large Asian organization towards their corporate e-learning portal. Data on employees' perceptions of the importance and their satisfaction with the implementation of the e-learning portal were gathered by administering a survey questionnaire. Results indicate that the highest perceived importance and satisfaction was with the tacit know-how category of knowledge management tools supporting learning by doing. Progress report and lecture notes were regarded as the most important and effective individual knowledge management tools.

IMPROVING UNIVERSITY-INDUSTRY KNOWLEDGE PARTNERSHIPS FOR SCIENTIFIC RESEARCH AND DEVELOPMENT PROJECTS: A PILOT STUDY

QUAMRUL HASAN

Center for Strategic Development of Science and Technology (The 21st Century Center of Excellence Program on Technology Creation Based on Knowledge Science), Japan Advanced Institute of Science and Technology (JAIST), 1, 1 Asahidai, Tatsunokuchi, Ishikawa 923-1211, Japan

Beginning in April 2004, the new law for Japanese national universities turned them into independent public corporations. This recent change has increased pressure on them to look to industry for more support than ever before. Since JAIST is involved in a collaborative project with two industrial partners (one large and one small), we saw an excellent opportunity to conduct a pilot study on the university-industry knowledge partnership for a scientific research and development project in the Japanese national university setting. The purpose of our study was to identify both what areas or considerations have the most influence on such projects and how such projects can be improved. This paper presents our methodology and data results. Most importantly, it presents a list of specific suggestions for improving project performance. Although a pilot study with a small number of respondents, this study may still have significance in terms of suggestions for improving collaborative projects and/or in regard to the data-gathering methodology we used. We plan to provide results of the study to the project team members and recommend they apply the most important suggestions for improving their project. We also plan to do a follow-up study to determine whether or not the project is improved by the implementation of these key suggestions.

KNOWLEDGE MANAGEMENT SYSTEM: SOME METHODOLOGICAL REMARKS

GIANPAOLO IAZZOLINO

Dept. Business Science, University of Calabria, Via Pietro Bucci 3/c Arcavacata di Rende (CS) 87036, Italy

DOMENICO LAISE

Dept. Computer Science and Systems, University of Rome "La Sapienza" Via Buonarroti 12, Rome 00185, Italy

PIERO MIGLIARESE & SAVERINO VERTERAMO

Dept. Business Science, University of Calabria, Via Pietro Bucci 3/c Arcavacata di Rende (CS) 87036, Italy

The design of a Knowledge Management System (KMS) must take into account the congruence between the human and the technological dimensions. We propose a methodology to diagnose the failures of the organizational design of a KMS due to the absence of an equilibrium between these different dimensions. We argue that the disequilibrium comes from the existence of weak relations linking the agents of an organization. The Organizational Relation can be described through the following four attributes, which constitute the dimensions of the Organizational Relation: Organizational Goals (OG), Cultural Background (CB) of the agents, Organizational Rules (OR), Tools (T) (technological and organizational). For this reason we investigate the minimal set of conditions necessary for the existence of strong organizational relations, that is for the existence of a Knowledge Organization. A high performance of a KMS resulted when the design of human organizational relations is congruent with the design of the ICT System. The proposed methodology has been applied to two real cases (two research centers) for an organizational diagnosis.

References

Alavi, M. and Leidner, D.E. (2001) "Review: Knowledge Management and Knowledge Management Systems: Conceptual Foundations and Research Issues." *Management Information Systems Quarterly*, 25 (1), March.

Migliarese, P. and Verteramo, S. (2003) "Organizational based Method for Knowledge Management Systems Design." Proceedings of the 7th World Multi-Conference on Systemics, Cybernetics and Informatics, July 27-30, Orlando, Florida.

THE ROLE OF STRATEGIC HUMAN RESOURCE MANAGEMENT IN THE PROCESS OF A COMPANY'S KNOWLEDGE CREATION

GEORGE SURYA KENCANA

*George & Partner Consulting
449 Tampines Street 42, #02-90,
Singapore 520449
gsk062002@yahoo.com.sg*

The current business situation is influenced by globalization and fast-running firms. The consequence of such business environment is that there will be no competitive position safe from the possibility of replication or replacement. In order to survive, firms should always be adaptive and continuously develop themselves and their products. In other words, firms should continuously find ways to create and shape their values through innovation. The firms are able to increase their abilities in knowledge creation by building manpower that already have the relevant working experience with the industry, by motivating employees to mutually share knowledge they already have, and by keeping employees possessing valuable knowledge for the industry.

References

Buckman, Robert H., (2004). *"Building A Knowledge Driven Organization"*, McGraw-Hill Companies Inc.

Collison, Chris & Parcell, Geoff (2001). *"Learning to Fly"*, Capstone Publishing Limited.

Davenport Thomas H. & Prusak, Laurence (2003). *"What's The Big Idea?"*, Harvard Business School Press.

Marquardt, Michael J. (2002). *"Building the Learning Organization"*, 2nd Edition, Davies-Black Publishing Inc.

Nonaka, Ikujiro and Takeuchi, Hirotaka (1995). *"The Knowledge-Creating Company"*, Oxford University Press Inc.

BUSINESS INTELLIGENCE FOR KNOWLEDGE MANAGEMENT

VIJAY KUMAR

*Knowledge Management Group, Education and Research Department,
Infosys Technologies Limited, Bangalore, India*

Knowledge Management (KM), a concept nurtured in an anxious environment, has always been a point of debate, with questions on potential value addition and Return on Investment (RoI). KM preachers themselves have not been too sure of the ways of showcasing results in the absence of proper data to back the seemingly obvious implications. Tracking effectiveness of KM implementation in various segments of organization, geographically, functionally or otherwise, has also been another point of interest for KM implementers. In an attempt to alleviate these two main points, this paper tries to enable KM Practitioners with a solution to get the right data at the right time with the help of a Business Intelligence (BI) solution. Business Intelligence, an approach with its roots in Executive Information System (EIS) and Decision Support System (DSS), offers promises of helping in strategic decision making process by extracting easy to interpret information from the raw data. A case implementation at Infosys Technologies Limited, India has also been presented.

KNOWLEDGE MANAGEMENT AND COMMUNICATION CHALLENGES: DETERMINING WHAT INFORMATION PATIENTS REALLY WANT

KEVIN J. LEONARD & WARREN J. WINKELMAN

Department of Health Policy, Management and Evaluation,
University of Toronto, 12 Queens Park West Toronto, Ontario M5S 1A8, Canada

The development of Internet-based information and communication technologies (ICT) for patients with chronic illness is expected to improve access to medical information, ultimately improving knowledge and health outcomes. However, studies objectively measuring the effect of patient access to their personal health information on long-term outcomes are few in number, and most results are either contradictory or equivocal. One possible reason for these disappointing results is that the chronically ill patient's perspective on information is still not well known.

Herein, we present preliminary results of an ongoing qualitative study based on in-depth interviews and focus groups with a small roster of patients with inflammatory bowel disease. Self-Care, self-management and the maintenance of balance between illness responsibilities and life responsibilities appear to be the primary reasons that chronic patients seek information. In this self-care context, a conceptual framework for the patient's relationship with information is emerging; we have categorized their responses into three core areas: (i) general patient information; (ii) characteristics of an on-line patient accessible electronic record; and (iii) sources of information for the experienced patient.

UTILIZATION OF INFORMATION AND COMMUNICATION TECHNOLOGY IN AGRICULTURAL KNOWLEDGE MANAGEMENT: THE CASE OF THE PHILIPPINE NARS

RUEL V. MANINGAS

Philippine Council for Agriculture, Forestry and Natural Resources Research and Development (PCARRD), Department of Science and Technology, 4030 Los Baños, Laguna, Philippines

The Philippine Department of Science and Technology (DOST) through one of its five sectoral Councils, the Philippine Council for Agriculture, Forestry and Natural Resources Research and Development (PCARRD) joins the global arena in maximizing the benefits of ICT. ICT contributes to a qualitative difference in the way knowledge is generated and disseminated. Through ICT, there is a possibility for scientists/ researchers to interact with a much wider community of peers who work in the same field, with whom they can interact in real time, creating a new virtual community inclusive of extension workers and farmers. This creates a dynamic and proactive interaction and knowledge flow among intended stakeholders. Thus, ICT has been elevated as one of PCARRD's major concerns, adding value to its knowledge management activities.

PCARRD stresses the importance of access to information and organizing information into useful knowledge in a networked environment. The latest developments could attest to the sustained ICT efforts of PCARRD, doing more through efficient use of resources and synergy (Faylon and Delfino, 2003). This paper discusses the uses and importance of ICT in agricultural R & D and technology management in the Philippines. Some case studies are also discussed specifically focusing on the level of utilization of ICT-based products and services by end-users of selected R & D and knowledge providers in the agriculture and natural resources sectors in the country. Insights and future directions on ICT as a tool to enhance agricultural knowledge management are also tackled.

References

Burgos, B.M., D.P.A. Delfino, T.R. Javier & R.V. Maningas, 2004, *Application of Information and Communication Technology (ICT) in Agricultural Extension: The PCARRD Experience*. Paper presented during the FFTC Technical Advisory Committee Meeting 31 May to 04 June 2004, Oasis Hotel, Los Baños, Laguna

Maningas R.V. 2003. *Information and Communication Technology (ICT) Utilization by End-users of Selected Agricultural Research and Extension Networks in the Philippines*, Ph.D. Dissertation, University of the Philippines Los Baños, College, Laguna

THE LEARNING SPACE OF THE SERVICE FIRM AND ELEMENTS IN THE CO-PRODUCTION OF KNOWLEDGE: EVIDENCE FROM AUSTRALIAN SERVICE FIRMS

M. CRISTINA MARTINEZ-FERNANDEZ, CLAUDINE A. SOOSAY & KELL TREMAYNE

AEGIS- Australian Expert Group in Industry Studies, University of Western Sydney PO BOX Q1287 QVB Post Office, Sydney NSW 1230, Australia

Modern economies are increasingly realising that the key to their future competitiveness lies in their success in generating and applying new knowledge through a highly trained workforce. The term 'knowledge-based' or 'learning economy' has emerged to describe those economies in which the production, distribution and use of knowledge are the main drivers of growth, wealth creation and employment across all industrial sectors (OECD, 2001). In recent years the attention has been focussed on knowledge-intensive business services (KIBS) and research and technology organisations (RTOs) as the providers of knowledge-intensive services to both manufacturing and services companies and are critical to the modern economy (Hauknes, 2000; Hales, 2000; Miles, 1999). However there is limited literature on the relationship between knowledge management and innovation in service firms. This paper discusses the learning space of the service firm, the critical elements involved in the co-production of knowledge and how the management of these processes contributes to building innovation capability in the firm. The paper argues that informal transactions of knowledge play a critical role on the innovation capability building of service firms in addition to the role played by KIBS and RTOs. It also discusses the relationship of managing knowledge transactions with firm capability building and innovation. The paper present results from surveys and in-depth interviews that were conducted among 87 service firms in Australia

References

OECD (2001) *Innovation and productivity in services: Industry, services and trade*, Paris: OECD

Hauknes, J. (2000) Dynamic Innovation Systems: What is the Role of Services? In Boden M. and Miles I. (eds.), *Services and the Knowledge-based Economy*, London and New York: Continuum

Hales, M. (2000) Services deliveries in an economy of competence supply, Synthesis report work package 5 of *RISE – RTOsin the Service Economy*, CENTRIM: University of Brighton

Miles, I. (1999) Services in National Innovation Systems: From Traditional Services to Knowledge Intensive Business Services in Schienstock, G. and Kuusi, O. (eds.) *Transformation towards a Learning Economy: the Challenge to the Finnish Innovation System*, Helsinki, Sitra.

KNOWLEDGE SHARING ENABLERS: A REVIEW OF ORGANIZATIONAL STRATEGIES AND PRACTICES

LAILA MAROUF

Library and Information Science, University of Pittsburgh, 135 North Bellefield Avenue, Pittsburgh PA 15260, USA

This paper reviews organizational policies and strategies for effective knowledge sharing. Relevant body of research has been critically reviewed for examining the role of different KS enablers. These include: organizational culture (trust, collaboration, and care), organizational structure, reward system, technology, top management support, behavioral profile of individuals, characteristics of knowledge, and social relationships. Investing in social capital is crucial for facilitating knowledge sharing in organizations. The five possible avenues for creating social capital are: HRM strategies in building networks, a supportive leadership, physical setup, and support for communities of practice, and intelligent ICT applications.

KNOWLEDGE MANAGEMENT: FROM PRODUCTIVY GAINS TO STRATEGIC ADVANTAGE

SOURAV MUKHERJI

Indian Institute of Management Bangalore Bangalore-560076, India

Organizations operating in knowledge intensive industries need to systematically manage the processes of knowledge acquisition, codification, transfer and deployment. In their practitioner oriented paper, Hansen *et al.* (1999) observed that organizations operating in knowledge intensive industries broadly followed two kinds of knowledge management (KM) strategies, named 'codification' and 'personalization'. They argued that in order to be successful, organizations need to choose one KM strategy over another, since straddling is a recipe for failure.

This presentation depicts the challenges faced by a software services organization, in establishing an enterprise wide KM system. The case study research reveals how in the context of this organization, 'codification' and 'personalization' are stages of evolution, rather than being mutually exclusive. In order to deliver service efficiently, codification of knowledge is a necessity. However, codification does not help software service organizations in building domain competencies. This is due to the complexity and embeddedness of such knowledge. While codification is largely useful in increasing productivity, personalization is necessary to leverage organizational knowledge for solving complex problems, and for creating innovative solutions.

Thus, in order to leverage KM for strategic advantage, codification needs to be complemented by personalization strategy. Therein lies the future of enterprise KM initiatives.

References

Hansen, M.T.; N.Noharia & T.Tierney (1999) "What's Your Strategy for Managing Knowledge?" *Harvard Business Review* 77(2): 106-116.

DEVELOPING A KNOWLEDGE MANAGEMENT FRAMEWORK FOR SMALL BUSINESSES: A CASE STUDY

JOTHIMANI K. MUNIANDY

Information Services Business Unit, Bursa Malaysia Berhad, Exchange Square, Bukit Kewangan, 50200, Kuala Lumpur, Malaysia

This paper proposes a framework for developing a knowledge management (KM) plan for Rehanstat Sdn. Bhd. (RSB) which is a small market research company based in Kuala Lumpur, Malaysia. RSB is a client-based knowledge intensive firm, which recognises the link between KM and sustainable competitive advantage. In developing a knowledge management framework for RSB, first, the status of KM initiatives at RSB is analysed based on an adaptation of the criteria used for characterisation of KM starters, as proposed by Maier & Remus, (2003). The analysis shows that RSB is at a very basic level in KM initiatives and has not addressed any formal KM operational activities, nor established any KM goals, nor identified the potential of KM initiatives. An integral KM framework, as advocated by Beijerse (2000), is adapted for developing a KM plan for RSB. KM issues of structure, culture and human resources management aspects, at the tactical level, issues relating to KM goals at a strategic level, and knowledge work processes at the operational level, are addressed in a holistic manner in this framework. In discussing the application of the framework, a roadmap is defined and possible KM Initiatives for RSB are discussed The paper concludes by suggesting that RSB starts small, refrain form large investments in technology, and moves towards incorporating KM-linked processes and systems into its daily activities.

References

Beijerse, R P Int (2000) "Knowledge Management: Small and Medium-Sized Companies: Knowledge Management for Entrepreneurs" *Journal of Knowledge Management,* Volume 4, No. 2, Page 162 – 179.

Maier, R & Remus, U. (2002) "Defining Process-Oriented Knowledge Management Strategies: Knowledge and Process Management". *The Journal of Corporate Transformation,* Volume 9, No. 2, Page 103 – 108.

APPLICATION OF ADAPTIVE NETWORK BASED FUZZY INFERENCE SYSTEM FOR MODEL RECONSTRUCTION IN REVERSE ENGINEERING

D. NAGAJYOTHI

Lecturer, SOCIT, Inti College Malaysia Bandar Baru Nilai, Negeri Sembilan, 71800, Malaysia

Combining fuzzy neural network and laser surface data measurement, a novel model reconstruction methodology is presented. This model reconstruction scheme includes two main parts, one is surface data measurement system, and the other one is model reconstruction algorithm. The surface data measurement system consists of a vision system with a smart laser camera and a PC computer. The system is developed to measure data for freeform surface with complex shape. Using an Adaptive Network based Fuzzy Inference System (ANFIS), the model reconstruction algorithm is designed. For demonstrating the effectiveness of the presented scheme, a group points cloud data with good accuracy. This is measured by the presented data measurement system for an existing part and is taken as data sample for training the ANFIS. The trained ANFIS is taken as surface data model. By comparing the surface data, which is from trained ANFIS, with the data sample value, it can be found that the ANFIS model can match the real surface very well.

References

C. N. Huang and S. Motavall, Reverse engineering of planar parts using machine vision, Computers Ind. Engineering, Vol. 26, No.2, p.369 (1994).

J. S. R Jang, ANFIS: Adaptive-network-based fuzzy inference system, IEEE Trans. On Systems, Man, and Cybernetics. Vol. 23, No. 3 May/ June 1993.

V. K. Gupta and R. Sagar, A PC-based system integrating CMM and CAD for automated inspection and reverse engineering, Int. J. Adv. Manuf. Technol. Vol. 8, p. 305(1993).

T. Takagi and M. Sugeno, Fuzzy identification of system and its applications to modeling and control." IEEE Trans. Syst., Man. Cybern., Vo.115 p.116 (1985)

M. Sugeno, Ed., Industrial applications of fuzzy control, New York: Elsevier, 1985.

REVAMPING UNIVERSITIES - KNOWLEDGE MANAGEMENT: A MEANS TO EFFECTIVE PERFORMANCE

K. PADMINI

*Dept. of Library and Information Science,
S.V. University
Tirupati, Andhra Pradesh, India*

Knowledge Management (KM) is an audit of 'intellectual assets' that highlights unique sources, critical functions and potential bottlenecks, which hinder knowledge flow to the point of use. K M in universities should be focused on effective research and development of knowledge, creation of knowledge bases, exchange and sharing knowledge with colleagues, administrators, researchers, students, and community, providing awareness and training to the faculty and other employees, speeding up explicit processing of the implicit knowledge and realizing of its sharing. The present paper emphasizes the value of KM and its application in the universities to improve performance continuously to withstand the competition. It focuses on the multi dimensional profile of the University teacher who plays a pivotal role in the knowledge economy era. The article also highlights the process, components, technologies used and benefits to employees as well as to the organization. An attempt is made in this paper to pool up the roadblocks in introducing and implementing KM in universities and some measures are also suggested to overcome them. This article expresses the views relating to KM, which is still at the budding stage in the Indian educational environment.

References

Anjali, Gulati.(1999) " Knowledge management: An information technology perspective. " *DESIDOC Bulletin of information technology, 19(6):3*

Mongkhonvanit, Pomchai. (08.08.2002) *Knowledge management in higher education at the dawn of the 21st century.* <http://www.sims.berkeley.educorses/is213/s99/projects/p9>

Rajkumar,P.V.(2004) " Knowledge management: An untold need of tomorrow's world. " In T.A.V.Murthy and others(Eds.),*Road map to new generation of libraries using emerging technologies.*586-90, Ahmedabad: INFLIBNET.

Reid, Ian C. The web, knowledge management and universities. <http://www.ausweb.scu.edu.au/aw2k/papers/reid/paper.html>

INTELLIGENT KNOWLEDGE RETRIEVAL THROUGH COLLABORATIVE KNOWLEDGE SHARING

HATIM SALEH & SYED SIBTE RAZA ABIDI

Faculty of Computer Science, Dalhousie University, Halifax, Canada

The prevailing issues of information overload, lack of peer review and context identification tend to compromise the relevance and utility of knowledge resources present on the web. In the absence of definitive measures to ascertain the relevance of web-based knowledge content, we propose a collaborative knowledge sharing approach for determining the relevance of specific web-based knowledge content as per a user's interest and needs. The underlying idea is to leverage the expertise, commonality of interest and information retrieval pattern of an online community of practice to determine and to suggest the relevant knowledge content for a particular user. In effect, we aggregate the otherwise solitary knowledge retrieval efforts of the members of a community of practice to realize community-driven specialized knowledge clusters—where each cluster encompasses the individual knowledge resources validated by like-minded members of the community—that are used to assist specialized knowledge retrieval by all members of the online community. We present the notion of using *personal bookmarks* of expert-level community members as an implicit form of recommendation of knowledge content and a means of inferring user interest. The systematic grouping of personal bookmarks leads to specialized knowledge clusters; also the comparison of bookmarks allows to determine the commonality of interests amongst community members. Our proposed knowledge sharing solution is envisaged to provide the following opportunities: (a) commonality and expertise of users can be leveraged to support the ability to automatically "push" relevant knowledge to selected users; (b) the essence of bookmarks as a knowledge store can be enhanced through the development of a conceptual domain hierarchy derived from the analysis of how users tend to cluster their personal bookmarks

References

Kobsa, A., Stephanidis, C. (1999). "SELECT: Social and collaborative filtering of web documents and news". *Proceedings of the 5th ERCIM Workshop on User Interfaces for All: User-Tailored Information Environments.*

Terveen, L. (1997), "PHOAKS: A system for sharing recommendations - A collaborative filtering system that recognizes and reuses recommendations", *Communications of the ACM*, 40 (3), pp. 59-62.

GLOBALIZATION AND KNOWLEDGE MANAGEMENT: IMPLICATIONS FOR HRD

AVNEET SAXENA & S. WADHWA

IIT Delhi, India
avneetsaxena@rediffmail.com
swadhwa@mech.iitd.ernet.in

The purpose of this paper is to provide adequate direction to incorporate globalization and knowledge management in human resource development systems in order to meet digital era goals. Globalization can have far reaching implications for human resource development (HRD) and knowledge management practice to develop knowledge based organization. The paper suggests growing need for focusing on the influence of knowledge transfer in human resource development (HRD).We also propose an appropriate emphasis in HRD practices that enhance the sharing and transfer of knowledge.

References

Anderson, V. and Skinner, Organizational learning in practice: how do small businesses learn to operate internationally?, HRDI, Vol. 2 No. 3, September, pp. 235-58, 1999.

Davenport T.H., Prusa L., How Organizations Manage: what They Know. Harvard Business School Press, 1998, Boston.

Dessler, G., Human resource management, book, pearson education asia, 2002, India.

Nonaka, H. Takeuchi, 1995. The Knowledge-creating Company: How Japanese Companies Create the Dynamics of Innovation, Oxford Univ. Press, New York.

Tiwana A., The knowledge Management Management toolkit, Prantice hall. 2000.

Tiwana, A., Balasubramaniam, R., A design knowledge management system to support collaborative information product evolution. Decision Support Systems 31, 2001, 241–262.

Tolberta, A., McLean, G., et.al., "Creating the global learning organization (GLO)", International Journal of Intercultural Relations 26, 2002, 463–472.

Valkevaara, T., Exploring the construction of professional expertise in HRD: analysis of four HR developers' work histories and career stories, Journal of European Industrial Training 26, 2002, 183-195.

CONVERSION OF A HETEROGENEOUS EDUCATION SYSTEM (HEES) INTO A HOMOGENEOUS EDUCATION SYSTEM (HOES) BY USE OF KNOWLEDGE MANAGEMENT AND INFORMATION TECHNOLOGY

ASIF ALI SYED

Computer Science Department, Bahria University, 13-National Stadium Road, Karachi, 75950, Pakistan

The basic idea behind this paper is to convert the Heterogeneous Education System (HeES) into Homogeneous Education System (HoES) by use of Knowledge Management for the teaching engineering (information engineering) purpose using Information Technology ,Artificial intelligence and mathematical Modeling for the ease to teachers .

The purpose of this idea is (1) to provide the best possible education to students having vision and/or hearing disability so that they may achieve their full potentials in life, and (2) to advance and disseminate knowledge in this field of endeavor.

The technology itself is nothing but knowledge management is a basic thing through which we create technology. Computer technology is invaluable for assessing learning disabled students. It opens opportunities for developing innovative assessment tools in education. The nature of computers as information processing tools plays the role of user-friendly interactive learning environments. The possibility of designing instructional tools to meet individual needs of students, make computers potentially powerful tools for assessment.

The objective of this system is to provide high quality, innovative education to children with impaired vision and/or hearing , assist parents and families in catering special needs of the child. To engage in research, professional development and staff training relevant to the education of children with significant vision and/or hearing loss.

References

Bloomfield, B.P. and Danieli, A., (1995), 'The role of management consultants in the development of IT', Journal of Management Studies, 32, 1, 23-46.

Scarbrough, H., Swan, J., Preston, J. (1999), Knowledge Management: A review of the literature, London: Institute of Personnel and Development.

Stinson, B. (1993). Getting started with adaptive technology: Meeting the needs of disabled students. Florida Technology in Education Quarterly, 6(1), 71-76.

DEVELOPING A KNOWLEDGE-BASED ECONOMY: AN INVESTIGATION OF CULTURAL INFLUENCES

EILEEN TRAUTH

School of Information Sciences and Technology, Pennsylvania State University, 330E IST Building University Park, PA 16802, U.S.A.

PERRY WONG

Milken Institute, 1250 Fourth Street Santa Monica, CA 90401, U.S.A.

BENJAMIN YEO

School of Information Sciences and Technology, Pennsylvania State University, 307G IST Building University Park, PA 16802, U.S.A.

The cases of Silicon Valley and Ireland suggest that the development of information and knowledge-based economies are dependent on societal factors. This research aims to outline the cultural factors that influence the development of a knowledge-based economy in California's Humboldt County. Based on figures from the United States Census Bureau, Humboldt County had a per capita income of US$17,203, with 19.5 per cent of the population living below the poverty line, while the per capita income of California State was US$22,711 in 1999. Humboldt County has since deployed economic development initiatives, which includes the development of an information and hence a knowledge-based economy. However, there has been little evidence of success so far. Adapting Trauth's (2000) research framework on developing an information economy, we conducted face-to-face interviews in the summer of 2003 in Humboldt County, to analyze the relevant cultural challenges. We conclude that despite promising development initiatives, local business and political cultural factors inhibit the effectiveness of these initiatives. These findings can be extrapolated to Asian countries to emphasize the need to consider cultural factors in their economic strategies to develop a knowledge-based economy, against a back-drop of rich cultural and political diversity.

References

Trauth, E. (2004) *The Culture of an Information Economy. Influences and Impact in the Republic of Ireland.* Netherlands: kluwer Academic Publishers.

SUPPORTING COMMUNITIES OF PRACTICE: A RIPPLE DOWN RULES APPROACH TO CALL CENTRE MANAGEMENT

MEGAN VAZEY & DEBBIE RICHARDS

Department of Computing, Macquarie University North Ryde, NSW, 2109, Australia

One corporate sphere where the concepts raised by Communities of Practice (CoP) (Community Intelligence Labs, 2003, http://www.co-i-l.com/coil/knowledge-garden/dkescop/dcop.shtml) can truly strengthen workflow efficiencies is the customer Call Centre or Service/Help Desk. In this domain, where the operators' daily grind is to trouble-shoot vast volumes of sometimes simple, but often difficult, technical problems in a dynamic knowledge environment, ideas from CoP involving collaboration between knowledge islands and use of web-based repositories to access proven solutions can achieve huge efficiency gains in the acquisition and reuse of knowledge. In this project we are concerned with knowledge management in a high-technology Customer Call Centre with typically high staff turnover resulting in loss of expertise. To support the acquisition, maintenance and flow of rapidly changing knowledge we propose an extension to the multiple classification ripple down rules (MCRDR) (Kang, Compton and Preston, 1995) knowledge acquisition technique that not only provides a technological solution but an approach that is human-centered and driven. In this endeavor, we will extend two RDR variations: Recursive RDR (R-RDR) (Mulholland *et al.* 1993) and Interactive RDR (I-RDR). In our approach we practically apply the concept of value networks that places knowledge at the centre of the customer service organization's business model.

References

Kang, B., P. Compton and P. Preston (1995). Multiple Classification Ripple Down Rules: Evaluation and Possibilities. Proc. of the 9th AAAI-Sponsored Banff Knowledge Acquisition for Knowledge-Based Systems Workshop, Banff, Canada, University of Calgary.

Mulholland, M., Preston, P., Sammut, C., Hilbert, B. and Compton, P. (1993) An Expert System for Ion Chromatography Developed using Machine Learning and Knowledge in Context *Proc. of the 6th Int. Conf. On Industrial and Engineering Applications of Artificial Intelligence and Expert Systems* Edinburgh.

THE APPLICATION OF KNOWLEDGE MANAGEMENT IN PUBLIC SECTOR BANKS IN INDIA'S POST LIBERALISATION ERA

SURENDRA KUMAR VYAS

Department of Management & Technology, Engineering College, Bikaner, Karni Industrial Area, Bikaner, Rajasthan 33400, India

The Public Sector Banks in India are in a transition mode, due to the impact of reforms and globalisation. The new standards of performance are expected to take a new turn from the year 2005. The Banking industry is becoming knowledge intensive. Knowledge is the only input that can help banking industry cope with radical change and ask the right question before you attempt to find the answers. Unstable markets necessitate "organised abandonment." Your target markets may undergo radical shifts, leaving the bank in a disastrous position of being with the wrong product at wrong time, and in the wrong place. The impact of these forces has been witnessed most prominently in high technology environments and financial markets, and increasingly in other markets, as well. Knowledge Management lets you undertake what Drucker calls organized abandonment. You can reshape products, get out of projects and product line that can pull your business down, and get others that maximize growth potential. The PSBs would need to reckon not only with these challenges but also face pressure on net quality and return, retention of creamy customer, legacy systems, and timely development of suitable products for their varied and segmental clientele. The present paper attempts to study the application of knowledge management in one of the key area of banking i.e., Product innovation (Deposits). The common factors influencing Public Sector Banks-Post Liberalisation and product innovation are *Competition, Customers, Technology and Government Policies*. The paper interprets the comprehensive process of identifying, analyzing and adapting outstanding practices from organizations anywhere in the world to help the organization improve the *performance* and *process* through *strategic* changes in the *internal* and *external* environment.

References

Andriesz, Mike, Managing Knowledge, *The Scotsman*, Glasgow, Scotland.

Amrit Tiwana, *The Knowledge Management Kit.*

Davenport, T.H, *Process Innovation*: Harvard Business School Press, Boston.

Drucker, P.F, *Knowledge, Knowledge -Worker Productivity; The Biggest Challenge.*

IBA, Bulletins.

Kirk, R.E. (1996) "Practical significance: A concept whose time has come." *Educational and Psychological Measurement*, 56(4): 746–759.

Schumacker, R.E. and Lomax, R.G. (2004) *A beginner's guide to structural equation modeling.* Mahwah, N.J.: Lawrence Erlbaum Associates.

Wiggens, R.D. and Sacker, A. (2002) "Strategies for handling missing data in SEM: A user's perspective." In G.A. Marcoulides and I. Moustaki (Eds.), *Latent variable and latent structure models*: 198-220, Mahwah, N.J.: Lawrence Erlbaum Associates.

A KM AND E-LEARNING BASED ARCHITECTURE: AN INNOVATIVE APPROACH FOR SMES

S. WADHWA &
AVNEET SAXENA
IIT Delhi, India
swadhwa@mech.iitd.ernet.in

In today's world of increasing communication and global connectivity, e-services are fast becoming an important tool for the survival of Small Medium Enterprises (SMEs). As web-based services are rapidly increasing their scope to different avenues (e.g., e-marketing, e-banking, e-procurement, telemedicine etc.) and people are becoming more and more dependent on them, e-learning comes forth as a useful tool, especially for SMEs. E-Learning and KM offer a great number of advantages for SMEs that have been addressed in the paper along with its limitations. The KM and e-learning integration represents a step toward a real challenge in the near future. The paper discusses the existing E-Learning architecture. It then explains an application aimed at real time broadcast of animations and simulations on the internet and how it fits in the present e-learning architecture.

References

Brusilovsky P., 1999. Adaptive and intelligent technologies for web based education. Special issue on intelligent system and teleteaching, 4, pp.19-25.

Carr S., 2000. As distance comes of age, the challenge is keeping the students. Chronicle of Higher education, 46, pp. 39-41.

Chen C.M., Lee H.M., Chen Y.H., 2004. Personalized e-learning system using item response theory. Computer and Education, 6, pp.15-20.

CII (confederation of Indian industry)-opportunity, (2002), India, www.ciionline.org.

Lim, D., Klobas, J. E., 2000. Knowledge management in small and medium size enterprises. The Electronic, Library, 18(6), 420-433.

Nonaka, H. Takeuchi, 1995. The Knowledge-creating Company: How Japanese Companies Create the Dynamics of Innovation, Oxford Univ. Press, New York.

Tiwana A., 2000. The knowledge Management Management toolkit, Prantice hall.

MODELING A SIMPLIFIED KNOWLEDGE SYSTEM FOR TECHNOLOGY TRANSFER BETWEEN DONOR AND HOME PARTNERS

EADE WANG

CEO, DigiMedia Technologies Co., Ltd. University of South Australia

FU-SHENG TSAI

I-Shou University, Taiwan

SHIEH-CHIEH FANG

National Kaohsiung First U. of Science and Technology

There have been concerted efforts in the last three decades, on technology transfer (TT) as a means to stretch RD&E investment and develop greater use of the developed science & technologies in order to generate better economic return (Grant & Gregory, 1997; Bender and Fish, 2000). Major proven models for full TT include the Intel model "Copy Exactly" (McDonald, 1999), or Business Excellence Model (Shergold and Reed, 1999) practiced in western world, etc. However, a suitable model for non-US context and one that can really focus on compact technological-related factors is still emerging. Both are based on integrative modeling technique for past models, as well as the observations in practices. The aim of this paper is to respond to the gap aforementioned, by bringing absorptive capacity (AC) into scientific modeling toward a simplified and fit model pattern of TT. After the modeling, we also give some propositions for further research directions. Finally, implications are discussed.

References

Bender, S. and Fish, A. (2000), "The transfer of knowledge and the retention of expertise: the continuing need foe global assignment", *Journal of Knowledge Management*, Vol. 4, pp125-137

Grant, E. B. and Gregory, M.J. (1997), "Adapting manufacturing process for international transfer", *International Journal of Operations and Production Marketing*, Vol. 17, pp 994-1005

McDonald, Chris (1999), "Copy Exact", IEEE the advanced semiconductor Manufacturing conference

Shergold, Kevin and Reed, Deborah M. (1999) "Striving for excellence: how self-assessment using the Business Excellence Model can result in step improvements in all areas of business activities", *TQM*

KNOWLEDGE MANAGEMENT PRACTICES IN THE INDIAN CORPORATE SECTOR: AN EMPIRICAL STUDY

P. SUBRAHMANYA YADAPADITHAYA

Department of PG Studies & Research in commerce, Mangalore University, Mangalagangotri - 574 199, Karnataka State, India.

The aim of this paper is to report on the current trends and status of knowledge management (KM) practices in the Indian private, public, and multinational enterprises (MNEs). The survey findings are based on the responses obtained from 264 companies through a written questionnaire mailed to 804 sample units in early 2004. The results and discussions focus on the key dimensions of KM practices such as main responsibility for KM, causes and drivers of KM initiatives, perceived importance of knowledge domains and KM-strategy linkage, nature of KM application, KM metrics used to measure and assess the business value of KM, perceived benefits from and major challenges of implementing KM initiatives. The single most important challenge of KM is 'measuring and assessing the business value of KM'. Compared to the MNEs and the private sector, KM is in its infancy in the Indian public sector. Given the limitations of quantitative surveys to examine KM practices, the results of this study provide a starting point for future researchers to "dig deeper" and conduct more qualitative research into KM in Indian companies. Such an approach would also explain why KM is less likely to be found in the Indian public sector.

KNOWLEDGE SHARING IN THE ASIAN PUBLIC ADMINISTRATION SECTOR

L. J. YAO

Department of Business, La Trobe University Bendigo, Victoria 3552, Australia

T. KAM

Trade and Industry Department, Hong Kong Government, 700 Nathan Road Kowloon, Hong Kong

S. CHAN

College of Management, University of Massachusetts Boston, MA 02125, USA

General concepts of Knowledge Management (KM) were reviewed and discussed, with elaborations on the role Knowledge Management in the commercial and the public administration sectors. This gives an overview of Knowledge Management, especially knowledge sharing and characteristics of Asian culture, and its theoretical background in the context of both commercial and public administration sector Knowledge Management. Practices of Knowledge Management in Asia are lagging behind those in America and Europe due largely to cultural characteristics. Knowledge sharing has not been implemented to its fullest extend due to cultural factors. Challenges for Asian Knowledge Management in the public sector are discussed for future research.

References

"Knowledge Management" *Asia-Pacific News.* (2001) 1(2): July/August.

Chee, S. C. (2003) "Special Report: Dressing Down Knowledge Management," *Computer World*, May Issue, Hong Kong.

Chiem, P. X. (2001) "In the Public Interest: Government Employees also Need Incentives to Share What They Know," *KM Magazine*, August.

KPMG Knowledge Advisory Services. (2003) Insights from KPMG's European Knowledge Management Survey 2002/2003, January.

McAdam, R. and Reid, R. (2000) "A Comparison of Public and Private Sector Perceptions and Use of Knowledge Management," Journal of European Industrial Training, 24(6).

Nicolas, R. (2004) "Knowledge Management Impacts on Decision Making Process," Journal of Knowledge Management, 8(1): 20-31.

OECD Paper. (2003) Knowledge Management: Learning by Comparing Experiences from Private Firms and Public Organizations. Summary Record of the High Level Forum held in Copenhagen, 8-9 February.

Ritter, W. and Choi, I. (2000) A Pilot Survey on KM in Hong Kong, Poon Kam Kai Institute of Management, the University of Hong Kong, Hong Kong.

Schmetz, F. (2002) Introduction to KM in the Public Sector, Knowledge Board article in the following link: http://www.knowledgeboard.com/cgi-bin/item.cgi?id=95046&d=1&h=417&f=418&dateformat=%o%20%B%20%Y, October.

USA Federal Government. (2002) KM Tool for Government Practitioners, available at www.km.gov.

Yiu, D. and Lin, J. (2002) "Sharing Tacit Knowledge in Asia," KM Magazine, 5(3), Melcrum Publishing Ltd.

A MULTI-AGENT SYSTEM FOR SUPPLY CHAIN COORDINATION

XIAO YOU &
JIANXIN (ROGER) JIAO

*School of Mechanical and Production Engineering,
Nanyang Technological University,
Singapore, youxiao@pmail.edu.sg*

This paper provides a multi-agent system framework modeling and analysis of supply chain system, in which configuration agent (CA) is designed to interact with inside agents which represent legacy systems within company and outside agents which represent other companies. CA intensively manages and controls the supply chain based on the comprehensive information it collects from other agents. It makes quick response to adapt to the dynamic business environment and to coordinate other agents' behavior in real-time. A case study of mobile phone global manufacturing supply chain configuration is reported.

References

Ahn H.J., Lee H. and Park S.J. (2003) "A flexible agent system for change adaptation in supply chains." *Expert Systems with Application*, 25: 603-618.

Chopra, S. and Meindl, P. (2001) *Supply chain management: strategy, planning, and operations.* Prentice Hall College.

Fox, M.S., Barbuceanu, M., and Teigen, R. (2000) "Agent-oriented supply-chain Management." *International Journal of Flexible Manufacturing Systems*, 12(2/3): 165-188.

Fox, M.S., Chionglo, J.F. and Barbuceanu, M. (1993) "The integrated supply chain Management system." *Internal Report*, Dept. of Industrial Engineering, University of Toronto.

Maturana, F. and Norrie, D. (1996). "Multi-agent mediator architecture for distributed manufacturing." *Journal of Intelligent Manufacturing*, 7: 257-270.

Wooldridge, M. and Jennings, N. (1995) "Intelligent agents: theory and practice." *Knowledge Engineering Review*, 10(2): 115-152.